Introduction to
GROUP COUNSELING
and PSYCHOTHERAPY

CHARLES J. VANDER KOLK
University of South Carolina

WAVELAND
PRESS, INC.
Prospect Heights, Illinois

For information about this book, write or call:

Waveland Press, Inc.
P.O. Box 400
Prospect Heights, Illinois 60070
(708) 634-0081

Preface

The goal of this book is to present introductory material about group counseling and psychotherapy to the beginning student and those who are relatively new to the field. The organization is from the general to the specific. I believe interpersonal conditions, best explicated by Carl Rogers, form the foundation for successful group work in most situations. Systems theory provides a general frame of reference because it stimulates comprehension of human behavior at the intrapersonal, interpersonal, small group, organizational, and community levels.

Part 1 presents models of group counseling, chosen for their historical importance and current popularity, around which the reader may shape techniques for practice.

Part 2 concerns actual practice, with guidelines and applications. The content of these chapters delineates what appears to be common practice today and is based on my own model of group counseling—an integration of existing models. The breadth of information in Part 2 results because there is little evidence to support the superiority of one approach over another. I have collected significant material in the field and organized it so that it makes sense to the novice. Chapter 8 presents the basic elements of group dynamics. Without an awareness of group dynamics, the group leader would be lost. Chapter 9 includes information for organizing a group and keeping it going. This may be the chapter the beginning counselor finds most useful;

other chapters will take on greater significance with experience. Chapter 10 describes leadership styles as well as practical ideas on what and what not to do when leading a group. Chapter 11 provides a brief introduction to the systems approach.

Because group counseling and psychotherapy developed primarily in mental health settings, most of the information in Parts 1 and 2 applies particularly to mental health clients. Fortunately, much of the information is also useful with other populations, but Part 3 demonstrates additional ideas for working with disabled and disadvantaged clients, children and adolescents, and families and couples. The family is approached in two ways. First, the family is a small group, and consequently has a place in a group counseling text. Second, chapter 14 also includes ideas on multiple family counseling, an interesting combination of group and family counseling. Couple or marital counseling is approached exclusively from the perspective of working with more than one couple at a time.

Part 4, Special Applications, addresses topics of interest to many counselors. Vocational concerns make up a large portion of most people's lives, and are especially amenable to group counseling. Chapter 16, Vocational Development Groups, is applicable to high school students, college students, and adults. These groups are useful for people who are seeking their first job, who need job readiness skills, or who want a career change. Chapter 17 addresses those clients who need to improve their social and work adjustment skills.

I want to express my appreciation to the people who assisted in the work necessary to complete the book. My wife, JoAnna, has been the chief source of moral support as well as the person who helped make some sense out of the first draft by proofreading and editing. She also did a share of the typing, along with Betty Edmiston and Peggy Salsgiver. Gary Miller read an early copy of the manuscript and contributed many good ideas. The special chapters by Bob Chubon, Anne Chandler, and Steve Ostby have added much to the book's usefulness. We sincerely thank Dr. Louis V. Paradise of The University of New Orleans, Dr. James A. Fruehling of Northeastern Illinois University, Dr. Michael Waldo of the University of Maryland, Dr. Christopher I. Stone of the University of Wisconsin, Dr. Steve LeClair of The Ohio State University, and Dr. Harold Adams of the University of Iowa and the staff of Charles Merrill Publishing for their ideas and assistance.

Contents

1

Introduction to Group Counseling

Group counseling has developed in this century from the efforts of a few people trained in individual therapy and guidance. It now appears in multiple forms and applications and serves many consumer populations. An historical perspective shows us how much has been accomplished in a relatively brief time. Group counseling has only recently gained general acceptance as an effective and often preferred mode of assistance. Group leadership skills are now considered required for counselors who wish to be adequately trained.

Historical Perspective

Psychology's Contribution to Group Work

The major contribution to group work comes from the field of psychology. It has been the primary influence in theory, research, and practice. Group counseling is primarily a psychological activity, whether conducted by a psychologist, counselor, social worker, psychiatrist, or nonprofessional.

Joseph Hersey Pratt, a physician, is credited with starting the first psychotherapy group in 1905. Its members were tubercular outpatients at Boston's Massachusetts General Hospital, organized into groups of about 20 for "inspirational, persuasive, and supportive" purposes. Although the sessions dealt with some medical topics, the emphasis seems to have been mainly psychological. Pratt was the first to recognize some of the dynamics that occur in group therapy: the need for mutual support and the positive influence one member can have on another.

As psychoanalysis became more popular, its approach to working with individuals was applied to group work. The psychoanalytic approach offered a conceptual framework for understanding human behavior, a theoretical stance not previously available to the group therapist. Louis Wender observed transference phenomena in the group, and Paul Schilder applied free association techniques by encouraging group members to say whatever they wished.

Slavson's Activity Group Therapy resulted from his experience as a psychoanalytic patient, his involvement in progressive education, and the wish to work with children and adolescents in groups. He was able to get children to express themselves through various group activities and expanded his approach to include verbal therapy with older children. In the 1940s, Alexander Wolf worked with adults in therapy groups, and began the Postgraduate Center for Psychotherapy at New York Medical College in 1948. Wolf and his student, Emanuel Schwartz, eventually introduced the first certification program in group therapy. Slavson, Wolf, and Schwartz believed the group evoked psychoanalytic concepts more strikingly than did one-to-one therapy. The therapist's role as analyst and interpreter remained the same, but the interactions and dynamics in a group yielded more behavioral data. The individual remained the focus of treatment. "Multiple transference" was the one additional concept that emerged after the therapists observed that group members engaged in transference with other participants as well as with the group leader.

A subgroup within the psychoanalytic school disagreed with the orthodox view of group therapy. Foulkes, Bion, and Ezriel in Britain and Whitaker and Lieberman in the U.S. believed that group therapy varied significantly from individual therapy. They pointed out that different and more complex dynamics occurred, and new concepts for understanding group process had to be developed. Social psychology and respect for the group as a whole were necessary for effective group leadership. Shaffer and Galinsky point out the difficulty people have in perceiving the group as a distinct entity to be studied and understood apart from the study of individuals. Those who have previously worked exclusively in individual therapy often focus on the needs and behaviors of the individuals rather than on the dynamics of the group as a whole.

Another offshoot of the psychoanalytic model is European existentialism. Its proponents considered the group leader free to express personal feelings, attitudes, or concerns. Group discussion focused on the here-and-now, and there was more spontaneous interaction between group leader and participants. Ludwig Binswanger, Medard Boss, and others maintained the general psychoanalytic methodology and way of conceptualizing group behavior.

The most significant early divergence from the psychoanalytic model was that of Jacob Moreno and his Psychodrama Model. Although he had formulated his ideas earlier, in 1921 he formalized them into his Theatre of Spontaneity. In fact, Moreno was the first to use the term "group psychotherapy." He had observed how children were able to act out their feelings and thoughts, and decided to employ theatrical techniques with people who had psychiatric problems. One group member took center stage, acting out some important aspects of his present or past life. Other group members played the roles of significant others and auxiliary ego roles (different parts of the self). The group member and the leader "staged" the scenario, thus bringing psychological concerns into the here-and-now in a dramatic, concrete way. This action method allowed cathartic release, confrontation with the life situation, and prevention of avoidance or resistance. Moreno had a strong influence on Perls's Gestalt therapy as well as on other figures in the encounter group movement. Psychodrama is still taught at the Moreno Institute, and used in some form, such as role playing, by a large number of group therapists.

Another group approach, Gestalt therapy, was also action-oriented and called for the involvement of the group leader. Fritz Perls received psychoanalytic training, but came to disagree with many analytic concepts. He was influenced by Moreno's psychodrama, Zen, Gestalt psychology, and existentialism, among other concepts. He rejected the analytic emphasis on transference, going back to early childhood events, interpretation, and the more knowing stance of the therapist. Rather, Perls's groups dealt with the here-and-now, with the leader acting as facilitator/catalyst/describer of behavior. Perls placed the therapist-client relationship in a group context. He worked first with one group member only, using the other members only as observers, then encouraged interaction between the target member and other participants.

Behavior therapy had its beginnings in early experimental psychology that stressed learning principles as the best method for understanding and changing human behavior. The early work and concepts of Pavlov, Watson, and Skinner were adapted to psychotherapeutic situations. Stimulus-response, reinforcement, reward, contingency schedules, and other concepts could readily be used to plan modification of client behaviors. In the 1950s and 1960s, behavior modification approaches made a significant impact on counseling and therapy, especially in working with more difficult populations. This active approach continually sought behavior change as an objective, rather than relief of symptoms or talking "about" problems. The group soon became a good place to do behavior therapy. Structured group sessions were devised to deal with specific phobias, anxieties, efforts to stop smoking, and assertiveness training.

Growth and encounter groups are usually conducted for persons who function relatively well in society. Kurt Lewin's field theory of the 1930s and 1940s was the basis for the Tavistock small study groups in Britain, and the T-group (popularized by the National Training Laboratory) in the U.S. that became popular in the 1950s and 1960s. Although the Tavistock groups were similar to the T-groups in that they were unstructured and focused on members learning about themselves and group dynamics, the Tavistock group adhered to psychoanalytic concepts. Bion was one of the Tavistock group who focused on group cohesiveness and the regressive and progressive forces in a group. The small study group was to deal with its own dynamics and to understand itself as a group.

The T-group evolved from an emphasis on group relations within organizations to include interpersonal relationships and personal growth as legitimate group goals. Leading encounter group figures who emerged from T-group training were William Schutz and Jack Gibb. In the 1950s and 1960s, group objectives expanded beyond training in group dynamics and effective leadership techniques to enhancing one's personal growth. Stronger beliefs in humanistic principles and the more permissive atmosphere that encouraged greater self-expression and finding oneself, along with the need to cope with an increasingly depersonalized society contributed to the popularity of encounter groups.

In the early 1960s, Rogers used the term "Basic Encounter Group" and went beyond his previous group experience when training graduate students. His nondirective approach was in contrast to the gestalt and psychodrama groups, but shared many of the same basic beliefs about human nature. Rogers was the prototype of the group leader who believed in the person's ability to grow and function well if given the proper group environment. Perls and others also had this confidence in the group member and placed primary responsibility for growth on the individual participant. Encounter group leaders tended to deal with the here-and-now, had a phenomenological philosophy (valuing the perception of the person as his own reality), encouraged free expression, and tried to foster a close, supportive group environment. Systematic Human Relations Training and structured skill groups have evolved recently in response to society's wish to see concrete results from group work as well as abstract personal growth.

Group Guidance

Gazda (1977) traces the history of the group guidance movement to a 1907 class on "Vocational and Moral Guidance" in a Cedar Rapids, Iowa, high school. A course in occupational information was introduced at the high school in Westport, Connecticut, in 1908. Although these classes were instructional, they could be considered the forerunner of vocational group counseling. During the 1930s, classes like these became extremely popular throughout the country and led to the publication of numerous group guidance texts. At the same time, nonvocational themes appeared as part of the group guidance process. Homeroom teachers acquired a guidance function that included helping to establish relationships, determining student needs and abilities, and developing proper attitudes. Group guidance remained in the classroom until the 1950s. Gazda contends that because there were few counselors during this time and because teachers were not trained in group dynamics, classroom guidance was not very effective; since then, teachers have acquired group leadership skills and have become concerned with students' affective as well as cognitive development. School counselors are now better trained and able to consult with classroom teachers to facilitate students' personal development. It is not uncommon for classroom teachers to lead discussions about students' feelings, and to lead exercises for developing body-image. We now understand that knowledge of group dynamics is extremely important for the classroom teacher.

Group guidance and counseling outside the classroom is a more recent phenomenon. The few counselors there were before the 1950s did little group counseling, and very little of any kind of counseling as we know it today. Giving students vocational information, helping with selection of a college, discipline, and scheduling took most of their time. In some schools, counselors now lead counseling groups that go beyond vocational exploration, to focus on interpersonal, behavioral, attitudinal, and other dimensions.

Social Group Work

Social group work dates back to the settlement houses of the 1800s and early 1900s (Galinsky & Shaffer, 1974). The poor had so many problems besides their economic plight that social workers became a strong force in the attempt to improve their situation. Jane Addams's founding of Hull House in Chicago in 1889 was the highlight of this reform era. Group work was employed to address the many needs of the poor; thus, social workers were probably the first professionals to use group techniques for social and personal development. These group counseling procedures were not, however, based on knowledge of group dynamics; they resembled group guidance in that they served relatively large groups, were structured, sometimes had an outside speaker, and were usually formed to convey information or motivate participants. After World War I, social group work also dealt with teaching skills and values, often in youth service and community agencies, and often led by interested but untrained people.

During the 1940s, the focus enlarged to a treatment model. The influence of psychoanalysts, the desire for greater professional acceptance, and the opportunity to expand work settings to the many treatment centers changed the nature of group work. At this time social workers learned the psychoanalytic model of psychotherapy and often worked under the supervision of psychiatrists. They were able to obtain positions in mental health settings, child guidance centers, prisons, and other helping agencies. The methods and goals of social group work have changed over time. Originally, the concern was with changes in the environment, such as housing and jobs, that would benefit the individual group member. The psychoanalytic influence added an understanding of the individual to the existing concern with the impact of the environment on the individual.

Rehabilitation and Agency Group Work

Rehabilitation counseling with disabled persons began with the 1917 Smith-Hughes Vocational Act and the 1920 Smith-Fess Act. The Smith-Hughes Act initiated rehabilitation services to disabled veterans; the Smith-Fess Act expanded services to physically disabled civilians. Later, rehabilitation counselors added the psychiatric, mentally retarded, alcoholic, and nearly all different and deviant populations. There is no documentation of group rehabilitation work before World War II; however, the combined influence of group vocational guidance and Carl Rogers's group work led to the widespread use of groups in rehabilitation settings from the 1960s on. Group counseling is most often used in private rehabilitation centers and rehabilitation facilities, and sometimes in state vocational rehabilitation field offices. Counselors in field offices do not usually see their clients on a weekly basis, and use groups less often because of the emphasis on individual case management and coordination. Field offices are increasingly recognizing the usefulness of groups in helping clients develop positive attitudes toward their disability, explore vocational alternatives, find community resources, prepare for job interviews and related job-seeking skills, form job clubs, and cope with family and community attitudes.

The needs of the clientele are so diverse that one approach could not be satisfactory to all. Because vocational guidance deals with vocational needs, group vocational counseling is often found in rehabilitation settings. Groups range from very structured, intended to develop specific skills such as job seeking or work adjustment, to a more client-centered style that allows relatively free exploration of vocational interests. Other rehabilitation counseling groups include those that focus on adjusting to a disability, behavioral group approaches with lower functioning clients, such as the mentally retarded, severe psychiatric cases, and the brain damaged, and groups for learning daily living skills.

Definition of Group Counseling

The characteristics of a group have been explained in many different ways, depending upon the type of group and its situation or goals. Because we are concerned with group counseling, we will discuss the nature of groups in which counseling takes place, but even with this narrower focus, we still do not find a consensus among professionals as to the definition of a group.

We can probably agree that a group is a collection of individuals who meet and interact with one another face-to-face. Group members believe they belong to a particular group for the purpose of achieving a goal. They meet to satisfy personal needs and become interdependent because they influence one another. Events that affect one member have an impact on the others. There are thus individual factors, personal transactions, and a unitary fuctioning that clearly differentiates a group from one-to-one interactions. Furthermore, roles and norms become established in a group as a kind of structure develops among the members. Roles and norms evolve from sharing common attitudes, values, and beliefs. Members' personality styles, skills, and needs contribute to the group's roles and interactions. Depending upon the purpose and make-up of the group, it needs an appropriate number of members, a degree of motivation, a purpose, and, eventually, self-direction. Finally, groups go through stages that can be observed and described. For example, the beginning stage is often characterized by the members' getting to know each other, while being careful at first in revealing themselves. In the middle stage, a healthy group works at self-exploration and behavior change. The final stages of the group include termination and follow-up.

Gazda (1978) offers good general definition of a group:

> Group work refers to the dynamic interaction between collections of individuals for prevention or remediation of difficulties or for the enhancement of personal growth/enrichment through the interaction of those who meet together for a commonly agreed-on purpose and at prearranged times. (p.260)

Rationale for Group Counseling

Each model of group counseling, each group leader, and even group participants have a rationale for the group experience, whether explicit or implicit. Although political and economic realities require human interaction, we are most concerned with family, friendship, sexual, leisure time, or work relationships. These relationships produce stress, a sense of alienation, loss of meaning, low self-esteem, dissatisfaction with self and others, a sense of failure, or a desire to improve on a good life. All these situations are interpersonal or social, involving interaction in a group.

People live their lives in many groups of two or more, and happiness is to a large extent a function of how well these groups meet one's needs and how well one contributes to the good of the others and the group as a whole. If one perceives that she belongs, is accepted in, is loved by, can contribute to, and is safe in the various groups, the chances are good that one will have a sense of well-being and satisfaction with life.

The basic rationale for group counseling, then, is that it can improve or enlarge upon the real-life group experiences we confront every day. Group counseling is often the preferred intervention or life enhancement strategy because it most closely resembles real-life situations. It gives group members opportunities to express themselves, receive feedback from others, and observe, practice, and learn new behaviors that can then be transferred to group interactions in the real world.

Group counseling has many advantages over other intervention strategies. It can, on the one hand, be an intense experience that places a person in the spotlight, confronting his own feelings and pressures from other group members. On the other hand, a group member can choose not to interact and can verbally withdraw while maintaining involvement in the group process. It offers a great variety of experiences to choose from and allows participants to determine their own level and style of development. Members can get to know others relatively intimately if they wish and can reveal themselves in a safe environment. The relative safety of a group fosters trust, self-disclosure, and a willingness to try new behaviors. In the process, one receives valuable feedback from the others' individual perceptions. Thus, one is able to test interpersonal realities in a nonthreatening setting and receive the support of the group while doing so. When groups function well, the members are able to achieve a sense of belonging, emotional closeness, challenges to their old lifestyles and perceptions, and personal growth.

The counselor also finds advantages in the group experience. It enables the counselor to understand clients better as they interact in an array of behavior patterns, whereas one-to-one counseling provides quite limited information. The interaction among many different personality types gives more diagnostic information and allows the counselor to formulate strategies for each group member. The many dynamics in the group, the actions and reactions between members, and the members' coping strategies provide valuable information. In leading the group, the counselor has an opportunity to observe and assimilate the dynamics not present in individual counseling. The leader can employ many more techniques, which we will discuss in a later chapter, that afford greater opportunity to effect growth or change in participants. The group setting is a more realistic place to apply theory and concepts of human behavior because it resembles real-life situations. The final advantage is economic: when client-student numbers are high in proportion to the available counselors, groups are more efficient than individual counseling. Social skill development, job-seeking groups, clarification of life goals and styles, and other issues can be dealt with as effectively and more efficiently in a group.

Types of Groups

The range of counseling groups is so diverse that we cannot include all of them here. We will examine some of the more popular groups and a few unusual group types. Later chapters will give a more complete idea of what transpires in counseling groups.

Groups usually form because people with something in common wish to discuss ways of dealing with a personal, social, medical, or vocational aspect of their lives. Group types thus encompass the full range of problems and challenges human beings face in their daily lives. The first counseling groups were formed to help patients cope with a disease, and this type of group continues today in medical and rehabilitation settings. Support and therapeutic groups discuss how to deal with their disease or disability, how to accept oneself, and how to cope with family, community, and employers.

Groups made up of psychiatric patients and outpatients also have a long tradition. Sessions are directed toward the psychopathology that prevents individuals from functioning adequately in the community. Through discussion and interaction, group members come to better understand how and sometimes why they are dysfunctional, and ultimately to help each other engage in more adaptive behaviors. Psychiatric hospitals and community mental health centers house most of these groups. Another early form of group counseling was for adolescents. They may involve group activities as well as discussion, with the purpose of having young people display their behavioral difficulties in the group, followed by peer pressure and other techniques to modify the behavior.

Vocational and academic counseling groups are normally more structured, with specifically defined goals and more explicit expectations of group members. The leader has more control of the group, and there is greater emphasis on cognitive change and skill development than on emotional and interpersonal dimensions. Vocational groups in a school setting may explore career alternatives, places for further education, and job requirements for various occupations. There are also groups for developing job seeking skills, in which members learn how to find job leads, how to prepare a resume, and how to present oneself to an employer. The goal of the group is to have each member find a suitable job. Vocational and academic counseling groups include work adjustment groups in rehabilitation agencies, midlife career change groups, academic skills training groups, career exploration groups in college, and occupational information groups for low achieving high school students.

Other structured groups that have become popular include Parent Effectiveness Training, in which parents meet to learn better ways of relating to and managing their children. The leader is more directive than one would find in therapeutic groups; he teaches definable skills yet group interaction and support are key elements in a successful group. Spin-offs from this model include Teacher Effectiveness Training and Leadership Effectiveness Training, where again the emphasis is on skill development. Small groups for college freshmen give them an orientation to the school and allow them to express anxieties about their new undertaking and form relationships with classmates. Another structured group is that which offers information from group leader, speakers, and fellow group members to parents of handicapped children. A related though less structured group for parents of handicapped children provides support, and is most helpful when the children are severely handicapped. Parents learn they are not alone in their struggles, receive genuine understanding from one another, and acquire useful ideas for coping with their responsibilities.

The T-Group (training group) emerged after World War II as a method for training members of an organization or social system in human relations skills. Group counseling and therapy had not yet become very popular, but Kurt Lewin's ideas formed a basis for understanding organizational and social system dynamics. Although there was some effort to promote personal growth in group members, the emphasis was on developing leadership skills that would allow members to go back to their organization or social system and deal with group process. T-groups educated members through task-oriented experiences constructed to simulate real group experiences in an organization. These groups evolved from the task-oriented focus of the late 1940s and 1950s to an orientation during the last two decades in which interpersonal relationships in a group are considered most important. Systematic Human Relations Training is closely related to group counseling and T-Groups, and derives from the work of Carkhuff (1969), who used and expanded on Rogers's (1957) necessary and sufficient conditions for therapeutic success by conceiving a systematic method for training people in several interpersonal skills, such as empathy, respect, and genuineness. Groups of professionals, paraprofessionals, and lay people could be trained to exhibit human relations skills in a relatively brief period of time (Vander Kolk, 1973). The systematic approach was new to the field of counseling and therapy (with the exception of behavioral approaches) in the 1960s, and the emphasis on skill development was not held in high esteem at the time. Today, a focus on client skill development has become popular as an alternative to the medical model (that is, treatment of symptoms) often employed in mental health and other agency settings (Anthony, 1980). Groups are a particularly good environment for people to learn social and interpersonal skills. In Systematic Human Relations Training, specific skills are identified and illustrated; then, group members practice the skills until they reach the maximum possible skill level in the alloted time. These groups are used most often with counselors in training, in agencies as part of inservice education, and with clients in agencies, schools, and institutions.

Encounter Groups are diverse in their methods, group members' experiences, and leadership styles. Their common goal is to help the group member deal with himself and others more openly and honestly. The groups are both therapeutic and educative, focusing on the individual as well as on better contact with the environment, and employ traditional as well as contemporary group techniques. Carl Rogers (1970) evolved a form of encounter group from his client-centered therapy and related theoretical principles. Rogers, along with most encounter group leaders, provides minimal structure, allowing members to use their own needs and abilities to guide the group's direction. The leader primarily reflects group members' verbal and nonverbal expressions. Rogers employs few exercises to facilitate the group interaction. Schutz (1971), on the other hand, came from a psychoanalytic background to become one of the leaders of the sensitivity-encounter development in California during the 1960s. Schutz's open encounter model is characterized by open membership; use of communication games and exercises; recognition of the interplay of fantasy, imagery, body image, emotions, sensations, and the mind; and the leaders' providing an atmosphere of trust, growth, and support. Encounter or sensitivity groups are not normally used with a psychiatric population. Members are most interested in goals of personal growth, self-actualization, self-awareness, and enhancing their human potential. Marathon groups are a form of encounter or sensitivity group; some meet for 24 hours, while others meet for several days, adjourning to sleep and eat. The experience tends to break down defenses quickly as people become fatigued and/or learn to trust others quickly in the intense emotional environment. Interpersonal communication exercises are frequently used to hasten members' awareness of themselves, promote contact with their feelings, and promote increased group participation. Encounter and sensitivity group leaders require particular competence because of the potentially explosive emotional situations that may arise.

Counseling groups have been formed for numerous special populations; for example, group treatment of alcoholics and drug abusers is often preferred over individual counseling. The format for these groups varies from relatively nondirective and accepting to confrontive. Group counseling may be specially designed for minority groups, the aged, women, mentally retarded, or business executives. Some group types are consciousness raising, communication skills, interpersonal and social skill development, child management, rights advocacy, and human relations skills.

Ethical Guidelines

Any therapeutic or guidance intervention strategy has the potential to help or harm. Group counseling takes many forms, in many settings, with many different types of participants, various goals, and leaders with diverse training and experiential backgrounds; it is not possible to generalize about the limits and dangers in all group counseling situations. There are, however, limits and potential dangers for leaders and participants to be aware of before they become involved. Professional organizations have formulated ethical guidelines for practice, and you should carefully examine the ethical codes of your professional organizations. Ethical standards are devised to protect the interests of the group participant, not to inhibit the legitimate skills of the professional counselor therapist, and standards can be considered only guidelines, since one cannot anticipate all possible situations. The counselor or therapist must ultimately use his own judgment to make decisions that have ethical implications. When in doubt, it is best to consult a colleague and weigh other opinions before making a final decision.

The casebook of the American Association of Counseling and Development (AACD), formerly the American Personnel and Guidance Association, covers general practice and ethical guidelines for group leaders (Callis, Pope & DePauw, 1982). A counselor is expected to adhere to the general ethical standards of his professional association and to specific ethical guidelines for group practice.

The AACD casebook (Callis, Pope & DePauw, 1982) presents cases to illustrate each standard. AACD standards include the following:

Continuous professional growth throughout one's career. This implies ongoing education and inservice training.

Maintaining a high caliber of ethical, professional conduct and services.

Reporting knowledge of unethical behavior on the part of colleagues.

Stating professional qualifications accurately. The public and fellow workers have a right to be informed as to a counselor's professional training and experience.

Giving only unbiased and objective information to other parties. Client information, for example, must be presented accurately.

Respecting the client and guarding individual rights.

The ASGW guidelines for providing information and group services include these general responsibilities. For example, members have a right to know the group's goals, the leader's qualifications, and how the group will function. Individual and group goals are expected to be compatible, and potential members should have an explanation of group procedures: number of members, degree of structure, expectations of members, role of the leader, and group activities. The leader's qualifications should be conveyed in writing, although even that does not fully protect the consumer from a group leader's potential negative influence. The leader will need the skills and knowledge appropriate to a particular group and a certain amount of training and supervised experience before they lead a group of their own.

A solid graduate program that covers the many aspects of human behavior, such as personality, counseling theory and practice, and assessment of behavior, is a good foundation for group work, with theory, research, and practice in group work under supervision as the second phase of training. Ideally, the trainee would have experience as a group participant, then as a co-leader with an experienced group counselor, and finally as a leader under supervision.

Unfortunately, some group leaders have not accurately assessed their competence to lead counseling and therapy groups. One cause for the problem is inadequate training—participating in group counseling or attending a workshop does not qualify one as a group leader. Another factor is personality. Some professionals do not have the patience or inclination to allow a group a degree of control, or are too aggressive and directive. Yalom and Lieberman (1971) found that aggressive, authoritarian, confrontive leaders, and leaders who were distant and emotionally cool produced the most casualities. The leader has a responsibility to recognize his limitations and engage in only those situations he is prepared to handle.

Another guideline addresses screening and orientation for group membership. The ethics of *screening* concerns the potential benefit or harm that can derive from the group experience. The selector, usually the group leader, must try to select members most likely to benefit from the particular group and screen out those who will detract from the group. Some professionals believe that very disturbed persons, those in crisis, those in individual therapy, and those with a medical condition should not be included in sensitivity or therapeutically oriented groups. Yalom and Lieberman (1971) found measures of self-esteem, self-concept, growth orientation or expectations, and coping-ego-defense scales to be the best predictors of potential group casualties.

Group counseling may not be appropriate for certain types of problems, and some clients could be destructive to the group process. Aggressive individuals who act out verbally or physically are usually not good candidates for a group unless addressing those particular problems is the purpose of the group. People who are delusional, hallucinating, or otherwise have marginal contact with reality are unlikely to benefit from group counseling.

People who do not want to be in a group are less likely to benefit. When attendance is required in a mental health setting or by court order, the individual will probably exhibit additional resistance and hostility. Feelings about required attendance should be dealt with first. Mentally retarded or brain-injured persons usually do not benefit from traditional therapeutic group counseling. Others who would probably derive more benefit from individual counseling include, for example, a person who has just completed a battery of vocational and/or psychological tests, and probably needs to receive the information in one-to-one sessions with the counselor. Certain adolescents with behavioral problems in school and at home may need to be seen individually and with the parents to work on behavior management. At some point, group counseling can supplement the individual work for these clients.

Selecting members for a group will be discussed in chapter 9, but we can say here that members should be chosen according to whether group goals and other potential members are appropriate for the individual.

After members have been selected, ethical guidelines suggest individual interviews to prepare each member for the group experience. This is the time to give more detailed information about the group, deal with individual anxieties and questions, and to make a contract with the client as to everyone's goals and expectations. Unrealistic expectations can be dealt with at this time. The group will not bring dramatic changes to one's life; rather, members make small but significant changes, or gain information about self and others, or grow in a way not possible for them without the group experience. The individual interview is also the time to address involuntary membership.

There is also a guideline that refers to the difficulty of handling confidentiality of information. Groups function best when the members and leader trust one another, and trust develops when participants believe that what they say will not be repeated outside the group. Group members are reminded before they meet, during the first meeting, and occasionally thereafter, of the rule of confidentiality: they are not to repeat revelations or experiences of fellow members to people not involved in the group. There are exceptions and modifications to the rule. A few professionals tell members that nothing is confidential, and that they should reveal to the group only what they are willing to have repeated. If the leader is employed by an agency that requires case reports on each member, the members should be informed of the leader's obligation and what type of information will be included in the reports. Usually, however, a leader does not have to reveal specific information, although parents often have a right to information regarding a minor child. Group leaders must be careful not to reveal information about a member that may have come from individual counseling sessions, although it can be tempting to use or allude to the information to force the member to deal with an issue in the group.

Other ASGW guidelines relate to communicating the services one can expect to receive from group experience, and special conditions or experiments that may take place during the sessions.

There is a danger that participants may try to translate group experiences into everyday experiences. After an intense group experience in which one has met with acceptance and trust and has behaved openly and uninhibitedly, for example, attempting to transfer the same interactions to the outside world can produce a shock. Openness and trust are not rewarded in the day-to-day world as they are in counseling groups. A related danger is that an ex-group member may feel vulnerable now that he has opened up, and with inadequate support and understanding outside the group, may experience emotional distress and confusion, or, his new awareness may lead to impulsive decisions.

Members should be aware that they always have the right to terminate with the group. If counseling is required, the member can be referred to another group or counselor.

Group leaders must inform members of plans to tape record sessions, and obtain information releases if the sessions are part of a research project or to be used in discussion with colleagues.

Group leaders are expected to help members avoid threats, coercion, intimidation, and peer pressure. The group can become a powerful influence on its members' attitudes, feelings, and behavior. The group attempts to make members conform to its norms and expectations; when the norms and expectations are not suitable to the individual one can expect conflict. There is often inappropriate pressure for closeness and intimacy. Coercion, coaxing, and intimidation to produce self-disclosure or involvement in group exercises is a destructive influence on the group.

The leader is sometimes tempted to satisfy ego needs, to "look good," or to keep group members in a dependent position. The leader needs to be careful not to impose his values and expectations on others.

The leader should be active to the extent of facilitating the opportunity of each member to benefit from the group's resources. One or a few members' monopolizing of group time, for example, must be treated as a behavior that limits other participants' involvement.

Each member is to be treated equally and individually. This implies setting individual goals, respecting individual styles of interaction, and acknowledging that attitudes and behavior change at different rates.

It is unethical for leaders of counseling groups to have an intimate relationship with a group member. Members are vulnerable to the leader's "power"; others try to manipulate the leader. Members, may, however, socialize with one another outside the group as long as they do not discuss group sessions and report the socializing to the group.

The leader must encourage members to increase their independence and discourage dependent and manipulative behavior.

Many group techniques require supervised experience before the leader should try them independently. Techniques for eliciting emotions and intense feelings have the potential for harm as well as good.

Use of drugs or alcohol in association with group sessions is not condoned; some groups may, however, perhaps have wine and cheese after a session for more informal social interaction.

Group leadership involves a commitment to help participants reach the goals they set for themselves by all reasonable means.

Group leader responsibilities are not confined only to actual sessions, since members may need consulations on matters that cannot be handled during the group. Also, events during a group session may not be resolved, and will require attention before the next session.

At the time of termination, members may need referral to other community services. After termination, the leader is available for consultation and possibly further counseling. It is commonly agreed that the leader must prepare members for what is often an emotionally difficult termination. Following up on members after termination helps the leader evaluate group effectiveness.

The final section of the ethical guidelines explains the steps to take when one finds that a colleague is engaging in unethical behavior.

Theory

Because group counseling involves human behavior at many levels, it is a complex phenomenon. The first level with which counselors are concerned is individual behavior—one's intrapsychic, internal, physical, mental, and emotional facets. At this level, theories of personality come into play. Another theoretical level in group counseling is that of interpersonal behavior, which helps in understanding interactions among members of a group. The next level to address theoretically is the behavior of the group as a whole. Group theory helps us understand the dynamics of group process. We need to know whether a group is working cooperatively or has antagonistic subgroups. Two sources of theoretical understanding are important at this level. First, social psychology studies the behavior of groups, and has contributed many concepts and principles that can be applied to group counseling. Festinger's (1957) theory of cognitive dissonance, for example, gives us one way of understanding how group members deal with information that contradicts their beliefs or values. The second theoretical source is that of group counseling itself. Counselors realized that unique features of group behavior required concepts and constructs derived from observation of the group as a whole. Moreno was a leader in this evolution, but the T-group experiences after World War II brought the conceptualization of group process closer to the forefront, and theorists such as Berne and Rogers soon constructed their own theories of group counseling.

The theories we will discuss in the next chapters integrate individual, interpersonal, and small group theories; some emphasize one level more than another. Gestalt theories tend to focus more on the individual; Rogers's encounter groups are more interpersonal; and Transactional Analysis focuses on the entire group. (Application of theory to group counseling practice is covered in chapter 10.)

Function of Theory

Group counseling theory influences the behavior of the counselor and of the client. Since theory derives from the counselor's personal characteristics, history (experiences), and philosophical background, it closely relates to and to an extent determines the counselor's actions in a group setting. Because the counselor elicits responses from group members, his behavior influences the clients' expectations and reactions. Theory thus has a direct impact on counseling practice.

Good theory serves many practical functions. First, it gives meaning to and a framework for understanding facts and experiences. Behavioral observations take on meaning when they are organized and integrated into a conceptual framework. When members need time and a certain atmosphere to work cooperatively, we arrange our observations of those needs systematically to understand their significance. Theory unifies facts and observations to help us understand their implications for counseling practice. Theory also makes our experience logical and reasonable, helping us to know what to expect in a variety of counseling situations and choose appropriate behaviors for those circumstances. For example, theories suggest that groups pass through stages. In early sessions the counselor expects little cohesion and, consequently, waits patiently for a sense of unity to develop.

A third function of theory is as a heuristic device, a tool to guide systematic observation and produce new information. The assumptions, statements, associated concepts, and constructs of a theory either explicity or implicitly predict what will occur in group interaction. Predictions must be observable and repeatable; that is, observers must be able to test and validate the theory. For example, if a theory proposes that an authoritarian leader will elicit two responses in group members, submission when the leader has power over them, and rebellion when the leader is perceived as having little or no power, the propositions must be publicly observed and tested to determine their accuracy. Merely making a proposition has heuristic value, and contributes to our knowledge of group dynamics.

Tasks of Group Counseling Theory

The term "task" here is a little more specific than "function." Theory serves several tasks that give a more detailed look at how a group functions. First, theory can describe and explain behavior at a particular time in the group process. As the leader observes group interaction, he relies on guidelines to understand the behavior at that moment. Theory provides rules for describing what one sees, classifying the behavior, and responding to the group behavior. If the leader observes silence in the group just as one member verbally attacks another member, counseling theory shows how to classify the behavior (for example, as hostile, self-protective), describe the behavior (verbal, abusive language), and intervene (for example, by asking the group how they have reacted to the attack, or pointing out the silence, or interpreting the verbal abuse, or remaining silent). Each theory has its own way of conceptualizing a particular group behavior.

A second task of theory is to describe the antecedent conditions relating to the group behavior. Both psychoanalytic and behavioral theories are concerned with the most detailed possible description of events previous to the behavior. Antecedent conditions determine the behavior of the moment. Other theories recognize that recent past behavior influences the present, but that group member behavior is also influenced by the individual's inner experiences at the moment. Theories will therefore differ as to the significance of antecedent conditions in understanding present behavior.

Theory also explains how behavior changes inside and outside the group; each theory selects what to observe in the way of expected changes in group members. Theory building is a subjective process, and the choice of group goals illustrates this subjectivity. One theory may look for evidence of a more positive self-concept or greater self-awareness; another may evaluate changes in community adjustment.

Barclay (1971) points out that two types of theories focus on different types of change. The humanistic group (Rogers and Gestalt, for example) are interested in the inner reality, or what the client experiences. The client's report of changes in self-esteem are most important. The environmentalist group (Behaviorists and Psychoanalysts) are concerned with outer reality, or what they can analyze as behavior change that conforms to predominant social expectations. We include psychoanalysts because of the influence of scientific realism and logical positivism. The humanistic group tends to be less specific in goals and expected change. Environmentalists attempt to be more specific, to measure behavioral skills that can be readily observed inside and outside the group.

A fourth task of theory is to explain what contributes to behavior change. When change occurs, we want to know why; theory helps simplify and select from the many variables that could affect group and individual behavior modification. Group dynamics are so complex that without a theory, the group leader would be overwhelmed in determining what caused changes in the group. A unique feature of group counseling theory is the interaction of each member with other members, and the influence of the group as a whole. One member affects another member, the leader affects each member, and the group as a whole affects each member. Gestalt theory suggests that the leader can stimulate changes in the individual, with modest influence from the group. The leader in behavioral groups acts as a technician who arranges contingencies for change; the group provides appropriate reinforcement. Encounter group leaders are facilitators, while the group plays a key role in bringing about change in its members. Analytic group leaders consider themselves and other group members symbols of people in an individual's past.

Characteristics of Theories

When we compare theories in terms of their characteristics, we find an array of classification systems.

- Group counseling theories are functional, in that experience provides their raw data. Theory is arrived at by deduction rather than induction.

- Theories differ as to their focus on universal versus individual differences. Analytic theory and Transactional Analysis suggest universal characteristics that we can observe in groups, and direct treatment toward modification of those personality traits. The more phenomenological theories, such as that of Rogers, attend to the individual and her peculiar needs and perception of the world.

- Each theory has its own way of evaluating human nature. Classical psychoanalysts portray human beings as "savages" who need to control aggressive and sexual impulses. Group counseling helps build ego mechanisms to screen and modify these impulses. Behaviorists view people as a tabula rasa at birth (although genetic factors cannot be ignored) and group counseling as a place to learn behaviors that will enhance adaptation. Self or phenomenological theories assume that people have an inherent capacity for growth and positive behavior, and that group counseling can provide the desired conditions for promoting personal growth.

- Theories are either mechanistic or humanistic. Mechanistic theories assume human beings are passive animals who respond mechanically to environmental stimuli. The extreme of this position is the belief that people are machines to be analyzed and controlled; more moderate positions ascribe a degree of self-initiation to individuals. Humanists assert that each person is unique, and can be proactive toward the environment: people act on the environment and are acted upon. Issues of determinism and free will enter the picture. Behaviorists and classical analysts tend toward the mechanistic and deterministic viewpoint; self-theorists identify themselves as humanists.

- Theorists analyze human behavior at *molar* and *molecular* levels. Molar theories examine larger units of behavior that may or may not be observable: thoughts, walking, smiling, verbal statements, and so on. Molecular theories study more specific parts of the organism, such as body chemical neurotransmitters or the muscles involved in body movements. Some behaviorists look not only at gross behavior, but also attempt to reduce the analysis as much as possible, believing that the more specific one can be, the better control we attain over behaviors. Gestalt and Encounter theories tend to be molar.

- Theories vary in the degree to which they emphasize structure and process. Structure includes size and composition of the group, leader training and skills, and the chosen outcome variables. Process refers to the group's interaction patterns: who exercises power over whom, how *A* is passive in relating to *B*, and how one subgroup rejects another subgroup. Theories emphasizing structure, such as Behavioral groups, tend to exercise more control and stress the importance of measured outcomes. Theories emphasizing process want to help people understand themselves and their interactions with others. How people feel about themselves is more important than measurable outcomes.

- A final characteristic is that of overt versus covert behavior. Behavioral theories deal primarily with explicit behavior, although most theorists recognize the presence of thoughts and sensations. At the other end of this continuum, psychoanalysts stress the significance of the unconscious. Self theories and Gestalt allude to unconscious behavior, but actually deal with conscious thought processes and overt behavior.

Group Counseling Theory

The beginning group counselor wishes to know what knowledge and skills are necessary to understand groups and to lead a group effectively. All theoreticians and practitioners will never agree on the generic concepts and techniques required in group counseling. We suggest as core knowledge and skills those that are receiving widespread, though not unanimous, acceptance. Deviations from the norm will be apparent in the chapters on theory, but representative common threads include these:

1. The leader can be a significant agent in facilitating or debilitating group process and outcome. Certain personality characteristics, educational-training prerequisites, and experiences enhance leader effectiveness.

2. The group is more than a collection of individuals. Understanding group process includes knowledge of group dynamics. Merely understanding each individual in the group is not sufficient.

3. Group members are selected so as to establish membership patterns that will facilitate reaching group objectives.

4. Group goals, in addition to and consistent with individual goals, are established early in the life of the group. While theorists may not agree on specific goals, they usually do set group goals.

5. Theorists and practitioners agree that groups go through stages of development, with normally an initial stage of getting acquainted and learning to trust one another, a relatively intense middle stage, and a final stage of preparing to disband. Some researchers and theorists count more than three stages.

6. Successful therapeutic group counseling usually involves certain relationships among group members and between the leader and group members, such as ability to listen and communicate, trust, concern for others, and regular attendance.

7. Certain dynamics in counseling groups are incorporated in or acceptable to nearly all major theories and practitioners, such as scapegoating (selecting a group member on whom to blame group problems), subgrouping, hostility toward the leader, monopolizing discussion, and cohesivenss (developing a sense of togetherness).

Suggested readings to augment understanding of theory include Corsini (1973), Strupp (1973), Patterson (1973), Morse and Watson (1977), and Garfield and Bergin (1978).

Summary

Group counseling emerged from the practice of individual psychotherapy, guidance, and social work. It is a relatively new field which needs much more research and systematic clinical observation to develop a better understanding of its usefulness. Group counseling is a preferred mode of intervention for many types of problems and situations. It has many advantages over individual counseling, and has gained acceptance as an effective treatment modality. Group counseling is now used in the traditional psychotherapeutic manner as well as for actualizing potential in basically "healthy" people. It is used with nearly all personal and vocational problems, and with very disturbed people, the socially different, the disabled, and with high functioning persons.

Ethical guidelines for practice are an important responsibility of the counselor, and theory is another tool for guiding group work. Knowledge of theory helps organize facts and experience so they make sense to the group leader, who is then able to understand group dynamics and make decisions about leader behavior. Theory provides a frame of reference for anticipating what will happen in a group, and usually contains a method for setting goals and evaluating outcome. A group leader who has a foundation of ethics and theory has the knowledge base from which he can develop skills.

PART 1

Models of Group Counseling

2

Psychodynamic Group Work

Psychoanalytic group work was the first to establish a theoretical basis for practice. Alfred Adler (1925) was an early advocate of group work; his student, Rudolf Dreikurs (1957; 1960), carried on the Adlerian method in the United States. Adler is grouped with the more classical analysts because he fits there historically and because he retained many of the basic concepts. He in fact deviated from Freud's theory more than did subsequent analytic group theorists such as Wolf and Schwartz (1962).

The extension of psychoanalysis into group psychotherapy did not occur until the second generation of analysts. Freud gave only passing attention to the psychological aspects of groups and families. He concentrated on the individual's attempts to control, mediate, or channel (the ego mechanisms); instinctual urges (id) that were socially unacceptable; and one's learned sense of right and wrong (superego). Fundamental to the classical psychoanalytic approach was the individual's intrapsychic dynamics. The social context was of less concern, and in the early days of this theoretical stance, group therapy was not considered. Even the inner circle of Freud's followers dealt exclusively with individual treatment.

New adherents to the psychoanalytic approach discovered a need to expand concepts and techniques to the group setting. Psychoanalytic group work initially took the form of treating the patient in the traditional one-to-one manner, but in a group setting (Wolf & Schwartz, 1962). The individual and the analysis of his unconscious remained the goal of psychoanalytic group therapy. Group dynamics and the perception of the group as a psychological entity remained for the next stage of psychoanalytic group therapists (Whitaker & Lieberman, 1965). Consequently, we now have two distinct forms of analytic group therapy, with variations in each of these camps. The first group remains true to the traditional one-to-one techniques of analysis; the second maintains the analytic concepts but adds techniques and ideas from group-dynamic therapists, and approaches the group as a whole psychological force.

The nature of these two analytic groups differs in terms of how they are led and conceptualized. Both usually have six to twelve members who are expected to verbalize whatever comes to mind. The leader assumes a passive stance, listening to group members' statements. In both analytic group types, the leader offers interpretations selected and timed for maximum impact. Individual members may also offer interpretations, although their interpretations may in turn be analyzed. One difference between the analytic groups is that classical analysts interpret the behavior of individual members, while group dynamic analysts interpret the behavior of the group. For example, the classical leader notices that one member continually disagrees with him in an angry tone of voice, and recalls the group member's unresolved conflict with his father. The leader suggests that the group participant has transferred his feelings toward his father to the group leader. The group dynamic therapist may notice that the group as a whole is hostile toward him, and in pointing it out, suggests that they have difficulty relating to someone they perceive as an authority figure.

In both groups, transferences and resistances are interpreted for the purpose of freeing up unconscious material and become the focus of the leader's attention. Another difference between the group types is that transferences and resistances can be viewed at either an individual or a group level.

Theoretical Constructs

These fundamental concepts of psychoanalysis were applied to group therapy by analysts who followed Freud.

Transference

The therapist-patient relationship is basic to the psychoanalytic process. Freud recognized this interpersonal relationship as the medium through which patient change would occur. Both parties play key roles in the analytic process, and Freud began the examination of that process. Although many authors give the impression that Freud and his followers singled out the dynamics of the patient as the grist for analysis, a student of Freud's, Fromm-Reichmann (1950), points out that the therapist's personal attributes contribute to the quality and course of the therapeutic relationship. She shows how the therapist's past experiences and current emotional state contribute to the vicissitudes of the relationship. Furthermore, childhood experiences are not the only ones to be understood in analysis. The patient can react to the therapist in a here-and-now relationship. Fromm-Reichmann gives the example of a patient who, after many sessions of rambling about inconsequential matters, finally reveals the core of his problem. The therapist does not hear the revelation, considering it a continuation of the previous babblings. As the patient realizes the therapist's indifference, he becomes hurt and angry. One could speculate that the therapist had a relative who rambled on about unimportant things and that as a child he simply tuned out this boring relative. The therapist is thus also vulnerable to transferring childhood experiences to the present, with the result that current experiences are distorted and handled inappropriately—an example of *countertransference*.

When transference attitudes and feelings from childhood go unresolved, they carry over into adulthood. The psychoanalyst wants to have the patient's former feelings toward parents transferred to him. Transference of early childhood feelings into the present, directed toward the therapist, provides the basis for a temporary neurotic relationship that must be worked through. The objective is to have the patient gain insight into his inappropriate transference and work it through to the point where he is no longer relating to the therapist on the basis of childhood experiences.

An example may help clarify transference. One patient soon began to view his therapist as a critical person who had a negative attitude toward him and his life-style. The analyst had in fact made no negative comments, maintaining a neutral stance regarding the patient's behavior. After a number of sessions it became apparent that the patient's mother had been extremely critical of him; he had never been able to completely please her. The patient transferred these feelings to the therapist. Later in the therapeutic process, the patient became angry with the therapist for what he thought was a posture of distance and lack of concern. It was revealed that the patient's grandfather, who lived next door, had been a cold, self-centered person. The patient had resented this for years, wanting more attention and affection from his grandfather. Attitudes toward the grandfather were now directed to the therapist.

The patient is not aware of the transfer of early childhood feelings to the immediate relationship with the therapist, yet this dynamic reality is a primary vehicle for the therapist to guide the patient's realization of how these distorted and inappropriately applied feelings and attitudes cause his current problems. The therapeutic relationship serves as a microcosm of the patient's other interpersonal relationships, allowing the two to work on their relationship as a basis for change in the patient's life outside psychotherapy. What the patient learns through understanding transferences will alter his relationships with other people in his life.

Since the patient is not aware of the connection between feelings toward the therapist and earlier experiences with significant people, one role for the therapist is helping the patient understand the pathology through the vehicle of interpretation. The objective is to have the patient relate to the therapist according to the reality of their own relationship. In this process, the therapist is primarily an observer, noticing distortions, inconsistencies, and contradictions in patient statements. The patient is expected to become frustrated with the therapist's role as observer—a degree of frustration is necessary for learning. At the same time, the therapist offers enough support to encourage the patient's work.

Analysts are sometimes portrayed as aloof and distant, occasionally interjecting an interpretation into the patient's never-ending verbalizations. Although this approach may be true of some, an effective analyst usually has more redeeming human qualitites. Contemporary analytically oriented psychotherapists advocate kindness, support, respect, genuineness, and a sincere concern for the patient (Menninger, 1958; Fromm-Reichmann, 1950). While Carl Rogers (1957) places understanding, respect, and genuineness at the center of his therapeutic process, the analysts view these interpersonal dimensions as only several to employ judiciously along with many others. Rogers would emphasize the "realness" of the therapist in a very human encounter; analysts search for the nature of the patient's transferred feelings in the relationship and carefully allow the "personal" aspect of the relationship to emerge, thus facilitating resolution of old and unresolved conflictual relationships. The therapist may therefore hold back if he judges it to be in the best interest of the patient.

The therapist need not point out transference reactions every time they occur, but only those reactions that repeatedly interfere with the patient's ability to deal effectively with real interpersonal issues. Key transference reactions will continually reappear, so the therapist has many opportunities to confront the patient's distortions. He must, however, be cognizant of all the transference reactions that occur. Analysis becomes more complex because the "real" feelings toward the therapist and the transference feelings are intermingled most of the time; it is important to correctly identify the respective feelings and disentangle them. Earlier classical analysts suggested that the patient's feelings of love toward the therapist were the critical transference reactions to resolve.

Freud believed the Oedipus complex was sexual, that sexual feelings toward the parent of the opposite sex or hatred toward the parent of the same sex were transferred to the therapist. Freud's followers, including Jung and Adler, and the neo-Freudians such as Sullivan and Fromm rejected what they considered an overemphasis on sexuality. Consequently, current analysts view the parent-child relationship as critical, but try to determine its nature without assuming it had a sexual quality. The relationship is more often viewed as a competitive striving for power and attention.

Later analysts also suggest that the hateful or malevolent aspects of the patient-therapist relationship be pointed out. These aspects usually result from resentment toward the significant others of childhood who did not meet personal needs, and this anger must now be worked through with the therapist as the object.

Free Association

Classical psychoanalysts believed free association was the most effective way to bring repressed material to the surface. A patient's associative thinking is "free" in the sense that there is encouragement to openly state all feelings, thoughts, and fantasies, discarding any conventional restrictions. As the analyst begins to formulate a picture of the patient's unconscious material, they are able to discuss its causes, dynamics, and character. In the strict sense of the term, free association is now used less frequently.

The actual content of free associations is now considered less important than the motivation behind the associations. What prevents the material from coming to awareness? What is the patient's reaction when repressed material comes to awareness? Analysts are now more inclined to listen carefully to patient statements and discern from the statements the need to keep old feelings and experiences below the surface of awareness. Focus on free association may also detract from patients' immediate needs. One can become overly concerned with the past and neglect current interpersonal needs. Immediate life conflicts and struggles can be just as useful in uncovering the causes of patient distortions and inappropriate dealings with others.

Resistance

In childhood, one dissociates oneself from feelings and experiences that cause pain. Resistance refers to the techniques employed to avoid confrontation with those earlier conflicts. The patient usually uses the same devices in adulthood that he used in childhood; in this respect, the patient regresses during therapy to this earlier stage of development. Resistance is noticeable in the patient's reluctance to communicate effectively with the therapist and in refusal to accept the therapist's interpretive comments. Accepting the interpretations brings the repressed material to awareness, and the patient fears confrontation with the anxiety and discomfort he avoided in childhood. The patient is not aware of his resistance early in the therapeutic process. For example, a patient has had problems at work; he believes the supervisor is unfair, but is unwilling to say anything to his supervisor. The therapist points out several times the similarity between this relationship and the patient's relationship with his father, which the patient denies are similar. He is not aware of his resistance, because admitting to the similarity would bring out the anxiety and resentment toward his father that he is repressing.

Resistance also occurs when patients fear that acceptance of an interpretation will reveal closeness to and acceptance of the therapist; they fear that rejection will follow closeness to another person. Others resist because they do not want to feel obligated to the therapist for his revelation. Patients may draw a blank, be inattentive, disparage the interpretation, or ramble on about the therapist's positive qualities. Silence, forgetting material from a previous session, missing appointments, and discussion of irrelevant material are also forms of resistance.

Interpretation of resistance is the second stage of the therapeutic process. One must first develop a relationship with the patient to the point that he hears the analyst's suggestions and does not take interpretations as reprimands. Resistance must be dealt with before moving on to other repressed material. Patients use a wide variety of defenses, and the therapist must be alert to each patient's ingenuity. Many analysts do not view resistance as a struggle between therapist and patient, but rather as a struggle between the patient's urge to remain the same, avoiding discomfort, and the coexistent urge to be healthier. The struggle is thus intrapersonal, with the therapist acting as an outsider supporting positive growth. Interpretation of resistance comes when the patient is strong enough to integrate the therapist's statements without suffering a high level of anxiety. Success is achieved when the patient can accept interpretation and integrate it into the many other things he has learned about himself. Integrating interpretations into an advanced understanding of oneself is *insight*. For example, a patient who had many difficulties on the job and at home was unable to attain a promotion at work because she made too many mistakes. Just before she took a test for promotion, she injured her hand, and at home, demanded help from her husband and older daughter by feigning helplessness at household tasks. The therapist had pointed out her dependency and "helpless" behavior, demonstrating that she had learned the techniques in her relationship with her parents. The patient was at first angry with the interpretation, accusing the therapist of expecting too much of her. After a time, she gradually recognized the dependent behaviors. True "insight" occurred when she dropped the resistances and saw the reality of her maneuvers to be taken care of. The repressed material, the childlike behaviors, had been brought to the surface. She then was able to try more effective ways of coping at work and relating to her family.

Interpretation

The primary purpose of interpretation is to bring to consciousness previously dissociated and repressed material. If the therapist can help the patient bring to awareness her true emotional experiences in past and present interpersonal relationships, emotional stability is most likely to result. When the patient unconsciously communicates early emotional experiences, connections between present and previous feelings, and distorted perceptions of relationships, the therapist translates them into awareness. The emotional reactions surrounding earlier events, rather than the events themselves, need interpretive clarification. The new-found awareness is then applied to present interpersonal relationships.

Repressed material continually appears in the therapist-patient relationship, and the connection between the patient's behavior in psychotherapy and early childhood experiences must be repeatedly worked through. Working through continues until understanding is transformed into curative insight, which the patient must then apply in consistent patterns of healthy interpersonal behavior. (All repressed material need not be brought to awareness, for our survival, certain experiences call for selective attention or repression. But when pain or anxiety interferes with our lives, we need to lift the associated repression.)

Various subgroups within the psychoanalytic school disagree as to techniques of interpretation, what should be selected for interpretation, and how to interpret. Content, process, or causal or motivational factors surrounding events may form the basis for interpretation. Sullivan (1953) emphasized interpersonal relationships for interpretation; others recognize the patient's cultural background as a partial determinant for repressed material, which consequently affects the therapist's interpretations (Fromm-Reichmann, 1950). Interpretation is ultimately a function of the personal and professional inclinations of the therapist and the dynamics of the patient-therapist relationship. There are no rules for interpretation. Some therapists are bold and confrontive, while others give "mild" interpretations, which go only slightly beyond the patient's current level of awareness.

In this example, the patient has been talking about his increasing resentment toward the therapist because the therapist doesn't seem friendly or outgoing. Some weeks before, the patient had related his angry feelings toward his father and how he had given up trying to achieve a close emotional relationship with him.

Patient: Every week I come in here and reveal myself to you. I go on and on about my past and what I am doing now. You just sit there and ask questions, or make some comment.

Therapist: Yes?

Patient: Like just then. All you do is ask a question. There has to be something more to this. Is this all I get from you?

Therapist: You want something more from me. Perhaps like you want something more from others.

Patient: Of course. If I'm going to be with someone, and I'm giving something, why shouldn't I deserve something in return?

Therapist: Can you think of other people, in addition to me, that have not given you what you think you deserve?

Patient: There you go asking a question again. How can I relate to you if you keep asking questions?

Therapist: Have you considered there is a reason why you do not like the questions? Maybe they bother you because you do not want to answer them.

This example demonstrates the therapist's attempt to get the patient to make the connection between his demands in the therapeutic relationship and his demands on his father. The patient avoids facing the connection; thus, he is resisting. The therapist's last statement directs immediate attention to the resistance. The analyst in this case made a mild interpretation; a more confrontive interpretation might have been, "You are asking for more from me, just as you did with your father." The therapist could go on to explain the unmet need for emotional closeness with parents, and how the patient was still seeking that closeness through others.

Fromm-Reichmann (1950) presents an interesting example of an interpretation as well as an analytically derived, dynamic birth-envy in a male patient. The man related the repetitional experience of taking a deep breath to fill his chest, retaining the air as long as possible, then feeling as if part of his body should be eliminated. This was a pleasurable experience that occurred at the time of his wife's third pregnancy. Sensing the need to understand this when it was reported, the therapist tried to duplicate the patient's experience. When she got to the point of trying to dispose of something connected to her body, she was at a loss. She concluded the patient must be trying to dispose of a part of his body which she could not identify with. She realized the man was trying to be like a pregnant female, to fill up his body and feel pleasure. Of course he was puzzled by it all. It was suggested that he wanted to get rid of his penis; the interpretation was "avidly" accepted, and he commented on his envy of his wife. The birth-envy was found to be an important aspect of the patient's psychopathology.

These guidelines promote effective interpretation (Fromm-Reichmann, 1950):

1. Interpretation is a collaborative effort with the patient. The analyst must convey respect for the ability to understand and to grow.

2. At the same time, the analyst asserts valid and correct interpretations with confidence and authority.

3. Formulations are presented as leads or suggestions for further understanding to a person who needs guidance.

4. Preaching or lecturing is not effective.

5. Interpretations vary according to the patient's needs.

6. Guiding the patient to self-discovery of the hidden meanings in his relationships has a stronger curative effect and instills self-confidence.

7. Intellectual understanding of an interpretation should lead to a full therapeutic understanding of oneself. Repressed material

must be worked through until the patient can make adequate connections and apply insights to real life.

8. Interpret resistance first.

9. Interpretation of repressed material occurs after the therapist has an overall understanding of the patient's personality, significant past experience, and present life circumstances.

10. Interpretations will have to be repeated over and over.

11. The analyst should give interpretations when they are near the patient's awareness.

12. Interpretations are most successful when the therapist-patient relationship is friendly.

13. Interpretations should be gauged to release only the amount of anxiety the patient is able to cope with. Extremely confrontive interpretations can set off serious symptomotology.

Two comparisons of psychoanalytic therapy with Gestalt and Rogerian approaches bear mention. In relation to interpretive efforts, Gestaltists discourage the use of "Why?" with patients. Menninger (1958) sees only a limited use of the term, and believes it can be a "cheap and irritating 'trick'" when inquiring into the patient's past behavior. He suggests using instead a statement such as, "What occurs to you about that?" Menninger also advocates having the analyst communicate some degree of understanding and sympathy for the patient. Although not as strongly as Rogers emphasizes empathy and respect, many analysts suggest responses to the patient that show they are listening, participating, and trying to understand. They also urge the therapist to behave naturally and spontaneously, with the patient's needs and concerns always in mind.

Advantages of Analytic Groups

Shaffer and Galinsky (1974) list ten advantages analysts see for patients in group work.

1. To see that he is not isolated and alone in having problems, that others have similar difficulties.

2. To discover in himself resources for listening to and understanding others that he had not suspected were there; this can be an important source of increased self-esteem.

3. To re-experience his early family relationships—but this time in a setting that is conducive to a more favorable outcome.

4. To demonstrate to the analyst in a much more vivid way his pattern of interpersonal relating, especially those things that he does to provoke in others reactions that he in turn finds problematic.

5. To experience in a more vivid way his distorted transference perceptions of the therapist, since many of the group members will perceive the therapist quite differently.

6. To experience, via transferences to fellow patients, early significant relationships that cannot be transferred to the therapist because of some of the latter's objective characteristics—e.g., age, sex, physical appearance, personality, etc.

7. To experience the indiscriminateness of his transference distortions, since he will probably project the same image onto several group members, none of whom—from an objective point-of-view—resemble one another.

8. To gain insight into the effects of his character resistances on others more quickly and more dramatically than he can in individual therapy.

9. To see that it is safe and acceptable to express intense anger—especially toward the therapist—since if he is timid in this regard he has the living example of others to spur him on.

10. To wean himself away from the kind of prolonged, excessively self-searching and increasingly dependent relationship to the analyst that can occur in individual therapy—by interposing the reality of other people, who force their way into what might otherwise become a patient-therapist symbiosis.*

Group Methods and Process

Adlerian Therapy

For Alfred Adler, the therapeutic process is a cooperative enterprise between the therapist (leader and group) and the client (whether child, student, or adult). Counseling and therapy are educative processes in which both parties analyze the life-style and construct a new, more satisfying cognitive map. Mistakes in the organization of the cognitive map must be corrected. The general goal is to liberate one's social interests by decreasing feelings of inferiority and self-interest. The client recognizes his equality with others and learns to contribute. Group counseling is especially helpful in moving from a "private logic" to a more rational, satisfying assessment of life. A

---

*J.B.P. Shaffer/M.D. Galinsky, MODELS OF GROUP THERAPY AND SENSITIVITY TRAINING, ©1974, pp. 64–65. Adapted by permission of Prentice-Hall, Inc., Englewood Cliffs, N.J.

group can offer a sense of belonging, a safe place to examine one's life-style, and a way to build self-respect.

The basic aims of Adlerian therapy are: (1) establishment and maintenance of a good relationship; (2) identification and clarification of client dynamics (life-style, goals); (3) interpretation leading to insight, and (4) reorientation. The first aim, establishing a relationship with the client, is similar to nearly every form of counseling and therapy. There must be a trusting relationship in which all parties are considered equal. In the group context, one builds social closeness by stimulating cooperation, mutual responsiblity, social interest, and informality. The group becomes a special place to work on relationships. Early on, the leader elicits goals from group members, to alter and re-examine as the group proceeds. In this early stage, the leader also begins to assess each client, and may even make an interpretive statement for the client to think about. The counselor encourages the client toward productive, cooperative games. Adlerian therapy is not concerned with transference and attempts to discourage such a relationship, for example, through the use of more than one therapist.

The group has an opportunity to explore members' life-styles and uncover dynamics. The leader and fellow members observe social behavior and interactions. They see transactions in the social field and the consequences of the behavior. Interpretation of behavior or goals is not confrontive; the leader acts as a role model by suggesting dynamics or making a tentative hypothesis. The counselor conveys an attitude of caring, so other group members can later assume the role of helping fellow participants. This approach avoids blame and causation. Sometimes called *teleoanalysis*, this method of investigation calls for understanding the life-style and determining whether it helps accomplish life tasks. Adlerians concede that some people live under abnormal conditions that cause suffering despite an adequate life-style, but that they can acquire an attitude to help them cope.

As a part of therapy, reorientation cannot be separated from exploration, interpretation, and insight. The client is expected to make changes in life-style and behavior. Intellectual insight and interpretation of dynamics in a group are merely therapeutic games, unless they accompany active change. When the group can confront its members' goals and intentions through feedback and personal influence, it serves a significant purpose. Members learn about other life-styles and behavior, which stimulate a reorientation for them. During this important aspect of counseling, one must realize that (1) each group member can achieve responsibility for her own behavior, (2) change will occur through cognitive reorganization of life-style and goals. The notion of responsiblity is similar to that of the Gestalt therapists, along with the belief that one's thoughts control one's emotions. Attitudes and beliefs about oneself, others, and the future establish how one feels, not vice versa. One goal of group counseling is to have members believe the group will be helpful, thus providing hope; another goal is to convince participants that the other members value them.

The following is an example of group counseling with a small group of high school students. This is the eighth session and the boys know each other well from classes and their group sessions.

Robert:	I finally went to the school basketball game last week.
Sid:	Well, what do you know. You finally got out of the house.
Counselor:	What made you decide to attend the game?
Robert:	These guys kept saying how I never did anything but study. So I decided to try a ball game. [*response to social needs and social pressures*]
Counselor:	Is that what you really wanted to do?
Robert:	I don't know for sure. Maybe I was curious about it. It was all right.
Counselor:	You must have had some feelings about giving up your Friday night. [*technique of probing and making individual obtain insight into himself*]
Harry:	He probably hated not studying. He probably hated every minute of it.
Robert:	Like I said, it was all right. I could have spent the time on biology. But I found time on the week-end to do it.
Sid:	You always have to study. Always trying to get *A*'s. You'd think the world would fall apart if you didn't get an *A*.
Counselor:	Does that sound right, Robert?
Robert:	A lot of people get *A*'s. I'm not the only one.
Jack:	You just have to be the best in the class. You want everyone to know you get straight *A*'s, and if you get

a *B* you cry. I don't know why you think you have to be the best.

Harry: I think it's okay to get *A*'s, but Robert has to lord it over everybody.

Counselor: What do you think about that, Robert?

Robert: I don't think I lord it over anyone. I just like to get *A*'s.

Jack: Ha, you stick your nose in the air like you're better than the rest of us. But I don't see you trying to do anything except your school work. You don't try out for sports and you don't like girls.

Counselor: I guess people are saying your life is too narrow, and you won't take a chance at anything else.

Robert: I like to study and get good grades. What do I need the other things for? They seem boring to me. Besides, I'd rather be real good in class than a goof-off like Sid and Jack.

Counselor: You want to be the best and couldn't stand to be average. Do you think that's why you don't try anything else?

Robert: Maybe that's true. I figured I just wasn't interested; but if I were interested, I'd want to be real good at it.

Harry: You don't do anything else because you're afraid. You have to be the best at everything or forget it. Even classroom games you won't play unless you think you'll be the winner.

Jim: I think Robert feels like he's better than the rest of us.

Robert: I don't think I feel that way. I never thought of that.

Counselor: Is it possible you would like to be better than the others?

Robert: I do like being the best at something. And I do want others to look up to me. Now I wonder if other kids do look up to me.

Counselor: You're wondering whether being so perfect is paying off.

> *Sid:* Hey, why don't you try to be one of the guys? Maybe you could pull if off.

> *Counselor:* What do you think you've learned today?

> *Robert:* I didn't realize how important it was for me to be the best. And I thought before that I was looked up to by other kids.

> *Sid:* I learned I'm a goof-off. Does that mean I'm the opposite of the best?

> *Jim:* Maybe we can get Robert to be one of the guys yet.

> *Counselor:* Thanks for contributing, everyone. Give this some thought and we'll meet next week.

This dialogue illustrates Robert's striving for perfection. He avoided areas where he did not think he could be superior. The group helped him clarify his life-style and goals. Socially, Robert became aware of other young people's perceptions, and the group invited him to become a "regular guy." Robert's sense of inferiority in all areas except academics led to a deficiency in the other tasks of socialization and sexuality. The group leader had established a good relationship with the participants, aided in uncovering the dynamics, and helped Robert gain some insight. At the next session, Robert will attempt to do something about what he has learned. The suggested interpretations got Robert to think about himself and his life-style. Later he does modify his style to become more social.

Classical Psychoanalysis

Orthodox analysts such as Wolf and Schwartz (1962) perceive differences for the patient in the group process versus individual analysis. Because of the group's support, the patient is able to assert herself more easily than in one-to-one therapy. Members are frequently better able to express anger toward the therapist. The peer relationships that arise lessen the therapist's control or influence. The interplay of multiple transference affects ego development, because the patient has many relationships to work on that provide a means of increasing ego strength. Transference feelings are not directed only to the therapist; fellow group members become objects for transference, lessening the leader's significance as the recipient of unresolved conflicts. The presence of many members gives each participant different types from whom to unconsciously choose a "mother," "father," "sister," "brother," and so on. The variety multiplies the interpersonal dynamics, giving the leader more work to understand the dynamics. The leader can spend less time interacting and more time observing and understanding the many transferences and resistances.

The group experience allows realistic relationships with fellow members, whereas individual therapy is an artificially close relationship because transference causes the patient to feel unusually close to the therapist, but the therapist does not share that feeling. Conversely, in a group, members establish closer relationships with one another than with the group leader.

Group members form a reality base for one another through their natural responses to fellow participants' distortions, fantasies, aggressiveness, seductiveness, and so on. The group is not the relatively permissive one-to-one environment of individual counseling; rather, it is a more natural environment in which one is held accountable for one's behavior and where group members point out unacceptable behavior or distortions. One can learn social responsibility in this context, although of course, the pathology of the group or several members can be used to harm a participant. (The leader must point out such destructive behavior.) As the group develops, its members take more and more responsiblity for one another and the leader becomes less involved as members interpret each other's behavior and suggest more effective ways of relating. Thus, individual and group responsiblities form as each one learns correct and well-timed interpreting. A disadvantage of the group is that incorrect or ill-timed interpretations can be harmful to the patient.

To say that the group experience is less intense than one-to-one counseling suggests that a different dynamic is involved. Two factors contribute to the lessened intensity. First, the group's focus shifts from one member to another, so one person does not discuss her conflicts the full time week after week. Second, transferences are spread out, usually resulting in less intense regression to childhood behaviors. When the focus shifts to other members, a participant can integrate others' reactions to herself and contemplate her interpersonal relationships. A group relieves some of the pressure of continual attention of individual therapy, although the patient may thus be able to avoid meaningful interaction and revelation in the group. An observant group and a competent leader will notice this and point out the avoidance. The group is intense in another way, however; the patient must work on multiple transferences, relate to several people, has the opportunity to get close to more people, and is confronted by more than one person.

Role of the Leader

Adlerian Counseling

Various Adlerian therapists and counselors name these characteristics of the effective group leader:

1. Sincere and caring concern and accceptance of the client.

2. Openness; honest interchange with group members shows respect for them and serves as a model for group interaction.

3. Ability to instill hope in participants by projecting an anticipation of success; developing positive attitudes.

4. Good knowledge base for assessing each client.

5. Timing advice appropriately.

6. Willingness to attack "faulty premises."

7. Clarifying life-styles and goals.

8. Redirecting life-styles and goals by encouraging members to action.

The leader is, to a degree, directive and active, but balances his leadership with the notion that group members can and will decide what to do for themselves.

Analysts usually prefer a heterogeneous group because people of different ages and backgrounds promote a wider range of transference possibilites and more closely approach the nature of the family unit. Since analysis emphasizes early childhood and family relationships, the greater the group similarity to a family, the better. Non-analytic groups that are not concerned with transference are often more homogeneous.

Wolf first used the alternate session schedule, which analysts use most frequently—one meeting with the therapist, the next without. The absence of the authority figure gives some members more confidence to assert themselves; with support, they may eventually be able to confront the group leader. Alternate sessions also give the group an opportunity to develop greater responsiblity for itself, making decisions and acting independently, and transference feelings toward fellow members may emerge more readily without the authority figure's presence. The alternate session may be less attractive to a member who feels the need of the group leader's protection.

Limits are set for groups consistent with the analytic view that life's limitations are frustrating, but these limits also offer an opportunity to behave maturely and responsibly. Groups start on time, end on time, have a limited number of members, and usually prohibit certain sexual and aggressive behaviors. Many leaders believe they should not act as a parent, and that the group should set its own standards of behavior; it is more important for members to feel they can and should report sexual behaviors and fantasies to the group. Prohibitions that encourage a member to withhold feelings and reports of behavior defeat the purpose of the group.

Classical Psychoanalysis

The analytic group leader is not a full participant in the group. He does not interact as the members do. He is primarily an observer whose roles differ from those of the group participants. Some roles are similar to those of the counselor in one-to-one therapy. The leader attempts to establish an atmosphere in which members will be comfortable enough to interact freely, offers necessary support, notices and points out transferences and resistances, and interprets meaning behind repressed material or lets the group interpret. Slavson (1964) suggests additional roles, such as stimulating discussion when repression, resistance, or emotional fatigue interfere, or extending discussion by making connections between conscious feelings or attitudes and unconscious material.

The group leader may initially set a few ground rules, but thereafter he does not direct discussion, although he may interject a question or point out some dynamic. Responsibility for the continuing formation of the group lies with its members, facilitating their interaction with one another rather than only with the leader and giving them a sense of ownership of the group. As their interaction becomes spontaneous and supportive of one another, the leader can focus on transferences and resistances, directing comments to what he sees happening in the group without revealing his own feelings (which may be countertransference). The leader must be able to withstand a great deal of hostility in analytic groups as he becomes the recipient of member anger; whatever feelings the members project, the leader must be strong enough to deal with them.

In the following situation, we first see the group as immature, resistant, and hostile toward the leader. A later session demonstrates how they have matured. We enter the fifth session after they have spent ten minutes discussing the previous night's football game on television.

Ned:	I still think it was a mistake to try a field goal.
Bill:	It was the best percentage call to make. You disagree because it didn't happen to work.
Inez:	The game was on too late for me. I fell asleep at halftime.
Therapist:	You have talked over ten minutes about football. Perhaps you are trying to avoid something here.
Ginger:	Why do you always try to find some hidden meaning in what we say? Couldn't we just feel like talking about football?
Harry:	Yeah, you seem to want us to talk about something, but you never tell us what it is.
Bill:	He isn't going to tell us, and besides, what difference does it make? He hasn't done much in here anyway. I thought I would get something out of this.
Inez:	Well I thought the therapist was supposed to the be the *leader* of the group. Aren't you going to be a part of this group?
Susan:	How about it; are you going to just sit back? Will that be *all* you're going to do here?
Therapist:	I will make occasional comments.

The group's anger and demandingness come and go over the next sessions. They gradually focus on their own needs and how they can help each other, sometimes in an awkward or even self-serving way. The following is an excerpt from the 12th session:

Harry:	I think Mary needs to stand up to her husband. Mary, you kow-tow to him as if you were a little girl obeying the commands of your father. You've got to speak up.
Inez:	Yes. You can't keep being walked on. Do you have any self respect? You're not a child anymore.
Mary:	That's easy for you to say. But what if he acts even worse toward me then? Or what if he leaves me— then what do I have?
Therapist:	You had those same feelings in childhood toward someone, didn't you?

> *Mary:* Yes, but this is different. He might really leave. And I'd feel as if it were my fault.
>
> *Ned:* But all you're asking for is to be treated like a human being. What you want is reasonable. What's the matter with him anyway?

The group has begun to mature by focusing on fellow members rather than on the leader. The leader says less now, and in this case gives an interpretation by connecting transference feelings toward the husband to those experienced toward father. Mary does not yet accept the interpretation. The other members do not attack the leader for his comment because they are working to understand and help Mary. Ned has transference feelings for Mary. He sees her as his little sister, the one in the family he protected from men, and at times from his own father. He has taken up the same behavior with Mary by urging her to be assertive. Unconsciously he would like to step into the situation and resolve it himself. Bill saw his mother take the passive role in the home. He felt very attached to her, but resented her inability to stand up to her husband. Bill is not yet fully aware that he has another opportunity to get his "mother" to assert herself. Harry is not saying anything because he is rather uncomfortable; at the very edge of his awareness, he realizes he has been authoritarian with his own wife, yet is not ready to accept it. He hopes this topic will soon end. Inez is disturbed with Mary. Inez's mother was the dominant figure in the family. She said and did what she pleased, though not in a destructive way. Inez cannot accept the docility she sees in Mary and is ready to express her anger and frustration with her.

This brief analysis shows the multiple transferences taking place. Each person reacts to Mary on the basis of significant relationships they have had or, in Harry's case, now have. The leader may point out these transferences when it will not disrupt the work going on with Mary. Recognizing and understanding these transferences are part of his responsibility as he listens to member interactions. He notices that Harry is silent, and hypothesizes the reason; he listens to Inez's anger and frustration and tries to connect Mary's behavior and Inez's past experiences; he observes Ned's support and encouragement, his urge to make everything come out right. The leader also notices his own reactions to the group members and himself. He likes Ned's support of Mary but sees its potential for becoming overprotection. The leader is able to be patient with Mary, because she reminds him of another patient who was eventually able to assert herself. Inez's anger bothers him somewhat; she reminds him of his strong and capable sister for whom he has always had mixed feelings of love and jealousy. He vows not to allow his feelings of counter-transference to interfere with the psychotherapeutic process.

A Psychoanalytic Model

Although Irvin Yalom (1970) suggests that his is an eclectic approach to group psychotherapy, his early training and conceptual approach place him among those we can call "contemporary analysts." He has incorporated research findings and techniques from other schools of thought, such as sensitivity training, the National Training Laboratory, behavior therapy, family therapy, and group dynamics. Yalom's approach is representative of a large number of therapists in mental health settings who have an analytic conceptual framework yet integrate other methods and concepts to respond to various group situations. Yalom's traditional psychoanalytic base results in these techniques:

- Use of analytic concepts such as *transference*
- Use of medical terminology such as *cure* and *patient*
- Belief that the group is a recapitulation of the primary family group
- The group leader does not act as a full participant.

Group Methods and Process

Yalom (1970) lists ten factors that, to one degree or another and varying with each group and member, contribute to "cure" of an individual's pathology.

1. Imparting information
2. Instilling hope
3. Universality
4. Altruism
5. Corrective recapitulation of the primary family group
6. Development of socializing techniques
7. Imitative behavior

8. Interpersonal learning

9. Group cohesiveness

10. Catharsis

The educational process inherent in all groups may be explicit and planned or implicit and spontaneous. *Imparting information* is curative in that all people appreciate a cognitive understanding of themselves or events around them, partly to ward off anxiety. Knowing the reasons for one's behaviors or feelings allows greater control of life. In therapy groups, the leader or fellow participants give one another information in the form of feedback, guidance, or advice. Advice is rarely useful or curative for group members; however, for some groups, information giving is a significant part of their activity. Recovery Inc. was organized as a self-help group for former psychiatric patients; the meetings are highly structured and often focus on the teachings of Abraham Low. Alcoholics Anonymous and many other self-help groups have a strong didactic component. Yalom describes a group formed for preparatory guidance of pscyhiatric patients about to enter a group. Cognitive information made them more comfortable in early group sessions. Explaining a patient's illness and the patient's subsequent understanding have a curative effect in themselves.

Hope and the conviction that the group process will be helpful is essential to the patient's improvement. Those who expect help are more likely to benefit from group therapy. It is useful to mix group members at various stages of improvement; participants will have greater faith in treatment when they see improvement in others.

Many patients enter therapy thinking they are unique in some displeasing way, and experience social isolation, usually because their inadequate interpersonal relationships do not allow for frank feedback. Although people have unique constellations of personality dimensions, they do not realize the *universality* of problems and concerns and are relieved when they become aware of fellow group members' concerns. Yalom uses an exercise to help members realize common denominators. They are asked to write down, anonymously, their "top secret," the one thing they would not want to reveal to anyone. Each member draws a card, reads it aloud, and reveals how he would feel if he had such a secret. Yalom finds the three most common secrets to be a sense of inadequacy, a sense of interpersonal alienation, and sexual.

People have a need to be needed, and can act out their *altrustic* tendencies in the group. New group members usually believe they have nothing to offer, so giving support, understanding, and reassurance to another group member boosts self-esteem.

Group members bring childhood familial experiences with them and act them out in therapy, with the leader as the parental figure and group members as siblings. Yalom's conception of the corrective recapitulation of the primary family group is grounded in analytic theory.

Yalom also sees a need to *develop socializing techniques* within the group process, ranging from structure sessions in which members learn how to interview with a prospective employer to dynamic groups in which members give one another spontaneous feedback as to their social interaction skills and styles.

Imitative behavior is a strong force in group therapy. Participants may model behavior, verbalizations, and thinking after the leader or other group members, or observe positive behavioral changes in another member and decide to emulate him.

Interpersonal learning involves insight, working through the transferences, "the corrective emotional experience," and processes found only in a group setting. Harry Stack Sullivan is a major contributer to interpersonal understanding, offering a set of analytically-based concepts for analyzing group process. Borrowing the term "corrective emotional experience" from Franz Alexander, Yalom applies it to group therapy by requiring that a group member not only have intellectual insight into his problem, but go through an emotional experience that corrects previous experience. The problem must be treated in a real situation, and the group must be supportive and encouraging for one member to work through a problem. Asking patients for a critical incident that was helpful to them, Yalom found that the majority named another group member rather than the analyst as a participant in the incident. These critical incidents, whether negative or positive, helped the patient learn to express feelings, test reality, and become more involved in the group. As part of the notion of interpersonal learning, Yalom perceives the group as a social microcosm, joining group therapists who subscribe to group dynamics and the use of the group as a social entity. He believes members eventually reveal their social style in the group, and that the leader may wish to label the behavior according to his own school of thought. In the social microcosm, members, through consensual validation, become aware of the interpersonal styles. As the effects of transactions increase, awareness increases, and awareness leads to change. The participant is most likely to change if he is (1) uncomfortable enough to want to change; (2) wishes to be involved and accepted by members he respects; and (3) is not excessively rigid. A new cycle of learning can occur through feedback and introspection, and behavior will begin to change outside the group. Interpersonal distortions become less frequent as an "adaptive spiral" begins. The patient finds rewarding relationships, positive feedback from others, and elevated self-esteem.

Yalom accepts the term *parataxic distortions* to replace *transference* because it is broader and applies to more of the patient's interpersonal difficulties. Sullivan uses parataxic distortion to refer to any interpersonal distortion resulting from past interpersonal experiences *or* intrapsychic conditions. Thus, a patient may project his anger onto a fellow group member by accusing him of being hostile. The anger results from the patient's dissatisfaction at failing to be as assertive in the group as he would like. He perceives the other person as angry, but this parataxic distortion does not come from an early childhood experience.

Group cohesiveness, the analogue of "relationship" in one-to-one therapy, is the degree to which members are attracted to a group and remain in it. Explicit indications of cohesiveness may include an atmosphere of "we-ness," defense against external threats, participation, mutual help, and adherence to mutually established standards. Yalom considers cohesiveness a condition for cure, but not a curative agent in itself. The atmosphere in a cohesive group is such that members are able to share very personal matters, such as fantasies and illegal behavior, that they would not tell anyone else. At the same time, they are completely accepted and have no need to hide or pretend. In an effective group, members stick together no matter what happens in their lives outside the group, and one is able to establish positive interpersonal relationships and increase self-esteem.

Catharsis is curative when it takes place in an interpersonal context. Members seem to need to ventilate positive or negative feelings to fellow members, and in the process, facilitate group cohesion and correct previous emotional experiences. Catharsis must be integrated with other curative factors to be meaningful.

Role of the Leader

Yalom sees the group leader as more than a therapist performing individual therapy in a group setting. The leader's role is to develop an atmosphere that facilitates the curative factors and a cohesive group. The leader's influence becomes more indirect as participants take on more responsibility to cause change in one another. Fellow members can have greater impact on each other because they are not seen as authority figures nor as someone who is paid to be helpful. The leader must be aware of his strong influence in establishing rules and standards. The basic roles of the therapist are as technical expert, using knowledge and skills; behavior model; and participant, to help members work through relationships.

Yalom's perspective on self-disclosure differs from the orthodox analytic view. He advocates certain self-disclosures as contributions to the curative effect of group therapy. It is not necessary for the leader to remain aloof or convey an air of authority. The group leader can admit mistakes and that neither he nor his profession has the answer to every issue. The demystification of the therapist has taken place; he can express his own feelings and reservations. However, one must be careful in self-disclosure to avoid being destructive to the group process. One does not state all feelings, or insist that all in the group are equal, or emphasize reservations about oneself as a leader, because the group needs a leader who can be confident and skillful. Self-disclosure is helpful as a model for group members and helps them test their feelings toward the therapist.

Another deviation from classical analysis is Yalom's focus on the here-and-now of group therapy. He sees the interactional processes in therapy as the signifcant unit of understanding and examines the "how" and "why" of what is said, not just the content. In this historical approach that values the ongoing, immediate process, the therapist's task may be interpretive—he will occasionally need to direct the group from irrelevant discussion to the here-and-now. If, for example, a group is discussing deaths in their families, the leader might suggest that they are actually concerned about the termination of the group. Yalom's interpretations are either interpersonal (between group members) or directed to the total group.

Yalom formulated his analytically-based eclectic model on the premise that integration of research on group work and observations from clinical experience results in the best therapeutic approach. He borrows liberally from nonanalytic theorists and practitioners and employs empirical research findings to understand or modify his model for group therapy.

THE GRAND DAME*

Mrs. Cape, a twenty-seven-year-old musician, sought therapy primarily because of severe marital discord of several years' standing. She had had considerable, unrewarding, individual, and hypnotic uncovering therapy. Her husband was an alcoholic who was reluctant to engage her socially, intellectually, or sexually. Now the

---

*From THE THEORY AND PRACTICE OF GROUP PSYCHOTHERAPY, by Irvin D. Yalom. © 1970 by Basic Books, Inc., Publishers. Reprinted by permission of the publisher.

group could have, as some groups do, investigated her marriage interminably. They might have taken a complete history of the courtship, of the evolution of the discord, of her husband's pathology, of her reasons for marrying him, of her role in the conflict; they may have given advice for new behaviors, trial or permanent separations—but all would have been in vain. This approach not only disregards the unique potential of therapy groups but is also based on the highly questionable premise that the patient's account of the marriage is even reasonably accurate. Groups which function in this manner not only fail to help the particular protagonist but also suffer demoralization as the group becomes aware of its impotence. However, as one attended to Mrs. Cape's group behavior, several interesting patterns unfolded. First, her grand entrance, always five or ten minutes late. Bedecked in flamboyant, ever different garb, she swept in, sometimes throwing kisses, and immediately began talking, oblivious of the possibility that some other member may have been in the midst of a sentence, or indeed in the midst of a word. Here was narcissism in the raw! Her world view was so solipsistic that she did not consider that life might have been going on in the group before her arrival.

After a very few group meetings, Mrs. Cape began to give gifts in the group: to an obese female member, a copy of a Mayo diet; to a female with strabismus, the name of a good ophthalmologist; to a male homosexual patient, a subscription to Field and Stream magazine (to masculinize him); to a twenty-four-year-old virginal male, an introduction to a divorcee friend of hers. Gradually it became apparent that the gifts were not duty free. For example, she intruded in the relationship between the male member and her divorcee friend by serving gratuitously as a third-party go-between. In so doing she exerted considerable control over both individuals.

The therapist, too, became a challenge to her and various efforts to control him unfolded. The therapist by chance saw her sister in consultation and referred her to a competent therapist, a clinical psychologist. Mrs. Cape in the group congratulated him for his brilliant tactic of sending her sister to a psychologist; he must have divined her deepseated aversion for physicians. Similarly, on another occasion, the therapist made a comment to her and she responded, "How perceptive you were to have noticed my hands trembling." Now in fact, the therapist had not divined her sister's alleged aversion for physicians, he had simply referred her to the best therapist he knew to be available; nor had he noted her hands trembling. Entrapment was imminent: if he silently accepted her tribute, then he and Mrs. Cape became unwitting accomplices; on the other hand, if he admitted that he had not been sensitive to either the trembling of the hands or the sister's aversion, then in a sense, he has also been bested. In such situations, the therapist does well to concentrate instead on the process and to comment about the nature and the meaning of the trap.

She vied with the therapist in many ways. Intuitive and intellectually gifted, she became the group expert on dream and fantasy interpretation. On one occasion she saw the therapist between group sessions to ask whether she could take a book out of the medical library under his name. On one level, the request was a reasonable one: the book (on music therapy) was related to her profession; furthermore she, as a layman, was not permitted the use of the library. However, in the context of the group process, the request was a complex one in which she was testing limits, and which if granted, would have meant to her and the rest of the group that she did occupy a "special place" vis-a-vis the therapist and the other members. The therapist clarified these contingenices to her and suggested further discussion in the next session. Following this perceived rebuttal, however, she called the three male members at home; after swearing them to secrecy, arranged to see them, and engaged in sexual relations with two: she failed with the third, a homosexual, only after a strenuous attempt.

The following meeting was a horrific

one. It was extraordinarily tense, unproductive, and demonstrated the axiom that if something important in the group is being actively avoided, then nothing else of import is talked about either. Two days later Mrs. Cape, overcome with anxiety and guilt, asked to see the therapist and make a full confession. It was agreed that the whole matter should be discussed in the next group meeting. This meeting was opened by Mrs. Cape, who said, "This is confession day, go ahead, Charles!" and then later, "Your turn, Louis." The men performed as she bade them and later in the meeting received from her a critical evaluation of their sexual performance! Later in the course of the group Mrs. Cape accidentally let her estranged husband know of this event and soon he sent threatening messages to the men in the group, who then decided they could not longer trust Mrs. Cape and she was thereupon voted out of the group—the only occasion I have known of this. (She continued in therapy with another group.) The saga does not end here, but perhaps we have gone far enough to illustrate the concept of the group as a social microcosm.

To summarize, Mrs. Cape clearly displayed her interpersonal pathology in the group context. Her narcissism, her need for adulation, her need to control, her sadistic relationship with men, all unfolded in a dramatic sequence. Finally she began to receive crucial feedback as the men, for example, talked of their deep humiliation and anger at having to jump through a hoop for her and having received grades for their sexual performance. They began to reflect that "No wonder your husband avoids you! Who wants to sleep with his mother?" etc. The female patients and the therapist also reflected their feelings about her insatiability, about the tremendously destructive course for her behavior—destructive for the group as well as herself. Most important of all she had to deal with this fact: she had started in the group with a number of troubled individuals who were anxious to help each other and whom she grew to like and respect; yet, in the course of one year, she had so poisoned her environment that, against her conscious wishes, she became a pariah, an outcast from a group of potentially intimate friends. It was the facing and working through of these issues in subsequent therapy that, in part, enabled her to change and to employ much of her considerable potential constructively in her future relationships and endeavors. (pp. 25–27)

This example demonstrates a number of notions central to Yalom's approach to group therapy. The interpersonal relationships are focal to understanding the life and progress of the group. Mrs. Cape's relationship with the group members and the leader are studied and dealt with carefully. In doing this, the current life of the members and the here-and-now happenings within the group are discussed rather than the historical antecedents. Also note the attention paid to three levels of analysis: the individual, interpersonal dynamics, and the group as a whole. One learns about Mrs. Cape's intrapersonal characteristics (i.e. narcissism), interpersonal style (i.e. manipulations), and the cohesiveness of the group in spite of Mrs. Cape's maneuvers. Yalom then recognizes characteristics of this group as a whole. Finally, the therapist must be careful of his relationships with each member because it will affect the other group members. He had to be aware of Mrs. Cape's attempt to manipulate him, then he had to make a wise choice as to how to handle it. He employed the rule of thumb to bring all decisions, and to report interpersonal experiences with group members back to the group as a whole. In the end, Mrs. Cape learned to be more effective in her interpersonal relationships.

Summary

Psychodynamic theories of group counseling and therapy appeared in the 1920s and 1930s. This early work by Adler, Dreikurs, Wolf, and Schwartz set the stage for subsequent additions and deviations from these theoretical beginnings. These people advocated small group work when it was not fashionable. Later formulations built upon analytic concepts, such as the work of Yalom, and incorporated the findings of many other theorists and practitioners. Rigid adherence to psychoanalysis is no longer required of psychodynamically oriented group leaders. Basic analytic concepts have been modified to suit the needs of group settings. Group process and the role of the leader vary considerably according to the particular psychodynamic school of thought. Adlerians look more closely at social forces and the group member's striving for superiority; the leader is an understanding and involved participant. Classical analysts look for transference relationships and seek resolution of early family conflicts; the leader's role includes interpreting member behavior. Contemporary eclectic theorists are concerned with a wider range of group dynamics that contribute to a curative effect on members, and the leader assumes a varied facilitative role.

Discussion Questions

1. Explain how certain psychoanalytic constructs used in individual therapy have been applied to group therapy. To what extent do you think they explain what happens in group therapy? How are they helpful to you?

2. Who were the major contributors to psychodynamic group work? What were their unique contributions?

3. How does the group leader role differ among Adlerian counselors, classical analytic counselors, and Yalom-style counselors?

4. Explain how Yalom's curative factors actually work to the advantage of the group participant.

3

Transactional Analysis

Transactional Analysis (TA) has a natural affiliation with group counseling and therapy because Eric Berne developed his therapeutic model from his experience with groups (Berne, 1961). During World War II Berne initiated a group discussion among soldier-patients that was so favorably received he continued to experiment with group work. Berne's training was as a psychoanalyst, and analysts such as Federn and Weiss had a profound influence on him. He seems to view his own model as an outgrowth of nonclassical analytic notions. Berne recognized other therapeutic models and techniques, although he was willing to point out differences.

After clinical experience with the psychoanalytic approach, Berne became dissatisfied with it and embarked on building his own model. His approach differed from the analytic approach in several ways:

- There was absence of the use of the "unconscious" as a useful concept in therapy.

- It was less deterministic, in that group therapy centers around what one can do now, and the belief that one is capable of change.

- Much less time is required for analysis; patients are seen once a week for a matter of weeks or months, not every day for a year or more.

- It discourages transferences that promote dependence.

- The group leader is not considered an authority figure, although she must know more than the group members about transactional analysis and the counseling process. Leader and members are considered equals and interactions are more spontaneous than formal.

- The group leader is active in the analysis, interacting with clients and as a group facilitator.

- The group leader is also a teacher, often using a chalkboard to explain concepts and dynamics.

- Group members are encouraged to read about and learn TA concepts and to use the concepts in helping each other.

- Transactional analysis can be used with a broader range of clients, such as offenders, alcoholics, children, and the mentally retarded.

Berne retained certain aspects of the analytic model: the belief that early childhood experiences are the basis for life scripts the client uses into adulthood and that analysis, or cognitive understanding of oneself, is the basis for making changes during the therapeutic process. Berne's ego states—Child, Parent, and Adult—resemble Freud's concepts of Id, Superego, and Ego. Berne has contended they are really not the same because Freud's labels referred to hypothetical states in the individual whereas Berne's are based on actual behavior and experiences.

Transactional analysis is an educational, or didactic, approach that is highly structured, and both analytical and interactional in its therapeutic procedures. The educational value lies in the counselor's attempts to have the client understand his past and present cognitively using the TA concepts. Counseling is structured in that the group systematically follows steps in each participant's analysis. TA is analytic because it gets group members to examine their pasts, their current ego states, scripts, games, and so on. As a directive approach, it does not value members' "finding" themselves or engaging in unstructured self-exploration; interaction with other group members, the leader, and other significant people in one's environment indicate whether one is healthy or shows signs of pathology. Thus, one's psychological and social transactions become the focus of group counseling.

Theoretical Constructs

The first set of concepts has to do with the individual's motivational forces.

Contact-Stroke-Recognition Hunger

Contact/stroke/recognition hunger represents a need continuum from infancy through adulthood. The infant needs loving, caring physical contact with the mother and/or others. Physical contact with others is a form of stroking, and remains the most important or valued type of stroking throughout life. Other kinds of stroking, such as recognition, emerge. Everyone needs to be recognized, whether casually, as through greetings, or specially, as through a professional award. To some extent, then, human behavior is motivated by the need for rewarding physical and interpersonal contact.

Strokes can be conditional on one's behavior, or unconditional. Strokes can be positive, negative, or mixed. A "mixed" stroke usually begins with a positive statement, followed by one that questions or negates the first. A parent who says, "You did a great job cleaning the garage—much better than last time," is giving a positive and reminding the child of the negative. Children grow up learning a pattern of strokes that motivates them toward one type or another and sets the stage for a unique method of receiving strokes.

Structure Hunger

Most people have time to spend in activities other than those necessary to survival and must structure this additional time to meet individual needs. People usually choose social activities that will generate needed strokes. Failure to take control of one's time shows an unwillingness to take risks, and the amount of risk one is willing to take is directly proportionate to the strokes and satisfaction one expects to receive. At one end of the risk-satisfaction continuum, one may be "withdrawn" or participate in "ritualistic" social amenities. In the midrange of the continuum, a person engages in "pastimes," discussions of what one would do or plans to do—that is, generally talking about rather than engaging in an activity. "Activity" is also in the midrange: work and hobbies are examples of energy "directed to external sources." Next are "games"—more complex interpersonal transactions that lead to a payoff for both parties. The final way to receive strokes is through "intimacy," a loving relationship based on trust and sharing.

Leadership hunger is closely related to structure hunger and is found in those who are able to help others structure their time in rewarding or stimulating ways.

Excitement Hunger

Given a choice, people opt for an exciting activity rather than a dull one. Thus, we seek recognition, excitement, and activities to obtain the strokes that satisfy a need for intimate relationships with others. When this need is not met, the TA group can help one with self-analysis and finding ways to meet needs.

Life Script

Early in life, a child selects a "life position" based on how he can best adapt to his environment. He has four choices for a life position, based on whether he believes he is an OK person and whether other people are OK:

I'm OK—you're OK

I'm OK—you're not OK

I'm not OK—you're OK

I'm not OK—you're not OK

According to the selected life position, the child devises a life plan that guides decisions about how to use time and how to obtain strokes. A life script evolves that is often unrealistic, distorted, and irrational because it is formed so early in one's development.

In the "I'm OK—you're OK" script, there is little, if any, game playing. Relationships are honest and emotionally fulfilling for all parties. One who is critical of others, projects problems and blame on others, and uses games to support a sense of superiority is in the "I'm OK—you're not OK" position. The "I'm not OK—you're OK" position can be seen in one who feels inferior, has low self-esteem, and/or is depressed. Games such as "Kick me" and "Martyr" support the life script. When the position is "I'm not OK—you're not OK," varying degrees of withdrawal, fatalism, regression, self-harm, and poor coping skills appear.

TA groups offer the opportunity to analyze life scripts. Group members are encouraged to understand their own scripts and to see how they have been locked into a programmed and often unrealistic method of obtaining strokes. They can rewrite their scripts, cast themselves in the new position of "I'm OK—you're OK," and divest themselves of ineffective games.

Ego States

Berne's term "ego state" describes a state of mind and related behavioral patterns. Ego states are not vague constructs; they are a person's actual thinking, affect, and behavior at a particular time. Although found in adulthood, ego states form during childhood.

The Child ego state is one of spontaneity, joy, feelings, and impulses. A necessary ingredient in healthy functioning, the Child ego state takes on several forms. The Natural Child is the untrained aspect of ourselves, free of parental injunctions—our lively, impulsive, charming qualities. The Adapted Child conforms to the expectations of others in an attempt to gain acceptance. The Little Professor has the beginning use of reason along with intuition and creativity in moving toward the development of the other two ego states.

The Parent ego state results from mentally recording and accepting the injunctions, values, beliefs, and behaviors (including nonverbal gestures, movements, etc.) of one's parents. Childhood experiences have been recorded and are available to stimulate behaviors consistent with and often identical to that of one's parents. All the "shoulds" and "dos" are accepted without question. The Parent state helps one handle life's everyday demands.

The Adult ego state dispassionately evaluates information from the environment and from the other two ego states. It processes the information without feelings, tests reality, estimates probabilities, and tries to adapt the organism to the current real world. The Adult ego uses rational thinking to evaluate and update the Parent ego material, and determines whether the feelings of the Child ego are appropriate. Thus, it serves a regulatory function.

Games

People play games to experience a particular feeling or feelings. At least two people must be involved in a transaction that requires each to play a certain role. The roles are reciprocal; one cannot play without the other, and the transaction leads to an acceptable conclusion for both. Communication between the parties occurs at two levels, disguising the real intent of the transaction and resulting in a payoff termed "stamps," the feelings derived from playing the game. Each person saves a certain type of stamp, such as depression stamps or anger stamps. The type of stamps define the person's "racket"—someone may be in the "feel sorry for me" racket, another may be in the "I feel inadequate" racket.

People find others with whom to play the games by going through social rituals and pastimes. We establish transactions and try out games with people, and when we find people willing to play a game, we have the potential for continuing the transactions. According to Berne, some of these subconscious games are "Wooden Leg," "Schlemiel," "Ain't It Awful?," and "There I Go Again."

The most common game in group situations is "Why Don't You—Yes, But" (Berne, 1961). One player who is "It" states a problem to the group, and the other players are to come up with solutions to the problem. On the surface, the first player is asking for help or information, but he rarely accepts any solutions. At a deeper level, the player is trying to gratify another need.

Cynthia:	My son Bill just doesn't study enough.
Wilma:	Why don't you have him do the homework right after school?
Cynthia:	Yes, but he has football practice then.
Tina:	Why not have him do it right after supper?
Cynthia:	Yes, but he's tired then.
Mary:	Why don't you give him a reward if he does his homework?
Cynthia:	Yes, but I tried that and it didn't work.
Evelyn:	Why don't you tell him he has to stay in for the weekend if he doesn't study.
Cynthia:	Yes, but he plays football and I couldn't keep him home from the game.

The other players take on the parent role and the "it" player acts the child role, trying to confound the parents time after time. Group members may be trying to solve the problem at one level while unknowingly gratifying the child at another level. At one level, the "it" player presents a problem and at another level is saying that the parents cannot tell her what to do. A group member or the leader will notice the game and call it to everyone's attention, then they will analyze it.

Injunctions and Counterinjunctions

As the child develops, she receives parental messages in the form of injunctions and counterinjunctions. Parents communicate a wide array of "don't's": Don't succeed, Don't be yourself, Don't be intimate, Don't be well, and so on. These injunctions arise from the parents' frustrations, anxieties, and unhappiness. At other times, parents communicate counterinjunctions: "should," "ought to," "do." These are similar to concepts used in Gestalt counseling and Rational-Emotive therapy. The child cannot live up to all the parental expectations, which in adulthood cause one to expect too much of oneself. Portions of the relevant scripts include notions of "I should always do my very best"; "I ought to visit my mother every Sunday"; "I should always be nice to other people."

Parents thus write scripts for their children, and adults are to some degree victims of injunctions, life positions, and the games they learned to play. In TA, the participant learns about his script and learns to make decisions leading to a new script and to a reevaluation of injunctions and counterinjunctions.

Group Methods and Process

Transactional analysis is practiced primarily in groups. Screening and selection for the composition of a group is liberal, since nearly anyone can benefit from TA group counseling and the mix of participants is not important to the group's success. Berne believes many counselors screen certain people out of their groups either because of the counselor's snobbishness or the desire to have participants who will play only games the counselor is comfortable with, although Berne does suggest special groups for "remittent schizophrenics" and psychotics after they have received shock treatment.

A unique aspect of TA groups is the equality and openness between group members and the leader. Although the roles differ somewhat, it is assumed the client is capable of understanding herself and of functioning socially and psychologically at the same level as the group leader. The clients' confusion about their feelings, behavior, or thinking simply means they can work toward a better understanding of themselves in the group. Potential group members learn the basic TA terminology and concepts and are encouraged to eventually take on the Adult role in analyzing themselves as well as their fellow group members. The counseling process is a joint enterprise toward the client's attainment of social understanding and control; the client is expected to be aware of her goals and whether she is accomplishing them.

The Contract

TA is a contractual form of counseling in which group members must spell out what they wish to accomplish. Goals must be defined concretely and empirically so that any observer would be able to evaluate progress and accomplishment. Vague goals, such as "feel better about myself," are not acceptable. One can set goals such as "be more assertive and outgoing when socializing with others" or "not lose my temper every day with my children," but even these goals must be specifically defined as to the people involved, transactions, and exactly how the group member will handle them.

Clients thus take responsibility for themselves by determining their own goals and also by suggesting how they can make the necessary changes. The process of bringing about change is shared with the group leader and other members, but the individual is ultimately responsible for reaching the goals. He states what he is willing to do to bring about the change and must ask himself what he does to prevent the desired changes.

The seemingly simple contract is often complicated by the client's confusion and defenses. A client might contract to become more assertive with superiors, such as his boss at work, but it may become apparent in group counseling, that the client does not really want to be more assertive; he may be satisfied and prefer to be left alone on the job but has had others tell him to be more assertive. When clients want to contract to play the Adult role (the "shoulds" and "ought to's") or to change someone else ("I want my husband to stop drinking"), the leader must recognize and reject these and other inappropriate contracts.

Stages of TA

The traditional process of group counseling includes four stages: structural analysis, transactional analysis, game analysis, and script analysis.

Structural analysis involves the client's examination of his ego states. The client determines which ego state is predominant, its content, and how it functions. Since each person can function in the Adult, Child, and Parent ego states, the client seeks to understand each state and how one uses it in a healthy or unhealthy way. *Exclu-*

sion is the rigid reliance on one ego state to the exclusion of the others, functioning, for example, always as a Parent to the exclusion of the Adult and the Child. In this case, denial of the other ego states results in doing always what one should do, never feeling free to have fun.

Contamination is the term to describe the overlap of one ego state into another. Characteristics, content, or behavior appropriate to one ego state penetrate the boundaries of another ego state, usually in the form of prejudicial attitudes or beliefs of the Parent or Child states contaminating the Adult state. Delusions that others are not to be trusted, for example, are a contamination of the Adult by the Parent.

Transactional anlaysis is the examination of group members' interaction of ego states, that is, the interaction of one person's Child with another's Parent; for example:

> *Pat:* Nobody likes me. [Child]

> *Harriett:* Well, you should be nicer to other people. [Parent]

The leader and group members identify each person's ego state in the interaction and judge whether the transaction is useful or constructive. The leader acts as teacher; she may even diagram the transactions to illustrate them for the group.

Transactions may be complementary, crossed, or ulterior. A *complementary transaction* occurs when the behavior of one ego state elicits the expected response from the other person's ego state. Thus, if one's Adult elicits a response from the other's Adult, the transaction is complementary.

> *Joe:* Would you like to go to the lecture tonight? [Adult]

> *Mary:* Yes, I would. It's something I'm interested in. [Adult]

Person 1	Person 2
Adult	Adult

Crossed transactions occur when the response is not compatible with the initial behavior; one ego state initiates and another ego state responds.

> *Jake:* Sitting at this ball game is a waste of time when we ought to be painting the house. [Parent]

> *Susan:* Oh, I'm having such a great time! [Child]

	Person 1	Person 2
	Parent	Parent
	Adult	Adult
	Child	Child

Ulterior transactions take place when two messages are transmitted between people, one on the surface and the other covert.

Susan: The house painting needs to be done before winter sets in. [Adult]

Jake: Let's stay here. [Child]

Parent	— Overt —	Parent
Adult		Adult
Child	— Covert —	Child

In this case, Susan's explicit statement is Adult ego, which Jake does not accept. Susan's tone of voice communciates that she really wants to stay at the ball game and have fun, which is the message that registers with Jake.

The next stage of *game analysis* often takes up most of the group's time. Games are a series of ulterior transactions that lead to a negative payoff, such as bad feelings. The leader, with the help of group members, analyzes the ego states, the game, and the payoff, all of which must be exposed in the group. The exposed member is given permission to give up the game and substitute more rewarding interactions. The ultimate goal is to give up all games and engage in honest, real, intimate relationships. Group members help the person along by refusing to play a game or provide a payoff.

Berne describes the "Alcohol" game as a more complicated one made up of four players: persecuter, rescuer, dummy, and the one who is "it." "It" drinks excessively and uses various techniques to obtain and hide alcohol. The persecutor is usually the spouse, who abhors the drinking but, as in the case of all game participants, obtains primary and/or secondary gain from the transactions. The rescuer is typically a helping person (counselor or physician) who feels compelled to help. The dummy supplies alcohol, rather indifferently, for the "it." Since ex-alcoholics often understand the game, they can make the best rescuers. Berne notes that alcoholics will remain in a general counseling group only if the therapist is unaware of the manipulations, or if she can help the alcoholic learn to tolerate the frustrations resulting from others who do not play the game.

The final stage of *script analysis* ties together analysis of ego states, transactions, and games with an understanding of the life script one accepted in childhood. Because the life script involves unconscious factors and analysis of childhood dynamics, it requires a well trained leader and a group that has attained a high level of maturity. Early memories are explored to reveal members' early life-styles, usually some form of "I'm not OK." This early pattern will appear in subsequent games and transactions; for example, one who continually quits jobs after holding them briefly is in a life pattern determined during early childhood perceptions. This life position may be "I'm not OK—you're OK," and transactions may be Child to Parent, with the game set up to lead to failure, a sense of inadequacy, and reinforcement of "I'm not OK." The group analyzes the early life pattern to show how the member has played it out, so he can work to change the life script to one that is flexible and useful in adulthood.

Role of the Leader

The group leader must be a well-trained professional who is aware of her own ego states, games, and life script. Understanding of one-self and the impact of the leader's behavior on the group is prerequisite. The leader must also understand group dynamics, believe in the possibility of client change and growth, and be capable of stimulating group members' self-analysis. A group atmosphere must be created in which participants can discover for themselves how they are perpetuating useless thoughts and behaviors that may even be self-destructive; the atmosphere must be warm and accepting as well as challenging. The leader is protective in the sense of offering appropriate help and empathy so that members feel they are not alone and can face up to their problems; at the same time, the leader helps expose transactions and games that are counterproductive, so she is not accepting all group member behaviors. In balancing protectiveness and challenge, the leader's primary role is that of teacher. TA leaders attempt to enhance clients' cognitive understanding of ego states, games, and so on by applying their knowledge to human transactions in the group. They guide, direct, and encourage group members to obtain a better cognitive understanding of themselves, their feelings, and their behavior. Leader and client draw up a contract to set goals for this understanding and constructive behavior change.

Advantages

The major advantages to TA are its conceptual framework, methods, and leader-group relationship. Transactional analysis provides a well organized and developed set of concepts that help the counselor understand the cognitive and interactive functioning of group members. Concepts such as "games" help reveal group behavior that may be dysfunctional and provide a frame of reference for the counselor and group members.

There is also a fairly well articulated methodology for handling the group. Since the concepts developed from group experiences, they can be readily applied to the group process. Analysis of games and scripts, for example, provide a method for understanding each member's contribution to the group. Group members do not feel they are "sick" and incapable of handling their problems. Group counseling is an educational experience that involves each participant equally, including the leader, who assumes that everyone can learn the TA concepts, perform self-analysis, and help the others learn about themselves.

A disadvantage is that TA becomes overly cognitive if the group becomes immersed in analysis to the exclusion of spontaneous interaction and emotional expression; it has the potential to become merely an intellectual exercise. The following group discussion is one of a transactional group.

Jack: I've been very discouraged lately. I tried going back to work, but they put me on a job at the plant I couldn't do, so I talked to the foreman about it and left early. I can't go back to that job. And at home my wife expects too much out of me. She puts too much pressure on me.

Leader: Tell us about not being able to do the job.

Jack: Well, you all know my nerves are bad, and this job is sewing some vinyl strips together for car seats. It's hard work and you have to do it exactly right. When I even thought about doing it, my nerves went out on me. They can't expect me to do that job the way my nerves are. [*Child*]

Jodie: It does sound awfully hard to do. Couldn't they give you another job? [*Protective Parent*]

Jack: They said it was the only one open and I'm low in seniority, so it was that or not work.

Jodie: That's not fair. They should take into consideration your circumstances.

Jack: I think so too. They don't want to hear about my nerves.

Henry: If they have a job you're really capable of doing, they can't make someone else do that job so you can have an easier one. [*Parent*]

Jodie: But he could probably do some other job.

Jack: I don't want to take someone else's job, but I do think I should have some consideration for my nerves. After all, I didn't ask to have this problem.

Henry: I think you should try to do the job. They are paying you to work there and it's up to you to go ahead and do the work.

Leader: Is the work thing at all related to what is going on at home?

Jack: In a way. I feel the pressure there too. It seems like no one really understands me. They expect me to do all kinds of jobs, and at home my wife wants me to fix things around the house, play with the kids, go to the neighbors to play cards. It just goes on and on. She doesn't seem to realize my headaches and tiredness keep me from doing everything. I mean, I try to do as much as I can, but I need some psychological help before I'll be able to do much.

Martin: I sometimes feel the same way. I have trouble getting enough energy to do things. [*Child*]

Jodie: That's why you are in this group. You can't be expected to do much now. You've got to get your head together first.

Jack: Yeah. I need some time.

Henry: Who's to say anything will be any better in a few months? I think you should do more things now. What could be better for you than getting off your duff and being more responsible for yourself?

Leader: Jack, do you suppose there is *something* more you could do for yourself? [*Adult*]

Jack: Not really. I feel like I need people to leave me alone and let me settle my nerves.

Jack seems to be playing a form of the game "Wooden Leg." It is similar to a plea of insanity. Jack wants to be left alone until his treatment is ended; meanwhile, he can settle into a state of inertia. He appeals to the group members' and leader's sympathy, and succeeds with Jodie. This group is clearly in its early stages and must first analyze ego states. The leader must first guide the participants to examine their own ego states before analyzing the game. Jack and Martin are in the Child state, behaving immaturely, giving excuses for their behavior, and wanting others to protect them. Jodie acts like a protective Parent who wants to rescue and guard Jack from others' demands. The transactions among these three people are compatible and supportive. Henry's ego state is that of the Parent who tells Jack what he should do and what is best for him. This Parent-Child transaction creates some conflict, because Jack prefers the protective and not the authoritarian Parent. The leader adopts the Adult ego state by not reinforcing the childlike behavior; rather, he asks what constructive action will be helpful to Jack. There is no demand for specific action, yet some action is expected. TA theory suggests that (1) Jack is capable of doing something for himself; and (2) it is best to take action soon rather than wait until later. As the analysis moves along and the group matures, Jack's game and Jodie's need to protect will be expressed. Transactional analysis emphasizes, however, that group members are expected to take action to help themselves before analysis is complete.

Summary

Eric Berne devised a cognitive approach to group counseling. He significantly changed and expanded psychoanalytic concepts by focusing on consciousness, present behavior, and the members' responsiblity for taking charge of their lives. Most group members can learn his theory within a few sessions. Besides serving as facilitator, the group leader is expected to educate participants in TA concepts. As a counseling strategy, transactional analysis appears workable with a wide variety of problems and populations. TA differs from other theories in two ways: its emphasis on cognitive understanding of behavioral concepts and Berne's suggestion that any mixture of people can comprise a counseling group.

Discussion Questions

1. How does Berne's divergence from the psychoanalytic model influence the way he conceptualizes and practices group counseling?

2. Give an example as to how each of the following concepts could be illustrated in a group counseling interaction: Contact-Stroke-Recognition Hunger; Structure Hunger; Excitement Hunger; Life Script.

3. Give an example of ego state transactions that are (a) complementary, (b) crossed, and (c) ulterior.

4. How do "games" work to one's disadvantage?

5. Briefly summarize the role of the leader in transactional analysis.

4

Gestalt Group Work

Gestalt therapy results largely from the work of Fritz Perls, who developed, over a period of forty years, the basic tenets of a contemporary therapeutic approach. It is a unique synthesis of European, American, and Asian concepts that influenced Perls from the 1920s on. His early training was psychoanalytic, including work with Freud, Wilhelm Reich, and Karen Horney. Psychoanalysis gave Perls a conceptual framework from which he could eventually develop his own model for therapy. Reich's idea of a "body armor" gave substance to Freud's notion of resistance. Perls, always practical, used this notion as the basis for his ideas on neurosis. He eventually disagreed with or omitted significant aspects of analytic theory. The personality structure of id, ego, and superego, the unconscious, repression, psychosexuality, interpretation, transference, and the importance of going back to early childhood events were not part of Perls's thinking.

The term "Gestalt" derives from the preclinical European Gestalt psychologists, who studied perception and behavior in the organism as they relate to psychological and physiological responses to configurational wholes. Gestalt, then, refers to a pattern of perceptions integrated so as to form a functional unit whose character cannot be understood by knowing only the parts of the whole. Perls borrowed the concepts of figure/ground, the emergent and ever-changing gestalt, and the unfinished gestalt as organizing functions of the organism from the holistic theory of Kurt Goldstein and other Gestaltists. Perls also acknowledged the influence of Kurt Lewin's field theory. The German philosopher Sigmund Friedlander also had a profound impact on Perls with his notion of "differential thinking." Thinking in opposites, the ability to see both sides of an event, avoids a one-sided point of view. Thinking is thus paradoxical in nature rather than linear cause and effect. Differential thinking allowed Perls to make a connection with Eastern thought forms (such as Zen) and the concept of nothingness (no things to get in the way). These concepts also clarified Goldstein's notion of self-actualization, a term used decades later by Maslow.

Perls moved to South Africa in the early 1930s to escape anti-semitism. In South Africa, he encountered the work of Jan Smuts on holism, which supported Perls's evolving thoughts. Perls's break with classical psychoanalysis came in writing his first book, *Ego, Hunger and Aggression* (1941). He moved to America in 1947, but it was not until he moved to the Esalen Institute in 1963 that he was able to effectively communicate his theoretical formulations to a large group of people and establish gestalt therapy as a psychological technique.

Theoretical Constructs

It has often been said in Gestalt workshops that Gestalt therapy is a way of life. In many ways this is true, because Gestalt makes certain assumptions about man and offers guidelines for coping with virtually all of life's situations and problems. For Fritz Perls, Gestalt therapy was a philosophy of life. Its assumptions about people place Gestalt therapy in the humanistic, existential, phenomenological tradition.

1. A human being is a whole who *is* (rather than *has*) a body, emotions, thoughts, sensations, and perceptions, all of which function interrelatedly.

2. One is part of one's environment and cannot be understood outside it.

3. Humans are proactive rather than reactive; they determine their own responses to external and proprioceptive stimuli.

4. Humans are capable of awareness of their sensations, thoughts, emotions, and perceptions.

5. Through self-awareness, humans are capable of choice and thus responsible for covert and overt behavior.

6. Everyone has the wherewithal and resources to live effectively and to restore oneself through one's own assets.

7. One can experience oneself only in the present; the past and the future can be experienced only in the now, through remembering and anticipating.

8. Human beings are neither intrinsically good nor bad.*

Contrast with Psychoanalysis

One approach to the development of Gestalt therapy is through a comparison of Gestalt with psychoanalysis, since Perls had his early training in that therapeutic model. A fundamental concept in psychoanalysis is the unconscious, where thoughts, emotions, and past experiences are repressed. According to psychoanalytic theory, humans can be described psychologically as having many layers, with the innermost layer composed of the earliest repressed id impulses. Gestalt theory considers repression and the unconscious useless and inaccurate concepts. Rather, human beings only allow part of themselves to be "aware" of and in contact with their environment; like a rubber ball in contact with a surface, only a part touches the environment. People submerge much of themselves in the background or are preoccupied with fantasies (Simkin, 1976). Gestaltists are concerned with conscious behavior and expanding the client's range of awareness.

Emphasis on the "here-and-now" instead of childhood experiences marks another major break with psychoanalysis. Gestaltists do not ignore earlier lifetime events; rather, they understand them in the context of the immediate present. The client's current feelings toward and perceptions of past events become the focus in counseling. Previous experiences have meaning only in the immediate context.

Psychosexuality and classification into sexually described stages of child development had no particular meaning to Perls. Sexuality is one of many dimensions that form the whole human being. Perls refused to break the whole into elements as if each were a controlling force in the individual's development. Gestaltists believe that human beings create themselves; they are not victims of primitive instincts. Key developmental concepts in Gestalt therapy are the acquisition of

---

*From GESTALT APPROACHES IN COUNSELING by William R. Passons. Copyright © 1975 by Holt, Rinehart and Winston. Reprinted by permission of Holt, Rinehart and Winston, CBS College Publishing.

responsibility, maturity, and self-care of the individual. In all areas of life, one exhibits healthy development if one is moving toward taking care of oneself rather than depending on others.

Roles of therapist and client also differ in the two schools of thought. The analyst tends to be distant and passive, except when questioning or giving an interpretation. The client is supposed to free-associate, develop a transference with the therapist, and eventually gain insight into his problems. A Gestalt therapist is not personally involved with the client, but uses many active techniques, such as role-playing. Perhaps the greatest difference between the two schools is that the Gestalt therapist helps the client discover herself, and does not interpret unconsciously motivated behavior. Gestalt group leaders consider interpretations dangerous and often inaccurate. The client knows herself best, and in some cases must learn how to be aware of herself. If the leader or other group members interpret her behavior, she remains dependent on others.

Gestaltists consider the analytic division of the human system into three parts (id, ego, superego) artificial, inaccurate, and in violation of the belief that human beings are wholly functioning organisms that cannot be divided into separately functioning parts. The functioning of one part of the organism is interwoven with all other parts. They cannot be examined separately. Someone with diabetes, for example, can be affected not only physically by uncontrolled blood-sugar levels, but may also experience anxiety, depression, withdrawal, and loss of employment; thus, feelings, social relationships, and vocational factors are part of the total picture.

A final difference lies in each model's concept of human nature. Gestaltists reject the notion that man is an aggressive, sexual being who must be brought under control. They believe human beings have a desire to grow and learn, and simply need to remove blocks that prevent their full potential. People impose these blocks on themselves. Gestaltists are compatible with other humanistic therapists in this respect.

European Gestalt Derivations

Gestalt psychology in Europe was experimental psychology with an emphasis on perceptual and learning processes. Perls was able to apply certain Gestalt principles to the psychotherapeutic situation. Passons (1975) lists five propositions that Perls used:

1. *A person tends to seek closure.* People will attend to a gestalt that is incomplete until it is somehow unified or closed. The chapter

lost from a story must be restored, the dotted line will be perceived as a solid line, the host of a dinner party awaits the arrival of the last couple to begin the evening. Group members have an opportunity to bring about closure through the group process. Someone who has not completed the grieving process for a lost family member can do so in the group.

2. *A person will complete a gestalt in accordance with his current need.* Objects flashed in front of hungry people will be perceived as food, sexually deprived persons will view others as sexually interesting. When one desperately wants approval for a project, neutral comments will be interpreted as supportive. The person with unfinished work regarding loss of a family member has the need to complete the mourning, thus closing the Gestalt.

3. *The whole of one's behavior is greater than the sum of its specific components.* Appreciation of a great piece of art is more than the observation of colors, or of figures and shapes, more than understanding the artist, and more than the combination of these perceptions. Teaching a class is more than lecturing, giving information, and leading a discussion. The grieving group member is more than a person in sorrow, but rather, a whole person who requires understanding of how the grieving and other needs interrelate to form the whole.

4. *One's behavior can be meaningfully understood only in context.* A visit to a witch doctor seems primitive to us, but an African tribesman would find it hard to understand a football game. Observing two fully-clothed people swimming in a river has meaning when you learn that one fell from the bridge and the other jumped in to save him. A group member who weeps and screams at an imagined mother may at first appear to have an emotional problem. The context of knowing she is expressing grief and anger at her mother for dying helps her understand she is expressing normal feelings of grief.

5. *One experiences the world in accordance with the principles of figure and ground.* Figure and ground change as needs and environment change. When I am hungry, my stomach pains and the food I see are figure; the pool outside the window and the T.V. nearby are ground. After I eat and am satisfied, the pool and the T.V. become figure. Shall I go for a swim or watch a movie? The food becomes ground. The pain of losing a family member may be ground for a new group member. As people in the group express their painful emotional experiences, the loss become figure, and

in the foreground of awareness. This allows the person to express the pain and gain closure on the issue.*

This heavily phenomenological approach, which values the validity of each person's perception of his world, emphasized the individual's conscious perceptions. Those perceptions were considered the primary source for understanding the person. Perls focused on immediate perceptions and substituted the term "awareness" for "perception." To Gestalt psychology's "sensations," he added feelings, behavior, and thoughts. He believed problems arose when feelings, sensations, and so forth are blocked from awareness; that is, when they need to be figure, but are kept in the background. The group leader helps the client discover where he is blocked or is avoiding unpleasantness. When feelings, thoughts, sensations, and behaviors are brought to awareness, they form a gestalt, become "figure," and are fully confronted. They can appropriately move into the background as other needs arise.

Group Methods and Process

An unusual feature of Gestalt group counseling and therapy is an emphasis on one-to-one interaction between counselor and client. This interaction, called "working," is intense and active as the counselor orchestrates the events that take place in a group context. Ordinarily, members sit comfortably in a circle, the more informal the better. The counselor or therapist asks who wishes to work, and when someone volunteers, the initial interaction is between volunteer and leader, amounting to individual counseling in a group setting. The leader has the option to get group members involved with one another, and the degree of group process depends upon the leader's direction and how she chooses to address the member's problem area. Group interaction usually results from the leader's direction to the person at work to relate to other members as a way of trying out communications and perceptions and receiving feedback. Spontaneous group interaction seldom occurs in the traditional sense.

Although one-to-one interaction in a group was Perls's style, it is not itself fundamental to the theoretical principles of gestalt therapy (Polster and Polster, 1973). It does, however, have several advantages. First, the person in the "hot seat" "experiences an enhanced

*From GESTALT APPROACHES IN COUNSELING by William R. Passons. Copyright © 1975 by Holt, Rinehart and Winston. Reprinted by permission of Holt, Rinehart and Winston, CBS College Publishing.

sense of community." The vibrancy of the group deepens the experience of the figural person. The person has the opportunity to reveal himself to a larger number of people who can influence him through acceptance and rejection. The one-to-one approach can have a dramatic effect on participant/observers, who can apply the interaction between the one member and therapist to their own lives. Finally, the leader can broaden the range of experiences by occasionally directing the figural person to express something toward the group, or vice versa.

Addressing the advantages of a Gestalt group that encourages spontaneous interaction among members, Polster and Polster point out that free interaction reveals how people make contact with one another. Absence of good contact can be explored and resolved in the group context. People's problems and inarticulate methods of contact will receive some support from the group, and wisdom from the group as a whole supplements that of the leader. The figural person observes many alternative ways of thinking, feeling, and sensing.

The leader attends to verbal and nonverbal cues to indicate the approach or technique to be applied moment-to-moment with the client. Creativity, intuition, and attention to body cues play a large part in the leader's reactions to the client. The leader is directive only in the sense that she suggests client exercises, such as role playing, and statements, or describes client behavior she has just observed. She does not tell the client what to do, nor interpret behavior.

As the therapeutic encounter progresses, the group leader often asks the client to relate to individual group members or asks the group to give feedback (observations) to the target member. The group interactions can take many forms, the purpose of which is often to establish "contact" with the environment. For example, a client who has been working through the loss of a loved one two years before [unfinished business] may have isolated himself from others since the loss. After the mourning [crying and/or expressions of anger], the group leader may ask the client to make eye contact with each group member, or ask each member to make one statement to the client. This is one technique for bringing the client beyond mourning to reestablished relationships with the living.

The time allotted for each member is a function of the group's total time, how many people want to work, and the time needed to work at something. Individual time usually ranges from thirty minutes to an hour. Work usually terminates when the client has explored and reached a new awareness of the particular problem.

"Awareness" is a fundamental concept of Gestalt therapy. Awareness occurs in the client, while the therapist acts merely as an observer who guides the client toward phenomenological learning.

As needs arise, the organism automatically attempts to integrate feelings, thoughts, senses, and behavior into future awareness. This process is blocked or avoided when the organism anticipates suffering or other unpleasant experiences. As the organism becomes aware, new gestalts of figure and ground form and one comes in "contact" with the environment, meeting contact needs. When the organism is not fully aware, only partial gestalts form, pathology develops, contact is not made, and needs are not met. One then looks for support outside himself. As this process illustrates, the client is never "cured," he merely learns how to be aware so that he can make contact with his environment and meet his needs.

As an example, Jane has a need for affection and emotional closeness to others. In her apartment complex she meets people who make beginning gestures of friendship, but Jane's attention to some of these people is blocked because she is afraid they will hurt her feelings and possibly reject her. She turns down their invitations and sees them only occasionally in passing. Jane's need for affection is established, but it is blocked from awareness by her anticipation of hurt. The healthy figure-ground gestalt of people as friends in the foreground and other activities as background has not formed. She avoids meaningful "contact" with people and therefore her need is not met. The group leader will help her bring the need and feeling to awareness to form the healthy gestalt to meet the need. She will be aware of what she wants, and Gestalt theory assumes people do what they want when they are aware of what they want.

As mentioned, the client learns by experiencing himself and the environment in the present. While other models of therapy and counseling ask the client to talk about the past or about feelings and events, Gestalt urges clients to experience themselves in the here-and-now. The group leader asks, "What are you aware of now?" or "What are you experiencing now?" rather than "What do you think?" or "How did things go this week for you?" The focus is on full experiencing, including feelings and sensations. People normally tend to emphasize thinking, a limiting function often used to avoid full awareness. The leader continually brings the participant back to the immediate experience in the group, and statements about past events or relationships are brought into the present (for example, "What are you experiencing about that person right now?").

Gestalt therapists also focus on "what" is happening with a client, "how" it is happening, and how it could be different—they try not to use the word "why." Asking why calls for an explanation or a logical reason for behavior. Explanations are often distorted, as they encourage us to intellectualize about rather than face a problem.

Explanations also put the client on the defensive, making her feel as if she is being interrogated. Finally, explanations stress the importance of historical events that, if related accurately, imply that those occurrences caused what has happened in the present. Conversely, Gestalt therapists do not think in terms of cause and effect (deterministic models), nor do they want the client to have a purely cognitive understanding of self.

Asking *how* and *what* focuses on the present; there is no implication of blame or cause, and the client can employ senses and feelings. Thus, the therapist asks "What did you notice about your last statement?" or "How does it feel holding hands with him?" He does not ask "Why did you say that" or "Why did you hit your brother?"

The body does not lie; it communicates honestly, while the content of our verbal expressions are more often distorted, disguised, or untruthful. Gestalt therapy relies heavily on the client's nonverbal behavior as a source for psychological data. The client is urged to listen to his body, to be aware of sensations and feelings that are frequently ignored. Perls would urge group members to be aware of what they smell, touch, hear, see, and taste. The group leader must observe nonverbal behavior and point out what he sees when appropriate. Gestures, facial movement, posture, motor movement, tone of voice, and mannerisms give the leader much more reliable information than the content of what is being said. We often discover blocks and avoidances by focusing on nonverbal behavior.

Personal *responsibility* for oneself is a concept borrowed from existential psychology. The therapist or counselor frustrates the client's attempts to manipulate, blame, or force others to take responsibility for his behavior. If allowed to be manipulative and dependent, the client will remain unwilling to work at his problems and unhappy about his life. Gestalt therapy teaches responsibility and maturity. In group therapy each patient receives credit for his behavior, changes in behavior, and the work he does to make progress. People are able to deal adequately with their problems when they become fully aware of themselves and their needs.

The following example shows a client trying to make the therapist take responsibility, but the Gestalt therapist refuses to do so.

    Client: I don't know what to do. What should I do?

Therapist: What do you want to do?

    Client: I'm so frustrated. No one will help me.

Therapist: Say 'No one will help me' louder.

> *Client:* No one will help me.
>
> *Therapist:* Louder.
>
> *Client:* No one will help me.
>
> *Therapist:* What are you aware of?
>
> *Client:* That I didn't say it very loudly. I'm not sure I wanted anyone to hear me.

As the interaction progresses, the client becomes aware that she is actually asking herself for help. She verbalizes a split; one part of her wants others to help, the other part wants to help herself. The therapist has the client play both roles in a conversation by shifting back and forth between two chairs, removing himself from the focus of the interaction. An analyst, on the other hand, would have fostered a dependent transference. Instead of directly building a relationship with the client, the therapist guides her according to her own behavior and discoveries. He opts out of any struggle over who will be responsible, nor does he give advice; he simply shifts the work onto the client's shoulders, and she learns about herself.

The emotional split in this client's case illustrates the *polarities* in people, often seen in the form of top dog and underdog. Top dog is the part of the self that represents what society expects of us, the "shoulds" and "ought to's" we have learned from parents and others. Underdog is the part of the self that wishes to avoid things, put them off, and give excuses. Underdog usually wins, unless one is able to be aware of both and *integrate* the two into a gestalt. Polarities can prevent us from living fully, pulling us in two directions and creating conflict and wasted energy. A therapist usually has the client act out the polarities.

> *Client Top Dog:* You really should go to Mother's house on Sunday for dinner.
>
> *Client Underdog:* Well, I was there last week and I think that's enough for awhile.
>
> *Client Top Dog:* But she's expecting you.
>
> *Client Underdog:* Maybe she really isn't. Maybe she has other plans.
>
> *Client Top Dog:* She's very sick. How can you not go see her?
>
> *Client Underdog:* I won't have the money for gas anyway.

The therapist guides the interaction by encouraging the client to converse with himself, and eventually the two poles relinquish their extreme stands. Top dog states what would be nice to do rather than what "should" be done; underdog lets go of the excuses and says it would be nice of him to go. The focus finally becomes what the client "wants" to do. Awareness of what one wants often indicates integration of the poles. If the client goes to Mother's house on Sunday, it will be because he wants to, not because he feels obligated. Resentment is not involved, and the client feels in control of himself after making his own decision.

When polarities occur, when feelings, thoughts, and senses are not in awareness, when one is avoiding issues or not facing problems, he has reached an *impasse*. This appears most vividly in therapy when the client becomes confused or acts as if she cannot keep working. Failing to make a decision, withdrawing from others, and saying she can't do something the therapist asks her to try show that resistance has occurred. The therapist's skill is necessary to guide the client toward a *breakthrough*. If top dog and underdog continue in their extreme statements, there is an impasse. If the impasse continues after many tries to break through, the therapist may conclude that the client wants to maintain the impasse.

When individuals do not make effective contact with the environment and their needs are not met, they divert energy into thoughts or mechanisms that further frustrate healthy contact. These are resistant interactions: introjection, projection, retroflection, deflection, and confluence. The *introjector* passively accepts the environment, without questioning or confronting it. Energy is directed toward taking things as they come. The *projector* disowns part of the self by projecting that part onto someone or something in the environment and feels powerless to make changes since his energy is directed to pointing at others. The *retroflector* withdraws from the environment to some degree and reinvests energy into the intrapersonal system, attempting to be self-sufficient and separate from others. The *deflector* does not substantially or consistently invest energy in the environment, but has superficial or temporary contacts that do not last because they do not have focus. Through *confluence*, one goes along with trends and does not question changes, but gives up personal desires and values to conform to those of associates.

Role of the Leader

The primary tasks of the Gestalt group leader are to observe, listen, give feedback, and guide members toward greater self-awareness.

The leader assumes that (1) each member is capable of self-discovery, and the resulting awareness will make him more effective in this environment; and (2) it is up to each participant to work and take responsiblity for personal growth. The leader does not take responsibility for progress or lack of progress in therapy. The goal is greater self-reliance, self-regulation, and self-support. Group participants are to mobilize themselves and their environment for support and fulfillment of needs.

In facilitating growth, the group leader balances support, frustration, feedback, and guidance. Her support builds self-confidence and a sense of belonging. The leader believes in each client's capabilities. Because real growth occurs with an element of frustration, the client must be challenged and confronted. The leader points out manipulations and avoidances, and occasionally frustrates the client by refusing to play games. The leader or other participants give feedback on observable behavior, but as we have said, the leader merely describes the behavior, she does not interpret it; for example, "I notice when you talk about your mother you make a fist" or "Were you aware of how your voice sounded just then?"

The leader does not try to diagnose or figure out personality dynamics to lead the client; instead, he responds to what is happening at the time without concern for where the interaction will lead. This contrasts with most forms of counseling that emphasize determining the problem and setting objectives for treatment. The Gestalt counselor has no particular agenda, but leaves it to the client to determine where he wants to go at any time.

The leader's guidance function is based on Gestalt principles and the client's immediate behavior. Active orchestration of the unfolding drama is determined by the client's needs. Perls used the "hot seat" in his Gestalt workshop, with the figural member at center stage relating to the therapist. Role-playing is used differently than in psychodrama. With some exceptions, the client plays all roles, switching between them under the leader's guidance. A woman may, for example, direct statements to her "son," then switch to the other chair and play the part of her son responding to his mother, while the other members observe the interaction.

A favorite question of Gestalt therapists is, "What are you aware of now?" Other approaches include *repetition* ("Please repeat what you just said") and *exaggeration* ("Say that louder, or make the whining even stronger"). The leader focuses on bodily sensations, movements, and feelings to emphasize that the client must deal with himself rather than talk about others or outside events.

Certain behavior suggests avoidance and manipulation; the client's language, for example, communicates much about the form of resistance. "You" talk is a common form of poor communication that is best changed to "I"; when someone says "you feel so relaxed after drinking two beers," it is probably more accurate to say "I feel. . . . " "You" talk also makes assumptions:

Client: You'll just love this new book I bought.

Counselor: This is a book you're sure I'll like?

Client: I just know you will.

Counselor: What you mean is you liked it a lot.

Client: Sure.

Counselor: Then try saying "I like it and maybe you will too."

Choice of verbs often reflects poor awareness and lack of responsibility, as we see with the use of "can't" and "have to." "Can't" usually means "won't."

Client: I can't go to my boss and ask for a raise.

Counselor: Try saying "I won't go to my boss."

Client: I won't go to my boss.

Counselor: How did that "fit" for you.

Client: Well, I guess it's true that I won't.

"Have to" can be translated into "choose to" or "want to."

Client: I have to go to this party Saturday night.

Counselor: You *have* to?

Client: Well, my supervisor is giving it.

Counselor: Who decided you had to go?

Client: If I don't, it may affect my rating.

Counselor: So you would go to help your job rating.

Client: That, and I may even have a good time.

Counselor: You are choosing to go for a couple of reasons.

Client: I guess you could say that. Actually no one is forcing me to go.

Use of "shoulds" and "ought to's" fall into a similar category. When a client states a "should," it can often be converted to a "want to"; if the "want to" does not fit, then the statement surrounding the "should" needs to be further explored.

Client: I should go to work today even if I am sick.

Counselor: Who said you should?

Client: There is so much work to do.

Counselor: Try saying "I want to go to work today."

Client: I want to go to work today.

Counselor: How does that feel when you say it?

Client: I don't really want to go to work.

Counselor: Say what you want.

Client: I want to stay in bed and rest.

Counselor: And is there anything to stop you?

Client: No.

The range of techniques and experiments is as great as the counselor's imagination. You can ask clients to put on costumes; behave aggressively, then timidly; relate a fantasy; tell a story; tell a joke; lead the group in singing; roll up in a ball; strike a mattress, and so on. Never use techniques simply to be flashy, however, or because you do not know what else to do; techniques are to facilitate growth, and must be chosen for a specific purpose.

Advantages

Gestalt group counseling is particularly suitable for counselors who have a humanistic, existential approach to helping others. It is also appropriate for counselors who prefer not to impose a great deal of structure on a group, do not wish to diagnose members, and do not want to plan exactly what will occur in the group. Gestalt group work relies heavily on the leader's ability to sense at each moment what is taking place with a participant and what will facilitate awareness. Counselors who enjoy being creative may also enjoy Gestalt counseling.

Gestalt counseling puts responsibility for growth on the group member more so than do other theories, relieving the counselor of assuming too much responsiblity for the group and avoiding transference and related dependency problems. Gestalt techniques also minimize the possibility of countertransference and at the same time have the potential to create extremely intense group experiences. Because they can bring out strong feelings in group members, there is a danger of bringing out feelings too quickly for one to deal with or integrate them adequately.

Because of its powerful techniques and potential for showiness, the Gestalt approach can be dangerous in the hands of a poorly trained or unethical counselor. Techniques can be used to "show off" to the group, or they can be used in a mechanical way when the leader does not know what else to do. A leader who is overly directive and controlling can result in both a passive group and defeat the intent of producing a self-supporting individual. Gestalt groups frequently limit the amount of spontaneous interaction among members.

A Gestalt Group at Work

Leader: Who would like to work?

Susan: I would. My mother died three years ago and I can't get her off my mind. I think about her every day and it interferes with my work.

Leader: You said you can't get her off your mind.

Susan: Well, I haven't been able to.

Leader: Try saying, "I don't want to get her off my mind."

Susan: I don't want to get her off my mind.

Leader: What are you aware of now?

Susan: My eyes are getting teary. I feel a little nauseated.

Leader: Allow yourself to experience the tears and the nausea. What are you aware of now?

Susan: That I am fighting back the tears.

Leader: Allow yourself to be one of the tears. Let's put one of the tears here on the pillow. Now would you be the tear on the pillow and talk to Susan?

Susan: It seems a little silly, but okay. [She sits on the pillow]

Leader: What does the tear have to say to Susan?

Tear: [after a pause] I wanted to get out of you, but you wouldn't let me.

Leader: Now what does Susan have to say?

Susan: [moves to chair to be Susan] I didn't want you to get out. I didn't want to cry.
[Leader directs Susan between chair and pillow]

Tear: But you've kept me caged inside, when I needed to get out.

Susan: If you got out, then more would come, and more, and I might fall apart.

Tear: It's more important for me to get out. A whole bunch of us need to get out.

Susan: That's what I'm afraid of. I have to be strong, to keep the family together.

Leader: Who decided you had to be strong?

Susan: No one else would be strong. Everyone has depended on me.

Leader: Tear, ask Susan to be weak for a little while.

Tear: Please be weak for a little while.

Susan: I'm afraid to be.

Leader: Ask the group whether it's okay to be weak.

Susan: [Looking around the group] Is it okay for me to be weak?

Group: [Each member shakes his head yes; a few say "yes"]

Leader: How would you like to be weak?

Susan: I'd like to not worry about anything and not have to make any decisions.

Leader: Close your eyes and focus on your body sensations and feelings.

The leader then has Susan increase awareness of her body and how she physically holds back the tears. Within ten minutes, she is able to have a deep, intense cry. Further work reveals that Susan never let go of her very strong mother because she had fantasized that her mother would return and resume the leadership role in the family. This was "unfinished business" that was worked through. Later in the session, the leader got the group members more involved.

Leader: Susan, would you go to each person here and say, "I have let my mother die and now I am ready to live."

Susan: [Now very sober and drying her tears, goes to each person and makes her statement. A few members smile, one says "I'm happy for you," several others hug her.]

Leader: Is there anything else you want to say to the group?

Susan: Just thank you for being with me.

Leader: Shall we stop now?

Susan: Yes.

This example shows us these elements of the Gestalt group:

- Willingness to work
- Focus
- Guidance by the leader based on client information
- Requests by the leader for client experiments
- Creativity of the leader
- Role-playing both parts by client
- Taking care of unfinished business
- Reestablishing contact with mother as a dead person
- Use of the group to give the client support
- Use of the group to reestablish contact with the environment at termination
- Polarities of wanting to be strong and weak at the same time. (Susan learned there is a time to be strong and a time to cry, which was her definition of weakness.)
- Avoidance of past issues
- Awareness of mother's death freeing her to be herself

Gestalt Exercises

This sampling of the numerous Gestalt exercises will give you an idea of what they are like. In one, the group breaks into pairs. Each member is asked to tell, in turn, the other in his pair what he is good at and what is difficult for him. Each gives the positive, then the difficulties. Everyone returns to the group and tells the group as many of the positive things about the partner as they can remember. A group discussion follows ("I thought I would be bragging if I said more than three things"; "I listed more difficulties than things I can do").

In another exercise, the group breaks into pairs and the pairs take turns closing eyes and holding the other's hands. The directions are to learn as much as possible about the other person through their hands. After returning to the group, discussion centers around reactions to touch, sensations, and other experiences in the exercise.

A third exercise asks each person to fantasize about her current life and decide that if she could change life in one way, what change she would make. The members develop their fantasies with implications of the change and how it would affect them and their lives, then return to the group and share their fantasies. (J. O. Steven's *Awareness: Exploring, Experimenting, Experiencing* describes other Gestalt exercises.)

Summary

Fritz Perls broke from the psychoanalytic approach by rejecting the significance of repression, the unconscious, emphasis on childhood experiences, psychosexual stages, the aggressive-sexual notion of man, the id-ego-superego categories, interpretation, and the need for a transference relationship. Important concepts in Gestalt theory are the perceptions, or gestalt, of the individual, the here-and-now, people's holistic nature, and the need for people to make their own decisions. Gestalt group counseling is a humanistic, existential approach to helping people become more self-aware and able to achieve maturity. Gestaltists believe people are capable of growth and of taking responsibility for their lives.

Group counseling mixes individual counseling in a group context with leader-directed group interaction. The participant who volunteers to work must try to direct his awareness toward the physical, mental, sensory, and behavioral aspects of self and "discover" what is blocking growth or a desired way of functioning. By observing member-leader interaction, group members learn about themselves. Their degree of involvement depends on the leader's decision to direct interaction between the person who is "working" and the other group members, ranging from little to frequent and intense. The leader observes, listens, gives feedback, and orchestrates the therapeutic process, and give careful attention to nonverbal behavior, tone of voice, and the hidden meaning behind verbalizations. The leader is directive but not demanding in having a group member try techniques for increasing awareness. The real responsiblity for change is always on the group member.

Discussion Questions

1. Describe several major ways in which Gestalt group work differs from other approaches. For example, how does the one-to-one counseling in a group actually work?

2. Select two major Gestalt concepts, such as "awareness" and use of language, and explain how each is used in group counseling.

3. How might a polarity become integrated?

4. Explain the major tasks and roles of the Gestalt group leader.

5

The Basic Encounter Group of Carl Rogers

Carl Rogers offered the first significant alternative form of counseling and therapy to the psychoanalytic approach with the publication of *Counseling and Psychotherapy* in 1942. In subsequent books, articles, films, and workshops, he communicated his unique ideas regarding the therapeutic aspects of interpersonal relationships. Rogers's interest in groups evolved with the proliferation of many forms of group work from the 1950s to the present. To his assumptions of personality change and the nature of human relations, he added observations from therapeutic groups to formulate his ideas on group counseling and therapy. Rogers called his group a *basic encounter group*.

Theoretical Constructs

Goals

Rogers believes clients in counseling can have a number of possible goals, although we frequently associate him with Maslow's ultimate goal of self-actualization. Common psychological changes such as personality structure, greater integration of personality, reduction of internal conflict, more effective use of one's energy, and use of more mature behaviors are possible counseling objectives. Rogers's creative contribution to counseling is his perspective on what it takes to bring about these changes.

Necessary and Sufficient Conditions

All psychotherapeutic approaches assume certain factors or events are necessary to bring about change. Most schools of thought postulate certain roles for counselor and client, as well as specific techniques for the therapeutic process. Many roles, techniques, and therapeutic climates explain the dynamics of client changes. Rogers believes six conditions are both necessary and sufficient to bring about constructive personality change (1957): (1) a minimal relationship; (2) the client in a state of incongruence; (3) a congruent, genuine counselor; (4) the counselor's unconditional positive regard; (5) counselor empathy; and (6) the client's perception of the counselor.

In the *minimal relationship*, client and counselor must be in psychological contact; that is, there must be an interpersonal relationship between them. One needs to make a difference in the perceptual field of the other, although the parties may not be fully aware of the impact one has on the other.

The client must be in a *state of incongruence* and be vulnerable or anxious. Incongruence is a discrepancy between self-image and actual experience. Someone may, for example, have a fundamental fear and sense of inadequacy regarding taking on supervisory responsibility at work which is at odds with his concept of himself as capable and ambitious. He is aware of the distorted experience of his difficulty in passing the required examination for a supervisory position. As a result, there is a discrepancy between how the experience registers with him at the organismic level (sense of inadequacy) and in its symbolic representation (test inability). He has conveniently shifted the fear or sense of inadequacy to a behavior (test inability) that does not conflict with a self-image of ambition. He can tell himself he is capable on the job and would be a good supervisor, but that poor test-taking ability holds him back.

A differentiation is made between vulnerability and anxiety when the client experiences incongruence. The client is vulnerable to possible anxiety if he is unaware of the incongruence. Confronting experiences could leave him suddenly vulnerable. Anxiety arises when one barely perceives the incongruence. Slight awareness of the discrepancy may seem threatening. In counseling, one notices increased anxiety as a client becomes more aware of incongruities.

The *congruent, genuine counselor* must show consistency between experience and self-awareness. One does not present a facade, even if being open and genuine means being aware of negative feelings or attitudes (for example, "I'm not so sure I can be very helpful to this person"). The counselor need not express all she is aware of; however, if something may interfere with a helping relationship, it should be discussed with the client or a colleague.

Unconditional positive regard of the counselor is acceptance of the client and his experience without conditions or value judgments. One does not perceive a client as "bad" or "good," nor adopt an evaluative attitude. Approval and disapproval have no place in the therapeutic process. Both negative and positive feelings are accepted; the counselor genuinely cares for the client, yet is not possessive or overprotective.

Counselor empathy calls for true understanding "of the client's awareness of his own experience." The counselor strives to sense the client's private world as if it were her own. The counselor is often able to understand the client's feelings, thoughts, attitudes, and behavior more clearly than does the client. Communicating empathy to the client must accompany that understanding.

Empathy, a subject of much research and study, stands out as the single most important therapeutic condition the counselor can offer. Carkhuff (1977) demonstrates that empathy contributes more to dimensions of client change (such as self-exploration) than other therapeutic conditions.

The *client must perceive the counselor's acceptance and empathy.* He must notice in the counselor's behavior the understanding and respect that will facilitate change. Without recognition that he can freely express feelings in a nonthreatening environment, growth and change are unlikely to occur.

Rogers's conditions have been validated and can be defined and measured. One need not know the dynamics of the therapeutic process to test the efficacy of his hypotheses; the researcher can measure the conditions and positive changes. In measuring personality change, Rogers says the first condition is either present or absent; the other five conditions are present in degrees. He hypothesizes that greater personality change will occur as those five conditions are present in higher degrees.

Rogers considers the six conditions useful in all human relationships and can be found in special relationships in friendship and marriage. One does not need special training or intellect to provide necessary and sufficient conditions for another, nor does accumulating knowledge in professional training programs result in a trained therapist. One must have experiential training to become a therapist or counselor. On this premise, many paraprofessionals have been trained to provide therapeutic assistance, and research supports their effectiveness (Carkhuff, 1969; Vander Kolk, 1973).

Personality Theory

Rogers's concepts of personality evolved from experiences in counseling as opposed to a theory of human behavior. His is thus a field theory and a self theory, of which the significant element is understanding a person in the immediate environment of the organism. If one understands the internal and external forces that are operating, one can determine the individual's personality dynamics and interpersonal relationships.

Human Development

From birth, human beings demonstrate an innate desire to actualize themselves. They tend to value or choose experiences that will enhance growth, and to reject those that will not. Thus, in the presence of a warm, accepting atmosphere, a child is likely to engage in activities that promote the capacity for healthy development. The role of significant adults in the child's life is to offer the proper atmosphere for growth. We thus see the human organism as innately "good" and desiring to behave in a healthy way toward self and others.

Self-Concept

An infant gradually differentiates the self from others by discriminating between experiences that are a part of the self and those that are part of the environment. Development of self-concept depends on perception and evaluation of experiences in terms of how they reflect individual worth. Everyone requires affection and indications of acceptance. The organism is actually developing ways to determine *self-regard*. One way is through judging others' behavior as evidence of positive regard or lack of approval. Unconditional positive regard from others contributes to one's sense of self-worth; in the absence of positive regard, the organism may strive harder for recognition, become frustrated with interpersonal relationships, or engage in unhealthy self-perceptions and behaviors.

One must also perceive oneself with approval, manifested in self-regard. Rogers considers personal self-regard the more important of the two factors that contribute to the self-concept. Although the approval of others is helpful, it is of little benefit if one does not approve of himself. When experiences bring positive regard from others and are consistent with one's own sense of self-worth, one exhibits congruence and healthy functioning.

Conflict between regard from others and self-regard can cause maladjustment. Counseling helps one maintain or achieve congruence between self-regard and positive regard from others. Because self-concept, as well as the organism as a whole, is always in process, it is susceptible to change.

Optimal Adjustment

A fully functioning individual is open to experience and is nondefensive, allows inner experience and experience with the environment into his awareness, and his inner experience is congruent with experiences in the environment. He can therefore experience unconditional positive regard and use his capacities toward self-actualization; openness and awareness of experiences allow continual growth. Optimal adjustment implies constant growth and evolution of the personality through unique interaction with the environment.

Inconsistencies between self-concept and experience, or between self-regard and the regard of others, are usually not within one's awareness. Incongruence results in tension and anxiety, and one denies threatening experiences to one's awareness in an effort to protect oneself from pain. Maladjusted persons deny experiences, avoid relationships with others, distort experiences, perceive the phenomenal field selectively (preventing incongruent material from coming into awareness, or *subception*), and perhaps move toward personality disorganization. The low self-regard and defensiveness must be replaced with high self-regard and openness through a therapeutic relationship.

Group Methods and Process

Rogers's statement concerning encounter groups was a logical extension of his theoretical stance on individual counseling (1967). Since positive change takes place in the context of a therapeutic relationship, a group provides many relationships through which members can achieve positive growth. He suggests six hypotheses common to intensive groups:

1. Defenses and facades are gradually dropped as the client begins to feel safe in a relatively unstructured group that offers much freedom.

2. If they are on a feeling level, relationships will take place more often.

3. Understanding of self and one's relationship with others will become more accurate.

4. Personal attitues and behavior will change.

5. One will relate to others more effectively in everyday life.

6. Trust and coherence in the group will evolve after confusions, fractionation, and discontinuity.

Rogers identified common threads and sequential steps through which most groups pass, although these are not rigid patterns.

Milling Around   In the initial stage of the group, there is a great deal of superficial talk, confusion, frustration, and silence. Because members are given very little structure, they grope for goals, a leader, and a set of roles.

Resistance   People enter a group with a public self and a private self. At first they reveal only the public self, and genuine self-revelation by one member can threaten the others. Deeper self-disclosure happens gradually, fearfully, and with ambivalence. Revelations and a plea for help may emerge in disguised form, or perhaps not at all until the group builds trust.

Past Feelings   At first members will describe past feelings rather than reveal how they feel at the moment, taking the experience outside the group in time and place.

Negative Feelings   Feelings in the here-and-now will probably first be expressed negatively and directed toward other group members or the leader. Rogers suggests that members do so (1) to test the "freedom and trustworthiness of the group," and (2) because positive feelings are more "difficult and dangerous to express." Expressing positive feelings leaves one vulnerable to rejection.

Personally Meaningful Material   The next likely event in the group is for a member to express herself to other members in a personally meaningful way when she realizes there is freedom and acceptance and that no one has been hurt by expressing herself. This marks the beginning of trust in the group. These more meaningful revelations are usually of feelings toward significant figures in one's life. Acceptance is not automatic from all group members. Some may feel threatened by the revelation and attempt to ignore it, reject the other member, or change the topic; others will welcome honest self-disclosure and be supportive.

Expression of Immediate Interpersonal Feelings   At some point in the group process, a significant event is the emergence of feelings experienced in the here-and-now by one member toward another. Feelings may be negative ("I don't like the way you agree with everything") or positive ("I liked you from the very first session"). This marks the beginning of the exploration of genuine, current feelings that Rogers believes necessary.

Development of Healing Capacity   Some or all of the members display a natural ability to respond helpfully to others. Rogers notes sensitivity, perceptiveness, and healing attitudes in group participants that were seemingly awaiting permission to be released.

Self-Acceptance and the Beginning of Change   The personality begins to change when one begins to accept oneself. The group provides the atmosphere for becoming aware of one's feelings, then coming to accept those feelings as part of oneself. The client becomes more "real" and "authentic."

Basic Encounter   The group becomes less tolerant of facades and pretense. Participants become impatient with polite words and intellectual explanations; they want expression of genuine feelings. There is a natural movement toward deeper and more basic interpersonal encounters. Sometimes members become aggressive and confrontive in their demands to know another member, and may say something like "I don't really know you. You keep hiding behind all those words."

Feedback   Comments and behavior toward one another provide feedback as to how other participants perceive one. Significant people in one's life often give inadequate feedback. Self-awareness is greatly enhanced by the perceptions of others, in the way of statements such as "You make me feel warm inside because you don't make value judgements about my statements" or "I get irritated with you because you change the subject every time someone gets a little emotional."

Behavior Change   Rogers relies on self-report of group participants and research outcome data to support the efficacy of his groups. He believes the group experience has brought about many changes in individuals; the patient has greater spontaneity, empathy, tolerance, confidence, and honesty, develops closer relationships with others, and becomes more loving, genuine, and relaxed. Greater self-worth and congruence normally lead to better feelings about oneself and more effective interpersonal relationships.

Disadvantages and Risks

Rogers finds some disadvantages and risks in a group experience, which can apply to other forms of therapeutic group counseling as well.

Results may not be long-lasting.

Problems may be revealed with no opportunity to work them through, which can be damaging for a small percentage of participants.

When one spouse participates, marital tensions may come out that the other spouse is not as able to work on.

Strong feelings in the group can have a sexual aspect which can cause conflict when a person's partner is not in the group.

Experienced group members may try to impose their previous rules and experiences on members of the new group, detracting from expressiveness and spontaneity.

Despite the risks, Rogers sees the basic encounter group as an opportunity for rehumanizing interpersonal relationships. In contemporary society, many people feel isolated, and a group offers the intense I–Thou relationship in which one is no longer lonely.

Leadership Role

In Rogers's encounter group, the leader is a facilitator of self-exploration. The leader must first provide the necessary and sufficient conditions for personality change, in much the same way as in one-to-one counseling. The advantage in a group is that the leader acts as a model by demonstrating effective interpersonal responses. Group participants will observe and eventually emulate that behavior, thus constructing an overall therapeutic atmosphere. The leader is genuine, warm, and empathic in relating to the group members. Expressing feelings nondefensively and accepting whatever is said creates an atmosphere for members to do the same. Although there is some risk in open expression of feelings, unconditional regard for one another minimizes the risk.

The leader applies the assumptions of the client-centered approach to group process. He assumes members and the group as a whole will move at its own pace and deal with deeper issues as it becomes ready to do so. The leader deals with the group in terms of where the members are and what they want to work on. He is not directive in trying to move them from social chatter to deeper self-disclosure. It is up to the group to decide what it wants to do; however, this does not imply approval from the group leader.

Beyond the necessary facilitative conditions, Rogers does not support any techniques to promote group growth. He considers the leader an instrument for change and feels that additional techniques or games might impede the group's natural growth tendencies. The following behaviors of leaders from other schools, including other "self" counselors and encounter group leaders, do not appear in Rogers's approach:

1. Commenting on group process, which could make the group more self-conscious. Comment is left to the group.

2. Interpreting individual members' behavior.

3. Accepting transference relationships.

4. Suggesting a topic for discussion.

5. Having physical contact with members. The leader may, on rare occasions, hug or embrace someone, but physical contact should be natural and spontaneous.

6. Using warm-up games or exercises.

7. Directing members to do or say anything.

Advantages

The basic encounter group leader is expected to communicate the facilitating conditions skillfully. Skills such as empathy and respect can be learned, and form the basis for effective group leadership.

Rogers explains the process one goes through when growth occurs in the group setting; his explanation is a guide for the leader in understanding group participants. Rogers also describes a group's stages, to which the leader can refer when determining whether a group is making progress.

Led by a well-trained person, an encounter group can be helpful to educated people who wish to enhance interpersonal relationships and more fully actualize their potential. These groups provide a non-threatening atmosphere in which to explore oneself and attempt changes. Encounter is less useful with the mentally retarded, the severely brain damaged, the multiply handicapped or the severely emotionally disturbed, who need more structure and guidance.

EXAMPLE OF A BASIC ENCOUNTER GROUP

In this example, the first two sessions consisted of superficial banter. Members introduced themselves (they were college students from several universities and colleges), and spoke about their respective campuses and how they looked forward to this workshop. This constituted the milling around stage. The leader had told them it was their group and he was there merely to facilitate. They at first looked to him for direction, but when it was not forthcoming, they tended to ignore him. There were long periods of silence. Occasionally someone would ask what they were doing there.

Session Three (Abstract)

Nate: I came here to get something out of this. I don't want to just sit here and waste my time.

Susan: I agree. How come Dr. Smith doesn't say more and get us going?

Bill: Yeah, Dr. Smith. How about getting us going?

Dr. Smith: I can appreciate that you want to get something from the group. I don't think I'm the best one to decide what that might be.

Nate: You're the expert. You can tell us what we're supposed to do.

Mark: He told us this was our group. Maybe we could decide what we want to do here. I don't want to sit here and "shoot the bull" for hours. I came here to learn something.

Susan: I did too. I want to learn about the rest of you. Something besides where you are from.

Leader: You are asking people to reveal more about themselves than superficialities.

Susan: Yes. I can get that any time, any place. I'll bring something up. I have trouble with my roommate. She smokes all the time and plays the stereo when I try to study. I get real mad at her, but I guess it's her room too. I don't know whether I have the right to speak up or not.

Angie: Well, everyone has trouble with roommates. It's something you just have to live with. Does anyone want to go out to dinner tonight?

Robert: Now wait a minute, Susan has a problem and I don't think we ought to ignore it. At least it's something we could look at.

Bill: Is this the kind of thing we want to talk about?

This episode illustrates several things. For one, the leader offers *empathic responses* and at the same time directs *responsibility* for the group to its members. The participants are becoming restless with the superficial talk, yet are unsure of what to do. Their *ambivalence* is apparent when Susan tries to reveal something about herself. When Susan reveals *past feelings*, she is greeted with Angie's attempt to minimize the problem and avoid the feelings. *Negative feelings* toward the leader are expressed implicitly.

Twelfth Session

Bill: Here I am a sophomore in college and I've only had one date, and that one was when I was fixed up. I can't get up the nerve to ask anyone. I just don't believe anyone would want to go out with me.

Leader: It's hard to accept that someone would think enough of you that they would want to go on a date with you, yet you wish you could get up the nerve to ask.

Bill: That's the way it is. I know at least two girls I'd like to go out with. I talk to them, but I don't ask.

Nate: I had trouble with that, too. Maybe not quite so bad. What do you think is holding you back?

Bill: I don't really know. Maybe it's because I don't know how to act on a date. God, what would happen if she said no.

Norman: I know what you mean. When you think about asking, your stomach gets real queasy thinking about her saying she doesn't want to go out with you.

Betty: It does seem like it would be a real risk to ask someone. How would you feel, Bill, if someone said no?

Bill: I'd feel crushed. I'd think no girl wanted to go out with me. I'd feel terrible. I'd probably never ask again.

Leader: That first time you asked would be so important that it could almost devastate you.

Bill: Yeah. It would take so much

nerve that if it didn't work I'd never try again.

Angie: I think a lot of girls would like to go out with you. You're nice looking and you act real nice in here.

Susan: I know I like you and if we were on the same campus, I'd go out with you if I weren't going steady with someone.

Bill: I don't know. You're saying nice things, but how do I know other girls would feel the same way?

Leader: You are also saying something about whether you are willing to take a chance.

Henry: Yeah, how far has it gotten you by not asking? I'd take the chance. Besides, a girl would be lucky to be able to go out with you.

Angie: I wish you weren't so afraid of girls. You deserve to go out and have fun with someone.

Later in the session:

Bill: You're right that I'm afraid to take the chance. I don't want to be rejected.

Cliff: Is there anything we can do to help you do what you want?

Bill: You already have. I understand the problem more clearly and I know I have to go ahead and ask someone. I'm going to ask someone when I get back. Thanks for listening to me and encouraging me.

Personally meaningful material has now been revealed. Bill had never presented a problem before. To his friends, he has stated a lack of interest in girls and a need to get good grades for law school. His admission that he was afraid was a major step for Bill. He felt safe in doing so with this group of people. The participants gave him *feedback* as to how he came across in the group, gave him support, and revealed their feelings toward him. Their empathy reassured Bill that his feelings were okay, that others understood his problem. The other members also conveyed that they wanted him to do something to improve the situation.

Summary

Carl Rogers's encounter group is an example of the less structured groups sometimes called *sensitivity groups*. His approach assumes that people have a natural tendency to grow and improve themselves. Group counseling can provide an atmosphere within which members feel safe to reveal their needs and ultimately to improve their lives. Specific behaviors receive less attention than members' perceptions of themselves, their satisfaction with their lives, and their ability to establish meaningful relationships. Thus, examples of group goals may be to enhance self-esteem, reduce conflict with others, or to use one's energy more productively.

The leader sets an example for group members by providing facilitative conditions such as empathy, respect, and positive regard for others. This therapeutic climate brings about self-exploration, revelation of past and current feelings, and self-acceptance. The group atmosphere is one of acceptance and sensitivity. Members develop the capacity to respond helpfully to each other, leading ultimately to personality change. The leader is a facilitator and participant in the group, unconcerned with controlling the group or planning or directing group activity.

Discussion Questions

1. Rogers describes the sequential steps in group process. Give an example of what would or might take place in each step.

2. Rogers takes on a less assertive or directive role than many other models of group work advocate. In what ways is this true? What might be the advantages and disadvantages of his leader role? To what extent does this role "fit" for you?

6

Rational-Emotive Group Work

Rational-Emotive Therapy (RET) was founded by Albert Ellis as an alternative to the popular psychoanalytic, behavioral, and basic encounter theories of counseling and therapy. Ellis says emotional disturbance is the result of "crooked" thinking, poor logic, exaggeration of real situations, and a philosophy of life that leads to self-harmful behavior. To illustrate, he offers an A–B–C theory of personality. The disturbed person assumes that an Activating Event [A] causes an emotional Consequence [C]. For example, if one's children do not come for Sunday dinner, the parents believe their despondency [C] is the result of the children's not visiting [A]. On the contrary, however, their despondency is the result of how they think, or what they believe [B], about this event. If they believe the children should come to dinner and it is awful [B] if they do not, then they set themselves up for disappointment [C].

In counseling, the leader or counselor takes the role of instructor, explaining didactically and often persuasively the client's illogical and unrealistic thinking. The counselor is directive in the sense of taking control of the session, actively pointing out where the client's philosophies are counterproductive, and requiring the client to do something to change his crooked thinking. Thus, the client's thinking is disputed [D] by the challenge of the counselor or group members. Group members eventually learn to challenge their own irrational thinking.

Ellis's conclusions about the theory and practice of counseling result from integration of his clinical experience with portions of other theories he accepts as valid for understanding human behavior. His own training was as a psychoanalyst, but he soon observed the limitations of this approach and began to build a model that made sense to him. Ellis borrows liberally from philosophy, literature, and therapy and explains where he agrees and disagrees with each theory of human behavior and therapy.

Before formulating his theory in the early 1950s, Ellis had noted that over the course of therapy, his patients either did not completely lose their symptoms or created new symptoms. He concluded that adults retained the irrationalities, superstitions, and taboos learned in childhood, and that this thinking had to be altered for any real change to take place. Clients resist change because they are human; that is, their biosocial nature gives them a tendency to mislead themselves into believing that what they desire is what "should" happen. People thus tend to be perfectionistic, self-damning, and other-directed. Normal desire for love, approval, success, and pleasure are wrongly defined as needs. When desires are exaggerated, the person invariably has irrational, unvalidated ideas that will lead him into difficulties. Irrational beliefs were not noticably affected by traditional forms of counseling such as the analytic free-association technique and reflections of the client-centered school, while behaviorists dealt merely with immediate symptoms. So Ellis began to directly attack the client's unrealistic beliefs and values, focusing on "self-defeating ideas, traits, and performances." He advocates full acceptance of the client; the leader's strong caring, although not necessarily liking, for the client is assumed, but irrational assumptions and the behavior arising from them are rejected.

Ellis's RET is sometimes categorized with a relatively new movement in the counseling field, the cognitive-behavioral approach. A theory has not yet been developed, but themes and propositions that link counseling models have been proposed (Stone, 1980). It has arisen from psychology's stronger interest in cognitive functioning, as well as behavioral approaches such as Bandura's (1971), that allow for one's mediation of environmental stimuli. In fact, cognitive-behavioral counseling stresses the impact of "environmental variables on perception and performance," while at the same time seeing them converge with the influence of "mediational processes on personal adjustment" (Stone, 1980). Application of this model to group counseling has not been explicated for group counseling, except by individuals such as Ellis. (For more information on the cognitive-behavioral approach, you can consult Stone [1980], Meichembaum [1977], Mahoney [1977, 1974], and Goldfried, Decenteceo, and Weinberg [1974]. Another popular counseling approach that is cognitive in orientation is that of William Glasser [1965].)

Theoretical Constructs

Ellis (1979) explains eight propositions of RET:

1. Human beings have the potential to think and act in both helpful and self-destructive ways. We can think rationally or irrationally; we can be creative, sexual, loving, self-actualizing, and can learn from mistakes, organize, and relate well to others. On the other hand, we may also be unable to think ahead, and we can hate, shirk responsibility, be callous, intolerant, or perfectionistic.

2. People are, to varying degrees, gullible and highly suggestible, and are more vulnerable during their younger years when family and immediate community have a great influence. These factors contribute to a tendency toward "irrational thinking, self-damaging habituations, wishful thinking, and intolerance." Everyone also has inherent leanings toward certain types of thinking and acting that are biosocial, and everyone brings one's own unique qualities into a situation.

3. Perceiving, thinking, emoting, and behaving interact with one another and tend to occur simultaneously. Cognition almost always accompanies perception and behavior. Feelings are usually evoked by what one perceives and how one cognitively evaluates an event. The interaction of these four dimensions governs both normal and self-defeating conduct; therefore, the counselor must understand how the client perceives, thinks, emotes, and acts. Modifying or eliminating self-destructive elements requires a variety of methods that directly confront the malfunctioning elements.

4. RET is more likely to be effective in a shorter period of time than other therapeutic methods. Others may be somewhat useful, but the more action-oriented, directive, cognitive, disciplined RET approach is the most effective.

5. Therapeutic success does not depend on a deep or warm relationship between counselor and client. Transference or a "client-centered" relationship is ignored or discouraged. Of course, good rapport and full and unconditional acceptance of the client as a person are desirable. The counselor directs negative comments to self-defeating behavior and irrational thoughts. One can employ highly impersonal techniques in attacking the client's irrationalities. Although the counselor may be empathic, it is much more important to be firm and action-oriented in convincing the client to undertake a more self-disciplined life.

6. RET employs a variety of techniques, such as role-playing, asser-tiveness training, humor, persuasion, operant conditioning, and support to bring about fundamental cognitive change. Symptom reduction is of secondary importance; change in the symptom-producing, usually cognitive, factors is the real objective.

7. The reason people mishandle their reactions to obnoxious stimuli (point A) is because of their irrational, dogmatic, superstitious, magical, unexamined beliefs (point B), which lead to bad feelings and poor adjustment. Crooked thinking can be changed and elim-inated by rigorously applying the "principles of logic—empirical thinking." Irrational beliefs will not withstand the scrutiny of logical examination. A counselor can, for example, easily expose the self-defeating belief that "everyone should love and pay atten-tion to me all the time" and help the client wish to have "some people love me and give me attention some of the time."

8. The real cause of emotional problems is the client and what hap-pens to him. His irrational beliefs and evaluation of experiences actually bring about emotional disturbance. Psychological insight only helps one understand that a current problem has antece-dents and, of course, previous experiences do influence how one feels and thinks. The rational-emotive counselor helps one see previous experience in the light of one's beliefs about those expe-riences. The experience itself is not as important as how one eval-uated the situation.*

The client must take responsibility for persisting in irrational thinking; change in beliefs occurs only when one admits one's part in perpetuating them. The next step is a commitment to "hard work and practice" that calls for clear thinking and repeated activity to extinguish the irrational beliefs.

Irrational Ideas

Irrational ideas result from the interaction of both physiological and psychological factors. Rational-emotive psychology assumes that people have innate dispositions or tendencies toward growth, inertia, and irrationality. Ellis lists a large number of "biological tendencies to be self-defeating and socially uncooperative," including the ten-dencies to be overwhelmed by inertia, or trouble in changing one's

---

*Summarized material by permission of F. E. Peacock Publishers. Ellis, A. (1979), Rational-Emotive Therapy. In R. Corsini (Ed.), *Current Psychotherapies*. Itasca, IL (2nd Ed.).

thinking; to convince oneself that one needs or must have what one actually wants or prefers; to retain many of the prejudices learned in childhood; to feel one needs to prove superiority to others, even omnipotence; to jump from one extreme of an illogical view to the other extreme; to keep forgetting that something is noxious even in the presence of much evidence; to engage in a great deal of wishful thinking; to demand that others treat us fairly and dwell on the fact that they often don't; and to condemn oneself rather than the poor behavior. People thus have a natural but unhealthy disposition to demand that everything in life go as they want it to, and when it does not, they condemn themselves, others, or society.

Poor ideas also result from our beliefs and feelings about others. We overvalue what others think and how they perceive us. Disturbed people have a greater need for others' recognition and approval; their self-perception depends on the recognition of others, leading to depression, dependency, and anxiety. A healthy individual maintains balance between caring about others' opinions and realistic expectations. Unfortunately, society tends to reinforce the capacity to think and act irrationally. The result is a three-dimensional conflict between growth and self-defeating tendencies. Significant others, the individual's innate disposition, and his present functioning all interact to form healthy or unhealthy behavior. RET emphasizes the ability to counteract unhealthy forces, although it requires effort and dedication.

Ellis (1962) gives examples of irrational beliefs that cause and sustain emotional disturbance:

- "It is a dire necessity for an adult human being to be loved or approved by virtually every significant other person in his community." This belief is irrational because it sets a perfectionistic, unattainable goal; it creates anxiety because you worry whether others still approve of you, and how much they approve; it is impossible to be lovable all the time; you spend too much time trying to win approval; you give up your own wants and preferences; you are likely to lose respect and approval because you will behave in an insecure and annoying manner; and loving will be inhibited by the dire need to be loved. A healthy person strives for loving, creative living by seeking approval for practical reasons, building true self-respect, admitting that loss of approval is annoying but not devastating, ascertaining what one wants to do, and relating to others calmly.

- "One should be thoroughly competent, adequate, and achieving in all possible respects if one is to consider oneself worthwhile."

In fact, no one can be completely competent in all or most respects; undue stress and psychosomatic reactions occur when one compulsively tries to achieve; the need to be better than others is an other-directed and impossible task; the excessive need to excel violates the principle of intrinsically valuing oneself; and this "should" results in a fear of taking risks or making mistakes. Ellis recommends that one try to do well and enjoy the process of trying; do it for one's own sake; strive for *your* best; question whether striving is for one's own satisfaction; and welcome mistakes and errors.

- "It is awful and catastrophic when things are not the way one would very much like them to be."

- "Human unhappiness is externally caused and people have little or no ability to control their sorrows and disturbances."

- "One should become quite upset over other people's problems and disturbances."

Irrational beliefs such as these can lead to self-defeating behavior; they do not lead to rational decision making and long-term satisfying behavior. The counselor must identify a client's irrational beliefs, call them to his attention, and persuade him to act in ways that are rational and self-fulfilling.

Group Methods and Process

Ellis formed the first RET group in 1958 after observing the economic benefits and the fact that a client could take on the role of auxiliary counselor with another client. RET groups are often larger than other types, with as many as 14 members. Sessions are often livelier, there is "more new material, less stewing around in the same neurotic juices," more viewpoints available to someone who presents a problem, and more people are able to learn from a productive session. The larger group can also mean a smaller fee for each participant.

Contrary to some group approaches, Ellis opposes leaderless alternate sessions, and discourages socialization among group members, except perhaps to go for coffee without the counselor after a session. Overfriendliness, lying, and evasion interfered with group work when members were at first allowed to socialize outside the group. Ellis believes alternate sessions and socialization encourage participants to make therapy a way of life and to avoid facing and acting on their problems.

The group leader does not take up most of the time, as one finds in one-to-one RET. After a member presents a problem, the entire group becomes involved in questioning, challenging, and analyzing her thoughts and perceptions. The leader may model an analysis of the problem and move the client toward homework assignments to take action on the problem, but soon all members are welcomed as auxiliary counselors. Normally the group deals with one person's problem before moving on to another; however, a particular member's contribution may suggest a problem that must be confronted immediately. For example, the group may challenge someone who talks too much, too little, or is hostile toward other members, and the group's attention may shift. There are few exceptions to the group's content and language, and reluctant participants normally reveal themselves. If someone remains silent for long, she is questioned and brought out. Self-revelation is not elicited for its abreactive or cathartic effect, but to show there is nothing to fear in it.

Use of the A–B–C theory and pointing out irrational beliefs can have greater impact in a group because several people will point out the self-defeating thoughts. Ellis uses the example of a man who frowned and pouted in group sessions, but did not contribute to discussion. After being challenged several times, he finally admitted he was angry with one member whom he thought was self-centered, and with another who kept repeating her problems but never did anything about them. He was frustrated and angry and thought he was wasting his time. At first, some group members defended those he was accusing, then someone pointed out that the real question was why the accuser couldn't tolerate their behavior, try to help them, and help himself in the process.

Advantages of RET Groups

The first advantage of RET groups is their size—the challenge of 10 to 12 people to a group member's irrational belief system will have greater impact and be less easily edited out than will one person's verbalization. We also find that a great deal of self-teaching takes place when a participant assumes the role of auxiliary counselor. Through challenging other participants and observing their stubbornly-held thought, one begins to reflect on one's own irrational thoughts and stubborness; as arguments become convincing to others, one uses the same arguments with oneself.

When people enter a group, they often believe their problems are unusual and that they are worthless. Meeting members with similar problems or problems of the same intensity causes people to realize they are not alone, and seeing others improve helps people believe they can, too. Since there are no prescribed solutions, many people can share their creative ideas.

Clients who might reveal little in individual counseling are often stimulated to reveal problems in a group after they hear or challenge others' beliefs. Observing other people's irrationalities helps them recognize and discuss their own. A group is also more effective in persuading members to follow through on homework assignments. When ten people tell someone to express her wishes to her spouse, she is more likely to do so than if one person tells her.

The leader has a "real setting" for observing each client's behavior, in contrast to the limitation in individual counseling of self-reporting. A disturbed person also has the benefit of many viewpoints, ideas, and hypotheses about his beliefs and behavior than is the case in individual counseling. The fact that an RET session lasts an hour and a half gives one more time to explore and work on a problem than does a shorter individual session, and the coffee hour after the group allows more time to discuss a problem. After such an intense time, it is more likely that a client will continue to think constructively about the problem.

Action-oriented approaches, such as role-playing, assertiveness training, behavioral rehearsal, modeling, and other skill building exercises are, of course, best implemented in a group. Finally, a group gives each member an opportunity to learn how others view her, receive feedback, and learn what needs to be changed.

Ellis recognized disadvantages and limitations to RET group counseling. Every member of the group cannot be the focus of attention at every session, so concentrated persuasion and challenges can be diluted or occur less frequently than in individual work. And, not everyone benefits from group RET; some are too afraid; some too disturbed to stay with it; and some are too suggestible.

Role of the Group Leader

As we have mentioned, the counselor is an educator who uses a forceful, directive approach to make group members face their irrational beliefs and self-destructive behavior. The leader must be well versed in the many techniques, crooked thinking, and nonsense that members will use in the group process. The group must be challenged with thoughts that get them upset with themselves and others. The focus is on thinking and how it affects feelings, in contrast to leaders who focus primarily on feelings and how to express them. Ellis does not value the mere release of feelings; instead, the leader should encourage expression of feelings only to learn whether they are appropriate and whether crooked thinking has led to unnecessarily negative feelings.

The leader unconditionally accepts everyone in the group and, as appropriate, shows understanding, support, and encouragement for self-enhancing behavior. He also points out and tries to persuade (or coerces and expects) members to think and behave more logically. As an active, forceful leader he also encourages members to take on the roles of the leader.

The leader's objective is to help participants give up their demands for perfection. He directs them toward reducing self-defeating outlooks. Techniques range through cognitive, emotive, and behavioral. Ellis emphasizes cognitive techniques, such as persuasion, confronting, and challenging, but also uses emotive and behavioral methods such as role-playing, behavioral rehearsal, operant techniques, reinforcing straight thinking and realistic behavior, and expression of feelings.

Ellis (1973) directs the RET counselor to "always come back to and attack the person's irrational ideas, based on evidence from the client and people in general"; to "contradict and confuse the client"; to stay a step ahead of the client's "shoulds," "oughts," and "musts," and attack them; to use the strongest philosophic approach ("Suppose no one on your job liked you, what would be so terrible?"); to use feelings rather than sympathy to show how one upsets oneself; to explain how irrational ideas are self-defeating; to use strong words for dramatic effect; to listen carefully to what the client says to himself; to continually check to see if the client understands what is being taught; and to lecture only briefly and pointedly.

EXAMPLE OF AN RET GROUP

Leader: Who has something to bring to the group today?

Cindy: I'd like to have some help in the way my boss treats me. He is blunt, sarcastic, and doesn't listen to me or consider my feelings. He runs the place like a dictator. I've thought of quitting several times.

Leader: Have you spoken to him?

Cindy: No, I haven't. I don't dare to speak up. I know he won't listen. I'm so disgusted with him. He makes me so angry I could punch him.

Leader: Why do you expect so much of your boss? Do you realize you expect him to be nice to you? Actually, *he* is not making you so angry, *you* are making *yourself* angry. If you did not have the unrealistic idea that he had to be nice to you, you would not feel so bad. Tell us what is so terrible about his not being nice to you.

Cindy: I was brought up to be nice to other people and I think it is only fair that they be nice back to me. Why shouldn't he be nice to me?

Bud: So you expect him to be fair to you, and if he isn't you're going to be angry with him. It sounds like you set yourself up to feel miserable.

Cindy: I don't set it up. It's my boss who is so mean to me. He doesn't have any respect for women.

Kim: Maybe you'd *like* him to respect women, but who says he *has* to respect us?

Cindy: He ought to respect us. It's the gentlemanly thing to do. I think women should have more rights, but I also think men ought to be especially nice to women.

Leader: Why should men, or your boss, be expecially nice to you? What is so special about you that you should have special treatment? You think everyone should be nice to you all the time. This irrational thought has led you to expect, to demand, a lot from your boss. What is so terrible about his behavior?

Cindy: He ignores me, just coldly tells me what to do.

Leader: What's so terrible about that? Has he physically abused you or excessively criticized you? Does he not pay you the wage you agreed to?

Cindy: None of those things are true, but the work would be so much pleasanter if he were nicer.

Greta: You engage in a lot of wishful thinking. You wish things were better; they ought to be better. And when your wishes do not come true you feel mad.

John: Cindy, you have a hard time accepting your boss and your work situation as it is, and you don't do anything to change it.

How can you be so critical when you sit on your butt and don't do anything?

Cindy: I'm not the one who needs to change. It's up to my boss to behave in a more civil way.

Leader: You'd like to wave your magic wand to change it all. Since you don't have one, it's up to others to change. What would happen if you said to yourself 'I don't expect anything of my boss except that he supervise my work and give me my paycheck every two weeks'? Say that and see how it fits.

Cindy: I am saying that. It's not easy because when I do, I feel like I've let him off the hook.

James: So you couldn't criticize him and demand he be nice to you.

Cindy: Sort of, yes. Where would we be if we just let people do what they pleased?

Leader: Perhaps you are afraid of what would happen if you did what you really wanted. What would you really like to do?

Cindy: I'd like to tell him to quit acting like a pompous jackass and to act human. I'd like to punch him.

Bud: That's your anger coming out again; if you acted on your anger, what would happen?

Cindy: I'd probably get fired.

Joan: What you really want is to change how he behaves toward you.

Leader: And most often we are not very good at changing others unless we are willing to do something first ourselves. You want him to do something nice; are you willing to do something differently toward him?

Cindy: What can I do so differently? I do my job all right.

John: You still expect him to change, but you don't look at yourself and what you could do.

Cindy: I guess I could do something. Like maybe bring in some donuts with the coffee.

Leader: Let's work on a few things Cindy could do as a homework assignment that would get her doing something to change the atmosphere in the office.

In this example, Cindy's belief system was directly attacked by the group. Her unrealistic expectations of others, her wishful thinking, her denial that she played a part in the problem, and her excessive need to be treated with consideration were pointed out as self-defeating thoughts that led to her unhappiness and anger on the job. The leader questioned and challenged Cindy's beliefs. In the end, the leader showed concern by encouraging concrete steps for improving her situation. The group is fairly mature, as apparent by the cohesion they show when they pick out and confront Cindy's unrealistic beliefs. The tone in the group is to challenge her beliefs while accepting Cindy herself, and believing *she* can improve her situation by straight thinking and, possibly, by taking action. Later in the group, Cindy may be asked to role-play some interactions with her boss to practice for the actual encounter.

Summary

Rational-Emotive counseling and therapy asserts that most adjustment problems are a result of illogical and "crooked" thinking. Irrational beliefs, values, ideas, and expectations form a set of assumptions that conflict with the real world and how one can reasonably interact in one's environment. At the same time, people are capable of thinking rationally. They can discard self-defeating behaviors and take on rational thoughts that facilitate rewarding interactions. The focus of change is on the group member, not the environment. The group leader uses persuasion, reason, role-playing, and other techniques to bring about cognitive and behavioral change. He points out myths and crooked thinking and confronts group members with their irrational beliefs and behaviors. The leader is directive, challenging, and nonjudgmental except in pointing out irrational thoughts.

Group members participate in identifying, pointing out, and encouraging each other to acknowledge illogical thought patterns. A group member can work on problems that arise outside the group, but also displays behavior within the group that can be used as part of the therapeutic process. Members receive specific tasks for working on their problems through homework assignments, and group pressure increases the chance that a member will carry out the assignment. The RET group setting gives one an opportunity to compare his belief system with that of other members. The self-revelation and analysis of other cognitive patterns can bring group members closer to the reasonable thinking that will guide healthier behavior. The leader helps members give up expectations of perfection for a more realistic and tolerant way of relating to others.

Discussion Questions

1. Select an irrational belief, then show how Ellis might challenge the belief. How could you get a group involved in the challenge? What effects might the group challenge have?

2. What does the RET group leader hope to accomplish with individual participants and with the group as a whole?

7

Behavioral Counseling in Groups

Behavioral counseling in groups is complicated by the fact that it consists of a series group methods rather than one cohesive system. Methods vary according to theoretical orientation, the presenting problems of the client, and the group counseling setting. Therefore, we will first discuss the main theoretical contributions to behavioral counseling as background for the group techniques we will explain later.

Behavioral group therapy is a relative newcomer to the clinical helping field. It emerged from experimental psychology, which at first had a limited impact on the field of counseling and psychotherapy. Behavior therapy has its roots in the experimental laboratory work of Sechenov and Pavlov, who demonstrated how animals learn to respond to systematic stimuli in association with a reward. Conditioned responses were considered central to learning in both animals and human beings.

John B. Watson carried on the learning theory by establishing the behavioristic approach to understanding human and animal behavior. Since the 1920s, behavior therapists and counselors have used the concepts of "stimulus," "reward," "reinforcement," and "extinction" to systematically understand and change clients' behavior. They believe behavior is learned, and that behavior or problems can thus be understood as the result of all past experiences. In this way, behaviorists are similar to the psychoanalysts; both take the deterministic view that the past causes present behavior. Behaviorists differ from other theorists in how they conceptualize the past and present. All people are exposed to environmental and internal stimuli from birth, and perceive the stimuli and respond according to the characteristics of the stimuli, the situation, their own state, and so forth. Learning occurs through exposure to a series of stimuli and our responses to them. A young child learns language and emotional reactions primarily through interaction with parents; when the child verbalizes words the parents use, her behavior is reinforced and is likely to occur more frequently. If the child is punished for verbalizing in an unacceptable way, she may become anxious and, in the future, associate verbal learning with discomfort. This might interfere with school attendance or learning. A behavioral counselor has several strategies at her disposal. One approach assumes that an individual cannot be both relaxed and anxious at the same time (Wolpe, 1958, 1969). The counselor's role is to teach the client how to relax in situations that formerly produced anxiety; that is, acquire a new response to stimuli. With the child, learning how to relax when verbal learning is expected will bring about better functioning in school and when asked to demonstrate verbal ability.

The standard stimulus-response, or classical conditioning, model was later challenged by B.F. Skinner, who proposed an instrumental or operant approach to understanding behavior. This approach requires action in the presence of a stimulus, to be followed by a reward. The stimulus does not cause the behavior; it is simply there, and one learns that a specific behavior will incur a reward. A child might begin to use words in the presence of adults without their coaching her, and find that when she uses words, the adults give her a cookie. In this case, the child takes action on her own in the presence of the stimulus, the words spoken by the adults, and her action is rewarded with a cookie. If she were suddenly moved to another family that ignored her words, or withheld the reward, she would probably no longer say the words, that is, her behavior would be extinguished.

The Skinnerian model can be applied to group work in schools and institutions by using token economics, wherein desired behavior is rewarded with tokens which can then be exchanged for privileges.

Among therapeutic approaches, behavioral methods are most heavily researched to support their concepts and techniques. A close relationship with experimental psychology has contributed to the volume of research and the tendency to specificity and detail as to technique. Behaviorists value specificity as to symptoms and problems and methodically select the appropriate therapeutic technique. Counselor and client work together to determine counseling goals. The client must decide what she wants to change in her life; the counselor's responsibility is to come up with the technique or method to bring about the behavior change. Once counseling begins, both work openly toward bringing on the behavior change. Behaviorists are often accused of being cold and mechanical in the therapeutic process, yet, most consider a good relationship with the client very important. Early sessions are used to gather information and to develop a trusting relationship.

Behavioral therapy and counseling have several features that distinguish them from other forms of psychotherapy, some of which are a matter of emphasis and some unique:

Observable or measurable behavior is the unit of study, and the goal of counseling is to modify or change behavior.

Accepting that behavior is learned provides us with the process of study. If we know how human beings learn, we can teach them desirable behaviors.

The scientific method is more rigorously applied to counseling. Counselor and client seek to understand what the client has learned that presents a problem, then use systematic steps and techniques to reach specific and obtainable goals.

A variety of structured techniques are available to address maladaptive behaviors.

We assume conscious knowledge of one's behavior, as opposed to unconscious dynamics and the need for "insight."

There is no well-developed behavioral theory of personality.

Research documentation of counseling techniques builds a repertoire of methods to use with client problems.

Theoretical Constructs

Respondent and Operant Behavior

There are two types of human behavior. The first can be termed *reflexive* or *respondent* behavior: a specific kind of response elicited by a specific kind of stimulus, which always precedes the response. Pavlov's experiments demonstrated the conditioning of respondent behavior. If a person is fearful of dogs (unconditioned stimulus) and a dog is presented to that person at the same time you blow a whistle (conditioned stimulus), the person will learn to be fearful (conditioned response) when the whistle is blown without the dog's presence.

Operant behavior, on the other hand, is not preceded by a stimulus. If a behavior is followed by a reinforcer, the likelihood of the behavior's occurring again increases.

Reinforcement

Any event that strengthens the observed behavior is considered a reinforcer. The response is strengthened in that it is more likely to recur. In counseling, we try to reinforce the desirable behaviors by plotting how and when to introduce reinforcers.

Conditioning

Conditioning results when a response occurs in association with a stimulus that reinforces the behavior. Mother's smiling face (stimulus) occurs when her son smiles (response). If the mother's face serves as a reinforcer, he is more likely to smile when in the presence of his mother in the future.

In operant behavior, an increase in the rate of reinforced behavior is called *conditioning*. When a child participates more and more in class because he receives a piece of candy (reinforcer) each time, then he is being conditioned.

Extinction

When the conditioned response decreases in strength because the reinforcer is withdrawn, we see *extinction*. The behavior returns to the level expected without the reinforcer. If the candy is withdrawn, the child will return to nonparticipation in class unless another reinforcer, such as attention from other students, is substituted for the candy.

Generalization

After a response has been conditioned to a specific stimulus, similar stimuli may evoke the same *generalized* response. One who is severely punished by his father (stimulus) may experience fear (response) toward his father, then other adult men may also elicit a fear response. This fear response toward other adult men is *generalization*. The more similar the stimulus to the original, the stronger the response. Generalization has a number of implications; for one, people are likely to avoid situations in which generalization brings on discomfort. Thus, the young man will probably try to avoid close contact with adult males, a potential phobic reaction that could interfere with everyday life. Second, as an extinction procedure is applied to a generalized stimulus, extinction occurs more rapidly as the stimulus is less similar to the original. Therefore, as adult males are farther apart in age and appearance from the young man's father, it will be easier to extinguish the fear response toward these men. This procedure is the basis for certain behavior modification techniques.

Generalization is necessary so we do not have to learn a new response in every stimulus situation. On the other hand, we must and do learn to respond differently to certain stimuli that are similar in some ways and distinct in other ways. *Discrimination* occurs when behavior (a response) is reinforced in the presence of one stimulus but not in the presence of another. The young man's fear response is reinforced when he is with his father, but will not be reinforced in the presence of other men; therefore, he is differentially reinforced. The process of *differential reinforcement* leads eventually to a *differential response*, so that when the young man responds differently to other men than to his father, he is discriminating. Obviously, behavioral counseling will include teaching discriminating to the environment.

Counterconditioning

In the case of the young man severely punished by his father (conditioned stimulus), one may wish to bring about a response other than fear in the presence of older men. It is helpful, of course, that the older men not punish him (unconditioned stimulus) or cause discomfort, and even more helpful to have the older men behave in such a way as to elicit a pleasant response in the young man. They might invite him for a cup of coffee (new unconditioned stimulus). Replacing a new unconditioned stimulus for the old and a resulting response (comfort) that is incompatible with the original conditioned response (fear) is *counterconditioning*. The counselor's manipulation of new stimuli speeds the elimination of undesirable responses and can be effective where simple extinction procedures may not work. For example, without experiencing positive behavior from adult males, the young man may continue his fear response even though they never harm him.

Partial Reinforcement

Experimental testing has demonstrated that responses become stronger to inconsistent reinforcers than to continuous reinforcers. If a child receives candy for participation in class, he will participate more consistently if he receives candy intermittently rather than every time he participates. People usually respond more favorably toward others who give them occasional rather than constant attention. *Partial reinforcement*, then, means to withhold the reinforcer at times and offer it at other times.

Shaping

Shaping occurs when one wishes a particular response in an individual but decides to reinforce other behaviors that approximate that response, gradually reinforcing behavior closer to the desired response. One reinforces "successive approximations" of the desired behavior. Isaacs, Thomas, and Golddiamond (1960) used this technique to elicit verbal behavior in hospitalized catatonics. In a group therapy situation, two catatonics did not speak at first. The group leader noticed a patient moving his eyes toward a fallen piece of chewing gum; subsequently, the therapist held up a piece of chewing gum. When the patient responded by moving his eyes toward the gum, he was given the gum as a reinforcer. In later sessions, step by step, lip movement, a sound, and eventually expression of words were reinforced. The therapist must be careful to select correct behaviors and significant reinforcers.

Negative Reinforcement

Negative reinforcement is the removal of aversive stimuli contingent upon a response. The behavior that occurs when the aversive stimulus is removed is *escape*. For example, when a child has a temper tantrum (aversive stimulus) after being told he cannot watch television, and the parent then says "Go ahead" (escape response), the parent's behavior is being controlled by negative reinforcement. The child's aversive behavior is being reinforced. Although the parents may believe they have changed the child's behavior, actually they have simply escaped the child's aversive behavior temporarily and have been controlled by the child. When the parent does not give in at first but does give in later or intermittently, the child's aversive behavior is further strengthened.

Avoidance behavior is distinguished from escape behavior. In escape behavior, one responds so as to terminate an ongoing aversive situation; when we respond to, postpone, or prevent a situation, we engage in *avoidance behavior*. Ayllon and Michael (1959) were able to get psychiatric patients to feed themselves by discovering a situation the patients wanted to avoid. They wanted their clothes to be perfectly clean, so nurses were told to spill a little food on the patients as they were fed. To "escape" this aversive situation, the patients eventually fed themselves to "avoid" being spilled on again. Lovaas, Schaeffer, and Simmons (1965) have used painful electric shock as an aversive stimulus to force autistic children to engage in social behavior. In everyday life, many people work only to avoid a more aversive situation, such as not enough money for food and shelter, rejection by the family, or guilt. As long as the other undesirable situations are avoided, the work behavior is reinforced.

Modeling

Much of behavior is learned through reinforcement of imitative behavior. Development of language, motor skills, and social skills, for example, are heavily influenced by adults' reinforcing the child's imitative behavior. Adults act as "models" for the child. We learn to dance by imitating another person's movements. We also know that the consequences of the model's behavior influence the degree to which the model is imitated (Bandura, 1965). If the teenager who sells dope is able to buy fancy clothes and is looked up to in the neighborhood, other children are likely to behave in the same way. If parents are respected in the community, it is more likely children will imitate their behavior.

Advantages to Group Behavioral Counseling

Behavioral counselors have been wrongly accused of using groups simply because it is economical and of merely using one-to-one techniques in a group context. The group offers advantages beyond the one-to-one situation, however. In a group, the leader is not the only one to suggest alternative behaviors or to reinforce desirable behaviors; in fact, other group members may serve as more potent reinforcers.

The group also offers the opportunity for members to behave in ways that would not arise in one-to-one counseling. A participant may feel freer to try socializing or assertive behavior with certain group members and benefits from having more models from whom to learn imitative behavior. At the same time, each member has the opportunity to act as a role model or to teach skills, both of which can be rewarding.

Social interactions between members give the leader an opportunity to observe behavior and assess skills and deficiencies. Participants give responses to other members that would be unlikely to occur with the individual counselor. As members try different behaviors or learn skills, the leader can observe and evaluate their progress. Each member receives feedback on behavior at the time it occurs. Counselors have noted that changed behavior outside group sessions is not always accepted by family, friends, and co-workers, so the group provides support by continuing to reinforce positive behavior change.

These advantages apply primarily to groups that deal with social interaction problems. A group of this type usually has a heterogeneous membership and is less structured than those that deal with more specific behavior, such as a phobia. Goldstein and Wolpe (1971) believe the less structured groups offer unique possibilities for both behavioral analysis and therapeutic intervention. Lazarus (1968), however, reports effective group work with homogeneous groups dealing with impotence, frigidity, phobia, and the need for assertiveness.

Group Methods and Process

Techniques are fundamental to the work of the behavioral counselor or therapist. A theory of personality may be unnecessary, and one need not know the causes of the presenting problem. One simply understands the presenting problem—whether unwanted behaviors, new behaviors, or adapted behaviors—and selects a technique for changing the behavior. Behaviorists have not yet developed enough techniques to deal satifactorily with all human problems, but the range of techniques and the populations with whom they are useful have grown substantially in the past twenty-five years.

A major contributor to behavioral techniques is Joseph Wolpe (1958), who suggests that neurotic behavior is learned in the presence of fear-producing stimuli. The goal of behavior therapy is to reverse the fear response by substituting new emotional responses to the stimuli. From his assumption that one cannot be fearful and relaxed at the same time, Wolpe developed *systematic desensitization*. He taught clients to relax, then encouraged them to continue relaxing when confronted with the formerly fear-producing stimuli.

Aversion therapy (see Rachman and Teasdale, 1969) uses another set of techniques to alter behavior, including some unpleasant experience. Early studies used a strong electrodermal stimulus on alcoholics to get them to withdraw from alcohol (Kantorovich, 1929), and strong shocks on homosexuals to break them of a fetish (Max,

1935). Electrical shock was the aversive condition of choice until Cautela (1966) developed a "covert sensitization" technique. With this technique, the client imagines an extremely unpleasant scene in place of being subjected to a shock at the time of the undesirable behavior. Aversive techniques have been applied to socially undesirable behaviors such as alcoholism and sexual deviancies.

Another distinct approach is that of the social learning theorists (Bandura, 1969). Learning theory is applied to social-interpersonal situations to understand the acquisition of socially desirable and undesirable behaviors. These theorists' most outstanding contribution has been in conceptualizing "modeling" behavior as a way to learn social skills. Learning can occur from direct experience, vicarious reinforcement, or imitative learning, and the counseling group is an ideal place for modeling to take place.

Systematic Desensitization

Arnold Lazarus (1961) applied Wolpe's systematic desensitization to group settings. Remember that one cannot be both fearful and relaxed simultaneously; we cannot physiologically exist in both states at the same time. Fear is "reciprocally inhibited by the relaxation, resulting in its counterconditioning or extinction." The therapist presents the feared stimulus, such as a snake, and at the same time brings about a positive affective and physiological state by teaching the client relaxation procedures. Exposure to aversive stimuli is gradual; for example, the therapist teaches relaxation of body muscles, and if the aversive stimulus is a snake, sets up a series of graduated exposures to snakes, teaching the client to relax with the least aversive stimulus first. The client may be shown a picture of a snake a series of times until relaxation occurs, then be shown a snake through a window twenty yards away. The steps continue until the client is able to stand near or even handle the snake without fear. The client must, of course, want to overcome the fear. The method is systematic in that the counselor determines the aversive stimulus, plans a series of graduated exposures to the stimulus, and trains the client in deep muscle relaxation. The client becomes desensitized to the aversive stimulus; that is, it no longer elicits a fear reaction.

Lazarus formed groups of claustrophobic, acrophobic, and sexually impotent clients for systematic desensitization. Movement up the aversive stimuli hierarchy began when all group members were ready for the step. At first, each group was composed of members with the same problem. Lazarus later successfully worked with a group whose members had various phobias. After teaching the relaxation procedure, he gave each person a list of the items relevant to her anxiety hierarchy. They were told to read the description and imagine the scene in as relaxed a manner as possible with their eyes closed. Each member could proceed at his own pace. Comparing this technique with an interpretive, insight-oriented group of controls, Lazarus points out that insight did not change the control group's symptoms, whereas two-thirds of the behavioral group underwent change.

Another group included impotent men who had anticipatory fears of sexual failure. A series of sessions began with giving information to the men and their partners, separately, relaxation exercises, and group desensitization beginning in the third session. The hierarchy of conditions began at kissing and ended in changing positions during intercourse. Ten days later, each of the three group members reported a successful sexual experience. After one more session, participants reported consistent success in their sexual activity. A similar procedure was used with frigid women. Ten sessions were needed to complete the hierarchy. After 14 sessions, one woman reported consistent satisfactory climax, while the other two achieved it more than 50 percent of the time.

Other reports of desensitization therapy include Paul's application (1966). He selected people who were highly fearful of public speaking and placed them in five types of groups: systematic desensitization, insight-oriented psychotherapy, attention-placebo, waiting list control, and a no-contact control group. Significantly greater improvement persisted for the desensitization group after two years of follow-up. Paul and Shannon (1966) compared a group of chronically anxious people who received desensitization along with group discussion of "reeducative goals," insight-oriented psychotherapy, and attention-placebo techniques. Desensitization was most effective, and group desensitization had a more positive generalized effect than one-to-one desensitization therapy. The average therapeutic time per client was less than two hours. Other successful applications have been carried out by McManus (1971), Di Loreto (1971), and Sloane, Staples, Cristal, Yorkston, and Whipple (1975).

Modeling

Most traditional learning theorists believe fear reduction and fear development result from direct trial and error experiences. People develop fears from a traumatic experience or a set of aversive stimuli experiences. Treatment techniques such as desensitization expose the client to the stimulus to reduce fear. Bandura (1971a, 1971b) suggests that trial and error does not explain human behavior as well as his social learning theory. He believes observational learning (modeling, imitation, social learning, vicarious conditioning) explains how people learn language, familial customs, vocational roles, and religious practices. A child learns to dribble a basketball by watching older people play basketball, then trying it himself. He doesn't pick up the basketball and, through trial and error, learn it completely on his own. Bandura believes fear is learned in much the same way. Most people do not have direct, aversive experiences that lead to fear; instead, they learn it through social experiences. For example, few people who fear snakes have been harmed by snakes, but have learned to fear them because others do.

Three types of behavior or learning result from modeling. One can acquire new skills or response patterns, such as recreational skills, a new language, social skills, or job interview skills by imitating others. Second, one can learn not to respond in a certain way by observing the negative consequences someone else incurs. This learning leads to an inhibited response in the behavior repertoire. Showing a film of aggressive behavior and its consequences of social rejection gives overly aggressive group members an opportunity to learn how their behavior has left them socially isolated. Another type of response, *disinhibition*, refers to behavior of which one is capable but normally inhibits. A model then elicits, or disinhibits, the normally controlled behavior. The adult who becomes ill and engages in extremely dependent behavior disinhibits the behavior in the 20-year-old daughter when she becomes ill. The third behavior effect is *response facilitation*, in which a person who already performs a certain behavior now performs it differently or it becomes elicited in a certain situation, because a model serves as a discriminative stimulus. In other words, a behavior can be "prompted and channeled" by others' actions; an audience applauds when someone begins to clap appropriately, or people in a group begin to ask questions when one person starts it off.

A fearful individual inhibits her approach behavior, the behaviors already in her repertoire. Although she is able to climb a high stairway, or stand next to a snake, or talk to men, she inhibits the behavior because of fear. Disinhibition and eventually extinction of the fear occur when the individual observes a model in the aversive stimulus situation who suffers no negative consequences. Accurate information about the aversive stimulus reduces the fear; one is more motivated to try a behavior after watching someone else do it with no aversive consequences; and extinction of the fear response takes place when one observes model–aversive stimulus interaction, or *vicarious extinction.* These techniques and the social learning theory approach are particularly suitable for group situations because (1) many groups form so members can learn social behaviors, and (2) models inside and outside the group can be used in the group setting.

Group settings are ideal for many social learning theory techniques. Counselors preparing clients or students for job interviews may instruct them in the appropriate behavior and verbalizations for a successful interview, but no matter how detailed the explanations, the client may never fully understand or learn the behavior. Modeling is ideal for such situations; the counselor can use films of job interviews or role playing. He can point out the appropriate behaviors so members can observe as well as hear what is expected of them, practice the behavior and receive positive feedback (reinforcement) for successful acquisition of new behaviors. Social approval and immediate feedback facilitate the learning process. Fear of the interview process becomes disinhibited and new behaviors are learned. The leader must do some planning for this kind of group, first identifying specific job behaviors to teach (clean hair, appropriate dress, verbalizations), then ensure that they are displayed for the group members. Videotaping expected behavior and the participants' role playing as a means of feedback seems especially effective (Webster-Stratton, 1982).

Bandura and Menlove (1968) videotaped single and multiple modeling for children who were afraid of dogs. In the long-term, the group of children exposed to the multiple models displayed more positive behavior toward dogs than those exposed to the single model, and both modeling types were more effective than movies of dogs. In another study, withdrawn nursery school children changed their behavior after seeing videotapes of multiple models who were reinforced for social interaction (O'Conner, 1969).

Researchers have begun to explore what type of modeling behavior has the greatest impact. In the *mastery model,* one may behave in a way that shows great confidence in overcoming an aversive stimulus; in the *coping model,* one can model some hesitancy and gradual reduction of anxiety toward the feared stimulus. Meichenbaum (1971) compared these models in overcoming fear of snakes and found that groups exposed to the coping model displayed significantly more approach behavior than did those exposed to the mastery model. Although the results may have been enhanced by the fact that group participants considered the coping models similar to themselves, it is likely that members learned coping skills from the model that facilitated their ability to approach the snakes.

Social learning theory and modeling are appropriate for most settings and a wide variety of problems as the primary counseling method or as an adjunct to other approaches.

Cognitive Behavior Modification and Self-Control

Two major criticisms of behavior therapy have been its attention to remediation rather than prevention and its mechanistic quality. Recent techniques involve clients in developing skills to apply outside the therapeutic setting, thus addressing prevention by helping clients acquire coping skills for their everyday environment and reducing the mechanistic quality by forcing clients to rely on their initiative and cognitive processes.

Behavior therapists have generally dealt with clients as passive respondents to stimuli and ignored cognitive processes because they were difficult to objectify and quantify. With the emphasis on observation of behavior, it is understandable that behaviorists would avoid the study of behavior that must be either inferred or self-reported. The initial success of conditioning led many to believe that behavior could be changed and shaped with the client's participation, but it became apparent that operant techniques are not always effective, and techniques such as token economies might have only a temporary effect or could not be generalized to other environments. Also, theoretically acceptable explanations for the effectiveness of some techniques, such as desensitization, have not been forthcoming, so experimentation has come to focus on internal processes such as thinking. In the behavioral model, cognitive process is still considered the mediation between stimulus input and response.

Self-control techniques have met with success, can often be initiated and followed up in a group setting, and are efficient. Behaviorists describe self-control as *self-reinforcement*, a critical term in understanding self-regulatory procedures. To control one's own behavior, one must be able to withhold and present reinforcement contingent on the presence of a behavior or condition.

Behavior normally falls in a smooth pattern; however, the pattern changes if conflict occurs, if there is an error, or if one is prompted to make a change. Kanfer (1975) suggests that a three-stage self-regulatory process takes place under these conditions. First, one observes one's behavior in the relevant situation *(self-monitoring)*. For example, a client observes that she consistently gives in to her mother's every wish and command and would like to be able to say "no" to her. The client's observation is a necessary precondition to self-regulatory responses. Next, she determines the criterion for her behavior *(self-evaluation)*. She decides she would like to say "no" to her mother when she really does not want to do something. The final stage is *self-reinforcement*, giving a positive reinforcer or punishing stimulus depending on successful or unsuccessful performance. When the client says "no" for the first time, she gives herself a positive reinforcer, such as going out to dinner. She thus establishes the self-regulatory system and administers self-reinforcement. This is an example of *behavioral programming.* Thoresen and Mahoney (1974) use this term to refer to controlling responses (saying "no") that occur after the stimulus situation (mother tells her to come for dinner) by then administering the reinforcer (going out to dinner). Self-monitoring and self-reinforcement are key concepts in this process.

Behavioral programming has been applied in the classroom through token economy programs, but requires a great deal of time to administer and generalization outside the classroom appears limited. On the other hand, when appropriate training is given to all parties, student self-regulation has been successful (Drabman, Spitalnik, & O'Leary, 1973; Turkewitz, O'Leary, & Ironsmith, 1974).

Bolstad and Johnson (1972) employed self-regulation with disruptive children in the first and second grades. They established a baseline for frequency of disruptive behavior and created four groups: one to receive no treatment, one with external control, and two self-regulation groups. They put all treatment groups on a token system to decrease disruptive behavior. In the next stage, the self-regulation groups were taught to monitor their own behavior by comparing their record of disruptive episodes with that of the therapist. If the records were the same, the children were rewarded; if not, they lost tokens. After the training stage, the children were left to self-monitor and self-regulate. Self-regulation was found to be just as effective as external reinforcement by the therapist in maintaining lower rates of disruptive behavior. This and other studies show that students can participate in regulating their behavior.

A final example of self-regulation applies to weight loss. Bellack (1976) worked with overweight people to see whether self-monitoring (keeping a record of what one eats) or self-monitoring combined with self-reinforcement would result in weight loss. Of the two self-reinforcement groups, one reported back to the therapist periodically; the other group was not seen after it received instruction in self-regulation. The self-monitoring group did not do as well as the group that also used self-reinforcement. Furthermore, later follow-up showed that the self-reinforcement group continued to lose weight. Interestingly, the self-regulation group that did not see the therapist after instruction did as well as the group that saw the therapist periodically. The experiment showed that people can control their behavior and that there are ways to minimize therapist time in administering self-control techniques.

Training in Social Skills

Group counselors and therapists are interested in clients' social skills because social skills closely relate to other dimensions of effective functioning. People with poor social skills often have problems in interpersonal relationships, may be depressed, have low self-esteem, or derive less satisfaction from life, and may occasionally suffer severe forms of emotional disturbance. Social skill deficits apparently begin in childhood, where patterns such as withdrawal are first noticeable and often extend into adulthood. The behavorial group counselor has direct and explicit techniques to develop or modify social skill deficits.

Social skill deficits can be categorized into two general types. In the first, one knows what to do and when and where to do it, but is inhibited by anxiety. In the second category, one does not know appropriate social behaviors and must add them to one's repertoire. An example of the first category might be an 18-year-old college freshman. This student has socially active parents and has observed a range of social situations in an average middle class family. Although not an extreme extrovert, she knows the minimal social graces. In her first year of college, she becomes highly anxious about being on her own and withdraws into her room. She does not exhibit the social behaviors she knows about. She might well benefit from participation in a group to help her overcome her anxiety in the new social context. We might see the second type of social skill deficit in the psychiatric patient with a long-standing history of inadaquate social skills, withdrawal, and isolation from the community. This person has never learned the necessary social skills for developing and maintaining friendships. When opportunities for social behavior arise, she behaves inappropriately and is rejected by others. This client needs a group that will train her in social skills, assuming that a new set of behaviors is needed.

Many behaviorists use the terms "social skill training" and "assertiveness training" interchangeably. Assertiveness may apply to the expression of nearly all feelings, except anxiety. A more differentiated viewpoint is that we must distinguish assertiveness from aggression; *assertiveness* is desirable because it is a spontaneous expression of the feelings of the moment, whereas *aggression*, in the form of hostile, raging outbursts, results from accumulated anger or resentment.

A behavioral group is an excellent place for clients to work on social skills because they can practice modifying or developing behaviors that will carry over to larger groups. Hersen and Bellack (1977) define social skills in behavioral terms as:

> The individual's ability to express both positive and negative feelings in the interpersonal context without suffering subsequent loss of social reinforcement. Such skill is demonstrated in a large variety of interpersonal contexts (that range from family to employer-employee relationships), and involves the coordinated delivery of appropriate verbal and nonverbal responses. In addition, the socially skilled individual is attuned to the realities of the situation and is aware when he/she is likely to be reinforced for his/her efforts. Thus, at times the socially skilled individual may have to forego the expression of "hostile" assertiveness if such expression is likely to result in punishment or social censure. (p. 145)

Role of the Leader

Behavioral group counselors acknowledge the imporance of establishing a positive relationship with group members, although the type of group suggests the degree of importance given to this aspect of counseling. The counselor shows respect for clients by allowing them to identify their problems and become involved in the working stage of the process. The group leader facilitates learning by positively reinforcing the behaviors group members wish to acquire.

Most behavioral counselors proceed systematically in setting up and leading a group. An early step is identification of a problem in behavioral terms. A contract may be drawn to include the client's behavioral objectives and what he is willing to do to meet them. The client, counselor, and sometimes the group work jointly toward the objectives. The leader must use his judgment to place clients in appropriate groups. Next, the counselor selects appropriate clinical strategies.

The most common strategies are instruction, feedback, modeling, behavior rehearsal, social reinforcement, and homework assignments. The therapist gives specific *instruction* to the precise behavior, such as voice volume, expected in a particular context, for example, speaking to one's husband. The role of educator is consistent with the behaviorists' nonmedical approach. In group settings, members may come to a consensus in instructing a member to try certain social behaviors. After the client attemps a social skill, therapist and group members give him positive and negative *feedback*.

When the client has not previously performed the expected social skill, it is demonstrated, and the client is asked to imitate the behavior. Group participants, the leader, or videotapes can be used to *model* the desired behavior. In the behavior rehearsal technique, the client role-plays with the therapist and/or group members the interpersonal situations he finds difficult. These are usually verbal behaviors that call for expression of feelings and attitudes. Through *social reinforcement*, the leader compliments the client for a response that approximates the desired social or assertive behavior. Feedback and social reinforcement usually occur together, as in "You did very well when you asked your roommate not to smoke while you are eating." Behavior is shaped by giving stronger social reinforcement for behavior that comes closer to the target response.

Homework assignments are behavioral assignments the client may give himself or that the therapist or group members may give him to carry out between sessions. The purpose is to practice new or modified behaviors in the social environment. After role-playing the behavior, the client practices a behavior for which one would expect positive reinforcement in the environment. More difficult behaviors and those that may meet negative reinforcement are postponed to a later point in counseling.

This example shows the six clinical strategies we have described. A group member who has been dominated by her friends wishes to be able to express her feelings to them. They plan the social activities and expect her to go along with their plans. She always smiles, says she thinks the activity would be fun, and remarks on what a good idea her friends have. She tells her counseling group how she really feels and what she would like to say to her friends. The leader and participants give *instruction* as to the specific behaviors that would be most effective with the friends. Group members role-play a scene between the client and her friends as a *model* for her. She then does *behavioral rehearsal* by role-playing the scene with group members; in practicing the desired behavior, she receives *feedback* as well as *social reinforcement* ("That's very good!") for responding in new ways. Finally, the client is given the *homework assignment* of exhibiting the behaviors with her friends. She is told to try the least difficult behaviors, those most likely to elicit a positive reaction from her friends. The client tries the behavior, reports back to the group, and receives more feedback and social reinforcement.

Summary

Behavioral group counseling uses learning principles to understand and change behavior. It deals with observable and measurable behavior and a scientific and systematic approach to modifying behavior. A set of operationally defined concepts, such as reinforcement, extinction, and counterconditioning, describe the client and environmental variables. Among the available group methods are systematic desensitization, modeling procedures, aversive conditioning, self-control, and systematic social skills training. It is important to define each member's problem, set behavioral objectives, and, often, to have a counseling contract with clients. The goal is to bring about noticeable behavior change, usually according to what the client has defined as desirable. Systematic and specific behaviors require the group leader to plan carefully.

The group leader ensures that the group is correctly structured so as to modify the behaviors one wishes to change. The leader negotiates goals with group members, but determines the methods for meeting the goals. In a way, the leader is a technician—he applies the technique most likely to alleviate the problem. The many available techniques, whose effectiveness is supported by research, allow flexibility in determining what might work in a particular situation.

Discussion Questions

1. Explain the basic assumptions of behavioral counseling that distinguish it from most other models.

2. Describe how the following techniques or concepts could be applied to a specific type of group: Systematic desensitization; Modeling; Self-control. What are the advantages and disadvantages of each?

3. In what way do the behavioral concepts of learning, shaping, reinforcement, and generalization apply to group counseling? Given these concepts, how is the behavioral counselor's role perceived?

PART 2

The Practice of
Group Counseling

8

An Introduction to Group Dynamics

Group dynamics has interested many disciplines, including cultural anthropology, sociology, social psychology, and counseling, but the disciplines have reached only general agreement as to a definition—that of human psychosocial interactions in a group setting. In group counseling, the leader wishes to know about the interacting psychosocial forces that affect the overall nature of the group and its ability to meet individual needs and enhance the members' lives. A social psychologist would be concerned with the function and structure of psychological groups, how they form and change, and how they become self-directing units. Most disciplines would like a clear perception of how groups function and how they can be improved for society's benefit.

Kurt Lewin (1948) was probably the first to use *group dynamics* to refer to what took place in small groups. Lewin, Lippitt, and White (1939) examined the influence of leadership patterns on groups and group members. French (1941) followed with a report of a laboratory experiment that showed how fear and frustration affected organized and unorganized groups. Two studies (Lewin, 1943; Radke & Klisurich, 1947) examined the process of group decision making as a way to modify eating habits during food shortages. Lewin became the leading theorizer on group dynamics in an era of concern for the negative influence of authoritarian leaders and how populations might conform to immoral behavioral expectations. Issues such as leadership, decision making, attitude change, group discussion, and group productivity became topics of investigation.

Cartwright and Zander (1968) carried out a great deal of research on group dynamics. They define group dynamics as a "field of inquiry dedicated to advancing knowledge about the nature of groups, the laws of their development, and their interrelations with individuals, other groups, and larger institutions" (p. 7). Group dynamics is characterized as a process for analytical investigation, from which theories are constructed and subjected to empirical research. In group counseling, we are interested not only in the abstract theories and accompanying concepts that researchers suggest, but in how these theories and concepts will help us lead groups. Group counselors would agree with Cartwright and Zander's definition, but would add the notion of *applying* research knowledge to practice.

Understanding Human Behavior

To counsel a group effectively, the leader must have a sound understanding of human behavior as a basis for comprehending the dynamics of a counseling group.

The *leader's background*, in the way of education and personal experiences, comes with him to the group counseling setting and affects his impact on the group. He must be *open* to the group experience, keeping personal values, biases, opinions, and preferences from interfering with his understanding of the group members and their interactions. The greater his *ability to observe* transactions, verbalizations, and nonverbal activities of group members, the more effective his leadership.

The effective leader also requires the *ability to process information* he observes. Processing usually occurs in the form of hypotheses: What could it mean that Bill no longer sits next to Fred? Is it possible that Jane's quieter tone of voice this week is related to her argument with Lissa last week? That tone *sounds* like anger. It is usually unnecessary and dangerous to interpret isolated behavior, but once a behavior has some confirmation, through repetition or the participant's acknowledgment of its meaning, the leader can describe or label it. Ultimately, the leader takes *action*. When he has observed and processed a group dynamic, he may present it to the group. He may describe, suggest, state, or offer an observation on the dynamic. Action must be selective; that is, the leader presents the dynamic to serve a constructive purpose. In the case of one member's attacking another, for example, the leader might suggest, "I sense there is some scapegoating going on here," or, to get at the motivation, say, "There must be a reason for this scapegoating." To force the group to identify the dynamic, he may say, "Does anyone notice what is going on here?" or, to point out destructiveness, "This scapegoating is not very helpful to this group."

This chapter will emphasize the abilities to observe and to process information; action is discussed in chapter 10. As a framework for discussion, we will describe a counseling group and refer to it for each of the various dynamics.

A RESIDENTIAL CARE FACILITY FOR THE ELDERLY

As part of the ongoing program in a progressive residential facility for the elderly, there is a biweekly meeting for all interested residents to discuss conditions at the facility. Topics include food, medical care, program activities, transportation, and family visitations. Residents range in age from 60 to 92, with none needing intensive medical care. Everyone is able to move about the building, and most are able to go into the community independently.

Before this particular meeting, the facility director and a counselor in the community had discussed the possibility of offering group counseling to the residents as one option in their activity program. The director agreed to present the opportunity to the residents, without referring to it as "counseling." She was to describe it as regularly scheduled group discussions on issues of personal or social concern to the participants. The counselor would be brought in as a facilitator. At the biweekly meeting, the director informed the residents that there was the possibility of offering a discussion group to be made up of no more than ten people. Other details, such as information about the facilitator, the purpose of the group, and scheduling times were discussed.

Director: That's a general idea of what could be done with the group discussion, but it's up to you to decide whether or not you want the group. It should be directed to your personal or social concerns, but exactly what you set as the purpose is up to you.

John: I've never been in a group like this, so I don't know what to expect. It may be worthwhile, but I'm just not very sure about it for myself.

Jean: I think I have enough activities, and I already talk to most of the people here.

George: Now if it has to do with the social life here, I'd like to see us meet and do something about it. I think we could improve the social life. We're not so old that we can't have any fun, you know.

Lorin: I guess there are things we could talk about. I know I have some things on my mind that I don't say much about. I'd give this thing a try if there are some others who are willing.

Jack: I don't know. I wonder if it would really do any good. It could just be a waste of time.

Henrietta: I'll go along with it if the others want me to. It could be interesting.

Director: Those of you who are interested—do you have anything you want to focus on? George mentioned social activities.

Anne: That might be okay. I miss my family and maybe that has to do with being social.

Aaron: I'd encourage the ones who

Gert: want to do this. I haven't made up my mind.

Gert: I figure, what do we have to lose? If you know someone who is willing to come in and help lead us, I'll give it a try.

Stanley: I say if someone is willing to come in and meet with this motley crew, I'll give it a shot.

Anne: I'd be interested in how we could be more sociable. Let's at least meet and see what we can do. Maybe the leader will have some ideas, too.

Ron: Count me out. I don't like groups. I like one or two friends, and that's it. I don't even like to come to these, but I figure I better come and put in my two cents worth.

Kate: I'll join up. I'm pretty new here and this may help me get to know some people.

Director: Obviously some of you are interested and others are not.

Let me give you a day to think it over. Those who are interested can come to this room tomorrow at four o'clock and we can agree on a regular time to meet.

The residents' reactions were mixed, ranging from immediate interest to apprehension to immediate rejection of the idea. Eleven people met the next day, at which time they established an hour and a half to meet each week. Each person was scheduled to meet individually with the group leader prior to the first meeting. In these interviews, the counselor discussed the potential goals of the group and individual needs, and the elderly people got to know the leader a little. As a result of the interviews, the group was reduced to nine; one person decided not to attend because he did not want to be in a group that might discuss personal matters, the second was advised not to join because she was having surgery in three weeks and would subsequently miss three months of meetings. Within the group of nine, there remained a range of attitudes toward the group experience.

The following questions may help you understand group dynamics and its application to group counseling.

1. What are the various roles available to these elderly persons? What is the nature of these roles, and how do they come about?

2. What behavior will this group expect from one another? What rules will they set? How will they agree on the acceptability and unacceptability of certain behaviors?

3. What will be the communication patterns and styles in the group? Who will talk to whom? Who will be ignored?

4. What will be the pressures to conform to majority expectations? Will deviant expressions and behavior be tolerated?

5. Will the group develop a sense of "evenness"? Will members experience a sense of mutual support, trust, and unity? If they become cohesive, will there be a cost involved?

Roles

Roles that become established in the group show how behavior is determined to some extent by relationships to other members. Characteristic behavior in individuals can help the leader understand how each person fits into the interaction pattern of the group. Members assume roles that meet individual needs, such as acceptance, as well as group needs, such as open communication. Biddle (1979) defines roles as "behaviors that are characteristic of persons in a context." He suggests that definitions of roles as behavior in a group, or as expectations of behavior in various group positions, are too narrow. Role refers to behavior and, to some extent, expectations, but specifically to one's typical behavior in relation to a certain set of individuals in a particular context. Biddle's definition implies that role behavior changes as one interacts with different people, or with the same people in a different setting. One may also play several roles in the same setting or situation. In a small group, one may play a "supportive" role at one time, a "questioning" role at another time, and an "aggressive" role at still another time. Role change and flexibility can reflect the ability to adapt to changes in the environment.

We must also understand the difference between *ascribed* and *assumed* roles. The process of taking on a particular role is determined by many factors. In our group of elderly, George will act out the role of "playboy." He may have *assumed* this role as a teenager and found that it was reinforced, or others may have *ascribed* the role to him because he had a good sense of humor and did not take things seriously. Ascribed and assumed roles may be consistent with each other or exist without the other.

Remembering that "role" is borrowed from drama can also help us understand the concept (Forsyth, 1983). Just as an actor has a role in a play, each member plays a role in the group; the role to a large extent determines verbal and physical behavior. The "part" one takes is guided by the self-assumed role, which dictates a script that is followed with only minor deviations. Certain behaviors are expected of the actor, and major changes or inconsistencies bring chaos to the cast. In a counseling group, role instability results in disorganization. People want to know what to expect of others, and a particular group may wish to fill prescribed roles. If someone leaves a group, vacating a needed role, a new member will often fill that role.

When a group first meets, all participants begin with one role, that of "member." *Role differentiation* gradually occurs as members interact and experiment with various behaviors. Early on, the role of leader is differentiated from followers or members (Hare, 1976). In group counseling, a leader is normally designated at the outset; however, coleaders may be assigned or evolve from the group itself. The next stage in role differentiation occurs when members and leaders take on or are assigned more specific roles. One way to view these more specific roles is through organizing the group process in terms of tasks to be accomplished and/or emotional factors that keep the group functioning (Bales, 1958; Bales, 1955; Burke, 1967; Slater, 1955). A role taken on by the leader and sometimes by one or more group members is that of *task specialist*, urging the group to keep moving toward its goal by directing, suggesting, urging, guiding, and so on. Tension and stress usually result when other effective roles are not present to balance the group. Bales points out that the group may react negatively to the task specialist's prodding. Burke suggests that another role must then be assumed in the group to reduce hostilities and frustrations. Those who take on a *socioemotional specialist* role maintain harmony and positive interpersonal relationships. The roles of task specialist and socioemotional specialist are interdependent and necessary for group growth (Slater, 1955).

Bales (1970; 1980) analyzed group interactions into three dimensions: *dominance/submission*, *friendly/unfriendly*, and *instrumentally controlled/emotionally expressive*. (These dimensions were verified as important in understanding member roles in a number of studies [Schutz, 1958; Triandis, 1978; Wish, Deutech & Kaplan, 1976].) Using Bales's model, it is possible to describe someone's behavior as falling into one, two, or a combination of all three dimensions. He calculates group member scores based on their interaction patterns into 26 possible roles.

Roles describe behavior; they do not explain the reason for the behavior. We cannot say why a person acts as an energizer or a dominator simply by describing the role.

Group Task Roles

From the viewpoint that members either contribute or do not contribute to group goals, one can define certain roles as facilitating or coordinating the group's problem-solving activities; these roles help realize agreed-upon objectives. Table 8-1 describes facilitative roles, which are among the many possible positive roles one might find in a small group.

All the facilitative task roles will not be present in every group, nor are they all necessary to meet group goals. Some of the roles, however, normally appear in groups that achieve positive results.

Table 8-1 Facilitative Roles

Role	Description
Initiator	Energizes the group; presents new ideas, new ways of looking at things, stimulates the group to move toward some sort of action. Responses to the initiator may be positive, if the group is ready to move ahead, or negative, if it prefers inaction.
Information Seeker Opinion Seeker	Both request data of a factual or judgmental nature from the group. Information seeker simply requires cognitive information for clarification; opinion seeker focuses on values and the group's affective aspect. Each can be facilitative when data would be helpful to the group. An information seeker can dwell on data to the exclusion of affective concerns; on the other hand, the opinion seeker can put people on the defensive by pressing for value judgments and self-disclosure before a member is ready.
Information Giver Information Seeker	An information giver may spontaneously provide cognitive data, or respond to the information seeker. An opinion giver may also offer values or judgments on his own or in response to the opinion seeker.
Elaborator	Explains and gives examples of the topic, thus developing a meaning for what the group discusses; a rationale for group ideas evolves and the elaborator suggests how the ideas might work out.
Coordinator	Acts as a reality base for the group; ties ideas to practicality, prevents meandering into unrealistic discussions; pulls together group ideas; tries to have group organize its activities.
Orienter	Tells the group where it is in regard to goals and direction; summarizes what group has done and whether it is "on course."
Evaluator	Describes group's accomplishments and how well it is functioning; may evaluate usefulness or logic of a procedure, suggestion, or group discussion.
Procedural Technician	Carries out technical tasks (arranging chairs, brewing coffee).
Recorder	Writes down or remembers the group's decisions, plans, and suggestions.

Group Vitalizing and Maintenance Roles

Group vitalizing and maintenance roles build positive social-emotional relationships among group members and often result in attitudes that foster group cohesiveness.

Table 8-2 Vitalizing and Maintenance Roles

Role	Description
Encourager	Accepts others' ideas by praising, agreeing with, or stimulating ideas from participants; wants good feelings and a sense of security for the group. Excessive use of this role may direct attention from this person to the others.
Harmonizer	Attempts to mediate conflict and tension to keep group in harmony rather than polarized. May deal with subgroups in conflict. May brush real conflicts aside without a thorough working through.
Compromiser	Contracts with the harmonizer in cognitive orientation toward resolving group issues; may seek alternatives acceptable to the participants. When compromiser is part of the conflict, is often willing to give up status, see other points of view, or compromise in a way that resolves the problem.
Expediter	Oversees establishing group norms and guiding adherence to those norms. May try to get everyone to participate or suggest length of individual contributions. Role is similar to a leader's assistant or referee. Group members can become annoyed with someone who takes this role too seriously.
Standard Setter	Wants group process and goals to meet a criterion for acceptance by others. Sets high standards for norms and objectives. May evaluate quality of interactions. Often unsure of himself; wants high standards as a means of reassurance.
Group Observer and Commentator	Notes group process, relates observations or conclusions. Contributions may be descriptive, interpretive, or evaluative. In the extreme, this member may be distancing herself from the group, becoming a less involved participant.
Follower	Goes along with whatever group wants; quiet; offers little of self, preferring to be friendly observer. Usually too insecure and fearful to initiate ideas or discussion; not really a vitalizer.

Each role is adopted to meet the individual participant's needs and sometimes to meet group needs. To the extent that each person's needs can be met in a healthy, positive way, all roles will contribute to group progress. Where insecurity, lack of trust, and self-centeredness create unhealthy roles, the interdependent nature of the group is lost because members become preoccupied with themselves.

Anti-group Roles

Anti-group roles illustrate how emphasis on individual needs inhibits group progress and individual growth. Those in anti-group roles are the very ones who need a group experience. Their narcissistic or insensitive behavior has contributed to their problems in the first place, and the group is the best place to face their unproductive role behaviors. While these roles are often frustrating and irritating to the leader and other group members, they must help these members recognize their behavior and work toward healthier interpersonal styles. Greater participation results in greater involvement, which in turn brings a sense of being valued by others, with ultimately positive benefits for all. In rare cases, someone can benefit as much by being silent, but one must ask how this benefits the other group members.

The number of group member roles seems endless; for example, there is the *help-rejecting complainer* who extracts empathy and suggestions from others, then defeats the plan every time. The *doctor's assistant* tries to act in the ideal role of the group leader, to gain approval from others. With experience, one learns to identify many other roles. We can find examples of several group roles in our group of elderly people who are meeting to identify and work on social problems.

> *Gert:* Well, someone has to begin today. I'm glad we are having this group and I hope we get to know each other better. [*initiator*]
>
> *Henrietta:* Is that why we are here, to get to know each other? I'd like to know for sure why we are meeting. [*information seeker*]
>
> *George:* I'd like to see us come up with some ideas on how we can have more fun around here. It's kind of dull. [*opinion giver*]
>
> *Leader:* Our purpose is to evaluate our social needs, what we want from social activities, and what we can do to make our social activities better. [*information giver*]

Table 8-3 Anti-group Roles

Role	Description
Aggressor	Disagrees with ideas and discussion. May disapprove of behavior, feelings, and values. May impose beliefs or ways of doing things on others. May be jealous, insecure, need attention. Some groups fight back, others react passively.
Blocker	Stubborn about what should and should not be discussed; resists wishes of total group. Negativism can impede group progress.
Recognition Seeker	Boasts; engages in other behavior to attract group attention.
Self-confessor	Reveals feelings and insights unrelated to group's immediate dealings. Personal expressions distract group from concentrating on its task.
Playboy	Nonchalant or cynical toward group; engages in horseplay or other behaviors that communicate lack of involvement, thus disrupting group cohesiveness.
Dominator	Tries to manipulate others to recognize her authority; less aggressive than manipulative. Behaviors include interrupting, flattery, asserting status, giving directions. Interferes with sense of equality among participants.
Help-seeker Rescuer	Elicits sympathy from group by excessively dwelling on personal problems, confusions, and inadequacies. Giving attention may reinforce dependent behavior. Rescuers may meet own needs by accommodating help-seekers, but both roles unproductive.
Self-righteous Moralist	Has need to be always right and others always wrong. Authority on moral issues. Does not care to be liked; wants to be respected for moral integrity. Imposes moral standards on others. Will at first be quiet, then assert position persistently without conceding or admitting error. Projects image of moral superiority that soon alienates participants. Yalom (1970) suggests these people are disturbed by feelings of shame and anger, but usually believe they have no problems.

Table 8-3   Anti-group Roles   (*continued*)

Role	Description
Do-gooder	May be a modified form of self-righteous moralist who wants to do what is "right." Is helpful, kind, understanding toward others. Does not usually impose "good" behavior on others, but wants acceptance from others.
Informer	Possible variation on the do-gooder. Role occurs where group members interact and know each other outside group sessions; informer shares information about someone's behavior outside the group. Purpose of "squealing" is to enhance one's status with and acceptance by others, or as act of revenge.
Seducer	Uses manipulation, usually in the form of active or subtle attempts to control others by getting others to reach out to her or pretending to be fragile. Seductive behavior also avoids genuine closeness.
Hostile or Angry Member	Manipulates others by intimidation or avoids needs such as affection. Joking, sarcasm, and ridicule are signs of hostility. Result is greater self-protection on part of other participants to avoid attacks.
Monopolist	Talks incessantly about experiences, ideas, and information that is usually only tangentially related to group goals. Self-centered talk may be set off by similarity of another member's problem with an experience of the monopolist. May tell stories, relate what they have read, or relate personal upheavals in great detail. At first, group is relieved to have someone carry the ball; after several sessions, there is often fighting, absenteeism, and dropouts. Leader and group must deal with underlying anxiety of the monopolist.
Withdrawn, Nonparticipating, Silent Member	Opposite end of continuum from monopolist. Nonfacilitative group members may resent this member's seeming noninvolvement, or resent attention he gets when other members try to draw him out.

     Jack: Well I'm not sure we really need to do this. Most people here aren't going to change anyway. We can come up with all kinds of ideas, but it won't change anything. [*blocker*]

     Kate: I think we can accomplish something if we all try. But we need to agree among us and we need to put effort into it. We can make our social activities better. [*standard setter*]

  Stanley: I think we have a responsibility to better ourselves. I've been rejected by my family but I don't let that stop me. I still go to activities, I don't hide in my room, and I cooperate with the staff. If we do what is right we'll all be happier. I'd be glad to help everyone do what is right. [*self-righteous moralist*]

     Jack: Well, well. How can you people really believe things will be any different? Nothing has changed in the last year I've been at this place as far as I'm concerned. [*becoming hostile and aggressive*]

  Sophie: Now Jack, can't we all talk this out so we can work together? There must be a way that we can get an agreement on what to do in the group. [*harmonizer*]

Henrietta: I'd just like to know whether we have a reason to meet, and does everyone want to be here. I'm willing to go along with whatever the rest of you want. [*information seeker, follower*]

  George: Like I said, I just want to have fun. Is this group going to be fun? Maybe I can come up with a way for it to be fun. [*playboy*]

   Lorin: There are some good ideas here. And we all did show up. Maybe we want to do something to improve things. I'm interested in hearing what everyone has to say. [*encourager-expediter*]

    Anne: Maybe this relates to it, I don't know, but I feel stuck here all the time. My two children live 30 miles away and don't care about me. They never visit, and I feel awful. I wish they would get me out of here and take me to their house. [*self-confessor*]

Henrietta: I feel the same way. I cry in my room every night, thinking about living with my daughter. It's all so unfair. Don't some of you feel that way? I'd like to

know what I can do about it. What can be done?
[*help-seeker*]

Gert: First we were trying to discuss our goals, and now
we are off on personal problems. Maybe they are
related, but first don't we have to agree on whether
to work on social activities? [*orienter*]

Anne: I'm sorry. I just thought Jack and Stanley would
understand. You are so happy and I thought you
could help us. I do admire you so much. [*seducer*]

Arthur: As the senior member of these senior citizens I would
like to say that we have some very fine minds here
and there is no doubt that we can come up with ideas
for better social activities. This is a very fine idea;
however, only people who want to contribute should
be here. Those of you who have doubts can think
about it and decide whether or not to come to the
next meeting. [*dominator*]

Member Role Behavior

The role one assumes or is ascribed by others in the group is affected
or determined by many factors, some of which are historical and
some of which have to do with the immediate situation or even the
future. The individual's history in terms of experiences in the family,
school, community, and culture play a significant part in shaping
behavior in the group. The range of roles in the individual's repertoire will, at first, be limited to those learned from past experience.
For a particular person, there may be many roles or primarily just
one. One therapeutic goal of group counseling can be to change self-
destructive roles to growth-enhancing. A second goal might be to
restrict the choice of roles by developing the ability to choose what
best suits the circumstances.

As an example, Henry's adopted role in most social situations is
that of dependent help-seeker (and subsequent rejector). In the
group, he is deferential to the others, behaving somewhat passively
and dependently. He always seeks information but never gives any,
asks opinions but never reveals his own, attempts to have others
make decisions for him, and always agrees with the wishes of the
group. Henry is always looking for answers to his problems, and
agrees with suggestions and opinions as long as they require someone else in his life to change. If a suggestion would require that he
change in some way, Henry finds a reason it cannot be done. He
learned this role, with features of dependency, help-seeking, follow-

ing, and opinion-seeking, as he grew up. Henry had contracted juvenile diabetes in early adolescence, and the attitude of his close family and the subculture in which he lived was pitying. He was overprotected, waited on, and never given the opportunity to make decisions. A learned role of helplessness became his major mode of relating to others. It was what everyone expected, and the rewards were such that the role became fixed in all situations. School staff and peers learned to treat Henry carefully; he was not to exercise or be pressured in any way.

When Henry entered the group, he perceived the other members as a family that would take care of him. On the surface, he wanted to play out the dependent role that was most comfortable for him. But, although the other participants did not know it, Henry also resented his dependent role. He was uncomfortable with the lack of self-esteem, but did not know any other role. Thus, a member's past experiences have brought him to the group playing a constricted and self-denigrating role.

The role itself, or how someone acts out a role, is affected by dynamics within and external to the group. Despite emotionally harmful experiences, a member wants to be accepted by the others, so he may modify or exchange the role for another to gain acceptance. Henry will try to be accepted as a dependent person, which will not give him the highest status, but may help him avoid rejection by the others. He is willing to settle for middle-range status. At the same time, the composition of the group also has an impact on role performance. Homogeneous groups tend to restrict flexibility of roles; heterogeneous groups offer a wider range of roles. It seems that people with similar backgrounds and styles reinforce like behaviors in fellow members and are less likely to consider alternative behaviors. If Henry is placed in a group with others who are also diabetic and dependent, they will probably commiserate with each other and support each other's dependency. The dependency role is less likely to change. For example, dependent persons may focus their resentment on others who do not understand them, or who do not offer enough help. On the other hand, Henry may find himself in a group with members who are not disabled and a few diabetic persons who are not dependent. In this situation, his dependency role will not be as readily accepted. The nature of the group may influence him to modify his dependency—to be more creative in getting others to help him, or even to become less dependent. It seems the heterogeneous group would be more beneficial to Henry, because the group members can help him try new and more effective roles; their modeling will give him the confidence to try something new.

The impact of group norms on role performance can also be significant. Rules and expected member behavior can limit role opportunities or encourage role flexibility. If the norm is to establish rigid status lines, allow subgrouping, and discuss superficial material only, it is less likely that cohesion and eventual progress will take place. Roles will be extremely restricted. Henry may be assigned low status and grouped with another passive member. His need to reveal his resentments and assume a more assertive role will not be addressed because he will not trust the group, and the norm of superficial discussion will block personal self-disclosure. If the group norm is to value growth, self-revelation, and genuine caring for one another, Henry has a good chance to modify his role. This type of group will go through the usual developmental phases, and member roles will change along the way. Henry may try to be dependent at first, and someone may even take on the role of rescuer and opinion giver. Another diabetic may become the self-righteous moralist and preach to Henry about how he should change his life. Interaction of the various roles normally goes through a stage of conflict and confrontation. Eventually the group could move to the work stage and the members may carry out self-exploration and commitment to change. If these stages take place, a degree of cohesiveness develops. Henry would then have been confronted about his dependency in a supportive way, and the dependency would become less and less acceptable to the group. Henry would also reveal his resentments and might ask for advice less and less. His role would change as he began to make decisions for himself, and he might actually do something for himself, such as monitoring his diet. His roles in the group would become active—perhaps encourager and coordinator. By the termination stage, Henry would play the dependent role less often; he would have tried other roles and gain confidence in them; he would have developed greater self-respect; and he would look forward to changing his dependent role even more outside the group.

Norms

Group dynamics include norms that guide and influence members' behavior through a set of expected standard behaviors. Group norms refer to accepted and appropriate member behavior, including explicit rules such as punctuality and regular attendance. Norms also include implicit expectations that are not verbally agreed upon but evolve from interactions based on conscious and unconscious needs for certain behaviors by each group member. For example, members who want to move ahead quickly on a task will fall into normative behavior of attending to the task, rejecting distractions, listening to each others' ideas, and cooperating to perform the task. Another implicit group norm might be to avoid setting goals and to act hostile toward the group leader to escape self-examination. Thus, member beliefs and modes of conduct shape the norms, which in turn set guidelines for group interaction. When members follow group norms, they will be rewarded and accepted in the group; when they violate the norms, they may be punished and rejected. Certain norms are more important than others, and group reaction to a behavior is usually proportional to the importance of the norm related to the behavior. Self-disclosure may be less important in a task-oriented group and result in only a small reward for the member; in a healthy therapeutic group, self-disclosure will bring a noticeable reward. In this way the group brings about a certain degree of consistency and predictability among its members. Each person learns what to expect from the others, which lends a sense of stability and security in which to explore oneself. Forsyth (1983) summarizes the important characteristics of norms.

> First, norms are rules that describe the actions that should or should not be taken. Second, an evaluative element is involved, since norms usually suggest that certain behaviors are "better" than others. Third, in many cases norms are not formally adopted by the group, but instead result from a gradual change in behavior until most participants accept the standard as the guideline for action. Fourth, norms are often taken for granted by group members, becoming evident only when violated. Fifth, although people may obey group norms merely to avoid sanctions or to seem agreeable, when the group members internalize a norm it becomes a part of their total value system; hence, members often follow norms not because of external pressure but because normative action is personally satisfying. Sixth, while extremely counternormative behaviors are usually followed by negative sanctions, some degree of deviation from a norm is often permitted. (p. 121)

Norming has been considered one of the major stages of group development (Tuckman, 1965; Tuckman & Jensen, 1977); Tuckman calls it the third stage, following "Forming" and "Storming." Group structure develops at the norming stage, as well as stronger cohesion and harmony. Member roles and interpersonal relationships become more established, as members agree on rules, seek consensus on issues, and become more supportive of one another. The norming stage is followed by "Performing," in which the group has a task orientation, and the "Adjourning" stage, in which tasks are completed and there is emotional termination.

Implicit and Explicit Norms

Group norms must be recognized at a conscious or subconscious level before they become effective. Participants should discuss group norms and agree on rules and accepted behaviors to increase acceptance of norms and willingness to follow regulations. Norms apply only to areas of concern to the group; outside behavior does not fall under group norms, but member behavior in the group, shaped by the norms, affects behavior between sessions.

Implicit norms vary among members more than do explicit norms. *Explicit norms* are usually rules that apply to everyone, while *implicit norms* allow for individual differences. One member may be expected to assume some authority and guidance for the group, while another may be exempted from self-disclosure until she feels more comfortable in the group. Some groups have many rules that they follow closely. The leader in this more structured group establishes more rules from the beginning. Other groups have few norms (although they develop several implicit norms), and allow greater variation in behavior as well as modification of the norms. Therapeutic groups often have few rules initially and evolve norms out of the social context as they progress through group stages. The leader may try to impose rules and expectations, but the operating norms will be a function of the members' social interaction; they may or may not accept the norms presented to them.

Conformity

Norms exert pressure to conform. One concern in group work is the impact of norms on shaping participants' behavior. Members may be conforming, anticonforming, and independent. The conforming member goes along with the norms, an anticonforming member initiates behavior in opposition to the norms, and the independent member does not stress rules and expectations in choosing a behavior but makes judgments according to what seems best at the time. Conforming and anticonforming types are *field-dependent* and respond to an external locus of control; the independent type is *self-reliant* and focuses on an internal locus of control. Group norms and the power of each member are interrelated to some extent. On the one hand, more powerful members can exert pressure to conform, a function of their levels of real power and influence in the group. On the other hand, norms can modulate the impact of power and status in the group. Mutually accepted norms regulate excessive use of a few members' power and influence. They allow input and participation from less powerful members and encourage cooperation with the more powerful and perhaps more effective members.

At first members merely conform to the expectations of the group, but as time passes and behaviors become repetitive, members internalize the norm (Sherif, 1966). They personally accept the norm rather than merely try to please the other members (Kelman, 1961). For example, a group of adolescent boys may have a few members who must learn not to interrupt and to discuss topics other than sports. As they are rewarded for less aggressive behavior and discussion of more personal themes, the adolescents spontaneously engage in these behaviors. This situation also illustrates how group norms modify members' roles from aggressive to assertive and from negative or irrelevant to positive.

Sherif (1936, 1966) demonstrated that people develop standards for behavior through mutual influence, contrary to the belief that influence is used undirectionally to obtain compliance. Using Sherif's model, we find that groups begin rather ambiguously, but soon structure experiences and develop standards of behavior. This group norm arises through reciprocal influences, although it can occasionally be externally imposed. Group counseling leaders usually give just a few rules, so that members are free to establish their own norms. "The individuals caught in the ensuing experience of uncertainty *mutually* contribute to each other a mode of orderliness to establish their own orderly pattern" (Sherif, 1966, pp. xii–xiii).

Sherif's (1956) study showed how people in a group situation could be pressured to conform even when it meant giving up their initial accurate perceptions. He asked people to choose which line of several came closest in length to one they had just seen. In groups of three to fifteen, the subjects found other members choosing an obviously incorrect answer. When group answers were unanimous and subjects answered the questions publicly, they conformed to the group 32 percent of the time. If one member agreed with the subject or if answers were given privately, the conforming (incorrect) answers were substantially reduced. Other studies found that industrial workers set norms for production and workers who do not conform are sanctioned as "Rate Busters" (Homans, 1950); rejection of the deviant person is greater when the deviant behavior is more relevant to the purposes of the group (Schachter, 1951); and pressures toward uniformity in task behavior increase as the group goal and the path to the goal are clearer (Raven & Rietsema, 1957).

Types of Norms

One way to categorize norms is as methods of distributing rewards to group members; a norm is thus an accepted way to reward people for behaving in a way the group thinks desirable. The *norm of equity* portends that group members will receive rewards in proportion to their contributions. As they give more time, energy, and ideas, they are seen as deserving a greater payoff, on the assumption that people deserve to receive more if they give more (Walster, Walster, & Berscheid, 1978). A quiet person who is not helpful to others and has few ideas receives fewer rewards, in the way of attention, support, and status, than those who give more intellectually and emotionally.

Few groups operate solely on the norm of equity. More than one norm may operate at one time or they may operate intermittently. The *norm of equality* assumes that all members should receive an equal share of the rewards. In this case, one who is quiet and gives little may be perceived as needing rewards as much as the others in the group. Despite offering little to other group members, this member will receive attention and support as needed.

Other reward norms may be important (Forsyth, 1983; Lerner, Miller, & Holmes, 1976; Leventhal, 1976). When payoffs go to those who control the group, we have a *power norm*. Another norm (a Marxian Norm) is based on need; those with the greatest need receive the most, those with less need receive less. A similar norm is that of *social responsibility*, which expects those who have more to share with those less fortunate. These last two norms can present a problem in group counseling because the more fortunate or more giving members will feel they also have needs, and will often resent seeing a few members receive most of the time and attention. They will wonder why they should attend the group if they are getting little from it. The norm of *reciprocity* means that when a member gives to another member or to the group, he can expect a payoff of equal size. For example, when one group member gives attention and support to a quiet member, the quiet member is expected to give an equal, though different, reward of recognition.

Norms and Cohesion

To be cohesive, a group must have norms that promote trust, cooperation, affection, support, and individuality. Supporting positive behaviors and expecting them fairly consistently promotes closeness. The leader plays an important role in this process by recognizing positive norms and rewarding the group for establishing them. In a group's third session, for example, a member is the first to reveal significant feelings toward another member. The leader is immediately alert to this breakthrough and wonders how to handle it. Will self-disclosure become a norm for the group at this time? Should the leader reward the behavior by saying, "David, I know that wasn't an easy thing for you to do. I hope the group will support David in expressing his feelings"? Or will the leader wait to see how the group reacts, then comment on the interaction? The first response is an early intervention to try to shape the norm; later intervention gives the group more opportunity to work it out. Yet even here the leader influences the norm by encouraging group acceptance of David's feelings, or by pointing out unwillingness to deal with feelings. In this example, a self-disclosing norm leads to greater group cohesion.

Cohesion

Cohesion plays a large part in the development of a healthy group. A sense of togetherness, or "we-ness," suggests that members have a closeness that will enable them to behave supportively. Cohesiveness develops over a period of time as participants get to know and care about each other. Hansen, Warner, and Smith (1980) include cohesion as a stage in the evolution of a group.

Group cohesion occurs because people have a need to belong and be accepted by others. Many people who seek group counseling have had difficulty in interpersonal relationships. They have not found satisfaction in group situations, whether family, school, friendships, or workplace. The two most frequent sources of trouble are lack of self-worth and lack of acceptance. When one lacks a sense of self-worth, she feels she does not deserve to be intimately involved in a group, so she holds back from full involvement or avoids groups. If one senses lack of acceptance, she is experiencing rejection. She may be the family scapegoat or the "oddball" at school. Thus, one enters group counseling with ambivalence, anxiety, and a desire to be included and respected. Cohesiveness occurs when a group is attractive enough that members prefer to attend rather than terminate, they feel comfortable rather than anxious, and feel that the potential rewards make it worthwhile to remain.

When a group is "healthy," its members are able to listen to and accept all sorts of deviant behavior, fantasies, and attitudes. In contrast to usual social expectations, the group can include people with criminal, deviant sexual, or other kinds of acting out behavior. One's past becomes less important than the future. Depending upon whether the group has a therapeutic or task orientation, members are able to reveal experiences and feelings in the safety of the group, and participants realize that everyone has "hang-ups" and fears. Thus, cohesion interacts with other group processes such as self-disclosure, empathy, respect, and member roles (Bonney, 1974). Norms relate to cohesion either positively or negatively. Where group norms support free expression and individuality along with cooperation, cohesion is more likely to develop. In turn, the more a member conforms to a norm of mutual respect, the more likely she will be accepted as part of the group, no matter what she has done in the past. Group cohesiveness is enhanced by reinforcing statements that refer to "we," expressions of liking and wanting to continue with the group, interactive and cooperative talk, and other systematic means of social reinforcement (Krumboltz & Porter, 1973; Liberman, 1970). Cohesiveness is most powerful when there is also collaboration among the group members. Dailey (1977) suggests a model that makes cohesiveness and collaboration codeterminants of member productivity and effective responding.

To further understand the dependence of cohesion on other group processes, one can examine the relevance of group goals to its members, the past success of such groups in reaching its goals, attitude similarity of group members, the clarity of what is expected of members, how well members cooperate, and how well conflict is managed. Focusing on conflict management, we find that the group most able to bring negative feelings, such as anger, to the surface will be most cohesive and successful. Cohesion and open communication of both positive and negative feelings interact. A cohesive group can be open and honest, and as members feel safe relating freely with one another, they become more cohesive. Cohesion is not static, as it changes within each member over time, and individual members can experience very different levels of cohesion in the group. An individual experiences fluctuating commitment to the group, and group cohesiveness fluctuates depending on the type of group interactions, group membership (in open groups), and topics. The more cohesive the group, the less significant the fluctuations, although of course it takes time for a group to develop this level of maturity. Other benefits of group cohesiveness include increased capacity to retain its members, greater chance of reaching goals, lower turnover, lower absenteeism, greater participation of all members, greater commitment to goals, free communication, and increased closeness to group norms (Cartwright, 1968; Watson & Johnson, 1972).

Research and clinical experience have yielded many indicators of cohesiveness, including these behaviors or attitudes of an individual member:

1. Committed to group's goals.

2. Accepts assigned tasks and roles more readily.

3. Conforms to group norms more readily.

4. Pressures or rejects those who violate group norms.

5. More loyal to the group.

6. More motivated, persists longer at group tasks.

Group characteristics include these:

1. When the norm is productivity, cohesive groups are more productive.

2. Interaction is more friendly and democratic.

3. More likely to influence each other in making decisions.

4. More willing to listen to and accept opinions of others.

5. Pain or frustration on behalf of the group is better endured.

6. External criticism and attack on the group is defended against. (Johnson & Johnson, 1982)

As we have mentioned, some of the effects of cohesion are the greater tendency to attend sessions, to be on time, and to verbalize personally meaningful material. A longer-term effect is its impact on self-esteem. People with low self-esteem in a cohesive group feel a need to satisfy the group's wishes and expectations. They trust the perceptions and opinions of fellow participants. As the group expresses acceptance and liking, the member experiences *dissonance*, as Festinger (1957) describes one's cognitive state when he experiences two messages that are not congruent with one another. How to resolve the discrepancy between his low self-esteem and the group's high esteem? The greater the cohesion, the greater the chance that the member will revise his self-esteem upward to be compatible with that of the group. Conversely, when one values himself more than the group seems to value him, he may try other methods of resolving the dissonance, such as distorting or denying what the group is communicating in an attempt to maintain his self-esteem, or accepting the group values and reducing his self-esteem. Commitment to the group and respect for members' opinions influence acceptance of their judgment.

Several studies support the relationship between individual member attraction and participation in the group (cohesiveness), and positive outcome. Clark and Culbert (1965) showed that people who engaged more frequently in dyadic therapeutic relationships improved most through group sessions. The quality of group member relationships seemed an important factor, since the perceived member-leader relationship seemed to have no effect. In two studies by Yalom (Yalom, Tinkelberg, & Gilula, 1970; Yalom, Houts, Zimerberg, & Rand, 1967), cohesiveness was perceived to contribute significantly to assessed change in therapeutic groups. In one study, members perceived cohesiveness as one of the top three factors in helping them; the other study showed that members most attracted to the group (cohesiveness) and those most popular were most improved in terms of symptoms, functioning, and relationships. Cohesiveness has a profound effect on group members, and is frequently one of the most powerful influences on positive change in group counseling.

We have thus far portrayed group cohesiveness as a healthy process that promotes the growth of individual members. In the ideal, cohesiveness is beneficial because it also allows for individuality and occasional deviations from the norm. A mature, cohesive group is strong enough to allow for occasional differences of opinion and non-conforming behavior. It also does not place most of the power and influence into the hands of one or a few group members. This kind of group maturity is rare; in fact, cohesiveness is usually accompanied by excessive pressure to conform to group expectations.

The work of Janis (1971) on "group think" presents a classic example of pressure to conform when there is a seeming need for group cohesiveness. He found that groups that advise United States presidents exert strong social pressure against dissident opinions in the group. When there seemed to be group consensus, objections were quickly stifled. Although strong group norms and cohesiveness elevated group morale, critical thinking was lost in the process. When the group is involved in a decision-making task, it arrives at a solution that is quickly accepted by all. Several interesting dynamics occur. First, there is no overt suppression of opinion; rather, each member simply withholds dissenting ideas in order to maintain group cohesion. Even when the decision is implemented and its consequences disturb individual members, they maintain loyalty to the group decision. This type of group process is often characterized positively as *team play*. The dangers of "group think" and other pressures toward conformity always accompany the necessary ingredient of group cohesiveness.

When a person or group believes the individual in power has a reasonable right to expect and demand certain behaviors, we have *legitimate power*. *Referent power* occurs when one person identifies with, is attracted to, and/or respects another person. Analysts might regard a transference relationship as referent power. Referent power may also arise from a straightforward liking and respect for another person that gives the respected person the ability to influence behavior. *Expert power* usually rests with the group leader, who communicates possession of superior skills and abilities. To one degree or another, the leader may have all or a few of these types of power. Likewise, group members can have various forms of power over one another.

The effect of persuasive communication and the personal characteristics of those who receive the communication also tell us a few things about influence. It has been shown, for instance, that receivers with low self-esteem can be persuaded more easily than those with high self-esteem (McGuire, 1969; Watson & Johnson, 1972). If receivers are distracted while hearing the communicator's message, they are more susceptible to being influenced (Baron, Baron, & Miller, 1973). Receivers who are asked to actively role-play a stance previously unacceptable to them find that it becomes more acceptable (Watson & Johnson, 1972). People are also likely to be influenced by appearance, such as a uniform (Beckman, 1974). A charismatic person can stir people to intense loyalty and enthusiasm to follow a leader unquestioningly (Hoffer, 1951; Tucker, 1977).

Power and Resources

Johnson and Johnson (1982) explain the use of power in small groups. They consider power and influence as "one person's control over resources valued by another." When B believes A has resources B values, then A has power in relation to B. B will value those resources depending upon their availability somewhere else or at a lower cost, and according to their importance to B. One person's needs interact with another's resources. In a high school study skills group, Jamie has trouble with math, while Albert and Gwen have a better understanding of math. If Jamie values the ability to perform math tasks, he can be influenced by Albert and/or Gwen. If Albert causes more trouble or makes more demands than Gwen, Jamie will go to Gwen, who will be better able to influence Jamie regarding his study skills. In a therapeutic group, Chet may have a need to be helpful and protective toward others. The seemingly dependent Paula actually has power over Chet because she has a resource, dependency, that can take care of Chet's need. The more he values helpfulness and the less he can fulfill the need elsewhere, the greater will be Paula's power.

When group member goals are compatible and cooperative, influence can be positive, helping to accomplish tasks or personal growth. When members are competitive, there are power conflicts that lead to resistance. Resistance occurs when power is asserted offensively or threateningly, or when the desired outcome from the person in power does not occur. Others may fill the gap with their influence, or the group may fall apart because there are insufficient resources of power. Power must be *perceived* before it has an influence; members must recognize resources of knowledge or skill before they can be influenced. Someone who actually has few resources but is perceived to have many can greatly influence others. In fact, some would say the group leader does not actually have many more resources than the members, but because she is perceived as knowledgeable, "together," and skillful gives her much power in the group. When members do not perceive the leader this way, her influence diminishes.

Power and Manipulation

Influence and power may seem to infringe on one's rights because our society values the right to make decisions without coercion, to know what is expected of us, and to guide our own lives. Influence, however, is not purposeful manipulation to gain control of others; it can be mutually beneficial, enhancing cooperation in an open, trusting atmosphere. If Paula plays her dependent role as a deceptive way to seduce Chet, she is manipulating, or using power for a hidden purpose, to satisfy a selfish need. But if she truly feels she needs help making decisions and relies on Chet's advice and opinion, she can influence him. If they become attracted to each other in the process, no one has been coerced or deceived.

Everyone in a group has power of some type and degree in relation to someone else in the group. Ideally, power is balanced among the members, but in reality, resources are not evenly distributed. Certain members may have more types of power, such as the ability to reward, give information, or use personal appeal.

Managing influence properly contributes to group effectiveness. Besides a fair balance of power, the power must be based on competence, expertise, and information. Everyone has something to contribute to a group, and when the recognized resources are useful and positive, the group is likely to meet its goals. Power from authority or incorrect perceptions of resources can result in a superficial group marked with resistance. In a successful group, power patterns need to be flexible to meet the demands of the immediate task and the needs of the membership.

Use of Power Group members use a variety of tactics to "get their way" or to convince others of something. Attempts to gain favor, acceptance, or agreement, or to influence members' behavior implies the use of power. Falbo (1977) suggests two fundamental dimensions of attempts to influence others: *rationality vs. nonrationality*, and *directness vs. indirectness*. When a group member uses a nonrational strategy, she is using emotionality and misinformation not backed by logic; for example, an emotional appeal for others to condone her child-abusive behavior because she had been drinking, although she is also abusive when sober. Rational influence emphasizes reason and logic.

Direct influence includes threats and doing what you want to despite other people's opinion. Hinting and ingratiating are indirect methods of influence.

Powerful group members are usually happy with their position and use strategies to maintain it (Jones & Gerard, 1967). First, they legitimize their power and keep less powerful members in their place by making it wrong to change the status quo. They establish regulations and norms to maintain the power position; it may be a norm for other members to speak less often and to agree with the powerful member. Second, those with less power are made to realize that attempts to change the status quo will be highly risky. The powerful individual can maintain power through reward, such as recognition, or punishment, such as ignoring.

Less powerful members feel ineffectual, threatened, and often submissive or passive. Despite their frustration and uncertainty about the situation, they still direct attention and communication to the powerful member. Other results of their anxiety and uncertainty include:

Greater vigilance and trying to predict the high-power person

Perceptions of high-power person's behavior distorted

Both attraction and fear

Criticism of high-power member stifled

Not willing to clarify position

Attempts to gain rewards and liking through ingratiation, conformity, and flattery

Feeling vulnerable to exploitation because they feel they have no power to retaliate (Tjosvold, 1978)

Power and Obedience

Milgram (1963, 1974) demonstrated how willingly many people obey a directive even if it might harm someone. Volunteers in the study were led to believe that they had drawn the role of "teacher" by chance and must judge the performance of "learners," who were actually confederates of the experimenter. When learners made mistakes, the teacher, from another room, was to administer a shock, increasing the voltage from 45 to 450 volts as the learner made more mistakes. The volunteer believed he was actually administering the shock to the subject. Milgram wanted to determine just how much pain people would be willing to administer when coerced by an authority figure. When volunteers balked, they were told to "Please continue" or "The experiment requires that you continue." Despite predictions by helping professionals that most people would discontinue the shock at the 150-volt level, Milgram found that 26 of the 40 "teachers" administered shocks at the 450-volt level to the helpless subjects; none quit before the 300-volt level.

Milgram (1974) later found that several conditions affected obedience. Obedience declined from 65 percent as the subject came into closer proximity to the "victim." The level of obedience declined slightly when there was voice feedback from the victim (62.5 percent); significantly, when the volunteer was in physical proximity to the victim (40 percent), and to 30 percent when the teacher had to touch the victim to administer the shock. Milgram also found that the experimenter's prestige and ability to directly supervise the volunteer's behavior increased the level of obedience; only 20 percent of the teachers were obedient at the 450-volt level when they were not regularly supervised.

Using a similar experimental design in a small group situation, Milgram had the volunteer carry out ancillary tasks while a confederate pulled the shock switches. When the confederate refused to continue (as directed by the experimenter) and the experimenter told the volunteer to take over, only 10 percent of the volunteers administered the 450-volt shock. When two experimenters were present, one demanding that the volunteer continue shocking and the other directing that he discontinue, all volunteers obeyed the benevolent authority. Another group study of obedience found that people in the role of transmitting orders are much more obedient than those who are asked to execute the orders (Kilham & Mann, 1974). There are mixed results as to gender differences: Kilham and Mann found males more obedient, but Sheridan and King (1972) found women more obedient, and Milgram found no differences.

Obedience studies have several lessons for group counseling. Subjects were ordinary people, neither sadistic nor hostile, but the environmental pressures were such that people behaved in ways they would not behave under other circumstances. The power of the leader and other authority figures is conspicuous; many people are willing to do rather bizarre things when directed by an authority figure, such as swallow foul tasting liquids (Riess, Forsyth, Schlenker, & Freed, 1977), or immerse their hands in what they thought was acid (Orne & Evans, 1965). The power of a legitimate and expert authority figure is at the top of a social hierarchy.

Power and Conflict

The relationship of power and conflict is important in group work (Johnson & Johnson, 1982). Certain forms of conflict occur because one member expects something of another member, but does not have the power to effect the behavior. One member or the group resists another's wishes. If the member had enough power, he could make the other cooperate, and there would be no conflict. Also, there would be no conflict if the second person cooperated even though the first person had no power. We can see how influence is useful in resolving conflicts. For a group to function cooperatively, there must be changing spheres of power that can resolve or prevent conflict. When there is little mutual influence, there will be more conflict. Hostility and lack of trust reduce members' power and thus undermine their influence. Power of reward and authority rather than power of competence and information contribute to lack of trust, and coercive power increases conflict. Leader and members must work toward mutual influence to control conflict.

The degree and kind of influence is always changing in a group. As members move toward goals, they become more or less cohesive, invest more or less energy and emotion in the group, and find their needs met outside the group (Cartwright, 1959; Thibaut & Kelley, 1959). Individual members' influence waxes and wanes. The leader may have much influence at first, and relinquish power as members assume stronger roles and more responsibility. As the group becomes more cohesive, members have more influence on each other.

POWER IN A GROUP

To illustrate power and influence in a group, let us look at the second and the twelfth sessions of the elderly people we met early in the chapter. Note how the leader possesses "expert power" in the second session, and how George tries to wield "reward power." Lorin and Kate exert influence through rational means, while Stanley appeals to emotions. Sophie continues her influence as a harmonizer, trying to persuade everyone to get along. Henrietta and Anne attempt to manipulate the others through passive strategies.

Henrietta: I'm just glad we have Kevin [leader] here to lead us because I think we would be so disorganized without him.

George: I agree. We're glad you're here. We need an expert at this to help us get some action going.

Leader: I really appreciate the opportunity to work with all of you. Let me point out, though, that what we accomplish in the group will be a result of the contributions of everyone here.

Arthur: Yes, we must all take responsibility for the group, and I think it's time to work on the goal of examining our social activities. Who is ready to go over the list of our current activities? [Stated very authoritatively; Arthur is now trying to dominate the group.]

Jack: It's okay that we have a leader, but I also think we all need to take care of ourselves and speak up for ourselves. [Note how Arthur's attempt at securing power is being ignored by the others. Jack is not ready to let anyone influence him; he wants to maintain his individuality.]

Kate: I agree that each of us needs to speak up, but at the same time, I hope we will look out for each other and listen to one another. [rational, persuasive]

Lorin: Yes we need to work together here. I want it to be a pleasant experience. [Gert and Lorin continue to support each other with their rational and direct approach.]

Anne: I'll be as cooperative as anyone else. I don't have a lot of ideas, but I'm always there to help out. I like having Kevin here, and I think people like Gert and Lorin have good ideas. [Those who are looking for a follower should now have "spotted" one; Anne will now try to influence others by throwing her support to those she selects.]

George: I'm willing to "play ball" here too. As a matter of fact, if we come up with a few good ideas, I'll even throw in some money to support them. I'm not exactly hurting for money, and if some people can have a good time because of our ideas, I'll back them up. [George is fairly direct in his use of "reward power." Certainly the others will keep him in mind when they consider social activities, and some will be keenly interested in his support. George is using money as a form of influence.]

Jack: First we need ideas before we

worry about how to make them happen. [Gruffly]

Sophie: We don't need to argue. We are saying pretty much the same thing. We need ideas, and everyone needs to be involved. [Jack is experiencing a void in power, which prompts him to be critical of others. Sophie exercises influence by using her resource as a harmonizer.]

Leader: Yes, you seem to have some agreement about full participation. Are you all ready to discuss your social lives and whether they need improvement? [This is a legitimate influence to keep the group on task.]

Stanley: I think we must look at what we do to see if it's the kinds of things we really should be doing. I see some people smoking too much, drinking too much, gambling, and other things. We need to find a way to cut this out. If we don't, things will get real bad around here. Don't you think it's really terrible how some people behave? [Stated emotionally, this is an attempt to influence through threats, accusations, and guilt. Note that Stanley does not talk about himself and his social activities.]

Lorin: I'd like to see us discuss what the people in the group are doing and what else we want. I wish we had more things to do in town, for example.

[Moving now to the twelfth session, the bases of influence have not changed dramatically, but influence is less self-protective and directed more toward self-exploration than toward tasks. The leader is less directive.]

Arthur: I know I can be pushy sometimes. My wife used to tell me that, and I'd tell her that was the only way things got done. Maybe people shouldn't let me be bossy. [Arthur is mellowing just a little. He is trying to influence the group to change him, rather than working on himself.]

Henrietta: I kind of like a man who is strong, although it can be carried to extremes. Sometimes I like it when you speak your mind, Arthur. [One message here is that Arthur could have some influence if he would modify his authoritarian approach.]

Anne: I have the opposite problem. I'm too reserved in social situations. I just don't know what to say. Maybe I could trade some of my reserve for some of your boldness, Arthur.

Kate: Yes, wouldn't that be nice if we could trade an extreme with someone who acted at the opposite extreme? I think that's a good idea.

Lorin: Can we try that, just for fun, here? We could each think of something we want more or less of, explain it, and see what we could trade for. [Kate and Lorin are using reward power and rational influence. They have built their power to the extent that other members listen to them and follow their suggestions.]

Jack: That will take some thought on my part. I'm still not used to talking about myself. I'm more used to just doing things.

George: Well, I can see that. I'm more of a doer too. So we want to figure out what we need more or less of—about ourselves. [A statement about how George is like Jack is an example of referent power. When two people feel they have something in common, they are usually more able to influence each other.]

By this twelfth session, influence is used more to help each other; there is less conflict, less dominance, and less need for persuasion.

Communication

Communication in counseling groups is a complicated process by which members share information, feelings, and attitudes, all of which are necessary for personal growth and productivity. Communication is a process whereby a *sender* channels a *message* to a *receiver*. The message may be informational or affective, and direct or indirect. Messages are symbolic, conveyed through words or non-verbal behaviors.

Interpersonal communication involves senders and receivers whose abilities to send and receive clear and complete messages vary. Normally, the sender wishes to convey accurate information and expects a particular response in the receiver. The receiver attempts to recognize and interpret, or encode, the message. Group effectiveness depends partly upon how accurately messages are sent and received. Groups with interpersonal problems often show dis-

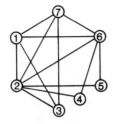

Figure 8-1 A Communication Pattern

crepancies between the intent and interpretation of messages. (Communication may be effective but limited only to negative feelings, which can also have a deleterious impact.)

Communication is multifaceted; each person in the group sends and receives messages from several other people. Everyone continually listens, expresses, and infers. The *communication pattern* varies from one group to another; for example, in a group of seven people, each will talk to a few others but not necessarily to everyone in the group. One pattern is diagrammed in Figure 8-1. In this case, person 2 communicates verbally with everyone, person 7 speaks with 1, 3, and 6. Person 4 speaks only with 2 and 6. We can thus plot verbal interactions in a counseling group and draw inferences as to the reason for the pattern.

Figure 8-2 shows another pattern in which the leader is the center of communication and all statements are directed to him. Bavelas (1948), Leavitte (1957), and Shaw (1964) describe these and other patterns or networks.

Communicating a message effectively is a major first step in building quality interpersonal relationships. Johnson suggests eight positive characteristics of message sending:

1. Clearly "own" your message by using first-person singular pronouns ("I" and "My").

2. Make your messages complete and specific.

3. Make your verbal and nonverbal messages congruent.

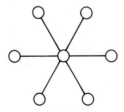

Figure 8-2 Leader-Directed Communication

4. Be redundant.

5. Ask for feedback concerning the way your messages are being received.

6. Make the message appropriate to the receiver's frame of reference.

7. Describe your feelings by name, action, or figure of speech.

8. Describe others' behavior without evaluating or interpreting. (Johnson & Johnson, 1982, p. 185)

"Receiving messages" has gotten a great deal of attention in the literature, especially as it relates to the counselor's need to understand accurately the content and feelings of client expressions (Carkhuff, 1969; Ivey, 1974; Rogers, 1957; Strupp, 1973). The principles from this research can be applied to members of a group; that is, certain listening and interpersonal skills increase the accuracy of the received message as well as the quality of the ongoing interpersonal relationship. The first step in receiving a message is accurate perception through nonevaluative listening. Content and feelings are perceived as the sender intends them. In the group of elderly people, Jack says, "This group may not be such a good idea. You say people are supposed to reveal their feelings and talk about themselves. I don't know whether I want to listen to all that." As Anne listens, she is thinking that Jack is really saying he doesn't care enough about other people to want to hear their feelings. This interpretation may have some superficial validity. Gert has been listening more carefully, however, and realizes Jack is afraid to express his feelings, and thinks the other group members don't really care to hear from him. So in one case, the intended message was not received accurately, partly because Jack sent it in a somewhat disguised form, but Gert received the message accurately.

The next major step in communication is to let the sender know the message has been received. Paraphrasing what has just been expressed is an effective way to let someone know what was heard— it shows someone was listening and communicates the receiver's level of understanding. The most useful paraphrasing contains the sender's intended content, feelings, attitudes, and meaning. Anne's response to Jack is, "Why don't you want to hear other people's feelings? It's important, you know. And maybe it could help you." This response not only misses what Jack was saying, but is interrogative. Gert's response is, "Maybe you're a little uncomfortable discussing feelings. I'm a little afraid myself, but maybe we can learn to be more open." This response picks up on Jack's apprehension, tries to reassure, and demonstrates empathy.

Communication assumes that interaction continues until all parties come to an understanding—merely speaking to one another does not imply communication. People in the group need to listen accurately, communicate their understanding, and then the sender must indicate whether they received the message accurately. Jack responds, "I guess it sounded like I wasn't really interested in anyone else, but you may be right, Gert. I never have talked about my real feelings with other people." This kind of exchange builds trust, understanding, mutual support, and helpful confrontation. Meaningful communication may occur sporadically; it requires a great deal of time and effort to achieve regularly. The leader can help in the early stages of the group by asking a member to paraphrase what someone else says, then ask the first speaker whether the paraphrase was accurate.

Among several important aspects of communication, *self-disclosure* appears to be an essential ingredient of therapeutic groups. In early sessions of a group, members usually show a degree of *resistance* as they try to determine how "safe" the group is and the level of trust they feel toward the group. *Competition* among members may act as a barrier to communication. Decision making is also essentially a process of communication, as is nonverbal behavior.

Self-disclosure

Self-disclosure refers to explicit communication of personal information that one would not normally reveal to others. We can understand self-disclosure in terms of its risk-benefit relationship. One takes a risk when opening up to others, although it seems to be significant in bringing about positive change. The more personal the material, the greater the risk. The risk is less when one believes other group members will receive the disclosure as intended and when they react as expected. An early personal revelation tends to be more emotional than cognitive. If others in the group understand it accurately and show warm acceptance after the disclosure, the risk to the individual is minimal and others will feel encouraged to become more intimately involved in the group.

Levels of self-disclosure tend to follow the group's developmental stages. In ordinary interpersonal relationships, one begins to reveal at a superficial level, then gradually discloses at deeper personal levels as the material is accepted by others. Other participants take on responsibility for the information, and in turn make revelations. The interaction continues to deepen until the parties reach a level at which they are comfortable. In more therapeutic groups, one hopes for more private disclosures, whereas structured, task-oriented, and informational groups require modest levels of self-disclosure, although self-disclosure is still important in dealing with issues of career choice or social activities.

Successful group counseling requires disclosure of personal information. Some self-disclosure is necessary in close human relationships, and close interpersonal relationships are necessary to benefit from most forms of group counseling. Appropriate self-revelation leads to acceptance by others, which facilitates self-acceptance. As group members reveal information about themselves they feel responsible toward caring for, and a wish to be helpful to one another. Research indicates that more self-disclosing group members tend to be most successful (Perez, 1965; Truax & Carkhuff, 1967). Sidney Jourard (1971) documents the importance of self-disclosure in effective human functioning.

Indiscriminant self-disclosure is not healthy. One must choose what to reveal, at what level, at what time, and in what circumstances. Personal revelation should fit the context of discussion. Self-disclosure should not be mistaken for impulsive verbalization of whatever one feels at the moment, nor continually associating comments to one's own experience, which tends to be self-centered attention-getting behavior. The level of personal material depends on what one feels comfortable revealing and the group's readiness to handle intimacy. A beginning group is usually not ready to process extremely personal material.

Group goals may also guide the type of self-disclosures. Disclosing everything about oneself to nearly everyone we know is not realistic; it can put others on the defensive, and not everyone is interested in our most personal experiences and feelings. Self-disclosure is necessary in therapeutic counseling groups, but should occur gradually and according to the readiness of the member and group to deal with it.

Resistance

Nearly every new member of a group experiences ambivalence about participation. Each person is usually drawn toward involvement that will enhance personal growth, and at the same time wishes to remain essentially unchanged. Examining oneself in the presence of others and attempting personal changes leaves one vulnerable and open to anxiety, and group members usually wish to avoid anxiety. The easiest way to prevent anxiety is to resist self-exploration and refuse to make changes. Since members are pulled in two directions, there will inevitably be times of resistance, which will lessen as the group matures. *Resistance*, then, is the methods one uses to prevent anxiety.

Anxiety refers to the discomfort one experiences when revealing personal information or attempting new behavior.

Resistance is a normal individual and group process that everyone in the group must cope with. This method of defending oneself may be acceptable at times or unacceptable when it is extreme or prevents personal growth. Resistance may be acceptable when the group or leader cannot be helpful; for example, group members may press too hard or too soon for personal revelations. The leader may not be competent to handle a particular type of counseling group. In both cases, a group member may decide to hold back because she does not like the "pushiness," or believes she will not obtain accurate information or feedback from the group.

Even resistance that blocks personal growth should be respected in the early stages of the group. When the group meets for its initial sessions, unhealthy resistance often occurs, in the way of negative attitudes toward the leader's authority and avoiding closeness to fellow members. This resistance usually results from application of past problems in interpersonal relationships to the social microcosm of the group, or transference. The leader evokes one's feelings toward authority, and resistance may emerge as excessive dependency or lack of cooperation. Feelings toward peers come out toward fellow group members. If one believes he is not likable, he will at first resist when other members reach out to him.

Some of the problem behaviors discussed earlier are actually examples of resistance. One must apply labels cautiously; they merely describe someone's behavior at a certain time in a particular place. A group member may attempt to monopolize discussion for several weeks or for only one session; that does not make him a "monopolist." In reality, no one is just a "monopolist," a "giver," or a "dependent." When behaving in one of these negative styles, the member is usually resisting; however, our concern is with the behavior and its underlying reason rather than with the label. A participant may talk a great deal, but we may never learn much about him because his use of words keeps us from getting close to him. This anxiety prevention may be a whole group phenomenon, with members conspiring to discuss safe and irrelevant topics. If the group is able to eventually develop, they will share feelings and attitudes in an environment safe from excessive anxiety.

Resistance may also appear as silence. A member may not speak because she is afraid to interact, thinking that any expression will leave her vulnerable to the others or the leader. More complex maneuvers are also possible; a member may discuss an interesting topic, such as sex, which is not part of his problem. A member with a disability may want to talk only about other disabled people. Anger can keep people at a distance. Methods of resistance include intellectualizing, avoiding topics, asking questions of others, always helping others, storytelling, and moralizing.

The underlying cause of resistance, prevention of anxiety, may also take many forms. One may have suffered shame at one time and doesn't want it to happen again. There may be fear of saying something that will make others angry, or fear of rejection if one reveals personal experiences. Others fear closeness because it also leaves one vulnerable. Still others feel they will receive no support, and others do not want to discover things about themselves that may cause upheaval in their lives.

We do not deal with resistance by confronting it directly, except in rare cases, but rather by providing a safe atmosphere and perhaps supportive confrontation. Without support and acceptance, the resistant individual is even less willing to take risks. Mild confrontation and challenge may be necessary to help the member loosen his defenses. Confrontation can communicate a desire to "get to know you better," to "get closer to you," to "be more helpful to you," which one hopes the member will regard as genuine concern.

A counselor may label group behavior resistive to defend against her own anxiety. If the group does not make progress, the group leader may blame members of the group (Saretsky, 1972) to avoid feeling inadequate and guilty. Supervision by a colleague can help a counselor examine attitudes toward the group and herself.

Competition

Competition also interferes with healthy group development. When members compete with each other, communication breaks down (Gibb, 1961); it may be absent, inadequate, or misleading. Defensiveness and lack of trust are proportional to the degree of competition.

Competition diverts energy that could go toward building mutually beneficial activities and interactions into self-protection, self-enhancement, and efforts to dominate (Walton, 1969). Defensiveness prevents accurate perception of others' motives, feelings, and values. It takes only one competitive member to arouse competitiveness in others, leading to hostility, resentment, aggressiveness, and dislike among members. The leader should encourage members to compete with themselves rather than with other members. Criteria for growth and change can be set up individually, then shared with the group. Cooperation is a matter of helping each other reach goals each has set. General group goals clearly require cooperation (DeCecco & Richards, 1974); competitiveness among members fosters unnecessary conflict and hard feelings about the group. Cooperation brings closeness and greater satisfaction both with oneself and the group.

Decision Making

All groups make decisions as to acceptable group behavior, goals, topics, and when to terminate. Many decision-making issues arise in group counseling, primarily in regard to the process of making decisions.

One hopes to make decisions after input from everyone, followed by final consensus. Research indicates that small groups make better decisions than do individuals (Holdman, 1965; Laughlin, Branch, & Johnson, 1969; Watson & Johnson, 1972). Individuals have incomplete information, narrower perspective, and tend to make more errors. Healthy groups allow everyone to state an opinion or desire and show respect for everyone's viewpoint. Through open communication and mutual concern, the group finally makes a decision agreeable to everyone. This usually requires some compromise, which is not possible in immature groups or groups with many rigid, defensive members. If everyone's viewpoint is not recognized, the group is likely to become polarized and resistance will occur.

Less useful, though sometimes more efficient, methods of decision making are voting, appealing to expertise, or simply having someone in authority, such as the leader, make a decision. These methods are for making quick decisions or for avoiding having the group take responsibility.

Many dynamics affect the decision-making process.

The less mature group has more trouble making effective decisions with consensus. (Watson, 1931)

Members may have different and conflicting objectives for being in the group.

Poor communication. (McGregor, 1967)

Self-centeredness that prevents giving to others. (Falk & Johnson, 1977)

Quick agreements that lead to superficiality.

Subgrouping that breeds unnecessary competition. (Gustafson, 1978)

The more homogeneous group has fewer resources with which to make a decision. (Johnson, 1980)

Dominance by one or a few members. (Torrance, 1954)

Too large a group to fully discuss opinions and alternatives. (Watson & Johnson, 1972)

Lack of motivation and involvement.

Too little time taken to present all views. (Fox & Lorge, 1962)

GROUP PROCESS

The following example of group process occurs in the fourth session of a group of seven mothers of severely disabled children. Vera's husband left her after the birth of a cerebral palsied son; Shauna is about to reveal how her husband treats her; Margaret relates at a superficial level and implies a great deal of support from her husband. One member says nothing. Note how Vera is criticized for "losing" her husband; she may be the group's *scapegoat*. Shauna self-discloses too much, too early in the sessions. There is competition as to who has the best or worst husband. Note the forms of resistance and that the group has trouble making a decision.

Leader: Last week we began to discuss how your husbands react to having a child with an impairment.

Agnes: From what I see, I think men just have a harder time accepting that they have a handicapped child.

Leila: Sometimes that's true.

Vera: That's why my husband left me. He didn't want no handicapped kid, so he just left.

Agnes: How do you know that? It could have been for other reasons.

Vera: No, I'm sure that's why he left.

Flora: Maybe he just didn't want any responsibility, or just didn't want to be married. Who knows what all was going on in your marriage?

Shauna: I don't know whether it's better to have the man leave or stay and treat you like dirt. I have to work, take care of my children and him, and I don't get any help from him.

Margaret: I sure am glad my husband is helpful because my son is 18 now and I couldn't handle him by myself.

Paige: Hmmm.

Vera: You are lucky. Think of how bad off you'd be if you were in my shoes.

Margaret: I like to think I've done some things to keep my husband for 22 years.

Agnes: Yeah, it's a job to keep the children and a husband happy. [Agnes, Flora, and Leila reveal nothing about their relationships with their husbands]

Shauna: Mine stays married to me but he's hardly ever at home. I cook for him and sleep with him and that's it.

Leila: What do you stay with him for?

Shauna: I don't know. I've tried to leave. I almost did one time. I wasn't feeling well and he wanted, or I should say he demanded sex. I told him I just couldn't. He got so mad at me that he tied me to the bedposts and raped me.

Agnes: My god! How awful. [The others do not know what to say]

Vera: Maybe that's worse than not having a husband.

Margaret: That makes me even more thankful for John.

Shauna: Now he's doing something I don't know what to do about. When I'm at work he brings his girlfriend home and they do it in our bed. At least I know it happened twice.

Agnes: My god! What's the matter with him?

Flora: Does he spend any time with your son? [Flora wants to avoid the personal material]

Shauna: Very little. He did before the hearing impairment was diagnosed. Now he acts like he doesn't have the time.

Vera: Well, it's his son too!

We can see how Shauna threatens the group with revelations they are not prepared for, and they try to avoid her problems for several more sessions. As they develop closeness, they try to get her to see how she contributes to the marital problem, and if the marriage can be saved. Vera receives more and more criticism because she is of lower income and less articulate than the others; she finally drops out. The others remain competitive for several sessions until they eventually reveal more about their families and become more cohesive, even phoning one another during the week to help each other through stressful times.

Nonverbal Behavior

Nonverbal behavior makes up more than 50 percent of messages communicated in social relationships. People tend to believe nonverbal cues that may contradict verbal statements even if they are not conscious of the cues at the time. Verbal and nonverbal behavior interact either complementarily or contradictorily. Nonverbal behavior can illustrate verbal statements or substitute for verbal behavior. Tone of voice can modify or expand the meaning of a word.

Contradictions between verbal and nonverbal behavior are especially important to the group counselor. Content may convey one meaning while nonverbal behavior conveys another. A member may, for example, claim strong interest in the group but frequently miss sessions. A member may smile at another while speaking in a hostile tone. The leader may say he is merely a facilitator, but sit in a larger chair, point down at participants, and speak with unusual authority. Nonverbal behaviors are perceived as more honest than verbal content, so the leader and group members need to be especially aware of the total pattern that occurs in interactions. Nonverbal behavior is habitual and, to a large extent, a symbolic expression of thoughts, feelings, and attitudes. It is less vulnerable to conscious manipulation.

Nonverbal behavior falls into four categories: body behaviors, interaction with the environment, speech, and physical appearance. Body behavior is the expressive action of the various body parts with the eyes the primary source of interpersonal contact. They may focus on another person, look down, shift, glare, tear, sparkle, or be covered. The skin may blush, perspire, or have goose bumps. Facial expressions include smiling, wrinkles, turning down the mouth, biting the lip, and sticking out the tongue. Hands can say "stop," wave to say "hello," and motion someone forward or to pass by. Fingers can form a circle to say "it's just fine," and the forefinger can beckon someone or point to something. Arms extended and open show receptiveness, hugging shows caring, striking may show anger. Tapping the foot can indicate anxiety or impatience, while slouching or sitting on the edge of a chair also convey messages.

The body's orientation in the environment also conveys a message the group leader will need to interpret. Desire to maintain distance may mean fear or dislike for the group. Closeness is usually associated with intimacy. Cohesive groups are usually not afraid to be physically close and minimize physical barriers among one another. Movement toward or away from each other can be aggression or fear. Where people sit may indicate how they feel about each other or merely which are the most comfortable chairs. A member may sit back from the group or in a place that draws maximum attention. Arriving early or late or leaving early also tell something about a person.

In group counseling, everyone attends to the speech of fellow participants and consciously or subconsciously makes judgments based on it. Tone of voice may be energetic, warm, vivid, and firm, or flat, tentative, lifeless, and cool. It may be changeable, seductive, intrusive, or whining. One may speak loudly or softly, or alternate for effect. Speech may be careful and precise, or careless and casual, or influenced by regional speech patterns. One may speak quickly or slowly. We listen to someone's speech to gain clues as to how he feels about us, about the group, or about himself.

Physical appearance, including clothing and grooming, conveys much about a person. Dress can show normal concern, lack of concern, or overconcern with oneself. The leader and group need to pay attention to how members dress. Some people have a great need to be stylish, and so emphasize their appearance. Hairstyle and care offer a clue to personality. The meaning may be different for everyone, so the individual should probably give an interpretation, although members may suggest a possible meaning. For one person, a very short haircut may be convenient because of involvement in athletics; another person may have short hair because of a learned association with cleanliness. One may have a beard to hide what he considers an unattractive face, while another may wish to avoid shaving every day. Other indications of personality include amount and type of makeup and jewelry. We cannot ignore how appearance is influenced by diet, sleep, and exercise. We all know how we look and act when we don't get enough sleep; what, then, is the reason for the lack of sleep? Obesity and anorexia nervosa are extreme examples of physical clues to possible personality problems.

The Leader's Nonverbal Behavior

The leader's behavior is always under scrutiny by participants. They observe and interpret the leader's nonverbal behavior for clues as to how to relate to her. The leader must be aware of her nonverbal behavior and its potential effect on the group. Her verbal and nonverbal behavior must be congruent to avoid causing confusion and irritation.

Beginning sessions consistently late suggests a desire to minimize time spent with the group. Looking at selected members when speaking shows a preference for them. Accurate and congruent nonverbal behavior is particularly important in group counseling where a number of people are interpreting cues idiosyncratically. The leader must be aware of eye contact, voice tone, appropriate use of touch, and undistracting clothing.

Theorists have proposed various approaches to understanding the counselor's nonverbal expressions. Classical analysts did not want the client to even see the therapist, so the client would react to his own associations and experiences rather than to the therapist, so the therapist's nonverbal behavior was not an issue. Among the next generation of analysts, some faced their clients, but did so impassively and nonreactively. They believed nonverbal behavior should be neutral so the client could establish transference based on past experiences. There is now such a variety of viewpoints about nonverbal behavior of the therapist that we cannot generalize. Most would still view the therapist's nonverbal behavior as symbolic of unconscious processes which the leader should bring to awareness to be effective.

Rogers (1970) stresses revelation of feelings and attitudes in nonverbal as well as verbal ways, but ideally, the verbal and nonverbal behaviors are congruent with the counselor's inner experience. Behaviorists tend to take a less dynamic view of nonverbal behavior; they consider it a potential model for clients or a way to reinforce desirable behaviors in group members. Wincing when one member shouts at another cues other members that shouting is not desirable group behavior. A pat on the back can be a reward for speaking up in the group. The greater the leader's importance to the group, the more potent are her nonverbal reinforcers.

Carkhuff and his colleagues (1969) carried out a systematic approach to nonverbal and verbal behavior. Facilitative core conditions such as empathy, respect, warmth, and genuineness are communicated largely through nonverbal means. When the counselor nods her head rather than frowns, the client perceives empathy. Looking at someone rather than out the window shows respect. Smiling and leaning toward someone communicates warmth; insincere comments and fidgeting shows disinterest. Attending behavior is important in nonverbal communication. Walters (1978) makes these suggestions:

1. Keep eye contact regular but not continual. Do not be overly intense, jittery, or defiant.

2. Make your facial expression match your feelings; try for a smile or pleasant look most of the time, avoid a scowl or bland look.

3. Maintain space of approximately an arm's length from nearest group members.

4. Direct movement toward clients.

5. Keep posture relaxed, leaning slightly forward; do not sit rigidly or lean away.

6. Respond to comments at the first opportunity or soon enough to show involvement in the group.

7. Arrange furniture to draw members together.

8. Use gestures to highlight words.

9. Keep voice clearly audible, but not loud; do not speak impatiently or too slowly.

10. Demonstrate alertness throughout session; do not appear apathetic, jumpy, or pushy.

Member Nonverbals

The meaning of nonverbal behavior in the group is illusive and dangerous to speculate on unless it is integrated with other behavior and the member is involved in the interpretation. The same behavior in the same context by two different people can have two totally different meanings. Two people have tears in their eyes, a grimace on their faces, and fidget about. One is reacting to another group member's revelation; the tears show understanding of the pain, the grimace is in anticipation of what will come next, and the fidgeting expresses the wish to end the story so as to reduce anxiety. The second person has just been fitted for a pair of contact lenses; the tears and grimace reflect his physical discomfort, and he fidgets because he wants to end the group and take out the contacts. Observing the behavior may not yield sufficient information to give meaning. It is usually best for the leader and other members to describe a behavior and let the person explain its meaning. If the member seems to be denying or avoiding awareness of the nonverbal behavior or its meaning, the group may want to give him their perceptions of the behavior. When a member denies an obviously hostile tone of voice, for example, the leader or a member might say, "I heard an angry voice even though it may not have been intended as angry."

The leader needs to be sensitive to each person's social-cultural background in interpreting nonverbal behavior. Cultures and subcultures give unique meaning to nonverbal behaviors. Some meanings are nearly universal, as with a smile or a handshake. Other meanings may be unique to a community, an ethnic or racial group, or to a part of the world. Voice volume may be louder in one part of the country than another. An individual's territorial boundary, that is, how close one may comfortably be to someone, varies in cultures and even families. A hug is an intimate expression with some people and a common greeting with others. Group members may misunderstand or misinterpret nonverbal expressions of fellow members.

Individual differences also account for variation in meaning. For one person, touching someone's arm can be a significant expression of affection, while for another it is a normal way to get someone's attention. Coming late to a group session expresses hostility, or perhaps chronic lateness.

The situation or context also influences the meaning of nonverbal behavior. One who acts the same way in two different situations does so for different reasons. Also, two people behave differently in a particular context.

The observer is also an important element in the meaning of nonverbal behavior. We all give meaning, even if only tentative, to what we observe. We may think someone who is snapping and making hostile remarks is angry with the group when in fact she is angry with her mother for becoming ill. Members must share observations to avoid faulty interpretations. Interpersonal difficulties can linger or arise from inaccurate interpretations of others' behavior and unwill-

Table 8-4 Behaviors Frequently Associated with Various Group Member States

	Head	Face	Mouth	Eye Contact	Hands	Posture
Despair/Depression	Down	Sad frown (eyebrows down at outer ends)	Tightness	Little or none; may cover eyes with hand	Autistic behaviors; body-focused self-stimulating movements	Approaches fetal position
Excitement/Euphoria	Mobile movement	Mobility of expression	Smiling; laughing	Tries to capture and to hold eye contact of all other persons ("Look at me.")	Sweeping, expansive movements	Frequent change; seductive
Fear/Anxiety	Stiff movement; chin down	Flushing	Tightness; clenching teeth	Darting glances to others; wants to keep watch on others by not meeting their gazes ("I'll watch you.")	Tightness; gripping; sweaty palms ("clenched and drenched")	Frequent movement; crouching; hunching shoulders
Hostility/Rejection Another Person Active/Overt	Head, and often chin, thrust forward and/or tilted upward	Angry frown (eyebrows down at center)	Lips tensed and pushed forward slightly	Defiant	Clenching; fist; thumping (symbolic hitting)	Poised on edge of chair
Passive/Covert	Down; turned away slightly	Squinting of eyes	Closed; normal	Aversion; blank staring	Body-focused movements; self-inflicting behaviors	Infrequent change
Dependency/Attraction toward Another	Head slightly down while making eye contact ("Poor Me")	Mirrors expression of other	Frequent smiling	Frequent	Reaching motions	Quasi-courtship
Resistance to Learning	Turned; rolled back	Rigidity of expression	Tightness	Avoidance	Clenched; looking at watch; body-focused movements	Held in; stiffness of limbs

ingness to share attitudes and feelings behind one's own nonverbal behavior.

Nonverbal Behavior in the Group

Group counseling situations are much richer in nonverbal behaviors than one-to-one counseling sessions. The leader is able to spend more time observing the nonverbal behaviors between group participants and model the observations and descriptions so members will begin to notice and express their observations. A group also offers greater opportunity for feedback. The leader's responsibility is to demonstrate and to keep the group from going too far with interpretations.

Nonverbal behavior gives a clue to the individual's inner state. One can hypothesize the meaning, then combine information from other behaviors to arrive at a conclusion. The first tactic, as mentioned, is to simply describe the behavior and allow the other person to explain its meaning; for example, "Jack, I notice the pitch of your voice goes up every time you discuss your mother. Does that mean something to you?" The second method is to gather various behavioral cues and suggest a meaning: "Jane, I've noticed you look down at the floor when the other parents talk about their children. You have never discussed your children. You are avoiding something here."

Even pointing out nonverbal behavior risks putting the member on the defensive and eliciting anxiety. A moderate amount of anxiety can motivate someone to work toward self-understanding, but excessive anxiety creates discomfort in the group. Interpretations also may not be accurate, or the member may deny descriptions or interpretations. Some members may be surprised and embarrassed. Others are so vulnerable to influence that they will accept interpretations too readily. Table 8-4 (Walters, 1978) shows a sample of meanings often associated with nonverbal behaviors and suggests relationships. We cannot say a specific behavior is always a clue to a specific inner state. Sweeping, expansive movements, for example, do not always mean euphoria; they may indicate anxiety and agitation.

Kagan (1967) provides evidence to support his model for understanding nonverbal behavior. He describes three aspects of nonverbal behavior: source, levels of awareness, and duration. The source may be affect or content; nonverbal behavior can relate to one or the other but usually not to both at once. One may be aware of one's behavior, potentially aware, or unaware. Potential awareness means one is not attending to the behavior but could do so if directed. Unawareness means one would not recognize its occurrence even if it were brought to one's attention. Duration records whether a behavior takes place in a fraction of a second, or for minutes, or is repeated for a period of time; factors such as intensity and habit formation can be analyzed.

Summary

The beginning counselor will probably not fully absorb the many concepts of group dynamics until he sees them in practice. After leading a group session, one can refer to this chapter to define the *roles* of each group member. Who was an initiator? Who gave opinions? Were the roles stable over sessions or did other group dynamics, such as *influence*, modify individual roles? Which people took on positive roles, and which assumed roles that held back the group? The leader can plot the frequency with which each person directs or receives communication from all other members of the group to show who initiates, who receives messages, who are most active, and which members others prefer to speak to. The counselor can also chart a more complicated behavioral analysis, categorizing each interaction in some way: positive or negative, helping, critical, opinionated, informative, evaluative, aggressive, dependent, and so on.

Each group's *norms* differ from those of another group. The beginning group counselor should observe a variety of groups to take notes on rules, values, and expectations. Focusing on one dynamic at a time makes it easier to analyze what takes place in one session or over a number of sessions. Does everyone succumb to the norm? What pressures are used to make members conform? How do norms change over time? Other dynamics, such as cohesion and power, can be observed similarly. The best way to learn about these dynamics is to first observe and take notes, then discuss your findings with a supervisor.

Nonverbal behavior is particularly interesting to observe because most people usually pay little conscious attention to it. There are several methods for collecting observational data on nonverbal behavior. First, the counselor can sketch the physical location of group members from week to week to see who prefers to sit next to whom, how close people sit to one another, who sits back from the group, and so forth. You can also record nonverbal signs of increasing cohesiveness, as people attend to each other, smile more often, touch one another, lean toward one another, and so on. You can also record individual nonverbal behavior. Your observations become more meaningful when you discuss them with a supervisor or colleague.

Discussion Questions

1. Give an example to show how the following "roles" or characteristics of roles might be seen in group counseling: changing roles, ascribed and assumed roles, role expectation, and role differentiation.

2. Of the helpful "roles" described in this chapter, explain which ones you think would be most useful in a group. Which roles would play a lesser part in terms of importance or time necessary to the group?

3. How would you go about avoiding or dealing with the antigroup roles?

4. Explain how group norms affect members' behavior. In what ways can norms be beneficial or harmful?

5. What kinds of norms arise? Give an example of each.

6. Explain how cohesion develops or why it fails to develop. How does cohesion help the group process? What can be done to encourage cohesiveness?

7. What are the types of power or influence, and how can they be used in a positive way? Give examples.

8. In what ways can a group member behave to improve communication?

9. What are some examples of appropriate self-disclosure in a group?

10. Why do members resist progess in the group?

11. Give several examples of nonverbals on the part of group members and the leader and discuss them. How might the leader use nonverbals to help the group?

9

Organization and Maintenance of a Group

The beginning group leader wants to know not only theory and concepts, but also the specifics of setting up a group and maintaining it until it meets its objectives. If the leader does not know how to select members, establish rules, recognize group stages, and terminate a group, the experience can be unpleasant for all parties.

Pre-Group Planning

There is a great deal of work to do before the group actually meets. The leader sets the stage for the first meeting by establishing a need for the group and preparing everyone to cooperate in meeting mutually agreed-upon goals.

A counselor who works in an agency, whether community or educational, should inform other staff members as to the purposes and procedures of group counseling. Cooperation from the staff tends to be enhanced when they understand the relevance of group work in their setting, and information alleviates fear of groups, suspicion that members are talking about them, and skepticism about the usefulness of group counseling. The counselor can explain the purpose of counseling, the goals, how groups are organized, and when they meet. Through this process, the staff may recognize ways to help the counselor. Teachers, for example, will be better equipped to make appropriate referrals, and community agency staff will be more willing to explain group participation to their clients. This is an excellent time to explain confidentiality, so the staff realizes they can report client-student behavior to the counselor but the counselor cannot reveal a member's group behavior to the staff. Illustrations, such as a commercial group counseling film, can be effective, as can role playing or group simulation. The counselor should also plan to communicate with the staff concerning the counseling groups' progress and contributions.

Group and Individual Goals

Goal setting is the next step in the sequence of organizing a group. General group goals are often obvious; for example, if one thinks clients need a group to help them understand their vocational abilities and interests, the group goal is apparent from the beginning. In a therapeutic counseling group, goals may be specific, such as mourning the loss of a loved one or going through divorce, or relatively general, such as self-awareness. The leader has these goals in mind before he selects members. In recruiting group members, selecting and communicating group goals helps them know what outcomes to expect and whether or not the group will be appropriate to their needs. Selecting a group goal before taking other organizational steps establishes a common purpose among members when they first meet.

Individual goals are agreed upon after member selection, ideally, before the first meeting. The group leader should meet with each member to discuss what each wishes to achieve in the group. Although each member has unique goals, they should conform to the group's overall objectives.

Individual goals will tend to be more specific than group goals. The leader can help members think about what are presently their most important and relevant objectives so they will tend to know at the first meeting why they are there and exactly what they need to do. Everyone can discuss member goals in the first session, and any time goals become unclear or need modification. Goals should flow from assessment of client needs, assessed from observation, self-report, testing, or a referral source. Individual goals should be based on these needs.

Selection of Group Members

Careful selection of group members relates directly to counseling success. Groups function best when members have a common purpose and ability to work cooperatively. Consequently, selection of members becomes a function of goal setting; for example, the goal of helping unwed mothers cope with their situation narrows the inclusion criteria.

Dinkmeyer and Muro (1971) and Yalom (1970) explain various exclusion and inclusion criteria. It is difficult to decide who should be excluded from group counseling because we cannot always predict someone's group behavior. Furthermore, diagnostic categories are either irrelevant in many settings or do not provide adequate information about potential group behavior. The type of group may be appropriate for one person, but not for another, or potential members may not be ready for or suited to the group, such as those who show extremes in behavior that will sap the group's energy and interfere with forming close emotional relationships. Extremes of hostility, aggressiveness, narcissism, paranoia, and verbal monopolization require some other form of help. Separate homogeneous groups may be useful for sociopaths and substance abusers. People who show lack of concern for others require individual counseling or another intervention strategy that emphasizes the consequences of antisocial behavior. Suicidal people need individual counseling and monitoring, and people who are out of touch with reality are unlikely to benefit from a counseling group. Severely disturbed people must be able to relate to other members in some meaningful way. Exceptions to all these categories can be made individually when leader and potential member can visualize benefits to the member and the group.

Beyond sharing a common goal, there are many factors to consider for inclusion in a group. Although there are exceptions, one expects prospective members to volunteer and to be motivated toward growth and change so as not to waste their time or detract from other members' learning. For most groups, members should be close in age to facilitate compatibility in developmental concerns. Teenagers share problems of identity, young adults are trying to establish themselves, and the recent retiree has different concerns. On the other hand, certain theme-centered groups, dealing with alcoholism, job-seeking, marital relationships, or obesity, can be composed of members in the full adult age span.

Personal characteristics also seem to enhance group success. Although they may be somewhat defensive and anxious at the start, members should be willing to disclose themselves to others and to become emotionally involved, to develop warm and trusting relationships. Another necessary quality is the desire to help others. One cannot enter a group to further only one's own growth. There must also be concern for others and a sense of responsibility for encouraging and understanding other members.

Selection may be done by the leader, the prospective member, or the group itself, although usually the leader interviews potential members and makes the final decision jointly with the prospective member. Members often enlist themselves; colleges and community agencies often advertise groups dealing with stress, assertiveness, or heterosexual relationships, and little or no screening takes place. Other types of therapy groups, such as RET, TA, and Gestalt, invite participation for two days or more, with little selection. Elementary and secondary school counselors may allow students to select a counseling group in which they are interested, and in some institutional and agency settings, clients may be required to attend group counseling as part of their program. In these situations, the leader must first confront the problem of motivation.

In rare cases, the group may select its members; for example, parents of handicapped children may start a group by finding a leader, then selecting additional members with whom they think they will be compatible. The open group can select new members by setting criteria and interviewing potential members. Whatever the selection method, it is important that members have similarities, so they will feel comfortable in the group, and dissimilarities, to create therapeutic anxiety and a basis for healthy confrontation.

Group membership is usually not absolutely homogeneous or heterogeneous. Gender can be one characteristic of the homogeneity/heterogeneity dimension. Therapeutic group leaders prefer a balance of male and female members, because sex differences bring forth varied perceptions of behavior, different ideas of how to confront problems, and alternative interpersonal styles within the group. Research on homogeneity versus heterogeneity shows that we need further investigation before we can accept the conclusions.

Furst (1953) studied the advantages of homogeneous versus heterogeneous groups. He considered a homogeneous group one in which there is similarity in pathology and psychodynamics among the members. He ascribed these advantages to homogeneous groups:

1. Group identification takes place rapidly and transferences are rapidly formed.

2. Reeducation takes place rapidly and insight develops quickly.

3. Psychodynamics are more rapidly laid bare.

4. Duration of treatment is lessened.

5. Attendance is more regular.

6. Interferences, resistances, and interactions of a destructive nature are lessened.

7. Intramural cliques are uncommon.

8. Recovery from symptoms is more rapid. (Furst, 1953, p. 120)

On the other hand, the advantages of the heterogeneous group are:

1. Heterogeneous groups by their very nature tend to take the therapist whether or not he so desires into deeper levels of therapy.

2. Character structure as well as symptom formation is influenced by the process of therapy.

3. Reality testing is more adequate and thorough.

4. Intragroup transference of a diverse and shifting nature can be formed readily in the heterogeneous group in accordance with individual needs.

5. Heterogeneous groups are easy to assemble and screening need not be as thorough. (Furst, 1953, pp. 121–22)

Despite Furst's conclusions, we suggest that leaders select members who are compatible with one another yet exhibit sufficient differences to arouse disagreement and divergent behavior patterns. A balance of personal characteristics creates a realistic social microcosm and provides contrasting behaviors for members to relate to. Too much similarity leads to dullness, and too many extreme differences discourage members. Moderate differences are stimulating and have a remediating effect, whereas extreme differences prevent cohesiveness.

To make decisions about selection, compatibility, and balance, the leader must interview and gather as much diagnostic information as possible about each prospective member. The initial interview and the later interview to prepare the individual for the group give leader and member a chance to begin an interpersonal relationship before beginning the group.

Gazda (1969) suggests a trial group as part of the selection process. The leader can form a large group and retain those members who seem most compatible after one or several sessions. He can see the others in individual counseling. Or, the leader can begin with a group twice the size he wishes to work with and divide it into two groups according to compatibility.

Closed and Open Groups

Closed groups establish membership by the first session with the intention of maintaining the same members for the life of the group. Selection and preparation of participants should enhance creation of cohesiveness and common purpose, so that the group will tend to continue and to meet members' needs. Overall, the closed group has the better opportunity to develop closeness among members.

Open groups begin with a set number, then add members as terminations occur or as the group can benefit from the addition of a certain type of person. Members understand from the outset that new members will be added. This policy is useful when members are likely to terminate at different times; one member may reach her objectives in ten sessions while others may need fifteen or twenty sessions. Open groups may be necessary in agency settings, where clients or patients are discharged at various times. Open groups offer the advantage of forcing members to relate to new acquaintances as we do in everyday life. A disadvantage is possible instability, accompanied by a low level of cohesiveness. Each time a member is added, each of the other members must adjust to the new arrival.

Adding Members

Whether the group is closed or open, adding a member will have some impact. Each group creates an atmosphere from its rituals, rules, limits, relationships, hierarchy, and distribution of power. A new member has the potential to disrupt the security of the status quo; on the other hand, the group may welcome a new member as a new stimulus. A rigid group tends to impose its established norms on a new member rather than see the member as a new and positive dimension.

It is reasonable to expect old members to feel ambivalent toward a new member and a new member to feel anxious about how he will fit into the group. Old members may be concerned about loss of power, slowdown in the group process, or loss of cohesiveness. Hostility may be overt or covert. The group may ignore the new member or encourage him to reveal personal material before he is ready. A more mature group tends to welcome the new member, offer support, and integrate her into the group, reducing the new member's anxiety and defensiveness.

Adding a new member is not a good idea when either the individual or the group is in crisis. A new member in crisis needs immediate and extensive help, which the group may not be equipped to offer (Lifton, 1966). In terms of group conditions, the best time to add a member is during a lull (Hansen, Warner, & Smith, 1980). A lull may occur when an emotionally relevant topic has been explored fully and the group is about to move to another topic. During a crisis or a time of high intensity, integration of a new member poses an extra burden or a distraction; the group can lose its focus, the new member may feel threatened by the intensity, and old members may resent the new member.

Group Sizes

Group size depends on many factors. Conscientious attendance varies from group to group, so to arrive at an ideal size, remember that members may occasionally miss sessions. Purpose also plays a role in group size. The best size for in-depth and intimate interactions is five to ten members. More structured groups or those with a guidance and information theme may range up to twenty members. Alcoholics Anonymous groups, which rely heavily on guidance and inspiration, may have many more than twenty members. The length of each session also affects size. Marathon groups work well with twelve to eighteen members. If a therapeutic group's single session is two hours or more, it can accommodate more than ten members. Age is also a factor in group size; preadolescent children appear to function best in groups of about five.

A group can be too small. The leader may engage in individual counseling rather than group work, and members' resources are fewer in the variety of personalities, reality bases, and sources of feedback. Richness of interactions is less. Participants sometimes need to pull back from the group occasionally, in terms of interaction or emotional involvement, and a very small group makes this option less available. Another possible effect of a very small group is an increased pressure toward conformity. The group leader may have to be more active than he wishes, and there may not be enough members to take on all the necessary responsible roles.

Ideal group size gives everyone the maximum ratio of comfort and anxiety, the correct level of interaction and intimacy, the opportunity to be different and to conform, a chance to arrive at consensus, and a sense of satisfaction about the group.

A group that is too large usually creates emotional distance between members, because of physical distance, because members do not have enough opportunities to interact. Deleterious subgroups are more likely to emerge in a large group and there is less chance for consensus. Generally, members tend to be less satisfied with large groups.

A rule of thumb, then, is to have a group of about five for preadolescents, five to ten for therapeutic groups, ten to eighteen for more structured groups, and eight to twelve for sensitivity and marathon groups.

Time and Place

One must consider the length of each session, the frequency of meeting, and the total number of sessions. The standard length of interactional group, growth group, and therapeutic group sessions is one and one-half to two hours. Although there is little research evidence to support this time frame, it is generally accepted in clinical practice. Groups need time to warm up, and an hour or less allows little intense discussion. Members may become tired, bored, or restless beyond two hours, so when more time is needed, more frequent meetings are better than longer meetings.

Marathons may last forty-eight hours, with breaks to eat and rest. The purpose of marathons is to reduce defenses and facilitate greater self-disclosure and intimacy. Some ongoing groups conduct occasional marathons to accelerate the group process. Children's shorter attention spans and abilities to absorb less in a given amount of time call for sessions of only one-half hour to an hour. The more intense and interactional a children's group, the shorter it should be. Regardless of session length, it should end on time, even when participants try to extend it.

The group's meeting time may be dictated by clients' availability and schedules, the counselor's schedule, or agency requirements. In some cases the group may be able to select the time, if the counselor is sure the time is acceptable to everyone. The counselor must guard against accepting a time that is inconvenient for her, because subsequent resentment or interferences can impair her effectiveness. Changes in time and place should occur only when absolutely necessary; a change can be disruptive, and members like the security of knowing where and when they will meet.

The purpose of the group and the needs of the members affect frequency. When the purpose is guidance, information, or maintenance, the group can meet as seldom as once or twice a month. Therapeutic groups work best meeting at least once a week, although more frequent meetings can increase cohesiveness and progress.

The number of sessions can vary considerably. An open group, to which members can be added while the group is in progress, may go on indefinitely, as in an out-patient group at a mental health center where members exit as they reach a certain level of stability or are rehospitalized. New members replace those who terminate. Members may remain too long and become unnecessarily dependent upon the group, but most clients respond well to limits, and make an effort to reach their goals within a specified time. A group with no end date encourages clients to avoid their issues week after week.

A closed group usually lasts a set number of sessions, perhaps ten to twenty meetings, as agreed in the first session. Some groups, such as those directed at vocational counseling or another specific theme, may meet fewer than ten sessions. Groups need time to warm up, get acquainted, carry out their work, then terminate. The number of sessions should not be so many that members become unable to break their dependency on the group.

The meeting location should be selected carefully; participants function best when they are comfortable. Soft chairs, a rug, proper temperature, and ventilation are conducive to group interaction and interest, as are privacy and protection from outside noise. Most therapeutic groups avoid using a table, which sometimes acts as an artificial barrier and blocks off nonverbal cues. If the group uses a table, it should be round, to keep members as close to one another as possible so they do not have to speak loudly and to promote easy communication and eye contact.

Pre-Group Interview

Before the group's first session, the leader needs to meet with each member to prepare him for the group experience. If the member is cognitively, behaviorally, and attitudinally prepared, he is more likely to be responsible and active. The client must understand group goals, the leader's role, his own role, and what he can gain from the group (Bednar, Weet, Evenson, Lanier, & Melnick, 1974). A preliminary group session (Corey, Corey, Callanan, & Russell, 1982) allows the leader to explain the purposes of the group and what will happen in the group. Members get to know each other before they make a final decision to join the group. Prospective members discuss specific goals and ground rules, such as confidentiality and attendance.

The first step in a pregroup interview is to inform the client about the group, as to:

- Time and place of meeting
- Number of expected members
- Descriptive information about other members
- Training, experience, and interest of the leader
- Number of sessions
- General goals
- Description of group format and procedure
- Techniques
- Fees
- Expectations of the client
- Ground rules
- Confidentiality
- Research that may be conducted with the group and whether sessions will be tape-recorded

- Opportunity to ask questions about the group
- Choice of joining the group
- Acceptability of fraternization outside the group

Prospective members have a right to know as much about the group they are about to enter as the counselor can convey verbally or audiovisually. A therapeutic group should not be disguised as a discussion group. The limits of the group, that is, what it will not do, should also be explained. As a general rule, the leader should explain the group as honestly and clearly as possible so the client has realistic expectations and guidelines for his own behavior. This is usually a time of high anxiety and susceptibility to misconceptions, so the counselor needs to be alert to the client's apparent understanding or confusion. He should ask the client to explain what he has learned about the group and encourage him to ask questions. Repetition of important points in this interview and in the first group session helps minimize misunderstanding.

Expectations for each member should be explicit. Some leaders give each member a written list of the expectations, such as those in the following list.

1. Do not join the group unless you have a commitment to participate and learn about yourself. Genuine interest will help you benefit from the experience.

2. Set goals for yourself. Think about what you wish to accomplish, then establish specific, concrete objectives that we can observe or that you can experience as change. If you want to feel better about yourself, for example, state precisely how you want to feel better.

3. Write down in concrete terms what you hope to accomplish in the group. Show this to the leader and the group as an agreement with them.

4. Realize that the group experience will be a struggle. It is not easy to look at ourselves, and even more difficult to change. It will take a lot of work and time. Be committed to the effort and be patient with yourself and others.

5. Be active in getting your share of the group time. You need time to focus on your concerns, and you must make that happen. Others will have similar concerns, and their work will probably be helpful to you.

6. You are responsible for your own behavior in the group. Do not blame others for what you do, say, or feel. It is exciting to be responsible; it means you can take credit for yourself. Reveal only what you want to reveal in the group.

7. Be as open as possible to your own behavior. This is an opportunity to learn about your feelings, attitudes, thoughts, and actions. Look at yourself and listen to the feedback from others.

8. Be open to close relationships with other group members and the leader. Listen to others and expect them to listen to you. Do your best to understand others. Be supportive, but disagree and even confront in a respectful way when it may help. Avoid giving advice and questioning extensively. Learn to trust group members and see your role also as a helper.

9. Practice new behavior in the group. This is your chance to try new things and receive feedback.

10. Try new behaviors outside the group, and share your experiences with the group.

11. Engage in therapeutic activities outside the group. These may include relevant reading, writing to express yourself, attending appropriate plays or movies, developing new friendships, evaluating your habits, and exercising.

Note the positive tone of the suggestions. It is best to focus on how the client can improve rather than on self-defeating behaviors. When the whole group accepts these suggestions, the group takes on a healthy atmosphere characterized by optimistic outlook, emotional closeness, and cooperation toward goals.

Discussion of ground rules can also be part of the pregroup interview. The leader mentions essential ground rules at this time, while those decided by the group, such as whether members may smoke, can be discussed at the first session. Therapeutic groups normally have a rule of confidentiality. Although it is difficult to enforce, members are asked not to reveal outside the group what they discuss in the group. It is especially important not to reveal what other members disclose. Leaders must clarify to the group what they are obligated to report to others; for example, agency and school settings may require a written report, and members, including children, have a right to know what will be revealed.

A few counselors do not set a confidentiality rule, on the premise that people learn to trust each other and will reveal only what will not be harmful to one another. Even these leaders make no promises of confidentiality other than to assure that they will not knowingly reveal anything that could cause the member harm. This approach allows the counselor freedom to intervene when a member engages in extremely destructive behavior, perhaps suicidal or homicidal. Other rules may include:

- No physical violence

- No drugs, particularly when coming to a session

- No sexual relations with members while the group is active

- Attendance at all meetings

- Decisions are made with input from everyone, ideally by consensus

- Everyone belongs and participates

- The leader will guard the rights and safety of members

Research does not tell us which rules are useful in what situations, but minimal rules appear necessary for structure. Children seem to function better with more structure at first, but otherwise, rules are up to the judgment of the counselor and the group.

Phases of Group Process

After the advance planning, the counselor is ready for the group sessions. Groups pass through phases, or stages, in attempting to meet their goals. We will label the phases Beginning the Group, Conflict and Dominance, Cohesiveness and Productivity, and Completing the Group Experience. These phases have various names and have been explained in many ways.

Beginning the Group (Phase One)

Now that the preliminary work is completed, the leader prepares for the first session. This can be a time of anxiety and anticipation for both the leader and the members. The counselor should have a good idea of what he wants to do as a leader before he enters the first session, and thus needs to reexamine his role, the purpose of the group, and the needs of the members he has just interviewed. His plan may be nonspecific, such as facilitating interactions in a personal growth group, or much more specific and structured, such as presenting videotapes and roleplaying in modeling interpersonal skills.

How to Begin A collection of individuals, all concerned with themselves rather than the others in the group, assemble for the first session. They are anxious and awkward; searching for structure is a threatening situation. Anxiety appears in nervous laughter, hesitancy in expressing oneself, and the polite, stilted talk common when people first meet. Some wonder whether they will be rejected or accepted, liked or disliked. They search for similarities and common ground with other members. There is a desire to learn what the others are like and how one can relate to them. People want to know how others are going to behave and what they will expect of them. Each person's role in the group is slowly defined, and individual identities begin to develop in the first session. This is an important time to establish social relationships, to learn how members will work with each other. The leader should expect all of this as normal. New members enter the group with ambivalent feelings. They want to participate because of desire to grow and improve their lives. The client realizes this is an opportunity to achieve something more in life, but at the same time, fears the unknown. There are fears of rejection, of acting stupid, of being unable to contribute, of criticism, and so on. The leader must recognize the members' fears and try to reduce them.

Discussion in the first session is, naturally, superficial. Usually the first session goes quite smoothly, because of the friendliness and the focus on information rather than affect. At first, members have only their pasts to rely on, so they relate to other members as they have always related to people like them. Perceptions of one another are based more on past interpersonal experiences than on each one's actual characteristics. Gradually, reality creeps into the relationships.

Each member's relationship with the leader will be unclear at first. Everyone will carefully observe the leader's behavior and attribute to him the characteristics they have associated with authority figures, so their initial responses may be respect, hostility, fear, or dependency. Members will then tend to look to the leader for authority, rules, and guidelines, which places great responsibility on him. Even when members take major responsibility for the group process, the leader shapes members' behavior.

Because members are so preoccupied with themselves in the first session, it is a good idea for the leader to direct comments to the group rather than to individuals. This relieves some of the pressure and communicates the leader's concern for the importance of the group process. Clients begin to consider themselves members of a group. For example, the leader may say, "Your comments show you have some uneasiness about being here." This sums up the feelings without singling out an individual. The leader might go on to say, "And I'm a little nervous myself." Self-disclosure at this time provides a model for the others, showing that it is all right, even desirable, to reveal feelings, and that they will be accepted by the counselor. Openness also shows that the leader is human, too. Leader role modeling responses of empathy and clarification show members what will be considered acceptable behavior, as well.

It is a good idea for the leader to involve everyone in the early sessions. Keeping member statements brief enlivens the discussion, and encouraging each person to speak gives everyone a sense of belonging. The counselor's responses should focus on what the group is doing rather than on the content of what is said. For example, after superficial talk about the weather, the leader could say, "I wonder if we are having trouble discussing what this group is about" or "Is this what everyone is here to discuss?" The leader role of keeping the group on task without being overly critical becomes apparent in the first session.

Initially, the counselor wants participants to interact as openly as possible so they get to know each other and begin to feel less anxious. Introductions can be handled in several ways. The traditional way is to simply have each person introduce herself, but there are more interesting ways. One method is to have the group split into pairs. Each person has three minutes to provide information to the other, then everyone returns to the group. One person in each pair is asked to introduce the other to the group, remembering as much as possible. The other person has an opportunity to add to or correct what was said. The dyadic interaction produces less anxiety, because it is easier to say things about another person than about oneself in a group.

In another exercise for a first session, the leader suggests that each member consider a response to a statement and tell the group; examples are:

How I feel about being here.

What I expect from the group.

Why I'm here.

What I'm afraid of.

An introductory exercise for children who are in the same school and already know each other is to have the children draw the name of another group member from a hat, then introduce that child to the group. Besides beginning some interactions, this technique reveals the children's perceptions of one another when they enter the group. When the leader facilitates discussion, he can elicit other perceptions of a particular child and that child's reaction. The leader must take care to see that descriptions are balanced in a positive direction, and that one child does not immediately emerge as a scapegoat.

The leader should choose exercises that address the group's needs at the time, fit the leader's concept of the group process, and which he is comfortable directing. Members should always have the right to decline to participate in an exercise. Exercises should not be used as gimmicks or to relieve the counselor's responsibility. Games can detract from genuine, spontaneous interactions, but they can serve as warm-up exercises when the group has reached an impasse. Even then, however, they should have a purpose and match the group's needs. (Some exercises that utilize touching or guided fantasies require extensive counselor training as well as supervised experience.)

Another topic for the first session is group and individual goals. The leader once again explains the purpose of the group and what he hopes will be achieved, then asks members whether they understand and agree. It is a good idea to have each member present her specific objectives to the group. Members can ask questions so they fully understand each other's objectives and begin to recognize what each person is willing to do to reach the objectives and how the group can assist in the process. It is important to instill a feeling of group involvement, a sense that they are pulling together rather than observing each other work. The leader can actively enlist the group's help in meeting each member's objectives. Finally, the group reviews the ground rules and adds whatever additional rules it feels necessary. The leader mediates to keep rules to a minimum.

Throughout the first session, the leader observes behavior and notes emerging interactional patterns. He can see who is assuming or receiving more power, who is leading, who is passive, and who is angry, as well as get a sense of the overall group dynamic—whether it is reticent, cognitive, task oriented, warm. This exerpt is from the middle of a first session.

> *Bruce:* How do we know that people here won't tell others what we say in here?
> [Silence]
>
> *Andy:* Guess we don't know for sure.

> *Susan:*   I'm not going to say anything to anyone else. I figure what you say is your own business.
> [Silence]

> *Jeff:*   Even though everyone agreed, it doesn't mean they keep everything to themselves.
> [Silence]

> *Jeanette:*   I'm going to say whatever I want 'cause I don't have anything to hide.

Some members of this group are concerned with confidentiality, while others are not. The frequent silences occur because members are reluctant to contribute. Note also that members address the entire group rather than individuals; allegiances and preferences have not had time to develop. The leader can acknowledge the concern of some participants by saying, "A few people are concerned about confidentiality. Is there anything we can do here to reassure each other that their statements will not go outside the group?"

Building a Group

During its early stage, one hopes to release a group's therapeutic and/or working potential. Any combination of people has the capacity to gain a great deal from a group experience or, on the other hand, to garner no benefits. The early stage may even be the beginning of a harmful experience. Each member's past experiences and expectations interact with the special combination of people in the group and with the leader.

To facilitate group success, a balance of comfort and anxiety should be established early. Anxiety needs to be reduced to a point where members are able to look more objectively at themselves and their interactions with others. Continued high levels of anxiety result in defensiveness. Comfort with one another enhances the openness necessary to work in the group. At the same time, an optimum level of anxiety motivates one to make positive changes. The principle is much the same as the relationship between learning and anxiety: modest levels of anxiety are associated with improved learning, whereas high levels reduce learning performance.

Peer influence is a factor in success. Members will have varying degrees of vulnerability to one another, but no one escapes some degree of influence from others. Early social interactions will set a theme; in therapeutic groups, one hopes peer influence will set an emotional theme of sharing problems (Bion, 1959), and in more structured groups, one looks for a shared desire to work toward the common goal.

Whatever the group theme, the individual and the group must work and progress together. The individual should begin self-exploration, which may be relatively superficial at first, during this early group stage. Each person begins to develop an identity with the group and a sense that he and the others can learn to work together; this is the foundation for later cohesiveness.

Dropouts

Dropouts occur most frequently in the early stage of counseling. Dropouts present several problems. The rate is quite high (25 to 57 percent), contributing to group instability, and the effect can be destructive; remaining members react with discouragement, self-doubts, and so on. If the group experience or interaction with the leader has not been beneficial, the decision to drop out may help the individual build his self-confidence and decision-making ability, and sometimes it is best to retreat from a situation one perceives as noxious. Occasionally, a group leader is reluctant to admit that a particular counseling group is not the best one for an individual; it is difficult to admit that selection was not appropriate, that the group has let the member down, or that the group simply was not suitable for this individual. Yalom (1970) provides us with a list of reasons for dropping out of groups, all of which are viewed as problems rather than healthy decisions.

1. External factors: Physical reasons to exit, such as moving out of town, which can largely be avoided in the screening process. Yalom found that most external reasons were actually due to group-related stress.

2. External stress: Turmoil in a member's personal life may leave him too emotionally drained to participate fully in the group.

3. Group deviancy: These members deviated from the group norm in several ways rather than just one. Yalom found no particular type or cluster of deviancy. He described, however, what seem to be people of lower status, lower ability to communicate, and who relate at a more superficial emotional level.

4. Problems of intimacy: Demonstrated in withdrawal, pervasive dread of self-disclosure, and expectation of quick intimacy. Ironically, some of these people could most benefit from the group.

5. Fear of emotional contagion: Occurs when the many problems of group members have a disturbing effect on one member. It can also be a reaction to the problems of one member. The affected person may become preoccupied with others' troubles. Yet another reaction is a lack of curiosity and concern for others; people drop out because they are not interested in other people's problems.

6. Inability to share the leader: These people want to be the center of the leader's attention, and find it difficult to sit back while other members have a relationship with the leader. They become frustrated and exit the group.

7. Complications of concurrent individual and group counseling: When group members are also in individual counseling, several complications may arise. It is important that individual and group counseling be compatible in methods and goals. Also, group members should not sit back and absorb what is happening, intending to be active in their individual session. Counselors need to be in regular contact with each other. When the individual and group counselor is the same person, sibling rivalry and resentment may occur.

8. Early provocations: Early on a member's behavior may be upsetting to others. Behavior that can cause dropouts include excessive hostility, aggressiveness, demanding self-disclosure of others, taunting, monopolizing, etc. A member may also be attacked by the group, resulting in a desire to escape the tension.

9. Subgrouping: Cliques are a source of conflict and rejection. Excessive conflict between subgroups or a feeling of exclusion increase the chances of a dropout.

Conflict and Dominance (Phase Two)

Moving from the early phase of beginning the group to a point of cohesiveness and work requires a transition phase. This intermediate stage involves more open attitudes and feelings, establishing status and role hierarchies, conflict among members and between members and leader, and resistance to progress. Each group experiences unique difficulties. One group may encounter all the common problems intensely, while another may experience one or two only briefly. Some groups become arrested at this phase; they either dwell on conflict, or ignore it and therefore never progress to a working group.

During this phase, members test themselves, each other, and the leader. Each one tests personal commitment and that of others to the group. A great deal of anxiety is still present as the participants wonder whether the group will be useful to them, what will happen if they open up, and whether others will try to understand them. Questions arise as to the relative threat of the other members, and how safe one is to be oneself. Thus, fear of learning about oneself as well as fear of others' reactions to personal revelations becomes a more important issue. By now, most participants have decided to stay in the group, but are unsure as to their role and how others will react if greater openness develops.

Some may reexamine their behavior and challenge, aggressively or passively, others' perceptions and reactions. Members now feel freer to criticize each other, and conflict arises as some members assert their viewpoints judgmentally or dogmatically. Mature give-and-take is less prevalent than opinions and attempts to establish influence. There will also be an undercurrent of attempts to avoid conflict, as some members remain quiet, try to change the subject, or try to mediate. Conflict should be brought into the open, yet dealt with in a way that does not discourage the participants.

Certain authorities (Yalom, 1970; Schultz, 1973) see control, conflict, and dominance as the essential characteristics of this group phase, during which members compete with each other and the leader for positions of power. There is rivalry, boundary testing, and establishment of a pecking order. A power and influence hierarchy emerges as each person jockeys for position.

The dynamics can be confusing to the leader as members behave inconsistently. Some are aggressive at first, then become quiet. Others are quiet and share only their "best" thoughts with the group. Some want power, but withdraw in the face of responsibility. Role modeling is in evidence; members behave like those they most respect. Members reveal their techniques for resisting influence as well as their need to be dominated and led. Someone may try to replace the counselor as leader. Pressure to conform intensifies and causes conflict because members are trying to maintain their identities while seeking acceptance. Norms and roles become solidified; those with greater power set guidelines for expected behavior. Each member eventually carves a role for himself.

Resistance is a major force in this phase. Resistance may be directed at the subject matter, the group, or the leader, in the form of withdrawal, absence, attacking other members or the leader, and questioning the purpose of the group. This defensiveness may originate from an individual or the whole group.

The leader must face the group's attacks and challenges, which will be both professional and personal. Some leaders seem to invite severe or prolonged attacks, while others manage to avoid them. Some leaders stay aloof from criticism, while others communicate an exaggerated need for the members' love and respect. The greatest problem for leaders is the personal threat of challenges. When a member criticizes ("you aren't helping us make decisions"), challenges authority ("we don't need you"), or attacks ("you rub me the wrong way"), it takes a good deal of personal strength to withstand the barbs. Yet the leader must resist the temptation to retaliate and accept criticism as a sign that members are working through their attitudes and comfortableness in the group. It is important to accept the challenges and deal with them openly.

Attacking the leader is common; some members are resolving a problem between dependency and independence. They want a leader to assume control, tell them what to do, and resolve all difficulties, or they demand independence—in the extreme, they want to get rid of the leader, or demote him to the status of "just another member." In this case, the group wants to rid itself of an authority figure and establish a totally democratic and leaderless group, although this rebellion may arise from hostile feelings toward authority figures rather from than a mature desire for a democratic group.

Other members defend the leader, either because they are mature enough to set realistic expectations for the leader or because they do not feel strong enough to disagree with him. Subgroups may emerge, one rebelling against and the other defending the leader. The group may select a scapegoat as a substitute for the attacks members are too afraid to direct at the leader.

The leader needs to recognize this situation and redirect the anger toward himself.

Cohesiveness and Productivity (Phase Three)

Conflict and competition decrease as members drop their preconceptions about the group and learn to accept one another. They identify more closely with each other and lose the sense of isolation they experienced in earlier sessions. Interpersonal respect and trust develop when they discover that self-disclosure does not bring catastrophe. The main concern in the early part of phase three, then, is intimacy. The group minimizes the power struggle, replacing it with greater closeness and cooperation. Emotional closeness becomes more than acceptable.

The new atmosphere shows cohesiveness; members become conscious of the group, in addition to individual concerns. They are able to listen and give support. There is an increase in morale, cooperation, and confidence in each other. The pendulum has swung from primarily negative interaction to positive interaction.

Cohesiveness brings higher-level communication patterns. Members show greater respect for others' statements and concerns, and listen more carefully to attitudes and feelings as well as to content. They express greater understanding of situations, problems, and feelings, and communication is less defensive, aggressive, or manipulative. As a result people are more genuine in what they say and are more willing to reveal personally significant material.

Everything, unfortunately, does not necessarily go smoothly at this stage. The group may tire of the conflict of the second phase and return to being too nice to each other. Members are supportive and understanding, and examine one another's problems, but they do not confront one another or allow open expression of negative affect, such as anger. They try to facilitate growth with kindness alone.

A second reality is that groups actually function with degrees of cohesiveness, with forward movement and regressions, with unity and times of conflict. Members may relate well most of the time, but have periods of disagreement in which they fall back on less effective, self-defeating behaviors. The group leader must expect times of adolescent behavior, denial, conflict, avoidance, and unconcern for one another; when these periods occupy the majority of group time, the leader must bring it to the group's attention.

As a third possible reality, the group may become stuck in the early part of this phase. A cohesive group may not move into action and behavior change. They self-explore, care about each other, even confront, but they do not encourage or challenge each other to make changes outside the group; they may even decide that outsiders should make the changes and learn to accept group members as they are. This misleading kind of support is destructive. A variation on this kind of group is that in which members are interpersonally close but fragmented and disorganized in terms of how they work or the direction they wish to take. They enjoy the relationships, but jump from theme to theme and problem to problem. The leader should confront the group and keep the group on focus, working toward a goal.

The significant element of this phase is productivity. When members are willing to explore important aspects of their lives and take action to improve themselves, the group has fully entered phase three. One looks for attempts, successful and unsuccessful, at behavior change or new attitudes toward others outside the group. The group has become a social microcosm for experimenting with new behaviors and attitudes. Members are more able to take responsibility and less likely to blame others for their problems or expect others to solve them. As a result of their close group relationships, participants are able to challenge one another toward constructive behavior change. They can evaluate each other more objectively; discussions have more give-and-take; decisions are arrived at more effectively. Members feel free to express any feelings without fear of punishment. Working through negative feelings toward each other instead of avoiding them marks a mature, working group. Members face crises inside and outside the group, discuss them, and work them through. They accept and include the counselor as part of the group at the same time they take on more leadership and maintenance responsibilities themselves. Corey lists the characteristics of an effective group at the productivity stage:

1. Trust and acceptance

2. Empathy and caring

3. Hope

4. Commitment to change

5. Intimacy

6. Personal power (tapping into one's inner resources to improve one's life; includes creativity, spontaneity, courage, etc.)

7. Self-disclosure

8. Confrontation

9. Catharsis (ventilating feelings, followed by discussion of the meaning it has for the member)

10. Cognitive restructuring (challenging and exploring beliefs people have about themselves and others)

11. Freedom to experiment

12. Feedback (Corey, 1981, pp. 44–48)

This phase of the group will make a real difference in the lives of the members. Time-limited groups need to reach this stage as quickly as possible, yet the counselor cannot rush it to this point. Groups of ten or twelve sessions may arrive at this phase in the last few sessions or not at all. Careful planning, selection, preparation of members, and skillful leadership enhance the chance of reaching this stage earlier.

Completing the Group Experience (Phase Four)

The ability to handle time and preparation for the ending, along with other elements, are characteristic of ending a session or group, but each requires certain techniques.

Ending Each Group Session The best use of time is necessary for participants to gain the most from the group. Realization that they have a limited amount of time and must work within those limits enhances members' motivation. Groups work most efficiently and provide more rewards when they begin and end on time. The counselor establishes this policy in early sessions, so that members quickly learn not to depend on an extension and to get right to their concerns. The leader must also discourage introduction of new topics near the end of a session. Most people cannot completely resolve an issue in one group session, so it is expected that members will leave with some unfinished business. The group can address a specific concern and bring out feelings, leaving the global issue for later sessions.

Although we prefer not to encourage new topics at the end of a session, clients are not so fragile that they will fall apart if they expose a concern and cannot deal with it fully in a session. The leader needs to help everyone recognize the concern, suggest ways to think about it between sessions, and encourage exploration at another session. On rare occasions, a client may require assistance between sessions for a crisis situation.

There is no rule for ending a session. Leaders frequently alert the group when twenty or thirty minutes remain, so they can plan the rest of the session. The group may move toward closure on a theme, or give one person time to focus on another matter. Or, the counselor may announce the remaining time and ask the group to reflect on that session. He can have each participant express perceptions of the session, with the expectation that each will focus on the group process. The leader may then comment on how well they stayed on a theme, how they interacted, or how the session compared with others.

The leader might also ask each member to reflect on the day's experience. What, if anything, had an impact on each person? What did they learn? Did anything disturb them? Those who were the main focus in the group can reveal their reactions; others can summarize feedback. The discussion can move to between-session activities and future sessions, encouraging members who have been the focus of attention to mention how they plan to work on what they have learned. The member, the group, or the leader can suggest homework assignments, in the form of new behaviors, ways to react to real life situations, and cognitive activities. This is the best time to discuss concrete ways of transferring learning in the group to real life situations, which is, after all, the purpose of group counseling.

Ending the Group Ending the group is a critical and often difficult experience for members and leader. It is best to prepare for the ending from the start. An open group can establish criteria for terminating a member; a closed group can agree upon total number of sessions or some other criterion as a guide to termination. Members can thus anticipate the ending and work within sessions at the speed and intensity to allow them to accomplish their goals in the allotted time.

As the end approaches, members of closed groups often want to deny that the group is temporary. They need to be reminded that the group was set up to meet certain goals, and nothing more. Reminders such as these discourage overdependence and help people realize their goals.

How members handle ending the group may reflect how they handle endings in their lives. Separations from people with whom one has interacted intensely and emotionally are rarely easy. There may be anxiety over functioning without the group's support, and disappointment about never seeing some people again. There may be anger toward members of the group or the leader. Love, jealousy, disappointment, hostility, and fear may all be present.

How group members deal with all of these feelings will vary. There may be denial of the impending dissolution, or agreements to meet in the future. Whatever the avoidance technique, the leader can help members face the reality of termination by spending one or more sessions discussing it to bring feelings and attitudes into the open.

The last sessions are a time to bring together what has been learned over the life of the group. New learning seems to be minimal at this stage; most growth occurs at the previous two stages, when members are most facilitative and intent on the work of the group. When they see the end coming, the activity level slows. They consider what was significant for them, where they stand now, and how to translate the learning into real life. The leader can facilitate major discussions: unfinished business, summary feedback, individual reflection, and plans for the future.

Before the last session, members may need an opportunity to take care of any unfinished business they have with one another, focusing discussion on interpersonal matters rather than outside concerns. Disagreements and conflict can be brought to their optimal level of resolution, though not necessarily resolved, and unexpressed feelings toward each other can finally be revealed.

Feedback summaries are useful in the last one or two sessions. Each member might summarize observations and feelings about someone else in the group, describing that member's progress. Specific feedback should be structured according to the individual's initial goals, and should focus on behavior; for example: "Terry, you came into this group laughing and talking a lot. You didn't stay on a topic with us, and I was annoyed by that. You wanted help in making friends and I think your flightiness and other behavior kept people at a distance. Now you listen much better and you can express your feelings more easily. I like you a lot better this way."

Feedback need not be 100 percent positive, but it should be balanced in that direction. The leader can set an example by focusing on individual progress, then telling the member what else he might work on. Excessive negative feedback will make the member defensive, and he will tend to discount the value of the whole experience. Members need honest feedback and encouragement to continue to work. The leader can also structure the feedback by giving members sentences to complete about each other: "What I like about you is . . . ," "I hope you will . . . ," and so forth. Everyone must also focus on himself, reviewing what he has done and learned. This is a time to summarize the experience in the group. Each person can have time in the last session to present her summary to the group. It can also be helpful to put the summary in writing so one can refer to it at a later date. Some people try to discount the experience later in life, and the written summary can refresh the memory of what was learned.

The final recommended activity is devising a plan of action for after the group's termination. The group, the leader, and each member, on the basis of the feedback and summaries, composes a statement as to what each will do to continue her progress in some area. The plan needs to be specific, showing what will be done and how. Others' expectations should not be part of the plan. An alcoholic may devise a plan to stay away from people who influence him to drink; a shy daughter can set up a schedule of increasingly assertive behavior for dealing with her mother. The group may want to meet in six months or a year to report progress and see each other again.

Follow-up, although rare, can be useful to both the former group member and the counselor. A follow-up interview gives the counselor feedback as to the group's long-term effectiveness. It also conveys to the former member the counselor's concern for transferring group learning to real life, and the need to function without the group. The anticipation of a follow-up session also motivates the member to function well so he can bring a favorable report back to the group. Continued contact among group members after termination can have positive results if it is not treated as an attempt to continue dependence on the group. Those who have developed special relationships with one another can continue their mutual supportiveness. The leader and fellow members can also suggest resources in the community to help continue growth, and the counselor can be available to refer or suggest other sources of support.

Summary

Planning before the group actually begins increases the chances of success. When counseling takes place in an agency, one must work with the staff to secure their cooperation. The group leader establishes general goals before the first session and helps each member articulate individual goals consistent with group goals. The leader also selects members, primarily for compatibility. Group size depends on goals: more structured, task-oriented groups normally accommodate more than ten members; children's groups, six or fewer; and therapeutic groups, six to ten.

"Closed" groups begin with a set number and rarely add new members after the first session; "open" groups add new members as other members terminate. Normally, the leader selects new members according to personalities—who will best fit with the group's dynamics. The leader usually also decides a time and place to meet. Arrangements, expectations, and goals can be discussed with each prospective member during a pregroup interview, at which time the client also asks questions and decides whether or not to participate in the group.

From beginning to termination, counseling groups pass through three or four phases. The beginning phase is characterized by getting acquainted, establishing roles and relationships, and finding where one fits into the group. A phase of conflict and dominance follows, in which disagreements, personality conflicts, jockeying for power, and establishment of subgroups occur. When the group is able to move through this troublesome phase, it becomes cohesive and productive, using its energy to work together on common and individual goals. Toward the end of the group sessions, members begin to consider that they will no longer see each other in the group, and must address the emotional factors associated with ending, summarizing accomplishments, and planning for future growth.

DISCUSSION QUESTIONS

1. As a class, simulate forming a group by setting up a hypothetical situation (such as a school or agency) and purpose for the group. Begin with pre-group planning and discuss each step in group formation. Explain what you would do, and what should be avoided, and potential problems.

2. List the important guidelines for selecting group members. What are the advantages and disadvantages of homogeneous versus heterogeneous groups?

3. In what situations would you want to have open versus closed groups?

4. What would you want to include in a pre-group interview?

5. As a group leader, what would you look for in the first phase of a group? What could you do to be helpful at this phase?

6. What kinds of conflicts occur in a group? How could you deal with conflicts as a group leader?

7. What seem to be the main ingredients that make a group productive?

8. What are the main tasks in terminating a group?

10

Group Leadership

A small group of high school seniors have agreed to participate in group counseling as part of their preparation for beginning college. They were screened and selected because school counselors and teachers believed these particular students might have difficulties adjusting to college life. Three students are overly dependent on others and may have trouble breaking from their families; two students appear to have little enthusiasm for continuing their studies; three have a history of behavior problems, including drug abuse and conflict with authority.

The group, led by two school counselors, meets once a week for an hour and a half. The counselors have interviewed each member to establish the group goal of discussing attitudes toward college and how each student feels about going away to school. The group meets in a comfortable room with soft chairs arranged in a circle, without a table. This excerpt is from the initial session:

Leader 1: Well, it's good to have everyone here today. Our purpose is to discuss your preparation for college. Going away to college can be a very difficult experience, and since you all have this to look forward to, we thought it would be a good idea to get together and talk it over.

Leader 2: I'd just like to say I am glad to be meeting with each of you, and I hope you will be able to share your feelings about college.

Leader 1: Why don't we begin with each of you telling us where you are going to college and what you want to major in, if you've decided yet. [Each student does so.]

Leader 2: Now we know where you are headed. I'd also like to hear how you feel about what you're doing.

Jim: I'm not sure what to think about it yet. I've been so busy I don't think about it a lot.

Leader 1: But it is something pretty important to think about, don't you think?

Georgia: Oh, it's important all right. I just think about how hard it's going to be, and all the new people I'll have to meet.

Don: It's going to be a new school and strange people. Only one other kid from here is going to the same school.

Leader 2: You feel some natural apprehension about going to a new place where you will have to establish new friendships.

Mary: Well, there's also the fact of leaving some people you care about. I've never been separated from my family.

Leader 1: Of course it can be tough. Yet it seems to be necessary, and something you can handle if you prepare yourselves.

Dennis: I'm not exactly broken up about leaving people. This may turn out to be quite an adventure. Maybe it will even be an advantage to go out of town to school.

Tony: Yeah, some of us may like to get a fresh start. I can't do much here without someone jumping all over me. I get blamed for everything. At least in college I won't have this reputation hanging over me.

Leader 2: College can be a new start, an opportunity to do something new with your life. Does anyone else feel this way?

Leader 1: Of course just going to a new school won't change everything. You'll have to look at how you will be different, too.

Jamie: I don't know if it will be any new start for me. I don't *mind* leaving here, but I'm not excited about where I'm going, either. I don't know what to think about it.

Bud: I'm looking forward to it because I'm going to have more freedom. No one telling me when to come in and what to do. I'll be glad to be on my own.

Mary: I wish I could say the same. I like to have people I know watching out for me. I like to decide things, but I also like some help in making the decisions.

Leader 2: I sense that some of you are reluctant to leave the people you know who are supportive, and others in the group can hardly wait to get away, to be on your own.

Leader 1: How about discussing independence and responsibility? These seem to be themes in what has been said so far.

Note that the leaders have quite different styles of relating to the group. How could you describe each style? What type of behavior does each leader exhibit? How might each leader help or harm the group?

In the sixth session, we find that leader 1 has changed his style of relating to the group because members were not responding well to his earlier style. Leader 2 maintains the same approach as before. The group has become more cohesive, more open about feelings, and willing to examine how they will cope with college.

Leader 2: I think we are having a good discussion of your attitudes toward college, and as we continue, I think each of you will be better prepared for college. Who can get us started today?

Dennis: I wasn't sure what you said last week about college not necessarily being a different experience.

Leader 2: You said again how you wanted to get where people did not know you. It may be that people will react to you there in the same way people react to you here—if *you* behave the same way. I'm concerned that college could be a bad experience for you if you don't work at making it a good one.

Dennis: This sounds a little like what Georgia said about my expecting others to be different while I stay the same.

	I don't know, this doesn't exactly fit into my way of thinking.
Leader 1:	It's something to consider, Dennis. Most people have trouble accepting change. It's whatever you want to do.
Tony:	Is it really up to Dennis to change if no one gives him a break? I mean, why should he hit his head against a wall?
Leader 2:	Tony, you seem to be struggling with feelings similar to Dennis's. You must have some feelings about your willingness to change.
Tony:	I've always thought, why should I change if no one else treats me any different? Shouldn't it be a two-way street? Now, when I think about college, I wonder if it's possible to be different there. I mean, no one there has dumped on me—not yet, anyway.
Leader 2:	You're leaving the door open for the possibility of being a little different. You're still unsure. A little like Dennis. How do others react to Dennis and Tony?

[The group gives support and encourages them. Now we move later into the sixth session.]

Leader 2:	If each of you were to change something about yourself, and you could experiment in this new place called college, what might you change?
Don:	I'd like to be able to make new friends without getting so nervous about it. I get so nervous I just don't even try.
Leader 2:	Can anyone help Don with that?
Bud:	I don't have any trouble making friends. Of course, I don't have any trouble making enemies, either. Everyone is one or the other. Anyway, I could help out—not sure just how.
Leader 2:	That's great, Bud, that you can use your ability with Don. How would you guys like to work on it together?
Don:	I'd like some of your ideas, Bud, but try to have some patience.

Bud: Let's talk after the group and we'll work something out.

Leader 2:   Don, let's talk some about what situations make you nervous, then Bud and the rest of us can come up with some specific ideas.

Keep these leaders' styles and behaviors in mind as we explain the various leadership concepts. We know that leader skill is one of the most critical elements in effective group counseling, and there are many possible leader skills and responsibilities. Group counseling requires adapting the skills of one-to-one counseling, as well as different skills. To date, training of group leaders has varied from virtually none to extensive formal education and supervised experience.

The Leader's Theory

Theory provides a framework for understanding group behavior and the events of group counseling. Without theory, we lack direction, and it would be difficult to explain client behavior. Theory also helps us choose our own behaviors in the group; leaders need reasons for choosing one action or approach over another. Theory provides a rationale for understanding the client and the group and gives the counselor direction (Lieberman, Lakin, & Whitaker, 1969). It helps the counselor examine client behavior and needs, set goals, plan, choose techniques, and evaluate. To determine the usefulness of a particular theory, the counselor must examine it in relation to each of the elements.

Client behavior and needs—What does the theory say about human behavior, the needs people bring to a group, and the concepts one uses to organize thoughts about human interaction? Does it help us make hypotheses about the clients and the group?

Setting goals—Theories differ as to goals for a group and individuals. Are the goals behavioral, attitudinal, interpersonal, or some combination of objectives? Leaders tend to select a theory whose goals are compatible with their concept of desirable group outcomes.

Making a plan—A useful theory suggests ways to achieve group goals. A plan can be derived from the theory's assumptions and concepts. The plan may include such factors as how many sessions are needed to bring about change, group composition, rules, desirable norms, and the role of the leader.

Leader techniques—What specific behaviors will help the group? A theory can suggest leader techniques such as aloofness vs. emotionality, degree of structure, frequency of verbalizations, interpretative level and frequency, use of structured exercises, facilitative vs. directive techniques, and so on. In practice, however, it is often difficult to trace leader behaviors to a theoretical stance (Parloff & Dies, 1977).

Evaluation—Theory can help at two evaluation points. The first is assessing the progress of an ongoing group toward meeting its goals. A theory helps the leader determine, for example, whether the group has bogged down or is at an expected stage of development. The second aspect of evaluation is determining whether a group has achieved its goals; a theory suggests how to measure achievement and degree of success.

Use of theory can be a building process whereby the counselor integrates previous experience, philosophical and sociological concepts, and knowledge of human behavior to arrive at a personal counseling theory. Before becoming counselors, people make implicit assumptions about human nature and form opinions of human behavior based on personal experience. Individuals also bring their own needs and personality into formation of a theory (Shoben, 1962; Stefflre & Matheny, 1968). Family, culture, and education are but a few of the influences on psychological theorists.

Counselors also acquire foundation for a theory from their professional training. By studying and applying contrasting counseling theories, one learns what works best. Few counselors accept one theory in its entirety; most rely heavily on one or two theories, and borrow from others.

Developing a theory is an ongoing process. It is best to be open to new ideas and to evaluate what one believes and practices. Formulating a useful theory requires continuous reading, training in workshops and courses, experiences as a leader, and discussion with colleagues.

Integrating various theories into a workable and systematic combination is an *eclectic* approach—a logical organization of related ideas from several theories. For example, a group counselor may rely heavily on the theories of Carl Rogers and the existentialists, but borrow from other theories as well. This counselor believes it is necessary to offer empathy, trust, respect, and genuineness for the group to meet its goals. He also believes only minimal structure and direction are necessary. Each person is responsible for his own behavior and has the potential to grow. Each member sets goals, usually of an interpersonal or self-concept type. This leader sometimes conceptualizes behavior in terms of psychoanalytic concepts—interpretation, resistance, unconscious forces—but does not verbalize them. He asks members to define their goals concretely and state how they can meet them. He also uses other behavioral concepts such as reinforcement and relaxation techniques and, occasionally, techniques from Gestalt, RET, and TA. With experience and added knowledge, the counselor continues to modify theory and technique.

Lieberman, Lakin, and Whitaker (1969) suggest guidelines in choosing a theoretical model.

1. A theory should explain group membership as members perceive it. How does a member's perception affect group process?

2. Theory must explain the leader's role and importance, including the source and extent of his influence and his motivation (needs, values, sociocultural factors).

3. Theory can explain the group's norms, values, and conformity as well as group stages and typical behaviors.

4. Theory can explain specific reasons for group success, the techniques and leadership style that are helpful under different conditions.

5. A general theory can describe the kinds of change to expect from group counseling.

6. A theory should explain how change transfers from the group to real-life situations.

7. A "help-giving" model is necessary to distinguish the efficacy of group counseling as opposed to other forms of intervention.

Leadership Style

Traditionally, leadership style falls into one of three categories: authoritarian, democratic, or laissez-faire (Lewin & Lippitt, 1938; Berman, 1982). This arbitrary classification is not wholly accurate, however, because a leader's style may vary according to the changing needs of one group or across different groups; yet the categories serve as a framework for examining leader behavior. A leaderless group implies no style, since the leader is not present; however, since it is often used in alternate sessions, it may be part of the leader's plan for the group.

Research and clinical experience offer functions, roles, typologies, and models of leadership (Lieberman, Yalom & Miles, 1973; Rogers, 1971) that help us understand specific group leadership behaviors.

Authoritarian, Democratic, and Laissez-faire Leaders

The authoritarian leader takes responsibility for the group by assuming expertise, knowledge, and ability. He believes members are in need of assistance and will look to the leader for guidance, direction, interpretations, correction, and planning. The leader does little, if any, self-disclosing. This is not a popular approach, although neophyte, poorly trained, and authoritarian counselors use it.

Yet, the authoritarian style, in modest degrees and specific situations, may be appropriate. Work with the moderately to severely mentally retarded or the chronically emotionally disturbed may require more direction and authority in the early stages—a somewhat parental stance.

The democratic leader takes less responsibility for the group, assuming members have information, expertise, and ability to contribute to the group process. Cooperation between leader and members is encouraged. One individual is not considered more knowledgeable than the others. The leader shares responsibility with participants; he acts primarily as a facilitator. This seems to be the most common leadership style in group counseling.

Democratic styles vary from the leader who hands over nearly all responsibility to the group to the leader who gives some structure and direction yet allows the group to make decisions within the limits of the general goals.

At the far end of the leadership style continuum is the laissez-faire leader. This leader gives members total responsibility for the group and expects them to set goals, develop norms, and find ways to meet goals. The "leader" is either another member or an observer; he may want to observe group dynamics, or fears taking on the leadership role, or hopes to be liked. With this kind of leader, the group usually never finds a sense of direction, so the laissez-faire style is rarely used in group counseling.

Leaderless Groups

Wolf (1963) first suggested leaderless groups in the 1940s. They are usually supplements to counseling sessions with a leader. Advocates (Wolf & Schwartz, 1962; Mullan & Rosenbaum, 1962) list a number of advantages:

1. Group members have greater opportunity to take responsibility and become less dependent on the leader.

2. Members are more likely to make decisions *they* wish to make.

3. Members become closer and friendlier.

4. Participation is less inhibited.

5. There is less competition for the leader's attention.

6. Members are more likely to be creative.

7. Members have more opportunities to act as therapeutic agents with others.

8. Transference and countertransference are likely to shift when the leader is no longer the primary focus of transference relationships.

9. Redistribution of influence and control may bring a new appraisal of the leader, authority figures, and group members.

Authorities disagree as to when leaderlessness should begin. It might begin in alternate sessions after the first one, or the leader may prefer to see a degree of cohesiveness develop before beginning leaderless sessions. The group needs a level of stability and an opportunity to first work through internal conflicts (Kadis, 1973; Berzon & Solomon, 1966).

Bieber (1957) and others express concern that the group becomes more social than therapeutic and that catharsis rather than interpretation and integration of material occurs. Some fear the group will act out in ways that are not beneficial to the members, or that more people will drop out. The maturity and needs of the members as well as the goals of the group determine how well they will function on their own.

Some propose self-directed groups. Cassette tapes provide directions. Self-directed groups have been used to develop interpersonal and management skills.

Leadership Roles

The two basic leadership roles are "technical expert" and "model-setting participant" (Yalom, 1970).

As *technical expert*, the counselor takes on the management functions of selecting members, setting meeting times, organizing rules, and ensuring an interactional pattern. This social engineering role incorporates various techniques, including asking for clarification, giving instruction, leading exercises, asking members to react to other's statements, and so on. The leader tries to get members to reveal their thoughts and feelings, to keep the group at work, to move it along, and to deal with problems. Through conscious and unconscious reactions, both positive and negative, to member behaviors, the leader acts as a "reinforcing agent." Participants learn to behave according to the influence of the leader. This responsibility should prompt leaders to plan what they expect from a group and behave in ways that will promote member growth. As a technical expert, the leader also interprets, to set norms for the group. Members can learn to apply this skill as effectively as the leader.

The leader is also a *participant* who *sets a model* for group members. Social learning research has demonstrated the effectiveness of leader behavior as an example for the group to emulate, and in fact, members do tend to behave in ways similar to the leader. Depending on the leader, the model may be more or less acceptable. Whether the leader is accepting, self-disclosing, and concerned with feelings and interpersonal relationships, or emotionally distant, defensive, and fearful, members will tend to behave similarly, thus affecting the group's success.

The counselor participates in one way or another. Should his role be as an equal participant or as an aloof leader? While opinions vary, most counselors reject either extreme. Self-disclosure, spontaneity, and showing concern and understanding humanize the leader, and make participants react to him more realistically as another human being with special expertise and knowledge. The leader is a contributing participant, while the group as a whole is the real agent of change.

Leadership Functions

The group leader's many possible activities may seem overwhelming to the beginner or even to the experienced counselor. The activities can perhaps best be organized into sets of functions. Dinkmeyer and Muro (1971) suggest a series of functions to help the group meet its goals. The first is *promoting cohesiveness*. A counselor must be "willing to take personal risks" in the process of fostering trust and cohesiveness. The counselor will have to work especially hard in the early sessions to help members perceive a sense of equality among themselves; he must be honest, open, and facilitate liking among members. Subgroups working at cross purposes should be avoided. Since frequent member interactions enhance cohesiveness, the leader needs to be sensitive to opportunities, or even create opportunities, for members to share feelings, attitudes, and opinions.

The second leader function is *summarizing*. Each group session will have one or more themes with a clear beginning and end. The leader can help the group find meaning and can facilitate progress by suggesting a summary of the group's discussion. Leader feedback to the group may take the form of identifying the theme, describing emotional level and interactions, or calling on members to summarize the discussion. Summaries are at first tentative, and should reflect the group's range of opinions and feelings.

A third leadership function Dinkmeyer and Muro describe is *resolving conflict*. Conflict inevitably occurs in a developing group because of "frustrated individual needs, conflicting goals, hidden agendas, disappointment in leader function, groping for structure, and anxiety over a new and novel situation." The leader must contend with divergent value systems and disruptive behavior. He pursues honest differences to a point where people can understand, if not agree with, one another, and must not permit unnecessary conflict such as teasing and scapegoating.

Guiding is a series of counseling techniques for promoting personal growth. Dinkmeyer and Muro list nine guiding activities:

1. *Tone setting.* Members to not automatically interact effectively; the leader can use self-disclosure to set a tone of expressing feeling and personal material. He can use exercises to promote listening, feedback, and interaction.

2. *Structuring and limit setting.* This reminds the group that they are there to share concerns and help with problems. Social interest and willingness to cooperate are emphasized.

3. *Blocking.* The counselor may need to block the efforts of group members; for example, if a subgroup asks the leader to get other members to quiet down, the leader demands that they express their own anger to the disruptive members.

4. *Linking.* The leader points out the similarity between statements or behaviors in terms of meaning. For example, if Faye lost her temper last week when the group accused her of keeping her feelings to herself, and this week June has yelled back at the group for the same reason, the counselor can say, "Faye and June have now both had experiences in which they became angry when the group demanded they reveal more of their feelings."

5. *Providing support.* The whole group or an individual may need the leader's support; recognizing someone's idea, encouraging a line of discussion, and approving of behavior are a few examples.

6. *Reflection.* These statements show the counselor's understanding of feelings and attitudes; he facilitates awareness by verbalizing what he detects in the participants.

7. *Protecting.* If a member is not ready to self-disclose or wants to minimize interaction, the counselor may need to step in protectively with a statement describing the group's demands or deflecting discussion to other members.

8. *Questions.* The leader may ask individuals or the whole group questions such as "What is happening in the group now?" "Who would like to react to that statement?" (Beginning counselors often use too many questions, so that members feel they are being interrogated.)

9. *Regulating.* The leader may have to moderate or, to some extent, control activity. He may need to quiet the monopolist so others have a chance to talk or remind members of ground rules and goals.

Lieberman, Yalom, and Miles (1973) conceptualize leadership functions differently. They present four functions, beginning with *emotional stimulation.* This function takes many forms, including challenging assumptions, revelation of feeling and attitudes, emphasizing release of emotions, and risk taking. The leader's personality and "intrusive modeling" stimulates the group experience. The second function, *caring,* includes protection, affection, friendship, and inviting support and feedback. The leader is accepting, warm, and genuine.

The third function Lieberman and his colleagues suggest is *meaning-attribution,* a primarily cognitive process whereby the leader gives concepts for understanding group behavior and how to bring about change. Cognitive labels can apply to group or individual behavior. When actual behaviors during a session demonstrate trust and closeness, the leader may describe it as a "cohesive" group that day. The last, the *executive function,* appears in activities such as setting goals, suggesting rules, pacing, managing time, interceding, and questioning.

There is considerable overlap between Dinkmeyer and Muro's and Lieberman's categories of functions. Lieberman's system has been used to characterize leaders in terms of the degree to which they are "executive," "caring" or "emotional stimulators," or "meaning-attributors." They found leaders most effective when they were moderate in amount of stimulation, high in caring, moderate in executive functions, and employed meaning-attribution. Leaders who were too high or too low in emotional stimulation and executive functions, and low in caring and meaning-attribution were less effective. Differences between group leaders did not relate to their theoretical stance.

Leadership Typologies

The Lieberman analysis also produced a set of six leadership typologies: energizers, providers, social engineers, impersonals, laissez-faire, and managers. *Energizers* are stimulating, high in caring, and high to moderate in use of the executive function. They have a strong belief system, are attached to a school of thought, are charismatic, and feel confident in guiding the group forward. *Providers* emphasize individuals, providing love, and giving information. They use caring and meaning-attribution most. *Social engineers* have a group focus and are concerned with how members deal with the social system. Meaning-attribution is emphasized, and leaders support and guide the group as a whole. *Impersonals* are aggressive stimulators, low on caring, meaning-attribution, and executive function. *Laissez-faire* leaders give little support or input and are not stimulating or guiding. There is some meaning-attribution; however, their ideas are not worked through using the other functions.

Managers use the executive function to an extreme, often in structured exercises. They exert maximum control over the group. The first three typologies were found to be the most successful.

Coleadership

The question of single versus multiple leaders for group counseling frequently arises. The efficacy of one over the other depends upon a number of factors, including economic considerations, advantages to the group, and counselor compatibility. Not every setting can afford the luxury of using two counselors in one group, since it might mean that one less counseling group would be available for students or clients. Group needs, membership, and goals sometimes suggest advantages in having two leaders. If a group has multiple leaders, they must respect each other and be able to work harmoniously with the group.

Multiple leadership advantages depend upon the group's composition, goals, and setting. It might be advantageous to have male and female leaders so that members can explore relationships with someone of the same and of the opposite sex, especially in a group with a heterosexual-relationship theme, although it can be helpful in most types of groups. In a vocational group discussing work behavior with peers and supervisors, some members may have trouble with male or female authority figures. The male and female leaders can serve as role models and provide opportunities to relate to a father or mother figure or to sisters, brothers, and lovers.

Coleaders also increase the chance that group members will identify or feel comfortable with a leader. A member may see one leader as a friend but have less emotional compatibility with the other leader. As they vie for attention or approval, members are more likely to feel accepted by one or the other leader. In general, the range of leader-member interactions increases. Members also benefit from more accurate and complete feedback; one leader is likely to observe dynamics the other leader misses. When the two leaders' abilities are well coordinated, group members benefit from the best of both. The quality of the leaders' relationship is crucial to group success; poor coordination and conflict is a poor model and has a destructive effect. Of course, some disagreement and difference in styles is appropriate.

There are also advantages to both leaders (Dick, Lessier, & Whiteside, 1980). Group dynamics are so complex and occur so quickly that it is virtually impossible for one leader to observe and assimilate everything; one can let the other take the lead while concentrating on the group's behavior and personal reactions to the group. A good team shifts back and forth in processing what is happening. Coleaders also receive feedback from each other, for which they need self-confidence and openness to constructive criticism. And, of course, merely observing the other leader's behavior is a source of information and learning.

Unfortunately, it is difficult to determine compatibility and complementary roles before the group actually meets, but coleaders should plan as much as possible to avoid problems. Coleadership is not always indicated for a group, and individual leadership is easier in many ways. One avoids competition, hurt feelings, jealousy, sharing rewards, and possibly threatening feedback. Multiple leadership almost always implies that one will be the primary leader and the other secondary. It is not easy to work out who will have greater authority, who will make final decisions, and to whom the group will listen. Leaders have different styles, experience, values, and expectations; each person must feel useful, draw on his strength, and receive rewards for a leader's work.

Certain techniques and qualifications enhance the likelihood of quality coleadership (Gans, 1957; Weinstein, 1971; Corey, 1981; Napier & Gerstenfeld, 1983):

1. Working within the limits of individual strengths and weaknesses

2. Avoiding conflict over control and authority

3. Experience in group work (except in training situations)

4. Flexibility in approach and adaptation to the other leader's style

5. Similar ability levels

6. Mutual respect, trust, and understanding

7. Recognition of each other's strengths, limits, and style

8. Anticipation of varying degrees of equality, group acceptance, and effectiveness

9. Predetermination of expectations, goals, and styles

10. Time for processing feedback, and planning

Some leaders find it advantageous to meet immediately after the group session while events are still fresh in their minds to share perceptions and bring out problems and issues. They can also meet briefly before sessions to reflect on the previous week, share additional thoughts, and decide plans or shifting roles. They can also let each other know how they're feeling in terms of fatigue or personal distractions that could affect counseling performance and agree how to handle it in the session.

The Leader's Personal Characteristics

Leader personality is a key element in the group counseling process (Shoben, 1962). Counselor characteristics vary in importance depending upon the theoretical framework and the type of group.

We have already discussed the "model-setting participant" as one role for the group leader (Yalom, 1970). This role calls for certain leader characteristics; for example, for group members to interact in a "confrontive, forthright, nondefensive, and nonjudgmental manner," the leader must exhibit this behavior. A counselor should offer acceptance and appreciation of members' strengths and problems. Yalom also suggests interpersonal honesty and spontaneity congruent with members' needs. The leader may sometimes have to restrain feelings, but rather than present a picture of perfection, the leader needs to admit errors and fallibility. No matter what the counselor's personal characteristics, members will, because of past experiences, add distorted perceptions of intimacy, competition, aggression, superhuman powers, and so forth that become part of the group process to be discussed and clarified.

Dinkmeyer and Muro (1971) list eight traits of an effective group counselor. First is the perception "by group members as being with them and for them as individuals." Members believe the counselor cares about each of them, and does not favor some over others. Second, the leader is "able to operate within the affective and developmental phases of the group." Awareness of group phases and ability to facilitate the phases are important, as, for example, offering acceptance rather than confrontation in the first phase. Third, Dinkmeyer and Muro believe group counselors need to be positive individuals.

Fourth, effective counselors are able to "affix a status role to group members"—that is, the counselor helps each member feel she has high status in the group. Fifth, the counselor is both specialist and artist—professionally knowledgeable, with the creative talents of a leader. Sixth, the counselor's "perception is influenced by the gestalt of the field," implying a desire for personal and interdependent relationships with group members. Seventh, effective leaders also allow participants autonomy, since the goal is to increase clients' independence. Last, leaders are most effective when their style and work level matches that of the group members. Dinkmeyer and Muro also consider flexibility, ability to develop cohesion, development of spontaneous interaction, and ability to understand member needs as important group counselor traits.

According to Corey (1981), the techniques of the counselor and the characteristics of group members are not enough to explain successful groups. To promote growth in the group, the leader must be living a growth-oriented life, and must have the characteristics he is trying to promote in the group. Corey's list of ideal characteristics includes these:

1. *Presence*—to respond and be moved by the painful and joyful experiences of others

2. *Personal power*—awareness of one's influence on others, and self-confidence

3. *Courage*—taking risks, admitting error, confronting with respect and caring, acting on intuition, sharing feelings, sharing power

4. *Willingness to confront oneself*—questioning one's needs, values, attitudes

5. *Self-awareness*—knowing one's needs, feelings, beliefs, weaknesses, strengths

6. *Sincerity*—"sincere interest in the well-being of others" and their ability to develop

7. *Authenticity*—to be real, congruent, and honest with others

8. *Sense of identity*

9. *Belief in group process*

10. *Enthusiasm*

11. *Inventiveness and creativity*

12. *Stamina*

Napier and Gershenfeld (1983) explain characteristics they consider important in group training and facilitating. Self-understanding can be the basis for excellent leadership; its lack is a major limiting factor. Complexities and subtleties of the group process will be lost to the counselor who is "unaware of personal needs, fears, and the influence of past life experiences." Personal biases interfere with accurate perceptions. To remain aware of one's own needs, the counselor must be open to personal feedback. Openness to feedback can promote leader growth and responsiveness to group members' needs. Napier and Gershenfeld also emphasize the counselor's intuitive ability to organize group information. He must be aware of how he comes across to the group. Dress, tone of voice, language, and expression of feelings all influence the group's attitudes, behavior, and outcome, to a greater extent than the technical sophistication and design of the group. In essence, the counselor's needs, values, self-understanding, and demeanor can be the major facilitating or limiting force in the group.

Kottler (1983) presents a "self-actualized" model for the group leader. He describes the counselor as busy, concerned with the well-being of others and oneself, an "action-oriented truth seeker" who takes risks, and is in an ongoing condition of positive change. These high standards for one's personal life relate to one's effectiveness as a group leader. The more personally skilled one becomes, the more professionally capable one becomes. The counselor must be open to self-understanding as the issues of group members unfold. In becoming better able to solve personal conflicts, the counselor also becomes better at working with group members' problems. Kottler emphasizes ongoing personal mastery and desirable characteristics such as self-confidence, humor, risk taking, honesty, energetic enthusiasm, and compassion.

We thus find general agreement as to the characteristics of an effective leader. Honesty and openness imply willingness to accept feedback and the leader's self-examination of needs and values to determine their impact on the group. These qualities suggest the leader's interest in personal growth and that of others. The leader can be nonjudgmental and accepting, values personal relationships, and has positive relationships. Behavior patterns are not narrow or rigid; rather, the counselor takes risks, is flexible and spontaneous, and has a healthy degree of self-confidence and enthusiasm.

Leader Techniques and Skills

Although roles, functions, personality, and technique overlap, we will define techniques as the specific procedures, detailed activities, and methods the group leader uses. Skills relate to the ability to carry out leader techniques and functions; roles and functions are more general descriptions of counselor activities or style. For example, evaluation is one function of the leader; techniques are the specific ways he evaluates.

The leader and the group have an interactive effect on successful outcome. Some writers, such as Napier and Gershenfeld (1983) believe the leader contributes more toward the group's effectiveness and success than any other factor. We can safely say that events in the group do not occur by accident; the leader's skill influences the participants' behavior. This power is a welcome responsibility to the counselor who wishes to positively affect other people's growth. At the same time, leader influence has little usefulness without the therapeutic effect of the group itself. Although the leader sets the process in motion, the group actually does the work; the group becomes the agent of change. We call on the leader's skill to facilitate the power of the group.

There is no formula to tell the counselor what to say or do in a given situation. Each group and each interaction is unique in some way. Less experienced or less competent leaders tend to rely on artificial techniques, "games," and pat answers. Knowledge of group dynamics, of group member needs, of oneself, and of principles of human behavior are the foundation for group skills and techniques.

Skills

Leadership skills can be artifically grouped according to those for (1) group organization, (2) group process, and (3) evaluation. The first organizational skill is the ability to accurately assess group needs. The pregroup interview, intake forms, and discussion during the first group session combine for this assessment. The skill of establishing clear and agreed-upon goals requires careful listening and coordination with all the group members. In this early stage of the group, the leader must be able to *plan* and *design* a group and group experiences that will benefit the members.

After the group begins, the counselor must draw on numerous skills. These process-related skills build cohesion and ultimate behavior change. Facilitative skills are basic to most group counseling stiuations, and include active listening, communicating understanding, showing respect for each member, and behaving genuinely. More active skills are interpretation, confrontation, questioning, suggestion, and persuasion. These active skills require timing and tact; the client must be ready to hear what you have to say, and is more likely to accept what is communicated warmly and caringly.

Summarizing shows the group what has occurred to give a general frame of reference for their behavior. The counselor pulls together important elements to give meaning to actions. Supportiveness requires the leader to be fully present with each participant, attending to their concerns, and ready to empathize. This does not imply condoning all behavior; confrontation may be necessary at the same time. The client particularly needs support at times of crises, conflicts, and anxiety about risk-taking. Initiating and redirecting skills relate to control of the group. The leader may open new themes or new ways to look at old issues. The group may need direction away from a well-covered or irrelevant issue to one they can address with greater energy. Other process skills include feedback, protecting members, and blocking.

The final skills are evaluation, recommendation, and referral. Evaluation is an ongoing process whereby the leader communicates individual and group progress toward objectives, during individual sessions and at the termination of the group. The final evaluation leads to recommendations as to how a member might continue to work toward goals. Certain members will want referrals to another group, to individual counseling, or to other community services.

Techniques

To begin the group and each session the counselor should have members talk about what they want from the group and how they feel about being there. The leader can express her purpose in being there and self-disclose immediate feelings about the group. This invitation and model often sparks discussion about what everyone is there for. Open-ended questions can also get the group started: "What are your feelings about being here today? What would everyone like to get out of this group?" The leader should be open about what the group can accomplish, the limitations, and what is likely to occur and not occur, and everyone should talk about fears, hopes, apprehensions, and desires. Warm-up exercises help members handle the same questions, with pairs reporting back to the others for a full-group discussion. The first session sets the stage for subsequent meetings. Members need to feel they can express their thoughts and feelings, and that the leader will recognize each person.

Individual sessions can also begin with a member's statement of his expectations for that day. The leader can ask about reactions or unfinished work from a previous session. The group can thus deal first with hidden agendas between members or between members and the leader and with experiences between sessions. Members can report progress or problems related to homework assignments. The leader should also feel free to bring up her reflections on the previous session or what is on her mind right then. The counselor can use these techniques to enhance member participation:

- Encouraging talk during the pregroup session

- Making participation a goal for each member

- Giving new members a positive attitude and sense of curiosity about the group

- Welcoming and introducing members as they arrive

- Avoiding the center of attention by getting members to speak to each other, not always to the leader

- Conveying the notion that everyone's contribution is important

- Letting members know that different ideas are welcome

- Calling on quiet members to ask for their thoughts or feelings

When the group is quieter than usual, the leader can divide them into smaller groups of three to five and give each a task, such as discussing a question or issue. The key to full participation is giving everyone an opportunity to speak and bringing into the open their reservations about participating.

Groups sometimes become lethargic as they continue in the same mode over several sessions. A change of pace and variety provide creative tension (Napier & Gershenfeld, 1983). For example:

1. The leader can increase *intensity* by giving the group 30 minutes to complete a 60-minute task. Give people limited time blocks in which to talk, followed by a period of listening. Give a block of time to discuss an issue. Allow a block of time to reflect on the group's work.

2. The leader needs to gauge the degree of *risk taking* a group and a member are ready for. Pushing too soon for intimacy puts people on the defensive, but the leader can challenge members to try things they seem ready for but reluctant about.

3. The leader may offer a presentation on a group-process concept, a fifteen-minute debate allowing questions only, with no responses, or a film.

4. The counselor can vary the type of interaction. The group might list talkative and quiet members, then have the talkative members only listen. Or, two group members who seem the most different might be put to work together on a task.

5. The counselor can also change the physical setting.

Changing seating arrangements, using or changing the food and drink, and alternating the meeting place can keep the group alive and awake. The leader must select creative changes that will have a positive effect; for one group, a break in the middle of the session may be refreshing; for another, it may cause avoidance of an issue that lay below the surface of discussion. Creativity and good planning alleviate some of the unproductive characteristics of group meetings—that they are often too orderly, too predictable, lacking in humor, too cognitive, too planned, boring, lack risk taking, nonsupportive, dominated by a few, and lack worthwhile outcome.

Resistance from the group can be dealt with subtly or confrontively. The leader usually begins with gentle statements such as, "What do you suppose is happening in the group right now?" This puts the responsibility for verbalizing the problem onto the group. With a more direct statement such as, "We seem to be having some trouble getting started here," the leader makes the judgment that there is a problem. The next level is interpretation: "As soon as we got to the topic of sharing deep feelings with other people, everyone quieted down and the subject changed." Normally the leader begins subtly so as to let the group do the work; interpretations can make members become even more self-protective.

Resistance is sometimes an effort to avoid negative behavior; they feel they face enough unnecessary criticism and competition in their everyday life. The leader can prevent this kind of resistance by breaking the group into pairs to list threatening behaviors that would turn them off to the group (Napier & Gershenfeld, 1983). There will be considerable agreement among members, which will then set a norm for positive interaction. Of course, the leader must be careful that the group does not set a norm preventing criticism or confrontation. Negativism can also be diminished by asking participants to focus on an issue's positive aspects. For example, discouraged job seekers can be asked what they have learned or gained from the experience.

The leader can use techniques that require action from group members. *Psychodrama* (Moreno & Kipper, 1968) forces members to act out their concerns within the group context. For instance, an alcoholic may play himself and assign other group members to play his *alter ego* and other significant people in his life; the group leader helps stage the social situations. A simplified version of psychodrama, *role-playing* is usually a one-on-one interaction in which one member acts out a real life scene with another group member, such as practicing assertiveness with one's boss. Asking a member to play the role of another member or a significant person in his life is *role reversal*, as when a member who shows little concern for the plight of a single woman with three children is asked to play the role of the woman while other members play the three children.

Modeling, discussed in other chapters, can vary from the natural behavior of the leader, to role playing a desired behavior for someone, to the use of films and videotapes. Modeling techniques are especially useful in building social and work skills.

Summary

The effective leader is able to integrate a dynamic set of person characteristics, experiences, and training so as to fill the roles and functions the group needs. Specific knowledge, skills, and creative application of techniques are necessary to facilitate cohesion and eventual success in reaching goals. The leader and the group share responsibility for behavior change and growth. The leader provides conditions, structure, and model; the members must work to reach their goals.

Returning to counseling excerpts at the beginning of the chapter, we can apply some of the leadership characteristics we have examined. Notice how Leader 1 is somewhat authoritarian in the first session; he is also a manager, a weak summarizer, somewhat impersonal, initially unaware of leadership behavior, does not share leadership with members, and lacks process skills. As the sessions progress, the leader realizes members pay less and less attention to his directives, opinions, and parental values. His strategy in the later session was to assume a more aloof and distant relationship with members by interacting minimally. The leader was unable to become involved in the group's affective development, was excessively task oriented, and lacked a positive approach.

Leader 2 was clearly concerned with members' feelings, attitudes, and behavior. He set a model for active listening, empathic responses, and respect, at times providing support and at other times, guidance. Healthy confrontation occurred at the beginning of the sixth session, in contrast to Leader 1's early and inappropriate confrontation in the first session. Leader 2 demonstrated caring, enthusiasm, and sensitivity. He occasionally directed statements to the group as a whole, encouraging a group rather than an individual or one-on-one process. He asked members to help each other. Leader 2 was more a facilitator and was accepted as a member of the group; he did not coerce, but reflected the expressions of participants. These characteristics reflect training as well as the personal characteristics of one who does not impose values and personal needs and wishes to see group members develop interdependent relationships. Coleadership under these circumstances can be quite difficult, and in this group's case, if Leader 1 is not able to respond more effectively, it may be better to have only Leader 2 work with them.

Discussion Questions

1. How is theory useful to the functioning of the group leader?

2. What effect do various leader styles seem to have on group performance?

3. What leadership roles and functions seem to "fit" for you? Which ones seem to be effective for other people? How do you think members would react to the various roles and functions?

4. How does a leader evaluate the necessary skills for leading various types of groups? What qualifications do you feel you need in leading groups?

5. What do you believe to be the most important personal characteristics of a group leader?

6. Show how various leader skills (such as listening, evaluation, persuasion, support, initiating, confronting) affect the group. What skills do you think you have developed or could most readily develop?

7. On a continuum from high structure to very little structure, where do you fall in terms of what you would be most comfortable with as a group leader?

11

A Framework for Planning and Assessment

In this chapter, we will examine the role of assessment in establishing and evaluating group counseling. *Assessment* refers to the various methods of collecting data and information about members and the whole group to help us comprehend group stages from initiation through the determination of effectiveness. Assessment includes interviews, observation, analysis of audio- or audiovisual tapes, standardized tests, and self-report forms. We will consider assessment at these group management stages: determining individual and group needs, establishing goals, analyzing group process, and evaluating outcome. We normally assess stages in that order; that is, we first determine needs, then set goals, conduct the counseling, and, finally, look at the relative success of the group experience.

A Systems Framework

The systems approach is widely used in human services to demonstrate the interactive effect of levels of human functioning. We relate to and are affected by many systems—the individual system (attitudes toward self), the interpersonal system (relationships with others), the small group system (belongingness to groups), and the community system. Levels of functioning range from interpersonal relationships to one's place in society.

A source of difficulty in determining group counseling needs, goals, and success is the complexity of the group process and environmental factors that interact to form complicated human behavior. We want to know the extent to which the leader brings about change, how much one participant affects the entire group's progress, and the extent to which the group milieu affects individuals. We also want to know how attitudes toward the agency, whether a school or mental health center, for example, affect members' progress. Finally, how does counseling success depend upon the environment to which members return between group sessions? We can schematically approach the variables that affect group needs, goals, process, and outcome by placing them in artificially separate categories. These categories interact both internally and with one another to form a highly complex set of reciprocal influences.

Systems theory provides an overall scheme for bringing together the many entities in human relationships that form and interact to define a system. One significant tenet is that change in one part of a system tends to bring change in another part. It is fundamental to systems theory that people process information about one another in a way that makes us interdependent; any time two or more people interact, they have an impact on each other that affects them individually and often affects their other human relationships (Newcomb, 1961; Capell, 1979, Durkin, 1981). Figure 11-1 shows how we can diagram a systematic approach to assessing group counseling. The levels of analysis are borrowed from Capell (1979) who did not apply it to group counseling, but we can incorporate the various models of group counseling into this framework.

The *individual level* in a human system can be seen in a person's attitude, self-esteem, psychosomatic problems, nightmares, self-satisfaction, and so on. We can immediately see the artificiality in breaking out these individual elements; for instance, we know that self-esteem depends to some extent on others' perceptions of us. Although

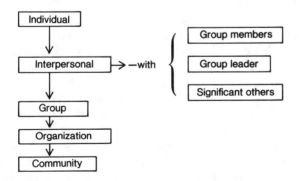

Figure 11-1 Diagramming a Systematic Approach to Group Counseling

each level interacts with the others, it is nonetheless possible to view self-esteem as an individual variable for measurement purposes. Essentially, self-esteem is one's positive or negative feelings and attitudes toward oneself. Remember that in setting up individual and group counseling goals, many fall into the individual category.

Many group counseling theories consider the individual level subject to change; the behaviorist might attempt to reduce psychosomatic symptoms, while Rogerian and developmental theorists might set promotion of higher self-esteem as a goal, and analysts and TA counselors work toward insight as a legitimate individual goal. In many groups, the intrapsychic goals are of primary importance, and the other levels of "interpersonal" and "group" are secondary to satisfying the primary goal. For example, one can imagine the group as the setting where members wish to learn to feel better about themselves; the group becomes the medium for raising self-esteem. The primary measure of outcome is self-esteem; however, one may also wish to measure interpersonal dynamics and group process to see how they might have contributed to success.

Interpersonal change involves three dimensions. First, individual group members have one-to-one relationships with one another. Second, individual members interact with the group leader. Third, each member has interpersonal relationships with significant people outside the group. Interpersonal relationships in one dimension affect the other two. For example, a member may be angry with the leader, but, fearing confrontation with the leader, directs the anger toward another group member. Change and learning that result from interpersonal relationships in the group will be generalized to improve relationships outside the group.

Virtually all theoretical positions advocate improved *interpersonal relationships* to one degree or another. Gestaltists may help one discover personal goals; the TA leader pursues the goal of honest, straightforward relationships. Behavioral group counselors sometimes focus on learning social skills. In assessing group counseling, interpersonal relationships are often considered the basis of what transpires at the other levels. They seem to be the keystone for understanding the "individual," the "group," and the higher levels of human systems. In an interactional approach that studies many variables in terms of their relationship with and effect on one another, however, one level does not unidimensionally cause phenomena to occur at the other levels. So, we identify the interpersonal variables of group counseling (assertiveness, empathy, warmth, withdrawal) and attempt to measure them in relation to the variables at other levels (self-confidence, group cohesiveness). One can begin at any level, identify the variable of interest, then attempt to show how it relates to and affects the others. If you are interested in group cohesiveness, for example, you might study how assertiveness or self-confidence grew as cohesiveness developed. Conceptualizing group process and outcome in terms of interaction rather than causative effects allows the leader or evaluator to understand what occurs in the broader scheme of human behavior. It also demonstrates how a simple analysis of one or a few variables must be placed in the framework of highly involved, interacting systems. For example, if we wish to evaluate the success of a group designed to help mothers learn child management skills, success will depend on the combination of many variables at the different levels of human systems: at the individual level, each member's motivation, self-confidence, intelligence, and so forth; how they feel about each other, the leader, and others, and their spouses' support of group involvement at the group level; their fears or the possible stigma attached to coming to the agency or school for the sessions at the organization level; and the belief that most may not believe the group is worthwhile and should be offered, at the community level. If the group is successful, it is helpful to know how these and other factors interact and contribute to the outcome of improved child management skills; there is not a simple causal relationship between presenting information on child management and increasing parental competence.

Group level factors such as cohesiveness, size, purpose, and roles are unique to group counseling. The influence of the group itself becomes the focus of attention. Some dynamics are unique to groups in general and to the group under study; something may happen in a group that would not happen in a one-to-one or large-group situation. We have examined the unique features of a group, such as status, power, sense of belonging, and norms, in chapter 8. We mention them here to remind you that study of the group must be placed in the context of the total human system.

Groups form within *organizations,* and we normally find more than one group in an organization. If we study an organization (a school, agency, institution, or business), we want to know as much as we can about the groups and people in that organization, and how the organization fits and functions in the community. Since our focus is on the counseling group, we are most interested in how the group and its members relate to the organization. In terms of evaluation, we may want to know how the organization contributes to the success of the group. Do other groups function compatibly with this one? We may also want to know whether our group contributes to the organization's objectives. Is it set up and run so as to be compatible with the organization's policies? For example, group counseling for alcoholics who attend a vocational rehabilitation center can be set up in many ways. To relate to the mission of the rehabilitation agency, must it have a strictly vocational emphasis? If the group has a therapeutic effect and many members abstain from drinking but still do not find jobs, does it mean the group has failed? Perhaps objectives have not been realistic, or techniques were not suitable to the agency and group objectives. In any case, group leaders and program evaluators must examine the group in its organizational setting and integrate group elements with organization elements.

We can use the same example in relation to the *community*. We can assume there are many different types of groups for alcoholics. Which community organization is best suited to offer which groups? Who decides what groups are offered? It is possible to have a coordinated community effort to offer five different groups. An alcoholism center might provide a group for alcoholics who are "drying out" and a second group at a later stage that is primarily educational. The mental health center might provide a therapeutic group for alcoholics, and Alcoholics Anonymous has its own support group. Finally, the vocational rehabilitation agency may provide a vocational group to explore careers, training and education, adjustment to work, and job-seeking skills. Thus, evaluating group success requires examination of the degree of coordination in the community, the appropriateness of the group in view of the existing community services, and the expertise of staff in the various agencies. A group is not an entity in itself; it is one intervention in one agency in a community that has certain resources.

Sociocultural Influences

The social milieu is sometimes included as another level in the human system, but as an influence on group process and change, it permeates all levels and defies placement in a hierarchy of categories. Awareness of the many social forces that affect each level of the human systems is crucial both to effective counseling and to accurate evaluation. Societal norms, mores, life styles, expected behavior, values, customs, and beliefs influence the individual, human relations, groups, organization, and community systems. While our concern is primarily with the social forces in the small group, we must be aware of group members' sociocultural background because of its strong influence on behavior. Without knowing participants' sociocultural backgrounds and values, the group leader may misinterpret, misunderstand, or use ineffective technique; the program evaluator may measure inappropriate goals or miss the actual effect of the group. We will illustrate sociocultural influences with three examples: individualism, male-female relationships, and racial attitudes. Remember that the group leader must be careful not to make value judgments about group members' sociocultural background or beliefs; respect for life style and norms is necessary to develop trust and meet the goals of individual members.

Individualism is a traditional American value. Most people in our society expect the individual to carry his share of the load and be responsible for himself; ideally, no one should have to depend on others. The values attached to work (high quality, self-reliance, and independence) are similar to those of individualism, the first level of human systems. In interpersonal relations, individualism dictates that we watch out for ourselves, avoid being taken advantage of, and assert our rights. In the group, the interaction style would be much the same—taking responsibility for individual behavior. The group is useful in meeting the needs of individualism.

In many Oriental cultures, however, individualism is not an acceptable value; the group or community is the valuable entity. One conforms to the expectations of the group, which in turn bases its expectations on the traditional customs and norms of that culture. Decisions are in the interest of the group, often made by an authority who follows the tradition of the culture. Each person has a role and status prescribed by tradition. Assertiveness is acceptable only in those of high status who are carrying out the values of the culture. Consequently, an individualistic American and a traditional Oriental in a group will function very differently from one another. Each will have different goals, and the leader will have to relate differently to each. The individualistic American tends to view the leader as an equal with specialized training; the Oriental tends to accord greater respect to the leader, behave deferentially, expect the leader to make decisions, and work more energetically for group rather than individual goals. At the interpersonal level, the American might become annoyed with the perceived submissiveness of the Oriental, while the Oriental might be confused by the American's individuality at the possible expense of the group.

The nature of male-female relationships varies significantly across cultures and subcultures. In some subcultures, roles for each sex are clearly and specifically defined. In many Indian tribes, for instance, the women grew the crops and tended to the children while men hunted and fought the wars. In counseling groups, one may find members who believe the woman should stay at home, clean the house, and take care of the children. Certain subcultural groups (and to some extent, our society as a whole) believe in a double standard for men and women. Men have more freedom as to what behavior is acceptable. In some cultures, women are valued no more than cattle. On the other hand, we know that women are also often protected, glorified, cared for, respected, and prized by men. Each group member brings personal values regarding male-female relationships, and these values influence relationships in the group. Different values in a group would be evident in the interaction between a traditional Hispanic man and a "modern" American woman. Although one must be careful of stereotypes, it is easy to imagine the Hispanic man as polite and courteous, while expecting the woman to defer to his opinions or decisons. She, on the other hand, is likely to express her opinion and do what she wants.

Racism and bigotry emerge as forces in most counseling groups, sometimes subtly and sometimes overtly. In addition to group member backgrounds, the actual mix of the group contributes to racism and bigotry as an issue. Where membership is cross-cultural, the significance of this dimension increases. Also, the purpose of the group determines to some extent the importance of racial factors. In groups that are more task-oriented than psychotherapeutic, racism and bigotry are a less important issue. For example, a vocational group that is learning to analyze the job market and acquire job interview skills will be less concerned with members' racial attitudes (the group level of human systems) than with the attitudes of employers (organization and community level of human systems). A therapeutic counseling group with members of different cultural backgrounds is more likely to discuss racial attitudes and feelings, unless the participants choose to avoid this important aspect of the group process.

Thus, sociocultural factors add another dimension to the difficulty of assessing change or success in group counseling. The evaluator needs to consider members' values in establishing group goals. It may not be legitimate to set a goal of greater independence for people who value interdependence and allegiance to the family.

We have thus far focused on social factors from outside the counseling group; there are also social factors within the group that help us understand group dynamics. Social influences in the group are a set of distinguishing variables that set the group process apart from other intervention strategies. These influences are neither positive or negative; they are characteristics that give people the opportunity to learn in a social setting where change can occur.

Each time a group forms, it has original qualities that are a function of the members themselves, and special characteristics evolve from the dynamics of those people. The social mix is different each time. Even if A and B both belong to the same two groups, their interaction is likely to differ slightly in each group because of each group's unique qualities. Members exercise some influence on one another associated with the atmosphere and norms of the particular group. One group may be slow in starting and resistant to opening up to expression of feelings, while another group may take very little time to warm up. The combination of personality types is one explanation of the difference between the two groups.

Status is another social influence in group counseling. One-upmanship often appears in one-to-one relationships; in group settings, this and other status games can be played, but the possible combinations become quite complex. In other words, in a group of eight to twelve people, there are myriad combinations of highest to lowest status. One or two may be considered the most intelligent, and the remainder of the group may establish a hierarchy of intellect. Yet not every member will have the same rank-ordering of intellect status. A sociogram can reveal how each group member assigns status to other group members. The same group may form a separate status hierarchy for beauty.

A third social influence, that of member role, emerges as the group progresses. As participants get to know and assess each other, each member is given or takes on their individual role. One may play the role of group clown, another of wiseman who speaks few but important words. Another becomes temporary coleader, and still another becomes the dependent one who must be taken care of. The leader must be acutely aware of the learned and assigned roles in the group because they can be either a destructive or helpful force.

Many types of stigma have a debilitating effect on the member and the group. Stigma attached to membership, such as a group for the mentally retarded, can sabotage the potential for good. Someone with a physical disability may be stigmatized and devalued as a member. Members of a counseling group in a prison will look down on the participant who is a child molester.

Cliques almost always form in groups. Several members may feel they have something in common, or some may band together to cope with other members. When cliques clash with other group members and become a means of holding power over others, they may have a deleterious effect; where they are used as a means of supporting, showing concern, or sharing commonalities, they can enhance group participation.

The final social influence, transference, is not used in the classic psychoanalytic sense. Here we mean that people learn interpersonal and social styles from the important people around them and bring these styles to the group. Feelings and attitudes toward people from the past or outside the group are often transferred to group members or to the leader. A man who has very positive attitudes toward women may now have and eventually express positive feelings toward the female group members. A young man who has had trouble with school officials or the local police may transfer his anger toward them to the leader or other adult members of the group.

A crucial question for the group leader and the program evaluator is: "What is the nature of these and other social influences at the beginning of the group and how can we evaluate their impact?" We can immediately see a problem, because most of these social factors do not emerge until the group is well along; thus, we cannot define the factors from the beginning, much less determine the nature and degree of influence. These variables expose themselves as part of the group process.

Measurement of Group Need

One must assess group counseling needs not only for planning but also to maximize effectiveness and demonstrate the usefulness of a particular intervention strategy. Careful planning and evaluation is required to professionally justify offering the service. One must first determine whether there is a need for the service, and if so, exactly what the needs are. Next comes planning, and third is actual service delivery. We are interested here in how the group process can be measured, to define precisely what occurs in group counseling that contributes to or detracts from success. Evaluation of the service, which usually occurs after termination and sometimes during delivery, is the fourth stage, when we are concerned with indications of progress, client change, or benefits to participants.

Needs Assessment

Group counseling usually takes place in an agency or institutional setting, although many groups function with private counselors and therapists. Whatever the setting, it is helpful to assess the needs of the particular population so as to provide appropriate services. In a mental health or rehabilitation agency, information on incidence and prevalence of needs helps to plan for the number and type of groups. In a secondary school, college, prison, or mental retardation facility, one can survey specific requirements. An early question to ask in designing a needs assessment is, "What are we going to measure?" That is, what information do we wish to obtain from the population? In a school, for example, we may want to know about acting out, social withdrawal, career information, or heterosexual relationships. In a rehabilitation setting, we may want to know the number of disabled people in the community, how many request services, what services they want most, and whether they want self-help, therapeutic, or career counseling groups. In a mental health setting, we may ask about the types and frequency of problems, how many clients seem appropriate for group counseling, and whether they are interested in group counseling. Because we want accurate information, the quality and relevance of the questions are vital.

Deciding *how* to measure needs is also critical because it affects the type of information we receive. Several alternatives are available: first, key informants can provide information. In a school, this may include certain teachers, administrative staff, and counseling personnel. In rehabilitation or mental health offices, the staff of referring agencies can answer questions. Community forums and committees of community leaders are another source of information. A second method of needs assessment is to utilize data already available, or to set up a data collection method within the setting. Agencies collect data on their clientele to document certain needs and problems; in other cases, standard data can be extrapolated, analyzed, and utilized to fill information gaps. School counselors can fill out weekly data sheets with number of students seen, presenting problems, and so on. The same type of demographic and problem-based data can be collected in nearly every setting. Community, state, and national sources of information are also available.

A third method of assessing needs is to survey the target population itself. Although the most costly, it is usually the most valid method. In a school or college, for example, one can select a sample of students and administer a needs survey to the representative group. A sufficiently large sample communicates student needs as they perceive them. A rehabilitation agency can survey a representative sample of disabled persons in the community or of new clients at the time of the intake interview.

The most important aspect of needs assessment is to collect and interpret accurate information for planning and decision making. Choices as to number and type of counseling groups depend on the availability of information regarding client need, although client need is only one factor in planning for group counseling. There always seem to be more needs than resources to meet them; likewise, whenever mental health services become available, a need for those services seems to magically appear and grow. Expertise, availability, and preference of professional staff, and social-political pressure on an agency, enter into program planning decisions. Nonetheless, needs assessment provides an important indicator for setting priorities in group counseling. Needs as perceived by professional and community leaders and clientele and other survey data offer a significant source of information for planning group counseling.

A final aspect of needs assessment occurs when the leader is preparing potential members for the first session. Although a few counselors prefer to know very little about group members previous to the first session, it is usually best to have at least minimal information. Therapeutic counseling groups are sometimes offered to the public with no screening or information gathering before the first session. In other cases, the group leader has a narrowly defined group purpose (such as to lose weight) and wants only certain types of people with specified needs, motiviation, and related information available (for example, a recent physical examination). The extent of assessment of member needs is a function of group goals, leader preference, and agency policy.

Although the general group goal may be established before selecting members, individual goals are normally formulated prior to or during the first session. Screening interviews or the first session can be used for setting individual goals, and an assessment at this time is recommended. The individual needs assessment (1) stimulates group members to clarify their needs and articulate them to others, (2) moves clients toward setting up measurable objectives, giving them each a goal and purpose for the group, (3) enhances client motivation as they clarify what they wish to work toward, (4) helps the leader integrate needs with the purposes of the group, (5) helps the leader plan techniques and methods to meet the needs, (6) facilitates intragroup support and commitment, and (7) enhances communication and coordination among all parties because they agree on and work toward meeting assessed needs.

Techniques such as a questionnaire or opportunities to discuss problems and concerns help clarify and list needs. It is usually better for the group participant rather than the leader to share problems and resulting goals with fellow group members.

Assessment of Group Goals

After determining needs, the next step is assessing group goals. All groups have goals, whether implicit or explicit, that help define the group and give shape to its activities. A classroom group may have the goal of gaining a certain level of knowledge or skill by the end of a term. One counseling group could set a goal of more open expression of feelings, while another group could work toward the acquisition of job seeking skills. An advantage of group counseling is that the range of possible goals is very broad, encompassing the potential psychological, social, vocational, and academic needs of most members.

One of the first tasks in establishing a group is to determine group and individual goals, which should be compatible with one another. There are at least two approaches to meeting this objective. The group organizer can interview or assess individuals, find what needs they have in common, then set group goals to meet the individuals' needs. In the second approach, a group may be proposed for a certain purpose (such as to develop independent living skills for adjustment in the community), and individuals are then selected whose needs are compatible with the group goals (for example, psychiatric patients preparing for discharge).

Purpose of Goals

An effective counseling group must have goals. Without them, or with poorly defined goals, or goals that are not compatible with group participants, the group's activity becomes aimless, vague, and of minimal benefit to members. Goals give a clear idea of what is expected of everyone, what activities they need to engage in, and how they can get the most out of the group process. Defining and agreeing on goals influences the activities, progress, and direction of the group and the commitment, motivation, and morale of the participants. The group's action plans, roles, and responsibilities are thus guided by its goals. Motivation and action are critical to success. Desirable goals enhance members' involvement in the group and increase the chances they will take action to reach those goals. Acceptance of group goals creates an inner drive to accomplish closure and achieve an objective. Cooperation is aided by group cohesiveness, which in turn is affected by group goals in bringing out cooperation, allowing judgment of what actions are for the good of the group and how members depend in some ways on one another. Six factors contribute to a member's commitment to accomplishing a group goal:

1. How desirable the goal seems
2. How likely it seems that the group can accomplish the goal
3. How challenging the goal is (a moderate risk of failure is more challenging than a high or low risk of failure)
4. Being able to tell when the goal has been achieved
5. The satisfaction or reward the member expects to feel or receive when the goal is achieved
6. The ways in which the member will relate to other members in working toward the accomplishment of the goal (some ways of relating to other members are more fun and involving than others) (Johnson & Johnson, 1982, pp. 141–42)

Goals also help evaluate the group's success. When specific goals are formulated in the beginning, one can evaluate group progress at various stages; when the group terminates, one can determine accomplishment of goals. This is helpful to the individual as well as to the group as a whole. Each member can examine her degree of success and her individual contribution to overall group goals. Group leaders and program planners are also interested in measuring the success, and therefore the value, of the group. Measurable goals help program evaluation and subsequent decisions such as whether to offer the same type of group again, whether it needs modification, and how its success compares with other services.

Types of goals depend upon setting, the leader's experience, training, and expertise, and participants' needs. Goals may be those of process (ability to listen, to express feelings), knowledge (learning about various community resources), skills (ability to fill out a job application), and attitudes (greater self-confidence as demonstrated in verbal expressions). Goals can also be established at different levels in the human system; that is, in the range from intrapsychic (less muscle tension), interpersonal (greater assertiveness), group (participating in a club), organization (understanding the purpose of the hospital), or community system (knowing the job market in the community). Goals may be set up to bring about development and change, or to learn something specific, or to accomplish a particular task. They may be set up to help participants become more effective in changing or using their environment. Goals are at times explicit, at times implicit, exist at differing levels of awareness with each member, and constantly change or modify as time passes. Ideally, goals are explicit and agreeable to all the members; however, implicit goals and hidden agendas are almost always present, and some can hinder success. If a few members agree to a group goal of greater personal independence, but are really attending only to appease a family member, they will not contribute to the explicit group goal. Each member usually has several goals and is not fully aware of all of them. A member of a group for alcoholics, for example, may consciously attend to gain support from others to control his drinking while subconsciously continuing his alcoholic game of manipulation. At one level he wants help, at another level, he wants to drink.

Goals change as members become aware of new goals or the need to modify initial goals. Needs are not always clear at first, and group participation helps clarify what members really want from the group experience. As members change and progress in the group, they may also wish to set new or higher goals. This is normal; the leader can handle reasonable changes, but must also evaluate the appropriateness of new goal directions. Members must not make goal changes only to avoid or deny other important goals. Radical changes may not be compatible with all members or with the setting in which the group is offered.

The various theoretical models differ as to the importance of goals. The psychoanalytically-oriented Slavson (1955) does not consider group goals and norms essential to a successful group. Behaviorists want operationally defined, measurable goals. Gestaltists tend to allow goals that relate to the here and now. From a humanist view, Otto (1967) set group goals based on enhancement of human potential. One may also use an eclectic approach, integrating various theoretical models, and come up with goals compatible with those theories. In Table 11-1, Corey (1981) compares the group goals suggested by major theoretical models. Goals for one theoretical model are not necessarily incompatible with another, so one can synthesize parts of the various theories. Also, certain models or parts of models may apply better to one group than another, and goals of one theory may be more useful to one group than to another.

Setting Goals

The need for clearly stated, specific, concrete goals for the group and the individual is a generally accepted facet of group counseling. Individual goals should be defined operationally so they can be observed and measured. The objective is to state goals so the group can take action to meet them. If the group can go through a sequence of

Table 11-1   Comparative Overview of Group Goals*

Model	Goals
Psychoanalytic groups	To provide a climate that helps clients reexperience early family relationships. To uncover buried feelings associated with past events that carry over into current behavior. To facilitate insight into the origins of faulty psychological development and to stimulate a corrective emotional experience.
Adlerian groups	To create a therapeutic relationship that encourages exploration of participants' premises and basic life assumptions and to achieve a broader understanding of lifestyles. To help clients recognize their strengths and power to change and to encourage them to accept full responsibility for their chosen life-style and for any changes they want to make.
Psychodrama groups	To facilitate the release of pent-up feelings, to provide insights, and to assist clients in developing new and more effective behaviors. To open up unexplored possibilities for the solution of conflicts and to lead to the experiencing of dominant sides of oneself.

Table 11-1 (*continued*)

Model	Goals
Existential groups	To provide conditions that maximize self-awareness and reduce blocks to growth. To help clients discover and use freedom of choice and enable them to assume responsibility for their own choices.
Person-centered groups	To provide a safe climate wherein members can explore the full range of their feelings. To assist members in becoming increasingly open to new experiences and in developing confidence in themselves and their own judgments. To encourage clients to live in the present. To develop openness, honesty, and spontaneity. To make it possible for clients to encounter others in the here and now and to use the group as a place to overcome feelings of alienation.
Gestalt groups	To enable members to pay close attention to their moment-to-moment experiencing, so they may recognize and integrate disowned aspects of themselves.
Transactional-analysis (TA) groups	To assist clients in becoming script and game free in their interactions. To challenge members to reexamine early decisions and make new ones based on awareness.
Behavior-therapy groups	To help group members eliminate maladaptive behaviors and learn new and more effective behavior patterns (broad goals are broken down into precise subgoals).
Rational-emotive-therapy (RET) groups	To teach group members that they are responsible for their own disturbances and to help them identify and abandon the process of self-indoctrination by which they keep their disturbances alive. To eliminate the clients' irrational and self-defeating outlook on life and replace it with a more tolerant and rational one.
Reality-therapy groups	To guide members toward learning realistic and responsible behavior and developing a "success identity." To assist group members in making value judgments about their behaviors and in deciding on a plan of action for change.

actions to achieve a goal, we say the goal is operational (Johnson & Johnson, 1982). Stating the goal in behavioral terms helps in evaluation of progress and results. For example, an individual's goal in a group might be to act more assertive by initiating conversations, saying "no" when he doesn't want to do something, and becoming involved in a social group or club. These goals are observable and measurable. Group members can see the individual initiate conversations in the group, and he can report behaviors toward the other two goals. At the termination of the group, the participant will be initiating conversations or not, choosing to say "no" or not, and be involved in a club or not. To observe and measure goals, they cannot be passive, nor as vague as "to feel better about myself," "higher self-esteem," "self-exploration," or "to grow," although these kinds of goals would be acceptable if they can be broken down into subgoals stated in behavioral terms.

The process of setting goals is facilitated by techniques that force members to think about specific needs. Potential group members are often confused or vague about what they wish to work on, and need encouragement to focus on and structure what they want to get out of the group. *Writing* is helpful to some people; it may take the form of an autobiography, or simply a list of one's assets or abilities and limitations or problems, and makes one think about and organize needs and objectives. A *journal* or diary makes one reflect on experiences, feelings, and thoughts that can lead to a clearer focus for group goals. *Reading*, usually recommended by the leader, can be directed toward the member's area of concern. Carefully selected self-help books and, in some cases, professional articles, help clarify appropriate goals. Of course, *bibliotherapy* is often a useful adjunct to group counseling. A structured *questionnaire* may contain questions about problems and concerns for the member to check, underline, or rank in order of importance, as with the Mooney Problem Check List, or the potential member may complete sentence stems to suggest primary goals. Examples of sentence completions are "What I want most is . . .," and "What really bothers me is. . . ." Corey, Corey, Callanan, and Russell (1982) give an example of a checklist for an adolescent group.*

> Directions: Rate each of the following problems (1–3) as they apply to you at this time and indicate the degree to which you'd like help from the group with them.

---

*From *Group Techniques* by G. Corey, M. S. Corey, P. J. Callanan, and J. M. Russell. Copyright © 1982 by Wadsworth, Inc. Reprinted by permission of the publisher, Brooks/Cole Publishing Company, Monterey, California.

(1) This is a major problem of mine, one I hope will be a topic for exploration in the group.

(2) This is a problem for me at times, and I could profit from an open discussion of the matter in this group.

(3) This is not a concern of mine, and I don't feel a need to explore the topic in the group.

- Feeling accepted by my peer group
- Learning how to trust others
- Getting along with my parents (or brothers, sisters, etc.)
- Getting a clear sense of what I value
- Worrying about whether I'm "normal"
- Being fearful of relating to the opposite sex
- Dealing with sexual feelings, actions, and standards of behavior
- Being too concerned about doing what is expected of me to the extent that I don't live by my own standards
- Worrying about my future
- Wondering whether I will be accepted into a college
- Trying to decide on a career (pp. 44–45)

Corey et al. also suggest the use of a *critical-turning-points chart:*

Another technique for preparing members for productive work in groups is to ask them to draw a road map of their lives and include some of the following points of interest: major turning points, major crises, big decisions, new opportunities, major accomplishments, key failures, important people, major disappointments. Members can then work in pairs, selecting whatever they would like to share from their charts. Or members can talk about critical turning points in their lives with the entire group. In addition to or in place of a chart, people can draw a sketch divided into three parts: "My Past/My Present/My Future." Much of their drawing may be symbolic. Again they can share what parts of their sketch mean to them in small groups or in the group as a whole. (p. 45)

The *survey-feedback* method of setting group goals requires the leader or organizer to assess members' needs and goals from the interview. In this process, member roles and responsibilities can be established, and short-term and long-range goals as well as the tasks or activities to teach the goals agreed upon. In the *critical path* method (or program evaluation and review) described by Johnson and Johnson (1982), a consultant helps the group set goals by first stating the end or long-range goal. The group chooses the subgoals and activities necessary for achieving the final goal, agrees on a time-table and resources, and assigns responsibilities.

Contracts are popular with some groups for clarifying goals, setting responsibility, and measuring success. Individual members write down what they wish to accomplish and what they are willing to do to reach the goals. The contract may be negotiated with the leader before the group actually meets, during the first session, or between the first and second sessions. Each contract is usually shared with other group members so they can help each other reach objectives and give feedback. Contracts can be reviewed periodically to evaluate progress and to consider modification. Members review contracts and evaluate relative success at the end of the group sessions. The real value of contracts seems to be clarification of goals and the responsibility each member assumes for reaching goals.

Assessing Process

Process evaluation occurs between the beginning of group sessions and the final session. There are two evaluation methodologies: one is the extent to which the group is moving successfully through stages toward the desired outcome; the other examines group counseling process variables—activity, interaction, reactions, behavior, and attitudes—at a particular point or points. The evaluator is free to select gross process variables, such as client satisfaction, amount of time a participant verbalizes, and frequency of positive and negative statements toward the leader, or other variables such as nonverbal behaviors, indications of cohesiveness, and affiliation patterns. One may also wish to examine the interaction of variables such as activity level of the group leader and group progress in self-disclosing, or dependency behavior and its relationship to a democratically-run group. The process evaluator is interested in selecting variables most likely to affect success; to add to our understanding of group counseling, we will examine several process variables: group member interactions, leader-member interactions, and group atmosphere.

Group Member Interaction. Perhaps the greatest amount of work on variables has been done on group member interactions. Bales (1950) devised an interaction process analysis for classifying group communication interactions into twelve categories, shown in Table 11-2. All individual interactions are classified as questions or answers and as positive or negative responses. The leader can use this classification system to analyze group process and the researcher to compare groups. Audio- or videotapes can record the data. Hill (1965a, b) devised another method of analyzing group process, the Hill Interaction Matrix (HIM), which assumes that a degree of homogeneity among group members is conducive to interaction and positive out-

Table 11-2 Interaction Process Analysis*

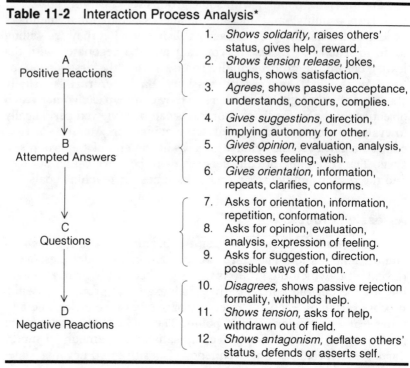

A Positive Reactions	1. *Shows solidarity*, raises others' status, gives help, reward.
	2. *Shows tension release*, jokes, laughs, shows satisfaction.
	3. *Agrees,* shows passive acceptance, understands, concurs, complies.
B Attempted Answers	4. *Gives suggestions,* direction, implying autonomy for other.
	5. *Gives opinion,* evaluation, analysis, expresses feeling, wish.
	6. *Gives orientation,* information, repeats, clarifies, conforms.
C Questions	7. Asks for orientation, information, repetition, conformation.
	8. Asks for opinion, evaluation, analysis, expression of feeling.
	9. Asks for suggestion, direction, possible ways of action.
D Negative Reactions	10. *Disagrees,* shows passive rejection formality, withholds help.
	11. *Shows tension,* asks for help, withdrawn out of field.
	12. *Shows antagonism,* deflates others' status, defends or asserts self.

*Reprinted from *Interaction Process Analysis*, page 9, by Robert F. Bales by permission of The University of Chicago Press.

come. The matrix consists of twenty cells that indicate a style or type of group member interaction. Verbal and other behaviors can be observed and recorded into categories of work-style and content-style. According to Hill, certain conditions are valuable to the group process: the wish to have a topic person much of the time, interpersonal risk-taking, and counselor's and client's assumption of roles of help-giver and help-receiver. As shown in Figure 11-2, group members discuss one of four possible content categories: (1) general topics, (2) the group itself, (3) personal issues or problems, or (4) relationship issues in the here and now of the group. Participants engage in five work-style categories:

1. Responsive—reacting to questions

2. Conventional—rather superficial and stereotyped

3. Assertive—the last of the prework levels characterized by revelation of a problem but denial of the group as a source of help

4. Speculative—asking questions and an intellectualized approach to the problem

5. Confrontive—members confront each other

Groups that engage in categories III and IV (personal and relationship) are those that work toward change in members; when members are more speculative and confrontive, the group is striving toward greater self-understanding. Thus, matrix boxes 13–16 indicate greater efficiency and potential growth for participants. Member interactions can be rated and placed in one of the cells; for example, when a group member says, "I liked the place we went to have coffee after the group session last week," it can be rated as pertaining to "group" and "conventional"—cell II B. If a group member speculates, "I wonder if maybe I should treat my husband better than I do," it is a "personal" issue—cell III D. By placing each interaction

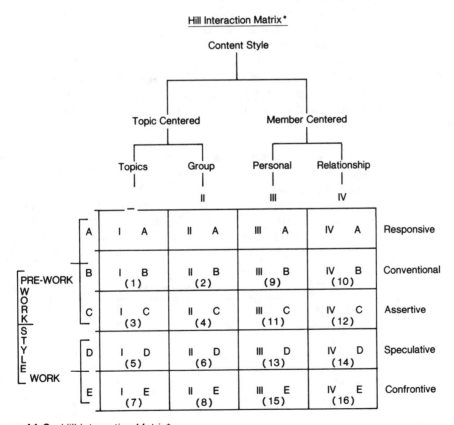

Figure 11-2 Hill Interaction Matrix*

in a cell, one can analyze the general style of each member and the group as a whole. Are members and group working? Are they moving toward objectives?

Hill also constructed the HIM-B to measure the member's degree of acceptance for each cell in the Hill Matrix, showing the member's preferred content category and work style. On the basis of the instrument's results, the counselor can select members he believes are compatible—whether one prefers to be group-centered and conventional, personal and confrontive, or relationship-oriented and speculative. One can also use the instrument while the group is in progress to determine changes or for research. Hill provides norms for the instrument, and percentage scores can be obtained for each cell (four test items are keyed to each matrix cell). Dinkmeyer and Muro (1971) advocate use of the HIM-B as one way to select group members; they assume homogeneous groups are usually most effective because of similar work styles and content interests, which produce more effective group interaction.

Luft and Ingham's (1969) model of communication is useful to group process. Their Johari Awareness model emphasizes the degree to which one is aware of his behavior and feelings, and the extent to which behavior and feelings are transparent or known to others. The four quadrants are based on awareness of self and openness to others. Diagrammatically, in the first quadrant, one is somewhat open to himself and others; in the second quadrant, he is blind to self but his characteristics are known by others; in the third quadrant, he is known to himself but his characteristics are hidden from others, and in the fourth quadrant, he is unaware of self and not known by others. Each of a person's many characteristics, feelings, attitudes, motivations, and behaviors could fall in one of the quadrants. The number of characteristics that fall in each quadrant varies among individuals. Normally, the "open" quadrant is largest in well-functioning persons and restricted in those who have many problems. A

	Known to Self	Not Known to Self
Known to others	1 Open	2 Blind
Not known to others	3 Hidden	4 Unknown

Figure 11-3 Johari Awareness Model*

purpose of group counseling is to help people decrease the size of quadrants two through four and increase the size of quadrant one. The larger size of quadrant one means that energy can be directed toward openness and constructive behavior rather than toward self-protectiveness, resulting in greater self-satisfaction, more interaction, and more flexible roles.

Luft proposes eleven principles for bringing about desired change:

1. A change in any one quadrant will affect all other quadrants.

2. It takes energy to hide, deny, or be blind to behavior that is involved in interaction.

3. Threat tends to decrease awareness; mutual trust tends to increase awareness.

4. Forced awareness (exposure) is undesirable and usually ineffective.

5. Interpersonal learning means a change has occurred that makes Quadrant 1 larger, and one or more of the other quadrants smaller.

6. Working with others is facilitated by a large enough area of free activity so that more of the resources and skills of the persons involved can be applied to the task at hand.

7. The smaller the first quadrant, the poorer the communication.

8. There is a universal curiosity about the unknown area, but this is held in check by custom, social training, and diverse fears.

9. Sensitivity means appreciating the covert aspects of behavior in Quadrants 2, 3, and 4 and respecting the desire of others to keep them so.

10. Learning about group processes, as they are being experienced, helps to increase awareness (enlarging Quadrant 1) for the group as a whole as well as for the individual members.

11. The value system of a group and its membership may be noted in the way unknowns in the life of the group are confronted.*

Sociometric measures have been a popular way to assess an individual's preferred interactions with others in the group by asking with whom one prefers to associate. Before a group forms the potential member can indicate from a list of names those he would like to have in the group. After the group has met, members can be asked to rank their degree of preference or liking for the other participants.

---

*The Johari Awareness Model and Luft's eleven principles are from Joseph Luft and Harry Ingham, *Of Human Interaction* (Palo Alto, California: National Press Books, 1969), pp. 13–14.

Another version is to chart the frequency of each member's interactions, both positive and negative, with the others to determine preferences and dislikes. The purpose is to assess members' social preferences to show the social status of each member's interpersonal patterns and the social organization of the group. Zeleny (1956) and others have found that group members are more ingenious, productive, and creative when they are allowed to interact with those they choose; on the other hand, the group leader has the challenge of handling the rejected participant. It is apparent that people who are rejected should not be placed with those who reject them, but should be placed in another group. Sociometric testing while the group is in progress also tells the leader about unspoken preferences, and can be used for feedback to participants. Bach (1954) offers more on sociometric measurement.

William Schutz (1966, 1971) concluded that three basic interpersonal needs explain human relationships: *control, inclusion,* and *affection.* The Fundamental Interpersonal Relations Orientation-Behavior questionnaire, (FIRO-B), with 54 items, indicates the degree to which interpersonal behavior is characterized by the three basic needs. The individual rates each item on a six-point scale to measure the valence (plus or minus) on each need, indicating on the need to control, for example, whether the group member wishes to control or be controlled or is rather neutral. Does she wish to belong to groups or avoid them? Does she wish to be emotionally close to others or distant?

The FIRO-B has been used to predict suitability for and compatibility of a group as one basis for selection. It also seems to predict behavior in certain situations, and group members are able to identify a description of their own group from the results of the FIRO-B.

Using the FIRO model and the measurement device, Yalom and Rand (1966) found that certain types of interpersonal homogeneity in a group relate to group cohesiveness. They also concluded that participants who are significantly different from the others in interpersonal style are more dissatisfied and tend to leave therapy prematurely. Compatibility thus enhances the togetherness and perhaps the effectiveness of the group.

The question often arises as to which incidents or interactions are most productive in group counseling. Yalom (1970) reports a follow-up study of twenty clients who were asked about their most critical incident or turning point. Incidents were emotionally laden and nearly always involved another group member; most common were:

Sudden expression of strong anger or hatred toward another member of the group

Expression of positive affect toward someone

Self-disclosure that led to greater involvement with the group

In regard to the first critical incident, expression of anger, De Cecco and Richards (1974) found that verbal expression of anger, handled skillfully, led to communication of issues that needed to be resolved. Mutual expression of anger brought motiviation to resolve conflicts and abide by agreements; anger had to center on issues rather than persons to be positive. Verbal anger toward a member led to threats and violence. Failure to verbalize anger or anger expressed by only one party increased tension and resulted in intimidation, coercion, and actions that could not be negotiated.

Vosen (1966) supports Yalom's point concerning self-disclosure; lack of self-disclosure in a group led to reduced self-esteem, suggesting that one must reveal oneself to others so as to be known and accepted by them, a necessary factor in building self-esteem.

Gibb (1961) studied competitive vs. cooperative behavior and discovered that one group member's competitive behavior fostered competition in the others, leading to defensiveness. Group members then devote more energy to defending themselves than to working on group goals. As participants become more defensive, they are less able to correctly perceive motives, values, and content in communication with others. Gibb found certain behaviors associated with a competitive orientation and others with a cooperative orientation. His findings might be categorized as in Table 11-3.

When group members describe behavior rather than make value judgments about it, they minimize defensiveness and enhance growth. The same can be said for addressing a problem rather than trying to control someone; behave spontaneously rather than calculatingly; express understanding rather than maintain aloof neutrality; communicate a sense of equality rather than of superiority; be

Table 11-3 Competitive and Cooperative Behaviors

Competitive Orientation	Cooperative Orientation
Evaluation	Description
Control	Problem orientation
Strategy	Spontaneity
Neutrality	Empathy
Superiority	Equality
Certainty	Provincialism

willing to work cooperatively; and experiment with ideas and behavior rather than exclude new information and alternative perceptions. The more cooperative group listens to one another, becomes more cohesive and productive, and works in a friendlier climate.

The quality of intermember relationships relates to positive outcome. Clark and Culbert (1965) found that participants in a T-group experience who entered into the most mutually therapeutic two-person relationships showed the most positive change during the course of the group. The nature and frequency of quality interpersonal relationships in group counseling thus significantly affects the value of the group experience.

Leader-Group Interaction Another aspect of group process is the interaction between group participants and the group leader. Although all models of group counseling address the dynamic role of the leader's interaction with group members, most models are derived from clinical experience. One of the earliest theorists in the quantification of group dynamics was Kurt Lewin. His first study (Lewin & Lippitt, 1938) concerned the group atmosphere created by the leader: authoritatian or democratic. When leaders were authoritarian, members tended to be more dependent on them, more hostile, and more apathetic; authoritarian-led groups, however, managed a greater quantity of group output. The democratically-led groups were less dependent on the leader, showed greater satisfaction with group activities, and felt their products were better qualitatively. The second study (Lewin, Lippitt, & White, 1939) added laissez-faire leadership and found that members were less dependent on the leader, but angry, aggressive, and less satisfied with group activities.

Since Lewin's time, studies have demonstrated that group members react differently to varying styles of leadership. Furthermore, the best leadership style depends on the circumstances, the purpose of the group, leader personality, and group member needs. In some cases, production quantity may be more important than participant satisfaction. With small groups whose main purpose is the quality of interaction, democratic leadership seems to work best. Reviewing the studies in this area, Stogdill (1974) concluded that:

1. Person-oriented styles of leadership are not consistently related to productivity.

2. Among the work-oriented leadership styles, socially distant, directive, and structured leader behaviors that tend to maintain role differentiation and let members know what to expect are consistently related to group productivity.

3. Among the person-oriented leadership styles, only those providing for member participation in decision making and showing concern

for members' welfare and comfort are consistently related to group cohesiveness.

4. Among the work-oriented leadership styles, only the structuring of member expectations is uniformly related to group cohesiveness.

5. All of the person-oriented leadership styles tend to be related to member satisfaction.

6. Only the structuring of member expectations is related positively to member satisfaction among the work-oriented leadership styles. (Johnson & Johnson, p. 48)

The Hill Interaction Matrix can be used to determine compatibility between the group and its leader by matching work and preferred content styles or as a diagnostic tool to show why a group and its leader are not relating well. The leader who confrontively urges discussion of relationships in the group will have trouble with participants who want to discuss relationships conventionally outside the group.

The leader has a significant impact on establishing group norms. As we have said, norms set the stage for acceptable or expected group behavior. Psathas and Hardert (1966) found the leader's statements had a seemingly implicit but strong influence on group norms; Shipiro and Birk (1967) showed the leader's multiple influence. A group member can become the center of attention when the leader responds to her actions and thus may assume a major role in future meetings.

Another aspect of leader-member interaction refers to the therapeutic conditions the leader offers and the effect of those conditions on participants. Carl Rogers itemizes necessary and sufficient conditions for personality change; Carkhuff (1977, 1971) has studied those necessary conditions and other facilitative conditions in both individual and group counseling. Facilitative conditions thought to enhance self-exploration or other forms of client change include:

1. *Empathy*—ability to understand what the client-group member has communicated

2. *Respect*—valuing the other person

3. *Genuineness*—congruence of the leader's feelings and thoughts with overt behavior

4. *Self-disclosure*—revelation of personal affect or information that can be helpful to participants

5. *Confrontation*—telling members what has been observed, such as discrepancies in member statements

6. *Concreteness*—simple, direct, concrete descriptions of member behavior

7. *Immediacy*—focus on the group's immediate interactions

Offering these conditions at high therapeutic levels contributes to positive change. The leader usually needs training to communicate these interpersonal skills to the group, and proper timing and selection of the conditions become part of the leader's skill. This model assumes that people become dysfunctional because of problems in interpersonal relationships. The group leader provides a nonthreatening, supportive relationship, and also models healthy interpersonal relationships. Group members learn to trust the leader and emulate the positive relationship skills.

Nichols and Taylor (1975) looked at three dimensions—facilitation, confrontation, and interpretation—offered to a group in its early stage and found that facilitation produced a higher degree of focusing. Simple facilitation encourages group participants to express themselves and interact. Interpretation and confrontation are more useful in later stages of counseling when people are more trusting and cohesiveness has grown. McMurrian and Gazda (1974) put the stages of group process in perspective. If the leader offers basic facilitative conditions of empathy, respect, and genuineness in the early stage, he prepares the group to be more active in the middle, productive stage. As a result of leader modeling, group members are able to work hard on self-concept and interpersonal relationships. A study by Mainord, Burk, and Collins (1965) illustrated the effectiveness of leader confrontation and immediacy. When the counselor used responses that diverted the group from discussion of personal issues, members were more comfortable, but did little to change behavior. Conversely, when leaders got participants to confront personal issues directly, immediately, and concretely, there were more behavior changes and successful terminations, although members experienced transient discomfort. Clients need to experience some anxiety to grow and change; temporary discomfort may necessarily accompany personal growth. The leader, however, must not induce unnecessary emotional pain, then justify it as a requirement for growth.

Group Atmosphere In addition to interpersonal relationships, group counseling features an atmosphere beyond that of individual dynamics. Each group can be distinguished from other groups and is more than the sum of its one-to-one interactions. The group atmosphere, or total group dynamic, moves through developmental stages. It can be described as "healthy" or facilitative in meeting group goals.

One of the better ways to assess group atmosphere is through observation of the group while in session, ideally through a one-way mirror. Videotape is convenient because one can stop and replay portions, allowing for more careful analysis. The presence of an observer who is rating or taking notes can interfere with the group's natural flow and openness, although observers on the fringe of a group have been used with no apparent contamination of group interaction. Group participants said they were not aware of observers once the group began and felt they would have been no more or less open without the observers. (This technique is useful for training group leaders.) The least desirable method of observation is the use of audiotapes; they are limiting because one loses much of the sense of the group without visual cues.

A classic study of the effect of *change* on group performance was that of Roethlisberger and Dickson (1940) at the Western Electric Hawthorne Plant. As working conditions such as lighting, rest, and varied workday were altered in the plant, workers' efficiency increased. Interestingly, productivity increased when conditions became less desirable as well as when they became more desirable, leading to the conclusion that change itself brings greater efficiency and that group members have a need for change. A more important lesson for the group evaluator is that observed or measured improvement in group members may not be the result of competent leadership or facilitative group dynamics; rather, altered behavior may be the result of group participation as representative of a change. For example, if an adolescent is placed in a treatment home because he chronically acts out at home and in the community, his behavior may change dramatically and positively. Can we say, however, that the group atmosphere in the treatment home had a therapeutic effect, or could we just as well conclude that a change in setting alone altered his behavior? Perhaps he would have done just as well in any alternate setting. When we study group atmosphere, we must be cautious in reaching conclusions about special benefits from certain total group dynamics and remain open to alternative explanations.

Group Stages Members usually receive information, instruction, or rules before the group actually meets, to create an atmosphere for positive group development. Bednar and Battersby (1976) studied the effect of pregroup messages on the early development of the group. Different messages were given to each of three separate groups: one message focused on obtaining group clarity; one was a persuasive explanation of the group; and one message focused on behavioral instructions—what to do in the group. The behavioral instructions were significantly more effective in bringing about group cohesion, work-oriented interpersonal communication, and favorable attitude toward groups. Clear and concrete instructions of expected group participation are more likely to produce a positive group atmosphere.

One study described stages of counseling groups as early, central, and termination stages (McMurrian & Gazda, 1974). The most productive atmosphere was found during the central or middle stage; the qualitative style associated with growth-oriented interchanges was markedly increased. In the termination stage, there was still strong identity with the group, but also conflicting feelings regarding cohesiveness, and awareness that the group would end. The level and frequency of interaction of the middle, working stage would not be appropriate for the ending sessions. Sisson, Sisson, and Gazda (1973) also found a decrease in interaction in the later stage, although the quality of therapeutic interactions was maintained.

The next dimension of group atmosphere is that of conformity or "groupthink." A result of group membership is that the very atmosphere demands a certain degree of conformity to rules and codes of behavior, and the balance between individuality and conformity is not always easy to define. Can the group function well and meet its goals if everyone behaves as an individual? To what extent are individual rights and creativity violated when the group pressures for conformity to rigid, narrow behavior patterns? Studies show that group members can be influenced to conform to others' norms or expectations of others, so in group counseling, norms and group pressure influence the behavior of members for better or for worse.

Conformity has also been studied in the form of "groupthink." The dissonant voice in a group can be muffled by other members' pressure. Janis (1971) showed that groupthink can prevent effective problem solving; one tends not to look at alternatives, but rather maintains the status quo and norms of the group process. The objecting member's ideas are considered irrelevant to the problem. The leader is instrumental in setting an atmosphere where disagreement is accepted as a nonthreatening aspect of group interaction.

Group cohesion is thought to be significant to group success. For example, Truax (1961) discovered hospitalized patients in the most cohesive groups were more likely to engage in deep levels of self-exploration. Others have found that group members report cohesiveness as a major therapeutic variable (Dickoff & Lakin, 1963; Kapp, 1964; Yalom, Tinklenberg, & Gilula, 1970). Yalom concluded that members of a cohesive group will:

1. Try harder to influence other group members

2. Be more influenceable by the other members

3. Be more willing to listen to others and are more accepting of others

4. Experience greater security and relief from tension in the group

5. Participate more readily in meetings

6. Protect the group norms and, for example, exert more pressure on individuals deviating from the norms

7. Be less susceptible to disruption as a group when a member terminates membership (Yalom, 1970, p. 56)

Assessment of Outcome

Group counseling is a complex and potentially powerful intervention strategy, and it is incumbent on professionals to demonstrate its worth. Consequently, we need to address the difficulties of analyzing the benefits of group counseling and some of the ways the leader or evaluator can determine success.

What are the factors that bring a successful outcome, and what shall we consider success? As mentioned earlier, the complexity of group counseling makes it difficult to determine which variables contribute to success and to what degree, the necessary circumstances, and the consistency of their relative importance.

We have discussed *process variables* that facilitate group interaction. We can assume these process variables also bring about positive change; for example, supportive statements, minimal competition, and respect for the leader readily contribute to real change in participants. In addition to the many process dimensions, we must also be aware of other variables. The leader's personality may be more effective with certain kinds of groups than another's might be. The leader appears to be more effective when offering certain facilitative conditions. A related variable is that of the group counseling model or approach. Of course, the purpose of the group may suggest the appropriate counseling model, and a tangible purpose, such as improving school grades, may be more successful than an abstract purpose, such as elevating self-concept.

Composition of the group is a significant variable. Some theorists believe homogeneous groups are more effective than heterogeneous, and it may be that mixing ages, problems, diagnoses, and maturity levels has an effect on outcome. It may be important whether membership is voluntary or required, and *context* or setting may have an effect. Factors such as ventilation, comfort, smoking, or members' attitude toward the agency can influence the group's success. Finally, *duration* and *size* of the group may be important. We might want to know how many times a group must meet to reach its optimum usefulness, or when a group seems to be too small or too large. Each of these variables and others interact with one another to geometric proportions, resulting in many combinations that influence group outcome. One group may differ from another on every variable we have mentioned. How, then, do we draw any general conclusions about the success of group counseling? It seems appropriate to conclude that group success depends upon the effective combination of facilitative process, a competent leader who is compatible with the group, and members with similar needs and motivation.

Corsini and Rosenberg (1955) list the group mechanisms they believe relate to success.

1. *Acceptance.* Everyone needs a sense of belonging. The group offers an opportunity for shared respect, trust, and understanding that serves as a foundation for later change in behavior.

2. *Ventilation.* Most group members have kept feelings and attitudes under control and have not felt safe about revealing themselves openly. These repressed feelings and experiences often prevent them from functioning as well as they could in the community. Expressing oneself in the group frees up internalized feelings and channels energy into more useful activities.

3. *Reality testing.* Participation in a group is a new opportunity for social relationships in which one can test interpersonal skills, attitudes, and feelings. Members can experiment with expressing anger or affection, for example, before trying new behaviors outside the group.

4. *Transference.* Strong emotional attachments can develop in a group that help members learn to deal with close relationships.

5. *Intellectualization and feedback.* Members derive cognitive understanding of themselves and their relationships, and feedback from other group members is one way to acquire knowledge about oneself.

6. *Interaction.* Interpersonal relationships reveal participants' goals and characteristics; as members learn about each other, they tend to progress toward their objectives.

7. *Universalization.* Through open communication, each member learns that she is similar to others in the group, is not alone in having problems, and that others understand one's problems.

8. *Altruism.* Most people wish to be helpful to others, and the group gives them an opportunity to be of service to members. The leader acts as a model for socially mature helping behavior.

9. *Spectator therapy.* One can learn by observing others' concerns and how others work on their problems.

Desired outcomes of group counseling are those regarding the group as a whole and those regarding individuals. Research into whole group outcome is normally based on the purposes of the group as set by members, leader, or researcher. At times, the goals of each may not be the same. Most goals relate to personality or behavior change in participants or accomplishment of a task. Personality changes might include greater self-acceptance, reduced anxiety, more expression of feeling, and control of delusions. Behavior changes might include greater assertiveness, seeking and finding a job, learning child-management skills, or developing more satisfying relationships with the opposite sex. Group tasks might be to make a management decision or acquire skill in leading counseling groups.

To establish group outcomes, one measure is used for the entire group, in other words, the criterion for change or progress is applied to all members in the same way. If the desired outcome is reduced anxiety, it will be the desired outcome for everyone and the same anxiety measure will be used on everyone. Success for the group will be a function of the total anxiety reduction for all members. This kind of desired outcome requires that members have the same goals and encourages the use of homogeneous groups. A disadvantage is that individual differences may be ignored in favor of a common group goal.

Some researchers advocate individualized outcomes, both for more effective use of group counseling, and for more realistic use of outcome research. According to this position, groups exist for the purpose of promoting individual growth or behavior change. When we look for group success, we really desire success for all the people in that group, so the important goal becomes that which the individual sets. Ideally, group placement is according to compatible, though not necessarily identical, member goals. Groups can thus be homogeneous or heterogeneous. Even when group member concerns are similar, however, their starting point, context, and relative issues will not be the same, consequently, desired outcomes will not necessarily be the same.

Let us use a nine-member adolescent counseling group as an example. With the individualized approach, one selects members who fall at different points on three dimensions. On the first dimension, three adolescents fall at each of three points on the continuum: acting-out, spontaneous, and withdrawn. On an academic continuum, the nine members fall as follows: above average grades, 2 members; average grades, 3 members; and below average grades, 4 members. On an anxiety measure, four scored very low, one average, and four scored high. The leader wanted a balance on the behavioral continuum so that acting-out members could interact with the average person and challenge the quietness of the withdrawn. High achievers could serve as models for the others. In regard to goals and desired outcomes, we clearly do not want one, two, or three goals for the entire group. We want a few adolescents to learn to control their behavior and several others to be more interactive. Even within each of these subgroups, goals may not be exactly the same. On the third dimension, one can say that several group members need to increase their anxiety levels while others need to reduce anxiety. We can use the anxiety dimension to illustrate how measures of group outcome can mask positive individual changes. If low anxiety group members increase their measured score at the end of counseling, the middle group stays the same, and the high anxiety group reduces its score, we would actually have no change in the overall group score. We might conclude that the group was not helpful in the area of anxiety, when we in fact achieved the desired changes in all participants. Individualized goals and measures may require more work for the group leader and the researcher, but often give a more accurate picture of group success.

Four methods of measurement predominate: client self-evaluation, leader evaluation, observer ratings, and paper-and-pencil devices. Although the validity of self-ratings is open to question because of conscious distortion or lack of awareness of change, self-ratings are quite popular and do offer one source of information. When group members can rate themselves and others honestly, they provide valuable data as to success. Self-ratings usually come from members' responses to questions posed, ideally, immediately after termination of the group and again six months to a year later. Corey and Corey (1977) suggest a sample questionnaire:

1. What general effect, if any, has your group experience had on your life?

2. What were the highlights of the group experience for you? Some of its most meaningful aspects?

3. What were some specific things that you became aware of about yourself, in terms of your life-style, attitudes, and relationships with others?

4. What are some changes you've made in your life that you can attribute at least partially to your group experience?

5. Which of the techniques used by the group leaders had the most impact on you?

6. What perceptions of the group leaders and their styles do you have?

7. What kinds of problems did you encounter upon leaving the group and attempting to do what you had decided to do in the outside world?

8. Have the changes that occurred as a result of your group experiences lasted? If so, do you think the changes are permanent?

9. What kinds of questions have you asked yourself since the group? Were questions of yours left unanswered by the group?

10. Did the group experience have any negative effects on you?

11. What kinds of individual and/or group experiences have you been involved in since this particular experience?

12. What effects do you think your participation in the group had on the significant people in your life?

13. Have there been any crises in your life since the termination of the group? How did they turn out?

14. How might your life be different now had you not experienced the group? Do you feel that you would have made any significant changes in your behavior?

15. Have you become more aware, since the termination of the group, of the part you played in the group process?

16. If a close friend were to ask you today to tell in a sentence or two what the group meant to you, how would you respond?

17. In retrospect, are you skeptical about the value of the group process or about the motivations of other people in the group?

18. Since the group, have you encouraged others to become involved in a group or in some other kind of growth experience?

19. How do you evaluate this form of group experience? What is its potential for helping people change in a positive direction? What are its limitations? Its risks? How would you recommend it be used? Do the potential gains outweigh the risks?

20. What are some other questions you think we should ask in order to get a complete picture of the meaning the group had for you? Do you have anything else to say about yourself and your experience either during or since the group?* (pp. 116–17)

After members return the questionnaire, the leader schedules a follow-up session during which members can clarify responses to the questionnaire and articulate the benefits they see in the group expe-

---

*From *Groups: Process and Practice*, by G. Corey and M. S. Corey. Copyright © 1977 by Wadsworth Publishing Company, Inc. Reprinted by permission of the publisher, Brooks/Cole Publishing Company, Monterey, California.

rience. The follow-up helps former participants extend what they gained from the group.

Counselor-measured outcome refers to the leader's ratings of group and/or members' progress. As with the self-ratings, one can question the leader's accuracy; the leader may be biased toward perceiving changes so as to enhance his apparent effectiveness, or he may rate certain members high or low according to personal feelings rather than objective observation. It is possible, nonetheless, for the group leader to provide accurate ratings.

Outcome ratings by observers tend to be more objective than those of members and the leader, particularly concerning behavioral outcomes. They are less useful in measuring clients' internal changes, such as degree of self-confidence. A last measure of outcome, paper-and-pencil instruments, include personality tests such as the MMPI, TAT, 16 PF, EPPI, and the Mooney Problem Check List, along with specific measures of anxiety, interpersonal communication skills, and marital relationships. Behavioral measures of introversion-extroversion, job-seeking skills, assertiveness, or academic achievement are also available. The assessment instrument should reflect the group's goals.

Summary

Assessing the steps in group counseling allows the group leader or evaluator to better understand the group's needs, behavior, and success. A systems approach is an effective way to conceptualize group counseling steps because it recognizes that individual, interpersonal, small group, organizational, and community factors interact. These levels provide a framework for understanding and analyzing groups. Individual needs, such as self-esteem, interact with interpersonal factors, such as social skills. Counseling occurs in a small group, but events in the group affect members' behavior in the community and vice versa.

The sequence for assessing group counseling focuses on needs, goals, process, and then outcome. One first identifies community, institutional, or group member needs in regard to the extent of need as well as the type of counseling service. One next determines group goals, either by assessing potential group members and basing goals on their common needs, or identifying organizational and community needs as the basis for setting group goals.

To assess the actual counseling, most research has been directed at group process. Of the various assessment methods, each specifies particular dynamics that appear relevant. Group process relates directly to assessment of group outcome, the last stage. Since group counseling is a service intended to make a difference in people's lives, we want to know if in fact it has had an impact on participants. Group process and outcome are extremely difficult to evaluate because of the many variables that are not always observable or measurable. The conceptual framework of systems theory, knowledge of the assessment steps, and use of assessment measures help the counselor work more effectively and evaluate his group's relative success.

Discussion Questions

1. Give examples of how a counseling group is affected by and in turn affects the levels of the individual, interpersonal relationships, groups, organizations, and the community.

2. Discuss examples of the effect of cross-cultural differences in members on the functioning of a group.

3. Explain how one might assess the needs of a community, agency, or group of people in terms of establishing a counseling group that addresses the needs.

4. Whay are goals important for a group? What are some legitimate goals for a group? How would you go about setting up goals for participants and the group as a whole?

5. Explain how you would go about evaluating the effectiveness of a counseling group. How would you measure process and outcome? How would you evaluate member participation and leader-member interactions?

Part 3

Special Populations

12

Group Work with Disabled and Disadvantaged Persons

In a maximum security prison, a group of inmates are exploring the source of the anger they had unleashed on their victims; in a large general hospital, several cancer patients are finding solace in sharing their concerns with one another; meanwhile, some black youths are providing feedback to their peers as they go through mock job interviews in an urban center in an economically depressed area. At the same time, a male with a spinal cord injury is decribing how he overcame his feelings of sexual inadequacy to a group of recently injured men undergoing rehabilitation. These situations depict the widespread application of group counseling and therapy to disabled and other disadvantaged populations. The use of group techniques evolved from the treatment of such special populations. An early example from the turn of the century was Pratt's use of educational sessions for tuberculosis patients, in which he observed marked improvements in morale (Yalom, 1975). L. C. Marsh's efforts to enhance the socialization of mentally ill persons, Lazell's use of group procedures to treat schizophrenics (Yalom, 1975), and Moreno's work in Austria with groups of prostitutes date back to the 1920s (Gazda, 1976). Following World War II, however, attention focused on group process issues and eventually merged with the per-

Contributed by Robert A. Chubon, Ph.D., Assistant Professor, College of Education, Rehabilitation Counseling Program, University of South Carolina

sonal growth movement of the sixties, detracting somewhat from the use of group techniques with special populations. Interest and application extended to a more general population and were heralded as a way to facilitate human growth and development. While public attention and the focus of research shifted, however, the use of group techniques with special populations continued to expand (Chubon, 1982). There are now probably few populations that have not been touched by the group counseling and therapy movement.

To those who have used the group method with special populations, its advantages are clear. Most of the problems incurred by disabled and disadvantaged persons have an interpersonal component, and group interventions have been found highly effective in ameliorating these problems. Although group counseling is often construed as "mass treatment," of which the primary advantage is efficiency, this factor alone would not account for continued reliance on and growth of this intervention were it not also appropriate and effective. Group techniques are now considered a primary, and often preferred, intervention strategy with special populations.

After dealing with these populations over a period of time, one realizes that a recurrent constellation of problems emerges that can be categorized as problems related to *change*, problems related to *loss*, and problems stemming from *difference*. Losses include those of function, social status, social support, and personal autonomy and control. Affectively, these losses become manifest as feelings of dependency, helplessness, guilt, anger, and a sense of isolation or aloneness. Aloneness is often compounded by actual isolation from the real world, imposed by the institutional confinement that typically characterizes treatment.

The change from one state to another, for example, from able-bodiedness to disability, often leaves the individual with a repertoire of coping skills that are no longer appropriate or adequate. Altered by disability or other circumstances, one is confronted with new and different problems with which one is unprepared to deal. These deficiencies are experienced as confusion, frustration, and sometimes fear; if unabated, these feelings can cause retreat or withdrawal that exacerbate the sense of isolation.

Disabilities and other conditions, such as belonging to a minority racial or ethnic group or economic or educational limitations all carry stereotypical perceptions of difference that have a stigmatizing effect. Those who suffer these stigmas face pressures that are intended to drive them from social visibility. Society tends to devalue these kinds of "differences"; when subjected to these attitudes, the stigmatized assimilate them and undergo a self-devaluing process.

Diminished self-esteem, limited interpersonal skills, and lack of *motivation* often become predominant.

Of the several problems common to the disabled or disadvantaged, the sense of isolation or aloneness is perhaps the most prevalent and among the earliest felt. Sometimes, simply exposing these individuals to others with similar problems in the context of a group provides immediate relief. Knowing that others are in the same boat seems to have a positive impact, perhaps because of the notion that there is strength in numbers or because one assumes that those with similar problems and pains will understand. Finding others who really seem to care can instill hope, which is often lost in isolation. Hope is a primary motivator for seeking help and sustaining the necessary energy. The realization that other members of the group believe it possible to improve one's condition enhances the sense of hope. The individual finds tangible proof that problems can be resolved or minimized.

Sharing solutions enables individuals to move forward more quickly than they otherwise might have. A competitive spirit toward problem solving sometimes evolves, which also facilitates progress. The group also provides an effective forum for the counselor or therapist to provide the information or correct the misinformation that is often a prerequisite to acquisition of new coping skills.

Sharing solutions and other helpful experiences can give members a sense of self-satisfaction. For someone who feels inferior because of a disability, helping others can be the first step toward regaining self-esteem. This altruism, or giving of self, is paramount in some groups, such as Alcoholics Anonymous, whose participants have somehow fallen to the foot of the social ladder and often show commensurate levels of self-esteem.

Lack of effective social skills often accompany disabilities and other disadvantageous conditions. Extended hospitalization can be ego-shattering; hospitals are typically based on a highly authoritarian structure, where acquiescence is a rewarded virtue and necessary to survival. Consequently, relearning to assert oneself may be essential to a successful return to the real world. Living a significant segment of one's life in a sexually segregated situation can also cause deficiency in other social skills. Isolation in an impoverished urban area may inhibit learning the social conventions and expectations necessary for functioning in the greater community. The highly social nature of a therapeutic or counseling group reveals these deficiences to the leader and others. The group then provides the opportunity to learn new behaviors through the leader's and members' feedback, and a safe place to practice.

Borrowing the behavior of a role model helps expand one's repertoire of social skills. Even an extremely nonverbal person has an excellent medium through which to learn, whether the model is a group peer or the counselor. Equally important is the need of some disabled and disadvantaged persons to learn appropriate ways to express affect. Without suitable learning experiences in the restrictive institutions and other oppressive situations in which these individuals often live, they are forced to suppress anger, frustration, and fear. A disabled person is often encouraged to "keep a stiff upper lip"; displays of anger are often deterred with threats of expulsion or other punitive action. Some institutions operate at the opposite extreme; the clientele are treated like children, and childish behaviors, including tantrums and inappropriate displays of affection, are accepted as the norm. The counseling or therapy group can initiate a focus on affect, and provide effective feedback to correct aberrant behavior and shape appropriate ways of expressing affect. Members find that it is acceptable and healthy to express fear and anger, or that physical displays of affection, such as hugging, are subject to social constraints. The group experience also offers opportunities to ventilate. Although no permanent therapeutic benefit is ascribed to catharsis alone, the temporary relief of getting things off one's chest is well established. It often keeps the individual functional until more global aspects of a problem can be resolved.

Group practitioners and theorists emphasize the necessity of developing cohesiveness, with its sense of belongingness and mutual responsibility for attaining goals. For the disabled or disadvantaged individual who may have endured a lifetime of rejection, the counseling group may be the first opportunity to experience sharing and caring. In the typically authoritarian institutional structure, cooperation is usually imposed or coerced, and stems from extrinsic motivators. Learning the value of self-control and direction may be the ultimate social skill necessary for the individual to live harmoniously with the rest of society.

Factors Affecting the Group Process

A number of factors affect the ability of disabled and disadvantaged persons to participate in group counseling and therapy activities and may adversely affect group dynamics. Attention to these factors is equally relevant in groups composed entirely of disabled or disadvantaged persons and groups that have one such member. In this latter case, attention to these factors may make the difference between the individual's functioning comfortably in the group or dropping out. Individuals frequently have multiple disabilities or problems that may require dealing with more than one issue at a time.

Mobility Problems

Transportation and mobility problems warrant considerable concern. For those who rely on wheelchairs, public transportation in many places is often inadequate. Often, private transportation must be provided, which can be burdensome. Architectural barriers often hinder access. Transportation and access may prevent regular attendance or make participation impossible. The economically disadvantaged or those who live in remote areas may have similar problems; they may not be able to afford transportation, or there may be none available. It should come as no surprise, then, that most groups for the disabled are offered in primary treatment centers or residential facilities. The message is clear; to provide group or other services after discharge, one must first resolve the mobility issue.

Mobility may also be limited within the group. Seating arrangements should take into consideration the needs of those who use wheelchairs or who have other limitations. The position of these individuals in the group is frequently dictated, to a large extent, by accessibility rather than preference, and the forced seating arrangement can affect performance in the group.

Medical Status

Mobility limitations are usually obvious among disabled persons, but other types of problems are more subtle, and apt to be overlooked. For instance, some people may have a limited sitting tolerance because of injury or limited stamina. The one-and-a-half to two hours that are typical for group sessions may be beyond some of these members' tolerance, so the format may have to be adjusted, perhaps to more frequent, shorter sessions.

Medications may be another consideration. Although antidepressants and mood elevators may enhance functioning, side effects of other medications may complicate the group experience. Valium is a good example of one of these medications because of its widespread use to relieve nonaffective symptoms, such as muscle spasticity; it does, however, have a significant impact on affect. The medication's effect on mood or affect can be quite pronounced, often producing an attitude of indifference. The client's resultant aloofness may not be typical, and misleading and confusing in the context of the group, underscoring the need for counselors and therapists to obtain pertinent background information on their clients.

Mental Status

Acute emotional problems may have considerable influence on group processes and cause disruption when these problems or disorders are not the focus of the group. Group therapy is used extensively with persons who exhibit the whole gamut of psychiatric disorders, ranging from psychosis to minimal neurotic problems. As mentioned, some of the earliest applications of group procedures involved psychiatric patients. Since symptomatic behaviors have interpersonal implications, group procedures lend themselves to treatment; however, when these problems appear in persons who are participating in groups that are not specifically intended to deal with them, they can be disruptive. Extreme mood swings are confusing to other members. Loss of contact with reality, for example, hallucinating, can be frightening to the unfamiliar. Extreme sensitivity coupled with the confrontation that often occurs in groups can result in withdrawal. Manic and hyperactive individuals can totally dominate the group and are usually difficult to control.

For the most part, however, these extreme emotional states are detectable during prescreening, and, unless the counselor or therapist plans to have the group address the related problems, it is advisable to exclude potential members from the group. They will probably benefit better from individual treatment until their mental status improves to a level likely to be tolerated by a more general group. The leader might also reserve persons with these more acute problems until there are enough for a special group. When such a member turns up unexpectedly, it may be necessary to remove him to preserve the integrity of the group. Such a termination can delay development of the group, but with assurance that the terminated member is receiving more appropriate treatment, the delay can be minimal.

A member's intellectual level, particularly when significantly low, is another factor that can have a notable effect on group process. If members function in the retarded range, it is reasonable to assume that cohesiveness and a therapeutic climate will evolve more slowly than is generally the case. It is not unusual for members who are retarded to exhibit a great deal of acting out behavior at the initial stages of the group. Some of this behavior is probably attributable to their needing to test the situation, but probably also stems from anxiety. Because the retarded may not have the ability or opportunity to develop more sophisticated, verbal methods for dissipating anxiety, it is more likely to become manifest in motoric behavior. Appropriate use of structure, such as limiting the size of the group and shortening sessions, can minimize related problems. It may also be helpful to precede group sessions with vigorous physical activity; after disseminating some of their pent-up energy, members may be able to better tolerate the restraints of the group session. Patience is vital when working with this population.

Counselors and therapists must also be prepared to meet the language limitations of many of these clients. Talking above their level of comprehension contributes to inattentiveness, boredom, and restlessness that result in disruptive behavior. Acquisition of appropriate social behavior, such as attentiveness and self-control, may be a natural first goal for such groups. In this regard, the group can be a forum for social and interpersonal skills assessement as well as training.

Problems can also arise if the intellectual level of the group membership is too varied. It may be impossible to conduct activities at a level suitable for all. Even if the leader can provide alternative explanations to facilitate understanding, the result will be bordeom and a strained atmosphere. Under such circumstances, it is difficult to maintain group momentum. Disparity in intellectual levels also creates "deviants" or subgroups, both of which are disruptive. Consequently, maintaining some homogeneity with regard to intellectual level may be necessary to help insure optimal group functioning.

Communication Problems

Because the counseling process revolves around communication, working with people who have communication impediments poses a challenging, but manageable, situation. Hearing impairment is probably the communication problem we encounter most often. Raising one's voice to be heard can obliterate paralinguistic cues to affect and can disturb the group process. The member with the impairment may be frustrated by the difficulty of trying to follow the conversation, or may ultimately be shut out of the group. If the group will include someone with a hearing impairment, the impact of the deficit should be minimized through strategic seating arrangements which are advantageous to the individual. Circular or semicircular arrangements can be effective, especially if the hearing-impaired member can supplement aural input with lipreading. If a group member has no functional hearing, sign language can be substituted. A sign language interpreter will probably be necessary, but counselors and therapists have effectively used sign language interpreters (Schein,

1982) without disrupting or inhibiting the group process. Experienced interpreters operate quite unobtrusively.

Someone with severe congenital hearing impairment frequently needs extra attention in dealing with feelings, because this handicap diminishes affective learning experiences. Without the verbal medium, it is much more difficult to learn intangible concepts such as love, hate, or friendship, and to associate them with a multitude of often subtle behaviors. Some deaf people become socially withdrawn because of the handicap and its resultant interpersonal strain, which further limits their affective experiences. The counseling or therapy group may provide an effective forum for dealing with related issues.

Other measures that help a hearing-impaired member to function in the group include discouraging more than one person from talking at once and eliminating extraneous noises such as those of ventilation systems or nearby traffic. The counselor or therapist can become sensitized to some of the difficulties of the hearing impaired with a few simple simulation exercises. For example, watching television or a movie with the sound turned off can suggest the impact of total hearing loss. Partial hearing problems can be simulated by keeping the volume of the television very low, trying to listen to a radio program with the radio tuned between two stations, or trying to carry on a conversation while wearing a headset tuned to high-volume white noise. Remember, however, that these temporary simulations do not begin to convey the lifelong psychological impact of hearing dysfunctions.

Because deafness and blindness are sensory impairments, they are often categorized together for study and treatment, with the assumption that they constitute similar handicaps. From a functional standpoint, however, the two problems are quite different, and in some respects, the consequences of the two handicaps are more logically seen as opposites. Although significant hearing deficiencies create problems with verbal communication, loss of vision has greater impact on nonverbal communication. Visual impairments pose a greater problem in relating to the overall environment than to people, although in terms of interpersonal functioning, the visually impaired may be cut off from facial expression, eye contact, body posture, and numerous other visual cues. The inability to see when another individual is pursing her lips in preparation to speak leaves the visually-impaired person in the awkward position of not knowing whether it is appropriate to enter a conversation. If the counselor or therapist does not deal with this predicament, the visually-impaired person may be inhibited in the context of the group. A sensitive group counselor or therapist can provide verbal cues to let that person know when he can speak and to insure that he is not excluded from other significant group happenings. It may be especially important to describe relevant nonverbal behavior, as well as other aspects of the group, such as seating arrangements, verbally.

Severe visual impairment also constitutes a mobility handicap. Merely getting to the sessions may be exhausting and emotionally draining. Seating arrangement can also be an issue; it may seem expedient to seat the visually-impaired member near the entrance or at the end of a row of chairs, but the arrangement must be evaluated in terms of its possible impact on group dynamics. Convenience should not result in isolation from the mainstream. Overall, vision impairment need not limit participation in the group process. In fact, Kennard and Shilman (1979) describe a successful therapeutic group in which members participated by means of a telephone network.

Expressive disorders constitute a third type of communication problem that can have an impact on the group. The most significant speech impairments are those stemming from brain dysfunction and are often manifested by victims of cerebral palsy, strokes, or head injuries. Speaking is a labored and frustrating process for these people; for the listener, comprehension is equally difficult and tiring. The pressure from this interpersonal strain causes the individual to struggle further, and speech deteriorates even more. Although supplemental or alternative modes of communication, such as writing or a voice synthesizer, can be used to compensate, there is no substitute for patience and a relaxed atmosphere. Under these supportive conditions, effective communication is possible; even gestures and pantomime have been effective in enabling group participation by persons with severe expressive handicaps (Sussman, 1979). Other expressive problems such as stuttering or limited vocabulary can be similarly dealt with.

Many people who need counseling or therapeutic services speak little or no English. Finding oneself in a group with whom one cannot communicate because of a limited grasp of the predominant language can be frustrating or even frightening. If the problem is not dealt with effectively, the group experience can exacerbate one's sense of helplessness and actually turn into a damaging experience.

One can address the problem of limited language with some of the techniques that are effective with other types of communication disorders. If the counselor is fluent in the member's language, he can act as an interpreter. Or, he might bring in an outside interpreter, although this is usually distracting because two conversations must often go on simultaneously. Even if willing, other group participants should not be given the burden of interpreting because it will distract from their personal concern and involvement. More than one member with the same language limitation complicates group dynamics by providing a strong basis for subgrouping.

Potential members who might be hampered by their language difference should be evaluated during prescreening to determine the extent to which the problem might interfere with group process and to ascertain the most effective way to deal with the problem. With proper preparation, it is usually feasible and desirable to include these individuals in groups if they seem strong enough to withstand the frustration; in other instances, it may be preferable to create separate groups for those with the language difference. If that is not possible, individual counseling may be the only recourse.

To minimize the problem of a language limitation, it is advisable to warn other potential group members of the expected difficulty beforehand rather than suprise them. This is equally true for the language-limited member. Forewarning members enables the counselor or therapist to gauge their reactions; if it appears that some potential members do not have the sensitivity or tolerance to make it a workable situation, they can be excluded from the group or given an opportunity to resolve their conflict before participating. When the group becomes operational, the counselor, through modeling, can establish an atmosphere of patience and support. Gestures and role playing often enhance communication in the face of limited verbal communication.

Cultural Differences

Skin color or some other aspect of appearance does not constitute sufficient reason to assume cultural difference. Many racially and ethnically identifiable persons have grown up outside the originating cultural confines and have assimilated their beliefs, attitudes, values, and customs from elsewhere. To be truly culturally different, one must carry attitudes, values, customs, and traditions that do not predominate in the associating population.

The counselor or therapist must be sensitive to cultural difference when it does exist, however. There is probably no substitute for personal contact in determining cultural status, and probably no more effective way to become knowledgeable about cultural differences than through personal, direct involvement with the cultural community.

Asking for or seeking help is contrary to some cultural systems. This value prevails in many rural populations, where independence and self-reliance have been keys to survival. A consequence of this value is resistance to activities that could be construed as evidence of weakness or an inability to solve one's personal problems. The implications for participation in counseling or therapy are obvious. In some instances, a group approach diminishes the resistance, especially if the member focuses on the social elements of the group. Members from some cultural settings, for example, Mexican-American backgrounds, have a strong sense of community, and homogenous groups readily develop cohesiveness and an atmosphere of mutual support. On the other hand, revealing personal problems to others inside the cultural group may be inhibited by other aspects of the culture, such as a highly active gossip system. Similarly, revealing personal problems to someone outside the cultural group, including group counselors and therapists, may be inhibited by suspicion and lack of trust. Meeting clients on their own turf may dissipate the suspicion.

Another cultural custom that may interfere with the group process is the practice of suppressing emotions and avoiding confrontation, characteristic of the traditional Japanese (Sue, 1980) and some Asian-Americans. In other cultures, silence is a sign of respect and may be a confounding factor. Different cultures give different attention to time. Some members will have difficulty accepting that group sessions must begin at the designated time because their culture does not value that kind of precision; it may also be considered rude to terminate ongoing activities just to be prompt at some other commitment. Time of arrival is also associated with status in some cultures, and lateness is a reflection of high social standing. Some individuals thus have a cultural basis for habitual tardiness and may not understand why others consider such behavior inconsiderate. These conflicting values contribute to the problems the culturally different confront. Attempting to impose change in persons with culturally-based problems is not likely to be successful, especially if the individual continues to reside in a community that supports the differences. Moreover, there is probably little justification for expecting someone to abandon cultural conventions just because they are different. Usually, a more appropriate goal is to enable the member to develop enough flexibility to adapt to the different cultural settings in which he must function. Exploring conflicting values in an atmosphere of respect and tolerance is probably the key to dealing successfully with culturally different group members.

Composing Groups with Disabled and Disadvantaged Persons

Practitioners tend to develop groups composed of members who are similarly disabled or disadvantaged (Chubon, 1982), probably as a reflection of the settings in which group counseling and therapy take place. These settings are generally institutions and agencies that serve discrete populations; when operating in a situation that deals with a specific population such as the mentally retarded, it becomes a matter both of necessity and convenience to limit membership to that population. Similarly, when a group is created to deal with a problem unique to some population, such as women who have undergone mastectomies, it is appropriate to limit group membership; however, the use of a restrictive approach to composing a group is probably overplayed. Often, the rationale for using homogeneity as a criterion for member selection is open to question. Homogeneity can facilitate cohesiveness, a necessary condition for effectiveness in most groups, but the price may be a group that focuses only on the superficial commonality that brought members together. It may be much more difficult for members to deal with diminished self-esteem, for example, when common physical ailments are a competing focus. In fact, research by Barch and Liberto (1980) seems to support that conclusion. Disability groups comprised of members with diverse diagnoses have been successful, further indicating that homogeneity is not of overriding importance.

A related question arises as to the inclusion of members with disabilities or some other disadvantageous condition in a group composed predominantly of members without these characteristics. The same rationale applies—there seems to be no research support for excluding an otherwise suitable candidate from a group simply on the basis of a disability or disadvantageous condition. The crucial issues are whether the individual's needs are compatible with the group's purpose and whether his interpersonal functioning is conducive to the group process. Yalom (1975) points out that some personality types may be damaging to the group process; for example, people who are highly manipulative or suspicious may constantly disrupt the group, and when others try to control this behavior, the disrupters are apt to become estranged, withdrawn, and ultimately to drop out. On the other hand, including disabled and disadvantaged members in growth-oriented groups can expand the issues the group is likely to explore.

Another issue to consider is the effect on group functioning of a disabled or disadvantaged counselor or therapist. This is a relevant concern since an increasing number of people with these backgrounds are entering the professions. So far, it appears unlikely that such chracteristics become an issue with groups. If the counselor is competent and comfortable with her personal situation, the group generally disregards the disabling characteristics. Although clients with characteristics or backgrounds similar to that of the counselor may more readily identify with the leader, somewhat facilitating the development of trust, those who do not share the counselor's characteristic rarely react unless the difference is at the crux of a personal problem. Since this strain will probably appear during the screening process, individuals who react adversely can be excluded from the group and dealt with through a more acceptable or comfortable alternative. Finally, although there are not many research studies in this area, even blind persons have proven successful group counselors and therapists (Benjamin, 1978).

Trust

The issue of trust emerges when developing group counseling and therapy programs for disabled and disadvantaged populations because many aspects of their life experiences have contributed to attitudes of distrust. Through institutional and other forms of oppression, some involving stigmatization and ostracism, disabled and disadvantaged people face an "us against them" predicament. Many of them have backgrounds filled with broken promises, exploitation, and outright abandonment during their efforts to sustain themselves in the "system." Sometimes group participation is involuntary, required by the institutional structure, which leads to skepticism and resistance. The alienation carries over to the attitude toward the therapist or counselor, who is identified as a member of the establishment.

Under the best of circumstances, genuine trust is difficult to attain, usually limited to a few lifelong friends or acquaintances. Before the leader deals with the issue of trust in the group, he should determine the relevance of high levels of trust to achieving the group's purpose. If the purpose is primarily informational, trust may be a minimal concern. On the other hand, revealing feelings of sexual inadequacy is likely to be contingent upon development of deeply felt trust.

The need for and benefits of trust can be brought into the open and explored, although simply talking about trust will not create it. The counselor's handling of the confidentiality issue is crucial to establishing trust. He must not make commitments he cannot keep. Particularly when a group is conducted under the auspices of the justice or corrections system, members will be suspicious of commitments of complete confidentiality. Recognition and admission of limitations can be a refreshing change to those who have encountered broken promises throughout their lives.

Used with discretion, the counselor's self-disclosure can also foster acceptance and trust. Self-disclosures show members that the group leader is human and understands their plight. This approach carries some risk, in that some members may seize upon revelations as an opportunity to discredit the counselor by focusing on apparent discrepancies or fallibilities; minimally, self-disclosure can result in a nonproductive focus on the counselor. Sometimes a leader who is not part of the system can more easily bridge the trust gap. In the end, probably the most effective way to deal with the issue of trust is an established record of trustworthiness; such a reputation spreads quickly among peers, diminishing the issue to an incidental level.

Trust among members, however, can be the more difficult problem, because the counselor will probably have little, if any, control over members' actions outside group sessions. Blackmail and betrayal are characteristic of many prison environments. In these circumstances, the only recourse is to deal with the issue directly, emphasizing that confidentiality is mutually beneficial and that a minimal amount of trust is necessary to remain functional, but one must expect intermember trust to evolve slowly. Members will test and retest each other until they perceive a satisfactory sense of security. An alternative is to screen out potential participants who have the most pronounced paranoiac views and deal with them individually until they are better able to meet the demands of the group.

Numerous activities and exercises are touted for facilitating development of trust, several of which involve blindfolding members one at a time and having them place their well-being in the hands of the other members. Although these activities seem to enhance interaction and cohesiveness, research has yet to confirm their effectiveness in enhancing trust.

Applications

To use group counseling and therapy effectively with the disabled and disadvantaged, it is essential to understand their needs as well as how their conditions may affect group processes. Their many needs often necessitate establishing intervention priorities. In addition, disabling and disadvantaging conditions are multiple and concurrent. The counselor must consider all relevant factors and formulate a workable strategy.

Alcoholism Treatment Groups

Group strategies in treating alcoholism are prevalent, to say the least. Although use of groups is extensive in this area, it is difficult to ascertain effectiveness. Group outcomes are not easy to discern from other interventions, such as individual counseling, usually conducted concurrently. Although empirical evidence is lacking, there seems to be strong support in the form of clinical impressions as to the utility of the group; unfortunately, the strong belief in the group approach has probably led to establishment of many programs that are not based on rigorous guidelines and are probably not effective.

The group program developed by the Alcohol Treatment Unit at the Texas Research Institute for Mental Sciences is exemplary because it is so well planned (Sands & Hanson, 1971). The multifaceted program has reportedly evolved as a result of considering specific needs of the alcoholic population, and includes orientation groups, singles' groups, spouses' groups, and couples' groups. Perhaps the most unique aspect of the program is its use of orientation groups. People who are admitted to alcoholism treatment centers vary in their state of readiness and willingness to receive help, and misplacement in the treatment program can result in attrition. Consequently, the Texas program's orientation groups assess motivation for treatment, provide information about alcoholism, assess ability to function in a group, and prepare clients to join a therapeutic group. The orientation groups meet weekly, for four to six weeks of 90 minute sessions, although clients can remain for an additional period if they not feel ready to move on to a therapeutic group. Others can be required to continue in the orientation group until they gain demonstrable control over sobriety.

A second tier of groups in the model program is that of singles' groups, formed because some individuals with alcohol problems have no interested family or relatives. Also, some people's problems may have little, if any, relationship to their marriages, and still others prefer to "go it alone." The groups have six to ten members who are unrelated married or unmarried persons. The therapeutic format is directed toward helping members ventilate feelings, comparing their situations with others', developing more effective interpersonal skills, learning coping skills from one another, and providing opportunities to try out and practice new behaviors. A supportive climate is maintained, and reported outcomes are (1) increased understanding of personal conflicts that contribute to alcoholism, (2) better ability to anticipate provocative situations, and (3) learning more effective ways to deal with problems when they occur.

Although spouse groups are intended to accommodate husbands and wives of alcoholics, only wives have joined the Texas groups. Initially, members have a chance to ventilate feelings arising from the fact that they may have suffered loss of support from the spouse or have been pressured to blunt the impact of the spouse's problem, may have been physically abused, and may have suffered financial hardship and childrearing problems, among others. As quickly as possible, the focus shifts to group members' behavior, particularly with regard to its possible role in sustaining the drinking problem. Members often express guilt because of the overriding belief that the member caused the spouse's problem. The therapeutic goal is to free the wife from responsibility for her spouse's behavior and help her come to rely on her own resources to live her own life rather than live in reaction to her husband. Once the wife is able to "let go," other problems emerge. Changes in behavior can result in estrangement, or sometimes separation; at the least, some may require additional or refined interpersonal skills.

When the problems of alcoholism have abated sufficiently that they are no longer a central focus, other issues take priority. Altered behaviors frequently call for interpersonal adjustments if marriages are to be salvaged, and when alcohol is removed as the problem, other personality factors are exposed. Sobriety, in and of itself, is not a panacea to all a couple's problems; significant other work may remain. If couples do not acknowledge the problems, the poor relationship may serve as an excuse for the alcoholic to resume drinking. Individuals enter the couples' program after they complete an orientation group or, in some cases, a singles' group. Sometimes the singles' group is a prerequisite for a spouse to become comfortable enough to withstand the more confrontive spouses' group. Members have opportunities to compare problems and solutions and to benefit from feedback.

The groups' format is designed to enable participants to take responsibility for their own termination. Essentially, the members determine when they feel capable of maintaining sobriety. Members are, however, expected to announce their decision to terminate early enough that the group can discuss the issue. Some members remain in the group for periods well beyond the point where sobriety seems stable and the member is vocationally successful, perhaps because of a need for continued support or because the member has no other safe place to ventilate.

Persons with Physical Disabilities

Common group purposes for those with physical disabilities include assertiveness training, sexual adjustment, mutual support, and personal adjustment. The problems are usually clearly attributable to the disabling conditions. In the face of their obvious needs, it is often easy to overlook the fact that disabled individuals also have the same needs as their nondisabled peers.

Recognition of such needs led Kriegsman and Celotta (1981a, b) to develop creative coping groups for women with physical disabilities. Unlike most group programs for the physically disabled, these coping groups were not part of a customary rehabilitative process.

One of the first needs was to find an accessible site, because the sponsoring agency's offices were not accessible by wheelchair. The group facilitator was a female counselor who was disabled; it was felt that having a facilitator who was disabled would be advantageous in developing trust and credibility. She collaborated, through postsession debriefings, with a counselor educator and psychologist.

Participants had various disabilities—spinal cord injury, cerebral palsy, birth defects, multiple sclerosis, and chronic pain. Those who appeared at screening to have severe emotional problems were excluded. Consistent with the personal growth model, the eight 90-minute sessions were essentially unstructured. In the early sessions, the women focused on issues such as feelings of self-worth, anger, and dependency. Other concerns that emerged were depression, embarrassment at asking for help, lack of acceptance of the disability, and difficulties in vocational and childrearing areas. Although sexuality was dealt with, this was a relatively unimportant concern for these women. The group explored ways to express anger appropriately and discussed positive changes in participants' lives.

Evaluation of group outcomes indicated that a disabled facilitator was an important factor in developing comfort in the group. Some members reported greater acceptance of their disability, as well as improvement in self-image and self-esteem. The improved self-concept was thought to be more consistent with views of the members as "whole women." Better acceptance of others and greater self-confidence in dealing with personal problems were also notable outcomes. The group experience appeared to result in acquisition of new coping skills, enabling participants to deal more effectively with their lives and futures.

The Elderly

The elderly experience a variety of problems that are amenable to treatment with group counseling or therapy. Several problems stand out. First, there are problems stemming from a wide range of losses: loss of spouse, family members, and friends through death; loss of job, home, and neighborhood following retirement. Other problems stem from the impact of aging on the body: loss of vision, hearing, stamina, agility, and mobility. Elderly people are also victims of attitudinal biases; they are often cast in stereotypes that depict them as inferior, incompetent, childlike, asexual, and burdensome. These problems are often compounded by isolation and loneliness, and the stimulus deprivation that comes from confinement to home or institution. This population also suffers from others' assumption that their problems are organically based, the result of deteriorating brain function, when confusion and diminished responses often stem from side effects of medications given for other problems. Finally, the elderly are also victims of theorists; the withdrawal theory, for example, holds that older people gradually withdraw from the mainstream in preparation for final separation.

Many of the problems one faces in one's later years are the result of limited socialization and interpersonal activities; others involve damaged self-image and self-esteem, all of which are readily treatable with group techniques. In fact, because of the strong interpersonal focus of the group, it is probably the most appropriate intervention for the problems of the elderly.

Capuzzi and Gross (1981) find the more common group types with this population are (1) *reality orientation groups* for those who are experiencing disorientation to time, people, things, and places; (2) *remotivation groups*, intended to stimulate those who have lost interest in the present or future; (3) *reminiscing groups*, built upon a life review process; and (4) *psychotherapy groups* for treating specific problems such as depression or anxiety.

For this population, it is important to choose a comfortable meeting environment, especially with regard to temperature, functional furniture, such as chairs that are easy to get in and out of, freedom from extraneous noise and other distractions, and awareness of the members' stamina, sitting tolerance, and mobility. The meeting times should not interfere with critical rest periods, and meetings held after dark can be especially hazardous to older people.

Altholz (1978) describes a therapeutic group she established in an outpatient clinic for mental health care and conducted for more than two years. Its purpose was to enhance socialization and enable members to share problem solutions. The number of participants ranged from five to nine; members had a common diagnosis of depression and were heterogeneous with regard to background. Therapy focused on three areas: adaptation to aging, reality testing abilities, and social interaction.

Coleaders were a female social worker and a male psychiatrist. Potential members were screened in individual interviews in which the group's purpose was described and personal goals developed. In the early sessions, a general contract was developed with the participants because it was felt that clear delineation of group purpose and functioning would help dissipate some of the confusion and apprehension older people often experience in such a situation. Sessions were an hour long, and although counselors stressed the importance of regular attendance, absenteeism was tolerated because of the many legitimate reasons for it among this population. Ultimately, members opted for an open-ended format with no specific termination point.

The group usually needed several minutes to "warm up" at the onset of sessions, so participants were encouraged to begin interaction as soon as they arrived at the meeting site. Cohesiveness developed rapidly, reflected in the members' concern for those who were absent. Members initially relied on the therapists for direction, but after a few months, older members began voluntarily assuming some of the maintenance responsibilities, such as orienting new members. There was a great deal of mutual support. General concerns included depression and suicidal thoughts, changing roles precipitated by aging, and difficulties in social relationships. Losses were among the most prevalent concerns. Altholz concluded that the elderly's self-worth increases simply by knowing that a group exists for them, and while they participate, they benefit from the social experience as well as from the other curative factors inherent in group therapy and counseling.

Visually Impaired Persons

Group counseling and therapy have dealt with a variety of the adjustment problems of visual impairment. Group purposes include enhancement of self-concept and self-esteem that often diminish in the face of dependency and mobility problems, and assertiveness training. Because the most frequent causes of visual loss, glaucoma and diabetic retinopathy, are associated with aging, the majority of visually impaired persons are also elderly. Other problems precipitated by aging become intertwined with the visual handicap and must be dealt with concurrently, as we see in the following group experience developed for the elderly, visually impaired.

This author has summarized the group experience reported by Harshbarger (1980) because it depicts a broad spectrum of the issues that need to be addressed when dealing with this population. Harshbarger (1980) developed a counseling group to supplement the life skills training activities in a community rehabilitation program for the visually impaired. Many of the program's clients were suffering depression as a result of their handicap. Mobility and transportation were not major issues, since the group setting was an established center that served the blind. Clients spent much of the day at the facility and limited transportation was available in the agency bus.

Elderly clients were fearful of anything that connoted "therapy" and its implication of mental illness, and were thus reluctant to admit their need or become involved. To overcome this fear, the program was called an "adjustment to blindness" discussion group. Although significant resistance remained, the staff was able to persuade a group of clients to try one session.

The initial group included both blind and partially sighted persons, about half of whom acknowledged depression as the reason for their interest and participation. The remaining participants reported reasons such as "curiosity" and "on behalf of a friend." An open-ended, ongoing format permitted admission and termination of members at any point. Generally, group size ranged from five to eight members. Harshbarger reported that sessions with fewer than five participants appeared to inhibit the group and increase anxiety, and more than eight members caused withdrawn individuals difficulty in interacting. Hearing impairments were common among participants, and the larger group size hampered participation of those with this additional handicap, because greater group size necessitated greater distance between some members. Members with both visual and hearing deficiences could neither hear nor see when others were speaking, and often unknowingly interrupted ongoing discussion. Smaller group size enabled these members to more quickly recognize others by their voices, facilitating development of cohesiveness. Rules of confidentiality prohibited members from discussing happenings outside the group membership, which irritated many nonparticipating clients at the agency and evoked curiosity in others, and may have contributed to their subsequent interest and participation. Once established, membership was sustained by a steady flow of new members. Because of members' heightened resistance, Harshbarger adjusted the format to allow potential participants to attend a "trial session" without making a commitment to join.

Clients were encouraged to focus on "feeling" issues, but they were not pressed. Some members became noticeably uncomfortable during confrontation that aroused strong feelings, and members often dealt more subtly with affect, such as depression, perhaps talking about it while relating difficulties in performing household chores. Participants were occasionally allowed to bring a friend or family member, which often precipitated discussion of issues such as dependency.

These procedures helped overcome initial resistance, and brought out salient issues such as adjustment to living alone, changes caused by the visual impairment, family reactions, and feelings of depression, aloneness, anger, inferiority, and guilt.

Positive outcomes included alleviation of the sense of aloneness, better understanding of others' blindness, and greater ease in asking for assistance from family and friends. General improvement was apparent in enhanced self-esteem and self-confidence, better acceptance of the visual impairment, alleviation of guilt and depression, and greater effort to resist the tendency to withdraw. This group demonstrated the range of problems amenable to group treatment and exemplified the considerations and adaptations necessary to make the group process effective with members who have disabling conditions.

Incarcerated Persons

Programs for people who are or have been incarcerated range from sensitivity groups to job clubs. Most are conducted postincarceration, because prison systems tend to emphasize punishment rather than rehabilitation and are thus antithetical to the treatment programs that might be most effective in that setting. Although we expect prisoners to reform before they return to society, society is still reluctant to "give" prisoners anything that might be construed as beneficial. Rappaport (1982) saw this conflict in his efforts to establish a group program for inmates of a state prison. Despite the apparent success of his therapeutic program, it was abolished when the prison administration changed to a less benign one.

Rappaport's rationale for group therapy with a prison population rests on the effectiveness of the approach in dealing with problems that involve relating to others, problems that are prevalent among criminals. Groups also provide a means for meeting other common needs, such as releasing pent-up feelings and coming to understand one's behavior. The group approach is also economical. Finally, Rappaport felt the group would facilitate members' insight.

The group format had an analytic orientation, with general goals of relieving symptoms (criminal behaviors) and restructuring personality. Techniques focused on exploring the intrapsychic, unconscious processes that underlie aberrant behaviors and on free association, that is, verbalizing whatever comes to mind. Resistance arises from ego threats, and part of the work of therapy is to cut through this resistance, particularly difficult in the prison situation. Resistance is heightened by the mistrust that permeates prison life, and self-revelation is clearly not valued. Similarly, many of the other curative activities of group therapy—ventilating, giving and receiving, being close to others, developing cohesiveness, acceptance, and seeing others "get better"—are inconsistent with inmate lifestyles. Messages that extol these activities meet with suspicion and skepticism, and compound the problem of overcoming resistance.

Rappaport established two groups, each with two therapists and ten inmates. Members were heterogeneous with regard to background, but were chosen because they were relatively articulate, considered capable of change, and had no history of mental illness.

Groups met weekly for 90 minutes, with focus on either intrapsychic conflicts or interpersonal relationships.

The initial group was highly suspicious of the program and of the therapists' and prison administration's underlying motivation. An overriding concern was the relationship between the group activities and the prisoners' paroles, the most crucial issue in their lives. Considerable energy went toward allaying fears that the opportunity for parole would be jeopardized by some aspects of the members' performance. After it became apparent that the first group suffered no retribution from the authorities, subsequent groups dealt more forthrightly with the trust issue. The fact that one of the therapists in the second group was not a member of the prison staff also helped to alleviate distrust. Therapists resisted the constant pressure to intervene on behalf of members under consideration for parole. They did, however, assume other advocacy roles; for example, they battled for continuing the group therapy program when prison officials threatened to abolish it, which seemed to enhance trust between participants and therapists. On the other hand, distance between therapists and participants could not be entirely overcome, because prisoners believed the therapists could not really understand their predicament, especially since the therapists were free to come and go as they pleased. Rage was not apparent in the sessions, perhaps because of the ever-present fear of retribution and the members' attempts to convince therapists of their rehabilitated state. Anger and warm feelings were expressed, although limited largely to verbalizations. Modification and control of behavior to this extent was considered therapeutic, since these constraints are necessary for acceptable social functioning. Warmth and cohesiveness were especially noticeable in member reactions after terminations.

The open-ended format was considered highly advantageous in that incarcerated members were able to see that some were "making it." In this regard, some members continued in the group after parole, and were able to relate their successes and difficulties on the outside. Paroled members used the groups as a sounding board to explore new problems, and overall, the group therapy program seemed to have a substantially positive impact on the participating inmates.

Culture Specific Groups

The lack of research on counseling minority and culturally different populations may reflect a reluctance to initiate group work with certain ethnic or cultural populations because of culturally-based resistance to treatment in groups. For example, Brower (1983), Sue and Sue (1983), and Ho (1981) outline cultural attributes that are likely to interfere with therapeutic group treatment for Vietnamese, Chinese, and other Asian-Americans, including constraints against public disclosure of personal problems and ventilation of feelings and unwillingness to be confrontive. The smaller number of studies may also reflect a lack of knowledge or flexibility for modifying or adapting the group process to overcome these resistances. Without knowledge and flexibility, leaders are doomed to failure, but on the other hand, with few published studies, it is difficult for the counselor to acquire the essential knowledge.

When problems are approached forthrightly, most culturally-based resistances to group counseling and therapy can be overcome. Schauble, Parker, Probert, and Altmaier (1979) report success at overcoming black college students' shunning of counseling services. This resistance, largely attributable to the black students' inhibitions about asking for help, especially from white-dominated services, and the passive stature of many counseling services, which expect students to come to them, was overcome by facing the issues head-on. In this program, intended to help black students develop more effective learning and coping skills, the services were taken to the students in their classroom settings. The program at first brought counseling psychologists into a special class for minority students, called "Psychology of Learning," with the objectives of teaching academic skills and principles of psychology and adjustment. This situation allowed the staff to clear up many misconceptions students had about the nature of counseling. A second step in the program provided smaller group experiences in which students could practice new learning and personal interaction behaviors, organizing the classes into small groups led by a professional counselor and a minority peer counselor. The peer leader bridged the black/white barrier. The small groups were a source of support for the black students and afforded them opportunities to share concerns and practice new academic and coping skills. Students also had the benefit of the peer counselor's positive role model. The large and small group experiences also allowed for individual counseling to explore personal, academic, vocational, and other needs. Taking the program to the students and gradually exposing them to the concepts of counseling overcame many of the resistances that stemmed from misconceptions and cultural values. The black students came to see counseling as something other than for "crazy and sick" people or a "white" service.

With the influx of Hispanic populations into the United States, there is a growing need to adapt and provide human services to them. Hardy-Fanta and Montana (1982) describe a successful group counseling program for adolescent Hispanic females. They reiterate the reluctance of some cultural groups to seek help and attend conventional treatment centers, such as community mental health centers, because of the misconception that counseling and therapy are for the "crazy." These authors also mention a dearth of published research dealing with group programs for Hispanic adolescents. They developed a short-term group counseling format in a school setting, directed toward troubled Hispanic females who were experiencing cultural and other conflicts. Problems included rebelliousness, depression, and withdrawal. Besides taking the program to the students in their normative setting, the bilingual counselors communicated in Spanish or English, according to the student's preference. The primary purpose of the groups was to give the Hispanic students an opportunity to share their feelings about being caught between traditional Hispanic values and mores and those of the mainland United States. Cultural conflicts were often intertwined with parental conflicts because parents adhered to traditional values while students were attracted to Americanization. As a result of counseling, students reported greater ability to tolerate anxiety, to express their cultural conflicts, and to depend on each other for support. Acting out behavior, depression, and withdrawal diminished among the students who participated.

Another group treatment focused on American Indian high school youths who had been in trouble with the law (Kahn, Williams, Galvez, Lejero, Conrad, & Goldstein, 1981). Culturally-related adaptations of the group technique included presenting therapy as hard work for which participants were paid, having an Indian mental health technician for a cotherapist, using didactic topics to provide structure, and developing much of the discussion in the third person, that is, talking about "someone else." Dramatic results appeared in terms of fewer subsequent arrests and less school absenteeism.

These three studies demonstrate the effectiveness of group counseling and therapy with culture-specific populations and underscore the need for counselors to familiarize themselves with the cultural characteristics of the populations they serve.

Peer Self-Help Groups

In general terms, peer self-help groups are composed of members with a common characteristic and problem focus, who maintain control over their group. In the past two or three decades, the number of self-help groups has burgeoned. The civil rights movement of the 1950s and 1960s probably gave impetus to other groups to take control over their own destinies. This was also a period of emergence of other types of social consciousness as well. The social programs of Lyndon Johnson's "Great Society," the philosophy of normalization in providing services for the handicapped, and emphasis on returning handicapped persons to the community through deinstitutionalization supported the assumption that disadvantaged individuals would take control of their lives to the greatest extent possible. Unfortunately, programs were often deficient and fell short of meeting crucial needs. As a result, people with common problems, disenchanted with available solutions, have banded together to take control of matters. These self-help services have gained acceptance as a vital supplement to existing services. Alcoholics Anonymous, for example, is used in conjunction with many alcoholic treatment programs. In other cases, peer self-help groups disavow relationship with professional service organizations.

The merits of self-help groups have been debated extensively. There is little doubt that many people benefit from them in terms of the mutual support they provide, the restoration of a sense of self-control, improved identity, and increased self-esteem. In terms of dynamics, cohesiveness and trust generally evolve rapidly. Experience sharing is important in dealing with problems; tried and proven solutions are passed on to neophytes or newcomers by more experienced members, often referred to as the "pros." Leadership models are diverse. Some groups elect formal leaders through democratic procedures, while other self-help groups seem almost leaderless, with control alternating from member to member. Sometimes leadership remains in the firm control of the founder. Selections and focus of goals are highly pragmatic and usually involve day-to-day living issues rather than personality change, although this is far from absolute.

Although self-help groups offer many benefits, they are not without critics. Some argue that members are removing themselves further from society; others feel these groups become so enmeshed in mundane issues that they overlook the broader aspects that are at the crux of their problems. Some self-help groups limit or prohibit public scrutiny, thus provoking suspicion. The most legitimate criticism is that most of these groups are not subject to objective evaluation, posing a particular dilemma for the professional called upon to recommend one of these programs. Is it ethical to recommend a program about which little objective information is available? Regardless of professional acceptance, self-help groups are probably here to stay and, in fact, are likely to continue to grow in numbers.

Discussion Questions

1. What changes, differences, and affective states must disabled and disadvantaged persons often deal with in group counseling? What are the problems of stigma and isolation?

2. How do lack of mobility, medical problems, communication limitations, emotional disturbance, limited intelligence, and cultural differences affect the functioning of a member and the group?

3. Choose a special population and discuss the unique features of forming, leading, and managing the group. What problems and special benefits do you anticipate with the group? How can you avoid problems?

13

Group Work with Children and Adolescents

Developmental Frame of Reference

A developmental model is one way to approach group work with children and youth. Young people go through maturational and psychosocial stages. Most counseling and psychotherapy models can be characterized as developmental to the extent that they recognize stages of human growth and development; for example, Freud articulated psychosexual stages. George Gazda (1978) integrated the work of numerous theorists into a framework useful for counselors who wish to emphasize prevention of psychological problems and the strengths of group members. It has special application to counselors working with children and youth or who work with adults through a developmental perspective.

This approach requires understanding of developmental tasks and stages so that, ideally, one can anticipate the tasks a person faces at various levels and attempt to prevent the potential failure that can arise out of each task or stage. Two features immediately become evident from Gazda's model: prevention becomes a real possibility and goal of group counseling; and emphasis is on the individual's strengths and capabilities at each developmental stage. The objective is to control the kinds of debilitating experiences that later require rehabilitation and remediation. The counselor is thus encouraged to devote half the time to prevention, guidance, and teaching functions. The group leader's specific task is to facilitate the learning of coping skills such as decision making, interpersonal skills, and family management.

Rationale

One of Gazda's assumptions is that human beings wish to interact in small, close groups to fulfill their gregarious natures; the logical extension is that group counseling will be the preferred intervention strategy. The individuals in a group have the freedom to make decisions for themselves; given the proper atmosphere, they have the inclination to do what is best for themselves. In the presence of unhealthy conditions, they may choose self-destructive behaviors that lead to failure. Some children are raised in conditions that give them greater freedom to choose, while others have more limited freedom. Whatever the environmental conditions, everyone learns to cope in his unique way. If members have not learned adaptive behaviors, the group leader helps them understand a wider range of choices and acquire new ways to solve their problems.

Group counseling must adapt to its members' age level and developmental tasks. Gazda pulls together several theories that contribute to our understanding of developmental tasks in moving from childhood to old age. From Havinghurst we see that normal development requires successfully completing each task before moving on to another. Failure to successfully complete a task causes difficulty with the tasks that follow, disapproval by society, and personal unhappiness. For example, if one does not learn in kindergarten and first grade to interact in the classroom, he is likely to be unhappy, rejected by his peers, and have trouble socially during the following years. In this case, group guidance and consultation with the classroom teacher is necessary, and the preventive approach is to design socialization and interpersonal activities specifically geared to the kindergarten child. The counselor arranges for nonthreatening classroom interactions; if certain children do not respond well to the classroom socialization activities, they can be brought into another activity group set up for this purpose and led by the counselor. The goal is to facilitate movement through the developmental task of socialization skills. There is a "teachable moment" for many developmental tasks; that is, intervention is most effective the nearer it is to the time the task would normally be addressed. Later intervention may be helpful, but will not have the same impact.

The five developmental domains, biological, intellectual, vocational, sociological, and psychological, each have their own tasks. Various theorists outline the tasks within each realm of functioning: for example, Gesell (Gesell, Ilg, Ames, & Bullis, 1946; Gesell, Ilg, &

Ames, 1956) discuss the physical-sexual realm; Piaget (1955) discusses the area of intellectual development; Kohlberg (1971) the moral or psychosocial; Erikson the psychosocial; and Super (Super, Starishevesky, Matten, & Jordaan, 1963) the vocational.

Knowledge of the developmental tasks and the required coping behaviors at each stage allows the counselor to assess achievement levels of each potential group member in the five developmental realms. Group guidance techniques can keep members moving along with the expected tasks. Guidance functions may include giving information, setting up developmental activities, and consulting with teachers. The counselor may train teachers in human relations skills or suggest class activities that promote growth in the developmental areas.

Direct intervention for a group of children or adults who have failed to master a developmental task may best take the form of group counseling. The counselor identifies the developmental lag and sets group goals for mastery of needed skills or coping behaviors. This intervention serves a remedial purpose; for instance, counseling for adolescents may address their inability to work cooperatively with others—remediation in the psychological and sociological realms. At the same time, these adolescents may also participate in another group that deals with vocational information, the work world, and exploration of vocational goals, a vocational guidance group organized to address another developmental area, but offered at the "teachable moment."

One must keep in mind the individual variation within each developmental area. Socialization abilities and physical maturation, for example, do not occur at the same time for everyone. Facial hair does not appear at the same age for every boy, and differentiation of self from mother and formulation of one's identity does not occur at a specified age. They do, however, normally arrive within a certain age range and follow a predictable sequence. For purposes of group counseling, Gazda names four phases: early childhood (ages 5–9), preadolescence (ages 10–13), adolescence (ages 13–20), and adulthood. Little is known about the value of group work before age 5, so Gazda omits this age group from the scheme. Males and females develop at different rates, so the age level for certain tasks will differ.

Gazda incorporates the use of nonprofessional helpers into his model, agreeing with Carkhuff (1969) and others that "helpers" without graduate degrees can be trained in human relations skills to assist clients who need or wish to master life skills. Indigenous workers are especially helpful with disadvantaged populations and where they share life experiences with their clients or students, as in the case of disabilities or alcohol or drug abuse.

Selection

The developmental model provides a systematic method for selecting group members. Selection is important because group member satisfaction appears to be largely a function of cohesiveness, and cohesiveness arises when members perceive that they have things in common with one another. Using the developmental model, one selects members who share certain developmental deficiencies or strengths. Gazda's description of the stages in each area of development helps the counselor diagnose the potential group member's developmental stage.

In each developmental area—intellectual, physical-sexual, vocational, psychosocial, and moral—a set of tasks follows a defined sequence. As an example, a typical eight-year-old would exhibit particular behaviors in each area. In the psychosocial, he is no longer identifying himself with adults; he is establishing friendships and giving love, distinguishing the adult from the child's world, and learning more roles and belonging to a group. In the vocational area, identification with significant others influences the child's self-concept. In the intellectual area, he perceives sameness of mass or substance and area with visual objects and is able to distinguish equivalence and nonequivalence in length; he begins to be able to classify things. In the physical-sexual, he is learning to be more "graceful and poised in movement and posture," more involved in physically daring activities, he evaluates new adventures, and is very aware of sexual distinctions between boys and girls. And in the area of moral development, he is beginning to establish values through fear of punishment; that is, he chooses his behavior to avoid pain.

Let us assume you are an elementary school counselor or a psychotherapist in a mental health center and plan to organize group counseling for eight-year-olds. As you interview each child and analyze school and family data, you will look for similarities among the children. You may determine that you wish to work on psychosocial and prevocational development; therefore, you will look for eight-year-olds who do not demonstrate the typical developmental levels for those two areas. One child may qualify because he is so attached to his mother that he refuses to make friends with other children and resists going to school every day. He does pretty much what he wants to do, preferring to stay close to his mother. His self-concept has not developed well because he has not adequately separated his identity from that of his mother. He also has an underdeveloped conception of work, the work world, and adult occupations. Evaluation reveals that he is growing adequately in the other three developmental areas.

The second potential group member is in conflict with her mother and her teacher, the reason for the referral. However, she perceives herself separate from her mother, has two good friends, and knows the rules of the class, although she does not always conform. She is able to identify with adults other than her mother and teacher, and understands the working roles of teachers, her father, and some other adults. Her moral development is even somewhat advanced for her age and contributes to the conflict with mother and teacher. She no longer behaves just to avoid punishment. Her mother has been unfair, demanding, and has unconsciously selected her as the scapegoat of family problems. This eight-year-old girl is rebelling against her mother; she needs therapeutic help but is not appropriate for this group because her problems are different. She should be referred to another group or seen in individual or family counseling. The group leader continues to screen until he selects five to seven children.

Empathic Approach to the Developmental Stage of Adolescence

This group of 13- to 15-year-old boys illustrates Gazda's approach. In practice, counselors see many more boys than girls.

John: We all skip school a lot, but Rocky skips so he can go and get drunk, and he wants us to get drunk with him.

Rocky: You act like you never get drunk. John, you drink when we cut school and you know it. You are just trying to blame me.

John: I drink some, but you try to get drunk every time and you get mad if I don't.

Rocky: No I don't. We skip to go and have a good time. Sometimes you're a drag.

John: I just don't want to get drunk every time.

Counselor: Well, group, what do you think about this?

Pete: Rocky has a lot of problems. He always wants to get drunk, and he tries to get us to do the same.

Rocky: Yeah, blame me for skipping school and drinking. You guys have to blame somebody, don't ya?

John: If it wasn't for you I wouldn't have cut school.

Ed: Neither would I. You just wanted to get a bunch of guys to drink with ya.

Counselor: It sounds like the group wants to blame Rocky for all the problems.

Ed: I think Rocky is the cause of it all.

Rocky: I never forced you to do anything. I've had it with you guys. Who needs ya anyway. You're a bunch of jerks anyway.

Counselor: Rocky sounds real angry at the group for blaming him.

Louis: Maybe he deserves it. I don't know for sure. He does have a big mouth.

Rocky: I'm gonna say what I have to say. I'm not gonna let you jerks push me around.

Pete: No, but you'll try to push *us* around.

Counselor: I hear a lot of accusing and not as much listening to each other.

Rocky: I've listened to too much already. Where do these guys get off pointin' the finger at me? They cut school and drank because they wanted to.

John: You talked us into it.

Louis: Maybe we got to admit we went along with it.

Counselor: Do some of you feel that all the blame isn't Rocky's?

Ed: It's mostly him. He's got a problem. Always getting drunk.

Rocky: And you don't have a problem? Who are you anyway? I've had it with you guys.

Pete: We want to help ya. We don't want to see ya drunk all the time.

The counselor is quite active in this group of early adolescents who are confronting one of the members, and the group has met enough times to reach this level of self-disclosure and genuineness. The leader shows empathy as well as mild confrontation. Eventually, members begin to show some warmth toward Rocky. Their concern becomes more evident in later sessions, and members become emotionally close. Rocky reluctantly concedes some of his emotionally distant "ringleader" status in exchange for greater acceptance. In the protocol, the members avoided responsibility for their own behavior and were actually saying they were afraid they might become like Rocky.

Preadolescents and adolescents are at the stage to learn to be productive and to master their environment. An adolescent must establish his own identity and learn to be loyal to friends and family. The perceptions of others are extremely important. The boys in this group are using self-defeating methods to establish identities. They feel rejected by adults and the mainstream in their school. They blame their deviant efforts on each other, illustrating their lack of loyalty to one another. As the group progresses, they begin to accomplish the tasks of ego identity, showing affection and concern, learning occupational roles, and thereby begin to adopt the "good boy" moral orientation.

General Guidelines for Working with Children and Adolescents

Although most general principles of group work apply to children, there are special considerations. The younger the children, for example, the shorter the session; a group for preschool and early elementary children may last 30 to 45 minutes. The leader must judge each child's attention span.

A second difference in group methods is size; the younger the children, the smaller the group, with a recommended size of four to six through age ten, because younger children are just learning to function in groups outside their immediate families. They also need greater structure; they need to be guided in their activities, and can be given greater responsibility for the group as they mature. The customary discussion of conflicts and concerns is less appropriate as we move down the age scale, so play counseling and play therapy are often used with younger children. Younger children are obviously unable to comprehend personal adjustment problems and normal developmental sequence.

Adolescents are often reluctant to confront their difficulties directly in a one-to-one or group discussion. Activity groups provide a chance for nonverbal expression and a setting for positive therapeutic changes in attitudes and behavior. This form of structured group activities is not used with adults; it permits the counselor to gather observational data for working with the child or consulting with parents and teachers. An example of an activity group is a group of eight boys, ages thirteen and fourteen, who meet once a week for two hours. The first hour and a half is devoted to structured recreation and crafts during which the coleaders direct the activity and interact continually with the boys, and the last half hour is spent having refreshments and discussion. During the session, group leaders point out positive and negative behaviors, encourage alternative behaviors, show understanding of feelings, and mediate conflicts. The leaders encourage the boys to talk about their relationships with one another during the discussion time.

Besides "activity groups," various other techniques are useful with children. Behaviorally-based social learning techniques such as modeling and skill building are used for nearly all age groups. Token economies have been used successfully with children in classroom and institutional settings, and self-reinforcement procedures show promise of making the token approach more efficient. For children with phobias and tension-related problems, group desensitization techniques may be useful. Structured educational-informational approaches, such as those that focus on study skills, learning styles, or medical information about a disability, have been successful. Vocational groups can be used through the teen-age years. Children's groups can also be structured for problem solving, conflict resolution, and decision making. The complexity of tasks and methods in each situation would depend upon the children's maturity and ability levels.

Work with Children

We can divide work with children and youth into two age groups: three through nine, and ten through adolescence, based on developmental needs and appropriate techniques. Essentially, the two major techniques are play therapy and counseling in groups and a group behavioral approach.

Fundamentals with Younger Children

The two main sources for guidance in group counseling with children are Ginott (1968) and Dinkmeyer and Muro (1971). Ginott's insights give the counselor a perspective for working with the younger age group; for instance, Ginott points out that adults normally volunteer to participate in a group and can drop out when they please, but a child is told he will have counseling and is required to remain in the group. Because the group may or may not be good for him and because the child is less likely to comprehend the notion that a particular group can be unhealthy, membership selection and evaluation of group effectiveness are especially important.

Ginott recommends play therapy for children three to nine. Younger children and those who have not differentiated self from mother have a weakness in this first attachment, and will not benefit from the strain of a group. They need to work with one adult to learn to establish relationships and form attachments. Admission to a group must also be based on a child's need for approval, which must be present before the group can exert influence—the child must wish to be accepted and to gain status with peers and therapist.

Members are selected from among children with dissimilar problems and needs so they will have opportunities to relate to children who are both different and complementary. Passive children benefit from the example of those who are more assertive; the quiet learn from the verbal. Ginott also gives age guidelines for group membership. Although there are exceptions, it is best to have members span an age range of 12 months. Less mature children can be assigned to a younger group. Ginott suggests mixing boys and girls at the preschool level and separating them from first grade on. His reasons will not be acceptable to those who reject differentiation of masculine and feminine roles, yet his concern for sexual identification is relevant in today's society because roles and expectations for girls and boys differ from time to time, and the counselor must select models, activities, and tasks relevant to current society.

With the exception of severely retarded children, various intellectual levels are compatible in play therapy. Certain materials and activities allow children at lower and higher cognitive levels to participate on an equal level. For practical reasons, children are accepted into a group at any time, although five is the limit for a play group because too much occurs in a larger group to allow the counselor to react to all the dynamics. One advantage of a group to the child is the relative ease in entering a situation with other children, whereas one-to-one encounter with an adult is often more threatening. Ginott suggests balancing a group with three quiet children and no more than two aggressive ones.

Ginott points out some differences in child-child and therapist-child relationships. First, in contrast to adult group counseling, the center of attention and the goals are directed at the individual. There are no group goals, nor does one seek group cohesion. Subgroups form and break apart; individuals can play by themselves. Group interaction helps children learn to give and receive and develop relationships.

Ginott lists several benefits of play therapy. Play and talk give the child an opportunity for catharsis. Vicarious catharsis can take place by observing other children, then active catharsis can follow. The group also gives the counselor a chance to facilitate insights. He can, for example, bring their behavior in conflict situations to the children's attention. They may have to reevaluate and perhaps try new behaviors as a result of peer relationships. These interpersonal situations with peers and therapist form a basis for reality testing. The group is a social learning situation in which the child can become less defensive, or less magical in thinking, or more verbal in expressing herself. Ginott feels a group offers more opportunities to sublimate pleasures by reducing the tendency to repeat the same activities. By observing others, the child increases the activity repertoire with water colors, finger paints, clay, and sand. There is greater opportunity to ventilate hostility and other feelings toward symbolic siblings. Sublimation occurs; throwing blocks becomes building a house, and attacking each other changes to shooting at targets.

The setting for play therapy is critical. Very small and very large rooms should be avoided. There should also be small windows, soundproofing, protected lights, windows, and other glass, waterproofed floor, durable and functional furniture, and no objects the counselor does not want broken. An array of toys the children will want to play with is an obvious requisite.

A therapeutic approach for group therapy includes:

1. Total acceptance of the child

2. A simple invitation to play without explanations, goals, reasons, questions, or expectations

3. Helping the child learn to express himself and enjoy respect

4. Permitting but not encouraging regressive behavior early in therapy

5. Permissiveness of all "symbolic behavior" with limits on destructive behavior

6. Prohibiting children from physically attacking each other

7. Enforcing limits calmly, noncritically, and briefly, mentioning limits only as necessary

8. Empathy

Dinkmeyer and Muro (1971) have additional suggestions for children's group counseling, some of which relate to groups other than the play therapy model. In contrast to Ginott, they suggest children be given an orientation to the purpose for the group and that the children discuss or work on agreed areas of concern. Puppets or a tape and slide presentation help explain the nature of groups. Initially, group members will be awkward, silly, and perhaps engage in horseplay. The counselor needs to accept this patiently; he might then use an unfinished story to stimulate discussion.

The use of media is common with this age group. Dinkmeyer and Muro list some useful items, such as open shelves from which the child can choose his own medium of expression; real-life toys to play out life situations and help the child express feelings toward his world, such as a doll house, doll furniture, dolls, farm and zoo animals, medical kit, cars and tricycles, and schoolroom toys; toys for release of aggression, such as guns and holsters; and toys for enhancing self-concept, such as erector sets, Lincoln logs, puzzles, and blocks (Dinkmeyer & Muro, 1971, pp. 225–226).

Through a relationship approach to media, the counselor expresses understanding of feelings without interpreting them for the child. Media are used to bring out feelings and attitudes, and the counselor's acceptance reinforces attitudinal and behavioral changes. (Axline [1947], Moustakas [1959], and Ginott [1961] elaborate on this approach.) Keat (1974) presents specific activities for children's groups, such as bibliotherapy, modeling, incomplete sentences, music, toy rooms, behavioral rehearsal, and games.

Behavioral Techniques

Cognitive behavior modification through self-control was utilized by Felixbrod and O'Leary (1973). Their work with second-grade children on solving arithmetic problems was based on the proposition that the child faced with a task can engage in self-reinforcement for the desired behaviors.

Felixbrod and O'Leary wished to determine whether self-reinforcement would be as successful as external reinforcement of correct completion of arithmetic problems. Children were assigned to one of three groups for six sessions. Those in the self-reinforcement group determined themselves how many problems they were to get correct in order to receive a point, with points redeemable for prizes. Externally-reinforced children were told how many correct answers were the criterion for a point. The third group, with no reinforcement, worked without incentive. Second graders in both reinforcement groups completed more problems correctly and worked longer on the task than did the control group, and the self-reinforcement group did as well as the external reinforcement group, supporting the notion that children are able to control their behavior over time and that children can set their own standards for receiving reinforcement.

Bolstad and Johnson (1972) used self-control with disruptive children. First and second graders were treated in their classroom for disruptive behavior. Baseline disruptive behavior was first established, and the children were divided into four groups: one with no treatment, one with external regulation, and two with self-regulation. All but the no-treatment groups were first placed on a token system to reinforce decreases in disruptive behaviors. They were to judge when they were disruptive, and make a record of it. When their records were accurate, they were reinforced as before. When the record was inaccurate, they received fewer tokens. In the next stage, the children were allowed complete self-regulation; that is, reinforcement was based completely on their own reports. In the final stage, the treatment groups were no longer reinforced. One of the self-regulation groups continued self-monitoring only. It was found that self-reinforcement was as effective as external reinforcement. The children observed behavior accurately and did not "cheat" on their records. Although we can see that children are able to participate in regulating their behavior, they cannot necessarily do so without counselor or teacher assistance, and historical social regulators, such as social censure for "cheating," also play a role. Bandura (1976) Kanfer (1976), and Turkewitz, O'Leary, and Ironsmith (1974) also discuss self-control.

Clement and Milne (1967) used an approach that combined play therapy with a token reinforcement system. Eight- and nine-year-old boys with social maladjustment and withdrawn behavior were assigned to one of three groups. One group engaged in play therapy, and members received both verbal reinforcement and tokens to exchange for candy and trinkets for social approach behavior, such as talking to another boy. The second group engaged in play therapy and received verbal reinforcement. The third group met in a playroom with no therapist. After 14 weeks, the token group showed greater change in social approach behavior than did group two, which showed greater progress than the third group. No changes were found in anxiety and other types of adjustment. A group approach that tangibly rewards desired behavior seems to be effective in changing social behavior. Changes in other types of psychological adjustment are likely to take longer than 14 weeks.

Modeling was used with a group of sixth grade students (Hansen, Niland, & Zani, 1969). A group of three boys and three girls contained one member of each sex who had received high sociometric ratings; the remaining members had received low ratings. Each session included discussion of a counselor-introduced social behavior topic. Bibliotherapy was also used. After eight sessions, the "modeling" group's low-sociometric-rated students made larger gains in social acceptance than a group with no models, and gains were maintained two months later. Modeling may also be effective for groups with children who have study problems and those who have good study habits; handicapped students with low self-esteem and those with high self-esteem; and for disruptive children and those without behavior problems.

Plenk (1978) describes an activity group for preschool children referred to as a *comprehensive treatment center*. These young children had problems of delayed speech, poor self-care skills, short attention span, immature interpersonal relationships, oppositional tendencies, autistic behaviors, and so on. Eight or nine children were heterogeneously mixed in terms of presenting problems and sex. Using a modified behavioral approach, therapists engaged in behavior management, on-the-spot interpretation, modeling, and verbalization of alternative behaviors, with the purpose of building the children's coping abilities. Plenk suggests that activity groups can be beneficial with a variety of psychological problems in young children.

A group learning approach has been successful in hospital settings to help children cope with adjustment to the hospital and anxiety associated with their medical condition. In one case (Cofer & Nir, 1975), therapists met with three to ten children three times a week to handle questions. Therapists relied on children to help each other in answering questions. Another child's experience was considered more valid than the word of the therapist. The group helped prevent distortions and fears arising from lack of information, confronted children's tendency to use denial, and gave support for acceptance of the illness. Frank (1978) used a similar format; Peterson and Shigetomi's (1981) approach was more systematic. Children and parents were invited to "Big Bird's Ice Cream Parlor" where hospital experiences were explained while Big Bird played the role of a child. A film modeled the child's experience. Children were also taught coping skills: deep muscle relaxation, distracting mental imagery, and comforting self-talk.

Techniques with Parent-Child Separation

Cantor (1977) suggests the school as an ideal place to provide group counseling for children whose parents are separated or divorced. She conducted a group of nine elementary-school children to discuss feelings about divorce, having to choose between parents, experiencing loss, relationships with stepparents, and problems with visitation.

Effron (1980) used role-playing, affective education techniques, and creative writing as techniques with children of divorce. Green (1978) reports an even more structured group where children engage in activities and discussion and read relevant literature. Vander Kolk (1976) describes a group for children who have lost their fathers through divorce and subsequent disappearance or death that used recreational activity, discussion, and listening to and talking about contemporary music related to the loss of a father. Sonnenshein-Schneider and Baird (1980) suggest a number of techniques for groups for children of divorce.

Work with Adolescents

Procedures with adolescents conform to this group's special developmental needs and problems. Adolescents must cope with crises in identity, extraordinary peer pressures, dramatic physical changes, impending career decisions, the desire for independence, and self doubts, among other challenges. These conflicts and pressures can sometimes best be dealt with in group counseling, where peer pressure from other group members can influence positive growth.

There are, of course, some difficulties in running adolescent groups. Effective groups may have to overcome certain obstacles (Schrader, 1979); for example, *motivation* is frequently absent. Many children and adolescents do not feel they have problems, or if they do, prefer not to discuss them with others. Some may feel a stigma in belonging to a group, leading to poor attendance, dropouts, and ineffectual participation. Allowing the adolescent to choose, careful pregroup interviews, and publicity for the group to reduce the stigma can increase motivation. *Deviant group norms*, with reinforcement of deviant behavior and punishment of appropriate behavior, can work against desired changes. The leader can insert a high-sociometrically-rated adolescent to encourage prosocial behavior, and a reward system for appropriate behaviors can help. Fear of the group situation and oppositional attitudes can result in *reluctance to self-disclose*. If adolescents refuse to discuss personal problems, share experiences, or role play, the counselor can reinforce those members who do self-disclose. Contracts with each member can prevent this from becoming a continual problem. *Scapegoating* and blaming others for one's problems is typical of adolescents; the counselor can point this out to the group, set a rule against it, or discuss taking responsibility for one's own behavior.

Poor group interactions are common because of poor communication skills: harsh feedback, interrupting, not listening, disruptions, simultaneous conversations, and irrelevant or self-centered statements call for systematic skill training. Adolescents have a particular problem in generalizing learned behavior outside the group. Homework assignments between sessions, a buddy system to encourage and reinforce new behaviors, and contracts facilitate generalization.

Skill Building Groups

Skill building models (Bedell & Weathers, 1979; Carkhuff, 1971; Goldstein, Sprafkin, Gershaw, & Klein, 1980; Ivey, 1974) suggest a teaching as well as a therapeutic role for the counselor and provide a systematic method for teaching and evaluating progress. Group counseling is an ideal situation for skill training, through sharing similar instructional needs, providing information and feedback, modeling, role-playing, and other active approaches.

Bedell & Weathers (1979) designed a *psychoeducational model* for skill training in groups. They first established four broad stages directed toward qualitatively different goals:

- Definition of the skill to be trained
- Awareness training
- Skill enhancement
- Generalization training

There are sequential steps within each phase of the program and evaluation of progress occurs at certain points. The steps may focus on communications, social interaction, or job-seeking skills, among others, with emphasis on the activities the group leader requires.

The second, closely related, skill approach is *skillstreaming* (Goldstein, Sprafkin, Gershaw, & Klein, 1980). Although not specifically intended only for group counseling, it is readily applicable to groups and effective with adolescents who need to learn prosocial skills. Structured learning is the overall construct, with components of modeling, role playing, performance feedback, and transfer of training. An advantage to the counselor of the Goldstein model is that it spells out detailed techniques and methods. For example, one chooses models who appear skilled, have high status, can control client-student rewards, are of similar age, are helpful and friendly, and are rewarded for displaying the desired skills. Goldstein et al. show how models should display characteristics, expected client-student characteristics, and the stages of modeling. They provide the same guidance for role-playing, performance feedback, and transfer of training and explain how to organize and carry out skill groups.

Activity Groups

Activity groups have been quite popular with adolescents. Egan (1975) explains the therapeutic mechanisms that operate in activity discussion groups. Gerstein (1974) reports his use of an activity group with 11- to 13-year-old boys and suggests modifying the therapist's activity according to the children's various problems.

Technology as Techniques

Videotaped feedback was used in a psychiatric setting with adolescents who presented a variety of symptoms (Corder, Whiteside, McNeill, Brown, & Corder, 1981). In alternate sessions, the group viewed short excerpts from the previous session, followed by discussion. While they analyzed the tapes, members reviewed the goals of discussing and handling their feelings and taking control of their lives. Two judges rated the videotaped sessions, and found that intimate statements and feedback occurred more frequently than in sessions not preceded by videotaped feedback.

Prevention

Developmental tasks can be dealt with directly in a group setting. Muro and Engels (1980) focus on helping group members know themselves, through which young people learn to develop self-acceptance, self-direction, decision-making ability, and sensitivity to others' needs. Another group approach tackles adolescent identity crises (Rachman, 1972) through encounter and marathon techniques including psychosocial play, fantasy, and exploration of ways to deal with conflict and decision making. Zimet (1979) proposes directing groups toward stages in the developmental process—sex role, social skills, identity, vocational decision making, parenting, and so on—as a preventive measure.

In another preventive effort, teachers served as group leaders for one hour a week for children with mild emotional and behavioral problems. The leader did not initiate activities, leaving children to explore, play, or interact, but provided a positive, secure environment. Positive changes in cooperation, relaxation, hostility, anxiety, and jealousy were noted. Teachers felt they were receiving support because problem children were being helped, and the leaders believed they became better teachers and more sensitive to the emotional needs of acting-out children. Maher and Barbrack (1982) used a behavioral group to prevent maladjustment in high school students.

Techniques with Behavior Problems

Schulman (1957) gives guidelines for working with a group of delinquents. He says that delinquents deal with anxiety by acting it out, have fragile egos and malformed superegos, are interested only in the present, and have their thinking limited by impulsivity. He says the counselor's role is to suppress members' aggressive impulses. Other writers suggest a variety of techniques they have found useful with delinquents (Kolb, 1983; Larsen & Mitchell, 1980; Phelan, Slavson, Epstein, & Schwartz, 1960; Sarason & Ganzer, 1973; Weinstock, 1979).

The adolescent with substance abuse problems presents what some consider the greatest challenge to the group leader. Many techniques have been tried, from a client-centered approach to confrontation. Bratter (1974, 1972) gives examples of a confrontive approach with drug abusers and alcoholics. He discourages the goal of insight; rather, he demands behavior change from group members using peer pressure to examine behavior and member involvement to enforce the norm of behavior change. At the same time, the leader fosters a positive relationship and commitment to the members. Ideally, the group becomes a caring community in which members come to depend on one another rather than the leader. Cohen and Rietma (1981) describe a four-week marathon group for substance abusers. Professional staff is with the group at all times. Members are diagnosed according to basic conflicts: independence versus dependence; activity versus passivity; adequate versus inadequate self-esteem; and resolution of unresolved grief. This information supplies the basis for interventions. Results indicate that members form a high level of cohesion, have peaks of self-awareness, become less defensive, work through irrational fears of the counselors, and carry over their motivation into later weeks.

Summary

Group counseling with children necessarily differs from adult counseling. With younger children sessions are shorter and groups smaller. Children usually require more structured preparation with learning theory procedures; group play therapy is less structured. Children's groups tend to talk less and engage in more activities.

A developmental frame of reference seems most appropriate for groups with children. Gazda mentions the developmental domains of physical-sexual, intellectual, moral, psychosocial, and vocational.

Younger children require special techniques that minimize verbal communication, as in Ginott's and Dinkmeyer and Muro's approaches. Adolescent groups are characterized by a combination of activities and verbal interaction. These groups are somewhat unique because certain features of group counseling are exaggerated; for example, adolescents often display inadequate motivation, deviant group norms, resistance to self-disclosure, and scapegoating.

Discussion Questions

1. How is a developmental perspective useful in understanding the members of a counseling group? What accommodations for selection, size, goals, and evaluation are recommended for each age group? What special developmental tasks for each age level could be addressed in a group?

2. What techniques are especially useful at each age level?

3. What kind of structure is useful at each age level?

14

Family Counseling

Family counseling can be viewed as a form of group counseling in the sense that it deals with the dynamics, problems, potential, and growth of a group of people who interact daily with one another. We will look at guidelines for family counseling in terms of assessment, setting goals, and intervention strategies. The final section of the chapter describes the unique approach of multiple family counseling with illustrations from a series of counseling sessions. This chapter is not a comprehensive presentation of theory and practice; the reader should take at least an introductory course in family counseling, followed by supervised practice, before engaging in independent family counseling.

There are interesting similarities and overlap between group counseling and family counseling. Some of the first group counseling practitioners, as well as current practitioners (the psychoanalysts), conceived of the group as a family. In the sessions, group members assume roles they have learned in relationships with significant people, primarily family members, and carry out these roles in the group; they perceive other group members as filling a family role. The perceptions and behaviors may be conscious or unconscious. Communication styles exercised in the family are exhibited early in the group counseling sessions. The leader helps group members understand these primary interaction patterns and make positive changes in them. In family counseling, strangers are not a part of the sessions, but the same interaction patterns and associated feelings are explored more directly. Group counseling attempts to bring about change in someone while he interacts with strangers, followed by individual change in the person's natural environment; family counseling tries to effect change in the family system, which in turn brings about changes in the individual.

Family and group counseling overlap also in their multiple dynamics, analysis of the whole versus the individual, similar expectations of the counselor, and possible techniques. Both family and group counseling contain a series of dyadic relationships and subgroups that lead to a complex set of interpersonal relationships. In both types of counseling, the counselor conceptualizes the process in terms of the unit; that is, the nature of the system as a whole. One strives for mutuality and cohesiveness, at the same time preserving the individuality of each family or group member. In both groups, the counselor uses techniques to facilitate the group's ability to take responsibility for itself. A family theorist such as Bowen and a group theorist such as Rogers want the clients to do most of the work. The counselor focuses on family or group process, does not align herself with particular members, and encourages clients to help one another. Certain techniques are common to both approaches; role playing, role reversal, videotapes, psychodrama, and guided fantasy, among others.

Definition and History

Family counseling is an intervention intended to change the nature of a family system. The counselor normally meets with members of the immediate family, extended family, or others who directly influence the family system. A crucial difference between family and other types of counseling is the counselor's perception and approach. Whereas in individual and most forms of group counseling the individual is foreground (the primary focus) and the group is background, in family counseling, the family is foreground and the individual is background. The family counselor is primarily, although not exclusively, concerned with dynamics and change in the family as a whole.

Approaches to family counseling vary on the basis of structure or method rather than theoretical differences. In *conjoint family counseling*, sometimes referred to as family group therapy, the counselor meets with a family to deal with total family problems and concerns. Usually the whole family is present, although it is not required. In *multiple impact counseling*, two or more counselors meet, perhaps over two or three days, with various combinations of family members for brief but intensive therapeutic sessions. The intensity of the intervention is thought to break down defenses and thus enhance change. *Network counseling* is based on the assumption that the family and family members have lost a sense of belonging to the community's social network. The counselor seeks to build effective connections between the family and its immediate social system by including friends, neighbors, or other significant people in the counseling sessions. Strengthening its social network can improve a dysfunctional family. *Multiple family counseling* involves more than one family in counseling sessions. It is thought that combinations of families seeking solutions to problems reduce the distance between counselor and family and allow families to identify with one another, imitate, and give support.

These approaches have evolved only in the past few decades; the significance of the family as a focus for therapeutic intervention was hardly recognized during the first fifty years of counseling and psychotherapy. Freud briefly utilized the family as the focus of therapy when he met with Little Hans's father to analyze the boy's neurosis, but in other cases, Freud was concerned only with the individual and primarily with intrapsychic dynamics. It remained for followers who modified the psychoanalytic approach to recognize the role of interpersonal and family dynamics in unhealthy functioning.

Adler was one of the first important figures to go beyond the individual, pointing out the greater importance of the social system. He perceived the interaction of the individual with society and the need to be a social being, accepted and recognized by others. He saw childhood as the first opportunity for acceptance and superiority through interaction with the family. In this respect, Adler viewed the family as the original social unit and the most important to the individual. Adlerian family work has attracted a substantial following in this country.

Harry S. Sullivan and Karen Horney also moved away from the classical psychoanalytic concept of instinctual drives as the explanatory mechanism for human behavior. Sullivan emphasized interpersonal relationships and believed that anxiety created in the mother-child relationship to be the original source of pathology. Horney believed that everyone seeks safety and security in their early relationships with parents and that these social-cultural forces contribute to adjustment or pathology. Both theorists saw the importance of the family in shaping personality, and their work provided a foundation for family therapists such as Nathan Ackerman.

Ackerman began his family work in the late 1930s and continues to exert great influence on the field. He observed the futility of diagnosis and treatment of the individual apart from the family context.

The assumptions we now make about families were avant garde in the 1940s and early 1950s. Ackerman blended useful analytic concepts with emerging concepts from social psychology, and *The Psychodynamics of Family Life* (1958) served as a comprehensive guide to one school of family counseling.

Another historical movement that began in the 1950s can be considered the major influence on family counseling as it has evolved to the present. It has formed into a general approach called "systems," and most of the people associated with it are termed *communication theorists*—Virginia Satir, the late Don Jackson, Jay Haley, Murray Bowen, and Salvador Minuchin. Ruesch and Bateson (1951) wrote on feedback and information theory in communication; Gregory Bateson and Don Jackson and others presented the "double bind" notion (1958). Communication concepts, the double bind, and Jackson's concept of family homeostasis became part of the framework for family counseling. These contributions and those of Michelfort (1957), Wynne (1958), Lidz (1958), and Brodey (1959) in the area of families with one or more schizophrenic members added to the early understanding of family work. At the same time, the work of Howells and Laing in England was consistent with the results of American investigators.

Family Counseling Concepts

Better understanding of family dynamics inevitably resulted in proliferation of psychological concepts. The revelation of family dynamics and ideas that clarified the interaction and impact of family members has allowed family counselors to better grasp family problems and, ultimately, to help alleviate problems. One of the first conceptual breakthroughs was the articulation of the *double bind*.

The notion of *double bind* derives from communication theory and the logical types developed by Bertrand Russell. Jackson, Bateson, Haley, and Weakland investigated human interaction in terms of its paradoxes, particularly in relation to schizophrenia. The *paradoxical injunction* was a form of interaction that left one of the interactors in a real bind. When someone states a paradoxical injunction, it leaves the other person no logical choice as to a response. For example, if your mother gives you two pair of slacks for your birthday and the next time you see her you are wearing a pair of the slacks, her saying "Didn't you like the other pair?" is a paradoxical injunction—you have no real choice of reply. Whichever pair you wore, your mother would make the same statement.

Jackson (1968) and his colleagues suggest five conditions, appearing over a period of time, for the double bind:

1. A "victim" and at least one other person must be present.

2. There must be a repetition of the paradoxical injunctions; one or a few have little or no lasting effect.

3. The injunction must be negative; punishment is implied for what the "victim" does or does not do.

4. A second injunction at a more abstract, often nonverbal, level conflicts with the first injunction.

5. Escape from the situation is closed off for the "victim" by a third injunction.

An illustration of the double bind is a family in which the mother has emphysema. When the child comes home from school, he asks how his mother is doing. "Oh, I guess I'll live. Don't worry about me" (with a sarcastic voice and a frown). The boy goes out to play, then later returns for dinner. His mother states, "You just had to go off and leave me alone!" The mother is giving a double message, and tries to cut off the child's method of escape. In another case, a wife's words show concern for her emotionally disturbed husband, but the tone of voice shows anger and coldness. "Yes dear, I'm going to visit you every day until you come home" (closed escape). "I miss you and I hope you miss me. This is all so very hard for me. That's why I forgot your magazines and bathrobe. You don't miss me, you're glad to be away from me. You don't even care." She then spills coffee over him.

The family counselor must observe the levels of messages and that two or three messages may be communicated at one time. He must determine the primary message and which one is understood by the victim. The sender is often not aware of the paradoxical nature of the message. The victim is usually confused in trying to comprehend the message. One can follow the injunctions literally or withdraw and ignore them all. Whatever his coping technique, the victim is trapped, because there is no logical response and no way to discuss the illogical communication. The double bind occurs even in nonschizophrenic families. Family members are unable to sort out the double messages because they change, and one rarely receives a clear message in terms of content, emotional aspects, and nonverbal cues. Communication is in the form of yes and no, love and hate, acceptance and rejection. The counselor must reconstruct the elements in a message and provide feedback to sender and receiver. A basic assumption to this notion is that individual family members become disturbed because they learn behaviors to cope with distorted and paradoxical communication. Because it is a family process, the family rather than the individual is considered disturbed. Family members are unconsciously selected to be the victim or scapegoat of disturbance in the family system; thus, the entire family must be treated, not just the victim.

Another family counseling concept is built on the notion that everyone needs to establish his own identity and to belong to a group. These needs can conflict as one wishes to break away from the family yet belong at the same time. The healthy individual balances these needs by having close relationships with others and at the same time maintaining a sense of self. This struggle can cover the lifespan—from infancy, where differentiation from the mother must occur, to the teenage years, when identity and belonging to a peer group are important, to old age, when one wishes to maintain self-esteem and closeness to family and friends.

Wynne (1958) first examined this dilemma in a family context by asking how the family contributes to a stronger sense of "I" and how it weakens that sense. A family absorption with having its members fit a prescribed mold rather than allowing for individual and different identities is termed *pseudomutuality*, an unhealthy attempt to have family members repress individuality and conform to expectations. Sicker families have rigid roles from which members are unable to escape; in these families, member roles are similar, there are sanctions against independence, and there is little spontaneity and humor. The one element of flexibility is that the family boundary can expand to include what is compatible, contract to exclude other things, and can change rules to maintain itself as the entire life-force of its members. Members, consequently, do not have to think for themselves. Disturbed members then have problems in identity, perception, and communication with the outside world. They are able to assume rigid roles in the family, and even identify with the family, but are not able to establish personal identities, thus causing the many adjustment problems. The repressive forces of the family interact. Reciprocal victimizing and rescuing are part of the whole family system. Unfortunately, pseudomutuality covers or masks the healthy need for individual identity. Wynn also suggests that positive need and feelings for intimacy and affection can be masked by family hostility which he calls *pseudohostility*. This surface hostility causes alienation among family members, which in turn destroys healthy communication.

Lidz (1958) coined the concepts *schism* and *skew* after studying disturbed families. For Lidz, parents play the key role in determining children's mental health. He assumed a *parental coalition* whereby father and mother must fulfill the roles of man and woman and husband and wife, thus offering the child an opportunity to identify with the parent of the same sex and to see someone of the opposite sex as desirable. This situation is necessary to maintain sex-linked roles. Finally, the generational boundary must be adhered to; that is, the child in no way replaces or takes the role of a parent.

A disturbed child is symptomatic of a marital relationship that is dysfunctional in one of two ways. Lidz describes marital schisms as unions in which role reciprocity is absent; husband and wife fail to achieve complementary roles; or in which there is an excessive attachment to the parental home. The result is constant tension and confusion for the child, leading to identity problems. The second dysfunctional marital relationship occurs when a strong partner dominates a weaker partner. Lidz suggests the father plays an equally significant role as the "adaptive-instrumental leader." The weak, ineffectual father is more harmful than one who is cold and unyielding.

Mother is viewed as the family's "affective leader." Lidz cited three aspects to mothering: first, the maternal nurturant relationship, characterized by warmth and eventual allowance for separation by the child; second, the need to form a parental coalition, fulfill her sex-linked role, and maintain generational boundaries; and third, transmittal of the language and values of the culture. When roles break down, when parents become irrational, and when communication is unclear, the quality of social interaction and emotional balance deteriorates.

Theories of Family Counseling

Each theorist addresses the issues and concepts of family counseling somewhat differently. Ackerman's theory evolved from an intrapsychic background to a recognition of role relationships and the family unit; the other theorists we will discuss belong to one degree or another to the currently popular camp of systems theorists.

Ackerman

Nathan Ackerman developed his system of family counseling based on extensive experience in a field with few guiding principles. He had to be creative in discovering the unique dynamics of family systems. Ackerman was perhaps the first to point out the dynamic aspect of the family, the exchanges and interchanges, many in the form of love and material goods, that transpire between the individual, the family, and society. Each influences the other in a lively, understandable interaction. The role of the theorist and the counselor is to discover the healthy and unhealthy interchanges.

Ackerman made several assumptions about family dynamics:

1. Many factors fuse to make up family bonds—biological, psychological, social, and economic; family members are interdependent across and within each of these factors.

2. The family is the biological unit for producing offspring and providing for their nurturance and training; it also fulfills sexual mores and needs, although they are less important.

3. The family is the product of evolution, adapting to the "biological bonds of man and woman and of mother and child," and adjusting to the mores, customs, and other expectations of the society; there is a basic continuity between individual, family, and society.

4. The family is an organism with its own history: germination, birth, growth and development, capacity to adapt, decline, and "dissolution of the old family into the new."

5. The family's internal organization and external position in the community determine the nature of its adaptations; internal tension and conflict can cause disharmony and hatred, while external threats to the security of the family can disrupt or can draw the family closer together. The quality of family interactions and loyalties can moderate outside negative influences.

6. The family meets two basic needs: it provides for physical survival and "builds the essential humanness of man." Humanness develops through social togetherness (affectional bonds), evolution of personal identity, patterning of sexual roles, integration into social roles, and cultivation of learning.

7. Values and emotions in the form of love and material goods are the units of exchange in the family, primarily given by the parents and received by the children.

8. A modest amount of frustration and disappointment are essential to the emotional growth of family members.

9. Subordination of hate in favor of love and identification with the parents helps the child grow. Tipping the balance toward love is most influenced by the parents' love for each other. The family's task is to socialize the child and help him form a separate identity.

10. Family identity evolves from the interaction, merging, and redifferentiation of the marital partners, who were drawn to each other through empathic attraction. Their emotional togetherness creates a unique family identity; the individuals lose themselves in the family, then find themselves again with a stronger individual identity.

11. The emotional give-and-take of day-to-day family relationships determines the relative health of the family. Expression of feelings, emotional security, safety from outside forces, and distinguishing fantasy from reality are most influenced by the interaction of family members.

12. Family roles (mother-wife, husband-father, child) and their interrelationships are interdependent and reciprocal.

Ackerman names three principles relevant to family counseling. First, disturbance in adults is rooted in current as well as past family experiences. Second, diagnosis and therapy require that the child be assessed as an element of the family unit. Third, disorders are best understood in the context of dynamic family patterns that change and interplay with the individual.

These assumptions are significant because they reject the notion that personality becomes fixed in early childhood. Ackerman believed instead that the continual interaction and reciprocal relationship of family members has an impact on one's mental health throughout life. He recognized intrapsychic factors, but emphasized the role of family in the formation of personality. In a sense, the family is the mediator between the individual and society.

Social role and personality is the concept that distinguishes Ackerman's thinking. He stressed the significance of social roles, learned in the family, as the bridge between intrapsychic life and social participation. He pointed out the importance of relationships with significant small groups and the wider society. Social role is "an adaptational unit of personality in action," one's social identity or outer self. Ideally, there is a smooth blend of the inner self and the outer self. The environment, though, may provoke disharmony between the two, shaking one's stability. A child may wish to engage in sports while the parents insist on violin practice and homework every day, causing inner turmoil, resentment, and depression.

Emotional stability also depends on consistency among assumed roles. Roles of father, husband, businessman, and school board member are harmonious, whereas the roles of church leader and bar owner would be in conflict in many communities and churches. Strain can occur at two levels. First, Ackerman believes consistency between personality and social role is necessary for healthy functioning. Can the same personality handle extremely divergent roles? Second, strain occurs when social roles are not compatible with the family's or society's attitudes.

People execute their social roles according to their personalities and behave differently in different roles. People also modify their role behavior according to circumstances.

The concept of social role in family counseling allows evaluation of actual family roles, expected family roles, dissatisfactions, and so forth. It also gives a basis for understanding reciprocal relationships, studying relationships, and identifying complaints. Misunderstandings, confusions, and distortions may be traced to a problem in role relationships, which can then be redefined. The counselor can suggest a more complementary alignment of social roles. Complementary roles may fail because of cognitive discrepancy (not knowing what is required), goal discrepancy, allocative discrepancy (one may be a victim due to age), instrumental discrepancy (such as earning capacity), or value orientation. The counselor can encourage family members to explain how they perceive their roles and the roles of other family members, bringing distortions and expectations to the surface. Role playing and role reversal are also effective techniques. The purpose is not only to facilitate communication, but to clarify differences in content as well. In other words, it is fine to understand one another, but the family must also work toward goals, try to come to some agreements, and shape substance into the agreed social roles.

Ackerman and other theorists use the concept of *homeostasis* to describe ongoing change in the family. Families and societies are always in the process of change, yet must maintain an equilibrium to remain functional. Homeostasis, or "dynamic equilibrium," is a capacity to adapt to change creatively and constructively. Individual and family homeostasis are interrelated. If one family member becomes disturbed, it affects the equilibrium of the other members and the family as a whole. Thus, one person's pathology reflects the whole family's emotional disturbance. Again, Ackerman stresses the family's reciprocal relationships; for healthy homeostasis to occur, family members must exercise flexibility in their roles and reciprocity or complementarity in role relations.

The family counselor is a teacher who helps clarify roles and moves the family toward a "new way of living." Other modes include freeing emotions and striking a balance between extremes of rigid and fluid roles. Continuity and usefulness of old roles are maintained along with openness to new ones. The first step in the family counseling process is to establish empathy with the feelings of hurt, doubt, and despair. Then the counselor examines affectional relationships and defenses to bring "sickness" from the individual to the family level. Members adapt or explore new roles. The role of the counselor may be that of an "activator, challenger, supporter, confronter, interpreter, and reintegrator." The family decides on a new value system and a new way of behaving to effect positive change.

Jackson

Don Jackson (1968), an early communication theorist, also considered the family a system maintained by homeostasis. Jackson observed the interplay of dynamic forces along with constancy in the internal environment; the balance of constancy and interplay of internal forces allow healthy family functioning.

Unlike earlier theorists, Jackson did not really address intrapsychic forces. Rather, he believed that communicative behaviors within the system and the nature of the relationships were the key to helping people. He replaced traditional views of psychopathology with a systems model in which object (people) attributes, relationships, feedback, and communication in the field (family) explain behavior. Traditional models asked why behavior occurred; Jackson is concerned with the "how" of behavior. How, for example, do relationships operate? Cause and effect become irrelevant concepts; concentrating on *how* behavior occurs forces us to examine the way each person affects others and vice versa. Multiple on-going as well as sequential relationships may form patterns within the system; for example, person A will affect persons B and C; then C affects D; D affects A, then B affects C and D, and so on.

Jackson emphasizes system interaction in his critique of Albee's *Who's Afraid of Virginia Woolf?* While other models of psychology might describe Martha as a sadist and George as a masochist, Jackson shows how the dyad relates with each one. A description of the interaction replaces clinical labels. To expand this type of analysis to an entire family, one assumes that each person's behavior depends upon and relates to other family members' behavior. This interaction pattern is more significant than and transcends the characteristics of the individuals. We see communication patterns in terms of content and process. According to Jackson, when a sender transmits a message to a receiver, the message is mediated by the form of communication. The statement, "It would be nice if you would stay home with the family tonight," seems quite clear; however, depending on the tone of voice and nonverbal cues, the message can convey love, sharing, sarcasm, or criticism. Counseling examines the series of such communications between family members.

Jackson suggests five axioms related to communication:

1. It is impossible not to communicate; silence and nonverbal as well as verbal cues send messages.

2. Communication suggests the presence of a commitment, which then defines a relationship. A message has a certain content, but the commitment or qualitative aspect of the message helps clarify the nature of the relationship.

3. The pattern of family relationships is circular rather than cause-and-effect.

4. Communication is verbal and nonverbal.

5. Communication exchanges are either symmetrical (those of equality) or complementary (one leads and the other follows); they are only pathological when they become extreme.

The role of the counselor is to observe and understand family interactional patterns. Intervention gives family members a chance to change the pattern. Jackson emphasizes cognitive understanding by all parties rather than recognition of the feelings that are communicated. In counseling, he prefers that the family discuss the nature of their relationships, with the hope of moving toward change, to reestablish healthy family homeostasis so the family system will exhibit "mutual responsibility, reward, security, and dignity." The counselor looks for inconsistencies in interaction, then disturbs the system by relabeling the family dynamics. He examines the interactions in the system as they exist now, not as they were.

Jay Haley

Like Jackson, Haley (1971, 1967) is concerned with family members' communication patterns, but Haley stresses the dynamics of power in family relationships. He believes each person maneuvers to gain influence and control over the social network, to "make the world more predictable." When the parties are considered equal, relationships are competitive, they are complementary when the parties are unequal. In any relationship, however, people struggle, define, and redefine its nature.

Haley makes two assumptions regarding communication. First, he agrees with other systems theorists that interactions are circular, not linear; people continually interact and have an effect on one another. Patterns of communication based on actions and reactions form the basis for rules of behavior. Second, Haley expresses the notion of levels of communication. *Metacommunication* designates the level that qualifies content, including nonverbal cues, tone of voice, inflection, intensity, and so on. True understanding of communication must take place at the levels of both content and metacommunication. A message is congruent and complete when the two levels are consistent; when the levels are inconsistent, the result is a double message. Qualified messages are often associated with emotional disturbance in a family. After communication has begun, the task is to define the relationship. This is where the power struggle begins. Problems include defining what messages or behavior will take place and who will be in control. Besides communication's content or factual component, the element of influence is equally important—how one party controls while the other submits or competes.

Haley believes the family system rather than an individual is pathological. The disturbed member is a family scapegoat. Family distress occurs when the disturbed member improves; that is, the members depend on one another, and change in one member affects the others. The role of the disturbed member is to hold the family together. Problems are not intrapsychic; rather, they begin in the system and affect the individual.

For change to take place, the client must be motivated and attuned to notice change. The counselor acts as an educator to help clients behave differently through the use of paradoxes.

Foley (1974) specifies the role of the counselor:

- To model behavior rather than tell the family how to act

- To take sides only temporarily, never aligning with one faction or another

- To control the relationship

- To point out the metacommunicative level

Foley also mentions several effective tactics; for example, the counselor should give the family ambiguous directives, such as asking for expression of feelings. Even ignoring this directive reveals feelings. The counselor should emphasize the positive, even by describing negative behavior in positive terms. He should also encourage usual behavior; the clients' resistance to the advice will bring about change. For example, telling a passive husband-father to remain out of the picture will bring his behavior to the foreground and may cause him to want to be more involved.

To bring about change, the family need not be aware of the causes of its problems, nor even of the present behavior that is related to pathology. The counselor is the agent who, through appropriate techniques and strategy, brings about change. He focuses on interaction patterns and points out what is actually communicated, with the expectation that the family is able to deal with new situations and produce new solutions. As change occurs, the family will stabilize at a new yet comfortable level.

Virginia Satir

Satir (1972, 1967) bases her work on the earlier conceptualizations of theorists such as Jackson and Haley but emphasizes family members' feelings. Satir concentrates first on emotional pain, without excluding cognitive and competitive dynamics. Satir assumes that people communicate in four wrong ways: blaming others, placating, being irrelevant, and being reasonable. Each method of communication is incomplete because there is a problem of feelings. "The blamer leaves out what he feels about the other person, the placater leaves out what he feels about himself, the reasonable one leaves out what he feels about the subject being discussed, and the irrelevant one leaves out everything." Distortion or absence of communicated feeling becomes the starting point for family counseling. Family members' emotional needs are the central concern of the counselor. When emotional needs are not met, disturbance occurs for one or more members.

An important concept to Satir is that of *maturation*. To achieve healthy functioning, one must be able to separate himself from the rest of the family. To do so, one must be in control of oneself and must take responsibility for making decisions on the basis of accurate perceptions. The mature person is aware of one's own feelings, able to communicate effectively with others, accept differences in people, and recognize differentness as an opportunity to learn.

The inability to differentiate oneself from the family is linked to poor communication and low self-concept. The child becomes dysfunctional because parental communication is disturbed, or parents have devalued the child, or they were poor models of communication. To survive, the child with low self-esteem needs to maintain an important role in the pathological family system. Family members send a continual message that one member is "sick," or at least a disappointment. Satir emphasizes more than other theorists the need for self-esteem and the importance of parent-child communication in developing self-esteem.

The evolution of family problems often begins with a couple's motivations for marriage. When two people decide to marry because they feel they will enhance each other's self-esteem and complement each other, the marriage has a good chance to be healthy. On the other hand, if two people marry because each sees the other as supplying what one is missing, a cycle of problems has begun. A period of dissatisfaction and disillusionment can set in that both hope will be alleviated by the birth of a baby; however, one or both parents will expect the child to fulfill unmet fantasies and desires. The child is seen as an extension of the parents, a way to meet their own needs as well as to project an image of worth. Acceptance is contingent on the child's conforming to the needs and fantasies of the parents. If the child tries to be an individual, he is rejected. These parents are usually in conflict, and the child cannot safely side with either one, nor break away from them. Siding with the parent of the same sex, and failing to admire or desire the opposite sex, or choosing the parent of the opposite sex and failing to identify with the same sex impairs the child's psychosexual development. This dynamic is based on the assumption that there are no three-person relationships, only two-person relationships that shift. If the parents' relationship is healthy, there is room for all other necessary two-person relationships; if it is not healthy, the parents vie for alliances with the children.

One acquires an acceptable level of self-esteem through relationships with parents. According to Foley (1974), Satir believes these conditions must exist in early development: (1) meeting physical needs; (2) a "warm, ongoing, predictable relationship with another"; (3) an experience of mastery over one's world; (4) validation as a distinct and worthwhile person; and (5) a sense and acceptance of what it is to be male or female. Satir takes a developmental point of view; the individual requires different kinds of support from the family during the various stages of development.

All families establish rules as guides to behavior. Satir emphasizes the family's rules about feelings. Are there things one does not talk about? Are certain members treated in certain ways? Can feelings be expressed? Under what conditions? Which feelings? Are the rules implicit or explicit? One function of the family counselor is to make the "feeling rules" explicit so they can be changed. Families are often dysfunctional because the members are not aware of the rules. A family may not allow expression of negative feelings; Satir teaches the family that feelings are normal and acceptable. It is okay to feel anger or affection. Many families, however, confuse feelings with action. Family members can learn how to express their feelings nonthreateningly. One may verbalize anger rather than strike someone, or hug another family member. The rules must change to allow expression of feelings. The counselor opens up this possibility to the family, then gives them the responsibility of doing something about it. This gives members the chance to understand the family interactions and to take pride in forming new communication patterns.

As one might expect, family change must occur at the feeling level of communication. Rules that are too constrictive must be opened up so members are able to say what they feel, perceive, and think about themselves and others. The family system must adjust to recognize each person's uniqueness and decision-making ability. Decisions should be explored and negotiated rather than arbitrary. Differences among family members must be accepted as an avenue for growth.

Satir's view of the family counselor is as a model for effective communication. Attention to, recognition of, and acceptance of each person's feelings, positive and negative, are prerequisites to helping a family. The counselor must communicate warmth and understanding and expose family rules and poor communication. Family members learn the difference between a communication's intended meaning and the received meaning. As the family interacts, the counselor points out covert, incongruent, or confused messages. The counselor thus teaches about communication and, through interactions with family members, acts as a model for healthy relationships.

The Practice of Family Counseling

Assessment

From the perspective that psychological problems result from family interactions, the assessment of these problems must be approached in a nontraditional way. Traditionally, a child or an adult with an emotional problem is evaluated by a mental health professional to determine intrapsychic or interpersonal conflicts causing the disturbance. Psychological testing and other assessment techniques produce a personality profile describing the individual's problems and strengths. The family counselor, however, sees emotional disturbance in an individual family member as an indication of family pathology. One member's deviant behavior is a symptom of a dysfunctional family. The entire family unit, and perhaps peers and others, is the problem. Assessment, then, is directed not at one individual, but to the functioning of the entire family; the individual's behavior is examined in the context of family relationships.

Because the focus of assessment is broader than the individual, its method is necessarily different. One analyzes the communication style, the roles of family members, and their feelings toward one another. Assessment is obviously more complex because we want to understand three or more people and the nature of their relationships.

Goals

An accurate and careful assessment leads to a set of counseling goals. If the counselor is able to describe the family pathology and the family is motivated to make necessary changes, then they can jointly set goals for the counseling sessions. These goals are more likely to be met if they are specific and can be observed by the family members. In most cases, the pattern of interaction and responses will be the early focus of counseling. The counselor attempts to alter the communication styles that have produced the pathology. The goals of family counseling need to be an ongoing focus of the sessions.

Perez (1979) suggests general goals:

1. To help family members learn and emotionally appreciate that familial dynamics intermesh among all family members

2. To help family members become aware that a family member's problems may well be the effect of one or more other member's perceptions, expectations, and interactions

3. To persevere in the therapy until a homeostatic balance has been reached that provides growth and enhancement for each member

4. To develop full familial appreciation of the impact of the parental relationship on all family members

He derives the more specific goals from the general, such as:

1. To promote each member's tolerance for the other members' idiosyncratic ways

2. To increase each member's tolerance for frustration when encountering loss, conflict, and disappointment within and outside the family

3. To increase the motivation of each member to support, encourage, and enhance each other member

4. To achieve parental self-perception that is realistic and congruent with the perceptions of other family members

Depending on the counselor's theoretical orientation as well as the needs of the particular family, other specific goals may be added. For example, it may be useful to have a father become less authoritarian, or give a son the opportunity to make more decisions about himself, or allow a daughter to express her true feelings. To bring about these more individualized goals, one expects to change the interaction style of the family as a whole.

Therapeutic Intervention

As in any form of counseling, certain basic conditions help bring about change. The facilitative conditions of empathy, respect, warmth, and concern toward the family members help the counselor gain their trust. Since the family and the counselor must work together toward positive change, a close and understanding relationship is essential. Even counselors such as Haley, who focus on the power dimensions of relationships, reportedly exude warmth toward their clients. Furthermore, if the counselor is to serve as a model for the family, high-level interpersonal skills are a necessity.

Another necessary dimension in the early stages of family counseling is borrowed from other forms of counseling—the concept of the participant observer, suggested by Harry Stack Sullivan. The counselor becomes a participant and an observer in the family, participates in their discussions, interacts, gives a point of view, reveals his values, and sometimes takes sides. A degree of involvement in the family appears to be necessary and effective, and demonstrates the counselor's genuine concern.

Even while he participates in the family, the counselor must also attempt to understand the family, moving moment to moment from professional counselor to involved family member. Professional distance can save the counselor from making mistakes. A family may place great pressure on the counselor to support their position, to condone dependency, or to blame a member for problems. One must recognize the obvious and subtle pressures and messages that come with joining the family, and combine skill, patience, and observation with one's true interest in the family.

The counselor's professional skill, perceptiveness, and ability to communicate form the basis of family work; techniques merely supplement skills and knowledge. The early stage of family counseling is a time for self-examination, not so much on a personal level as on a family-system level. One does not ask, "How do I feel about myself?" or even "How do I feel about my son?" Rather, one asks, "How does what I feel about my son affect him, and how does his behavior toward me affect me?" In other words, at this stage we explore the interrelationships.

Sculpting is a popular technique for revealing family relationships. Each family member is given an opportunity to arrange the others in the room, positioning the others in relation to herself and to the other family members. For example, a daughter places the father two feet away and facing her; the mother, five feet further away and facing sideways; and the sister, two feet behind and facing her. This is a nonverbal way of expressing how one perceives the family relationships. In this case, the daughter felt an open, close relationship with her father; she perceived the father as rejecting the mother while the mother wished for a better relationship, but was leery. The girl recognized her dislike for her sister, who in turn wanted and sought her love. Other family members then act out their perceptions. The counselor can explore why members are placed where they are. How does the person explain the positions? Questioning is usually necessary to clarify the reason for a placement; a person who is placed between two others might be perceived as a mediator or as a block to communication, for example.

Role-playing is especially effective. Most families have been locked into a pattern for years without questioning the pattern or trying to understand the other members. When one member plays another's role, she reveals her perceptions of the other's feelings, role, and communication style. Dysfunctional families have great difficulty with this; members often assume that other members perceive things as they do, or are confused about another's feelings. Role reversal (for example, having the son play the role of the father) has an impact on both parties. The son can learn about the father's feelings and communication style while the father learns how the son perceives him. The same is true when the father plays the role of the son. The other way to use role playing is to have a family member assume a new role; for example, a passive wife-mother can practice being more assertive toward her husband and children. The counselor must not only direct the role playing, but must support members' attempts to play different roles. Other family members may not accept the new role or the role reversal, and the counselor may need to protect the role player.

Although she must choose carefully, the counselor can also use *paradoxical* techniques. A paradoxical technique highlights an ineffective behavior, or, a highly resistant person may do the opposite of what is suggested. For example, one may suggest to a rebellious daughter that she pay no attention to her mother. Obviously, the counselor will suggest this only to certain children. Another example would be telling the passive mother to be even more passive, to look for ways to avoid expressing an opinion or standing up for herself. The effect is to get the woman to consider that she does have feelings and rights; by exaggerating her denial of them, one hopes she will come to her senses and attempt to gain greater self-esteem.

It is logical to teach the family effective communication skills. We are not born with the ability to communicate well; we learn it.

The best place to begin in counseling is in encouraging the family to listen effectively to one another. When the counselor notices that members are not listening or are distorting messages, he can ask one member what another has just said. At first the focus should be on listening to content, then on listening for feelings and attitudes.

Another facet of communication skill is *congruence*. Family members frequently send double messages, which at first the counselor will notice, point out, and then ask for a congruent message; eventually, the family should begin to notice its double messages and change them. A last important facet of communication is the receiver's ability to let the sender know he has understood a message. Family members frequently assume they understand one another without saying so, but it must be communicated. In this example, a mother is stating her concerns about her children and how she has tried to feed them well and keep their clothes clean; the counselor asks a daughter to tell her mother what the mother is trying to say:

Daughter: Mom, you want to be sure you are doing all the right things for us.

Counselor: Isn't something more being said?

Daughter: I don't know.

Mother: Well, it is more than preparing food and cleaning clothes. I do that because I love you.

Daughter: Yeah, I never thought of it that way. I just thought that's what mothers had to do. You never really said you loved me before.

Counselor: Isn't this an example of a message sent, but not received?

As the session goes on, work centers on sending a clear message and improving the daughter's ability to both understand the message and communicate her understanding to the mother.

Audio- and videotapes are also effective in family counseling. Family members are not aware of the verbal and nonverbal behavior they exhibit toward one another; a child may, for example, continually frown without realizing it; a father may speak gruffly and curtly but deny that he does so; a daughter may be syrupy sweet and manipulative but think she is straightforward. Ideally, the counselor videotapes selected family counseling sessions for the family to view. If the viewing is to be structured, the counselor asks the family to look for certain behaviors, consider them, and discuss them in a subsequent session. If the viewing is unstructured, one simply shows the tape and solicits reactions. The counselor, of course, is free to point out behaviors at any time to have them discussed. Tapes give the family an opportunity to discover for themselves their unhealthy family interactions. The objective tape can be less threatening than the counselor's observations, and family members may be more willing to "own" their behavior. They are also better able to see the impact each member has on the others. Double messages and obnoxious behavior are quite obvious on tape. The real benefit of the tapes is that family members can learn new behaviors and observe themselves acting in a more satisfying way.

Taping and other techniques bring out family members' attitudes, feelings, and interpersonal behaviors. In practice, behavior changes may occur while the family is still in the phase of self-understanding. In fact, certain behavior changes not only help clarify communication problems, they may also infuse sessions with greater energy and motivation. When one or more family members are willing to make a positive change, everyone feels more excited about the potential to improve family life. One advantage of family counseling is that there is usually a great deal of behavioral material from which to draw in jointly coming up with changes. As you might expect, family members are more than willing to reveal what they don't like about the behavior of other family members once rapport in counseling has been established. The skill of the counselor comes in identifying key family problems, then suggesting the changes most likely to alleviate the problems. Most of the responsibility for identifying problems and suggesting changes should be left to the family, to teach members how to discover and expose problems in the future. Furthermore, the family will become more mature and will function as a self-regulating unit. As much as possible, then, the counselor refrains from interpretations and suggestions, although they may be necessary in the earlier sessions of counseling. It is better to act as a facilitator, providing the atmosphere for self-examination.

In this example of a family of four, the presenting problem was the behavior of the fifteen-year-old son. His grades were below average, although he tested above average and had had above average grades in elementary school. The parents, especially the mother, complained that he took no responsibility at home. He only grudgingly and sporadically helped with chores, and "he has to be reminded every day to peddle the papers and collect from the customers." The son had been caught twice at or near school smoking marijuana. In counseling, he vacillated between an "I don't care" attitude and one of mild concern about himself. He complained about his mother's continually nagging him. His attitude toward his father, at first, was to ignore him. The sister was a "good girl" who seemingly caused no trouble. Although she entered the dynamics of the situation, we will not deal with her in this illustration.

The father's interaction pattern was

one of limited contact with the rest of the family. He worked, came home to read the paper, and watched television after supper. His wife handled discipline and most decisions. He admittedly had never been very involved with the family emotionally or in terms of activities. The mother-wife was a dominating person who believed that everyone would behave irresponsibly if she were not after them to do what they were supposed to do. She claimed to have their best interests in mind. She strongly believed her son would grow up not knowing anything and would never work if she did not insist on high grades and responsible work behavior. When the boy carried out the sculpting exercise, he placed his father in a chair with his back turned to all of them. His sister faced everyone. He put himself in a chair at a table with his mother leaning over his back. He said his mother would move from him to the same position over his father.

To summarize the sessions, it became apparent that the father tuned out his wife, but did the minimal tasks necessary to escape her wrath. He sympathized with his son, but never interfered or supported him. The mother felt both males lacked initiative. She had little respect for her husband's passivity, at one point admitting that she would respect him more if he told her to shut up once in a while, and did not want her son to become like him. The counselor used sculpting, listening, and communication skill training to help the family members become aware of their interactions. The son finally revealed that he felt as if he were in a power struggle with his mother and that whatever she wanted, he would resist. He resented the distance his father maintained. He felt he had been cheated by the blocked communication. A somewhat paradoxical technique was used with the mother in regard to the son's paper route. She was asked to do the opposite with him that she had done up to that time. She was to completely ignore his paper route, except to compliment him if he peddled and collected consistently. Her resistance to the idea was immediate:

Counselor:	Would you agree to try this for a month?
Mother:	Well, I don't know if I can.
Counselor:	I'm sure you can; are you willing to?
Mother:	If I don't, he won't peddle or collect.
Counselor:	So what!
Mother:	Then he'll lose the paper route.
Counselor:	What would be so horrible about that?
Mother:	Then he would have messed it up—he wouldn't have learned to take responsibility.
Counselor:	And you think he is taking responsibility now.
Mother:	Uh, well, at least he has the chance to.
Counselor:	Does he really?
Mother:	He could if he wanted to.
Counselor:	Yet, who is really taking all the responsibility?
Mother:	If he fails, then what?

The mother had put herself in a "no win" situation. By assuming her son's responsibility, he did not have the opportunity to do so. If she gave him the responsibility, she had to live with the fear that he might not succeed. In this case, she was sending the son a double message. On the surface, she expected him to be responsible, but at another level, she did not want him to be responsible. As long as she maintained control, she was in power, which satisfied her distorted sense of self-esteem. Thus, the son received both messages and was very confused. The relationship with his mother was one of resistance, but he could not confront her in a healthy, direct way because he never understood the underlying message. In the husband-wife relationship, the husband simply withdrew; he did not wish to communicate. The paradoxical intervention was meant to change the behavior and the communication pattern. One goal was to change from nagging to positive statements, and the mother needed support throughout this process to change behavior. She had to find other sources of building self-esteem and learn to live without a scapegoat. Of course, the counselor worked on behavior changes in the other family members as well. The son looked at his pattern of rebelliousness and saw how it contributed to the cycle of unhealthy interactions.

Each person can try a modified role as part of their commitment to an improved family, working with homework assignments and a contract. Many counselors find it useful to give family members assignments they have discovered might be useful, or that the counselor wishes them to try. The point is to get all family members involved in the planning and decision making and to give *everyone* an assignment, since problems are of the family, not of an individual, and everyone must modify behavior to alleviate the problem. The counselor must be sure the assignments involve changes the members are at least willing to try and that all members agree to the changes. Assignments should also be as concrete as possible.

The final stage in family counseling includes ongoing behavior change, practicing new interaction patterns, and eventually reaching a point where the family can diagnose its problems and take action on its own. One does not expect everything to be solved, nor that problems will never recur. When the family has made substantial progress in modifying the major problems and has learned to communicate openly enough to deal with its problems, the members are probably ready for termination. In the ideal situation, termination is mutually agreed upon; in practice, counseling often ends prematurely when a family member reacts negatively to the counselor or when too much anxiety is aroused in one or more family members.

Multiple Family Counseling

Two or more families seen together by a counselor or cocounselors is considered multiple family counseling. This variation of family counseling has certain advantages over individual family counseling, but takes many forms because counselors have different notions of the most effective way to structure family counseling. Focusing on dynamics, problems, and communication patterns of the family is considered family counseling whether one member of the family is seen or whether the entire family attends. Some systems theorists believe that intervention and change with one member of a family system will inevitably change the nature of the entire system. Murray

Bowen (1976) prefers to carry out family counseling with only the parents, and sees the children only for special purposes. Others, such as Laqueur (1976), work with all family members who are able to attend. Thus, some practitioners see one or two members of each family in a session, while others attempt to have all family members present. Most practitioners agree that parents, because of their degree of power and influence in the family, are crucial members of multiple family counseling.

H. Peter Laqueur (1976) claims to have initiated multiple family counseling with families that had a schizophrenic member. He found that including four or five entire families in a group not only saved time, but produced change faster than treatment of individual families. Bowen (1976), experimenting with multiple families with a schizophrenic member, tried several structures for counseling: all family members present, four cotherapists, and all staff present. After collecting data on family progress, Bowen concluded that it was best to work with spouses only, not to have staff present at sessions, and to use one primary counselor, with one or more others interacting only if they had something urgent to contribute or were called on by the primary counselor.

Bowen and Laqueur

Murray Bowen (1976) says that multiple family work is "exactly the same as working with a single family." He relates four main functions of the counselor: (1) defining and clarifying the relationship between the spouses, (2) keeping self detriangled from the family emotional system, (3) teaching the functioning of emotional systems, and (4) demonstrating differentiation by taking "I position" stands during the course of the counseling. In carrying out these functions, Bowen found himself teaching the same principles in sessions with different families. He was able to find three families with similar problems who agreed to participate in counseling. He wanted the families to come together, yet with a degree of emotional separateness among them so the spouses could work out their own emotional interdependence and family processes. He found that families made more progress when they were part of a research plan that included observing and recording sessions; members seemed to take more responsibility for themselves rather than rely passively on the counselor. Three or four families was an ideal number for multiple counseling.

Progress was about 50 percent faster than individual family counseling, primarily because family members found reassurance in the fact that other people had similar problems. Families saw progress in and learned from one another. Bowen eventually found that once-a-month sessions were more effective than once a week. Apparently, it takes about two years for a family to make substantial changes, and the once-a-month sessions are sufficient to keep them working while preventing dependence on the counseling alone.

Peter Laqueur (1976) structures multiple family counseling somewhat differently. He works with up to five families in a clinic or hospital setting where the group is open, that is, one family may terminate and be replaced by another. Counselors, cocounselors, and counselors in training are also present, so the total group number may be 20 to 30 people meeting for one-and-a-half hours. After first trying selection criteria, families came to be included on a random basis. The first task of the counselor is to explain to the group that disturbed interaction patterns in the entire family lead to problems in one or more family members; there is no such thing as a "primary patient."

Laqueur finds multiple family counseling unique because it allows the suprasystem, society, to be a part of the therapeutic encounter. In individual counseling, the counselor has access only to the client's perceptions; in group counseling, one observes peer interactions and individual perceptions, but lacks information on relationships with significant others or society. Even family therapy deals only with the narrow focus of the few people identified with a problem. In multiple family counseling, one can see how members and each family relate to their society, which provides valuable additional information and the opportunity for the larger system to give feedback to the family subsystem.

Laqueur suggests several techniques to facilitate progress in the group. In the first session, the mothers are asked to sit in the center and tell the group "what they think of themselves, and how they rate themselves as mothers and wives," then fathers are asked to do the same thing. This exercise helps people get acquainted and provides some behavioral data with which to begin. Children are asked to divide themselves into "good" and "bad" groups, and to relate their problems with the family. Laqueur also employs exercises that explore specific dyadic relationships and an exercise in which one family member stands on a chair as "boss" and decides who may stand close and who must stand far away, illustrating a family hierarchy.

Laqueur describes ten mechanisms of change: (1) delineation of the field of interaction; (2) breaking the intrafamilial code; (3) competition; (4) amplification and modulation of signals; (5) learning through trial and error; (6) learning by analogy; (7) learning through identification; (8) use of models; (9) creating a focus of excitation;

and (10) use of families as cotherapists. Delineation of the field of interaction is the counselor's attempt to "see the total field of inter-action between subsystems (patient, family) and suprasystem (the total social environment), and makes the participants in the group aware of the importance for sickness and health of this changing surrounding field." The counselor breaks the intrafamilial code when she discovers the secret meaning of messages between family members that have developed over the years, often with the intent of closing off discussion in a threatening area.

Members of the group can observe analogous conflict situations and learn from others who have worked out the conflict. Members also learn by identifying with fathers, mothers, or children of other families. The counselor also attempts to create a *focus of excitation* by having a family or family member behave in a new way and play-ing back a videotape of the behavior.

Summary

Family counseling is a form of group counseling. The various types of family counseling include conjoint, multiple impact, network, and multiple family counseling. Basic concepts for understanding family dynamics are the double bind, paradoxical communication, pseudo-mutuality, pseudohostility, schism, and skew.

Nathan Ackerman modified psychoanalytic concepts to fit work with families. Don Jackson was a leader of the communications approach; Jay Haley emphasizes family power struggles. Virginia Satir is a primary advocate of the affective approach to family mem-ber relationships.

Assessment and goal setting are early steps in family counseling that must be done with the entire family in mind. Rather than iden-tifying one person as the disturbed member, it is assumed that prob-lems arise because of family pathology, and intervention is directed to the family as a whole. Sculpting, role playing, paradoxical tech-niques, and communication skills are methods for changing family problems, with the leader acting both as observer of the family dynamics and participant in the process.

Multiple family counseling has evolved from conjoint family work and shows a number of advantages. It saves time, expands learning opportunities for family members, and increases the range of behavioral observations for the counselor. Multiple family coun-seling can take place with spouses only or with entire families.

Resources for other family counseling techniques include *Family Therapy* (Guerin, 1976), *Techniques of Family Psychotherapy* (Bloch,

1972), *Families and Family Therapy* (Minuchin, 1974), and *Techniques of Family Therapy* (Haley & Hoffman, 1967).

Discussion Questions

1. Give examples of these basic concepts in family dynamics: double bind, paradoxical injunctions, pseudohostility, schism, and skew.

2. Compare and contrast the models of group counseling. How are they similar and different? Which models make most sense to you? Why?

3. Give examples of various techniques the counselor exmploys in working with families.

4. What are the advantages of multiple family counseling? What techniques can you employ?

15

Marital Counseling in Groups

We include a chapter on marriage counseling in this book because of the recent trend toward seeing couples in a group setting. At one time, the treatment method of choice was to see each spouse separately, so that each would have a counselor to confide in and would not have to deal with jealousy or a feeling that the counselor was taking sides. Although one can still make a case for separate counselors, it has also been found that separate treatment increases the chance of divorce. Research does not tell us why this is the case. Both members of a couple frequently see the same counselor, and increasingly, several couples are seen in a group situation rather than as a couple-counselor entity (Alger, 1976; Papp, 1976). Ohlsen's *Marriage Counseling in Groups* (1979) describes this relatively new approach. His approach is based on a learning model whereby couples are helped to master normal developmental tasks. Emphasis is on prevention of major problems, diagnosis of early symptoms of self-defeating behaviors, and substitution of desirable behaviors for less desirable ones. Ohlsen sees a trend to using groups as a way for couples to improve their relationship skills, try new behaviors, and obtain feedback from others on newly-attempted behavior. Marriage counseling in groups is more likely to be short-term, and utilization of behavioral contracts is probable.

An advantage of seeing couples in groups is that exploration and self-revelation are more likely to lead to improvement because:

1. Other couples are more likely to see through the unproductive games.

2. Similar experiences can be the basis for giving helpful feedback.

3. Distressed couples can gain support from others with similar problems.

4. Other couples can insist on learning new and more positive behaviors.

5. Individuals can act as models for certain types of productive behavior.

6. It can be easier to learn how to gain support without being dependent.

7. Others' growth can be encouraging.

Purpose of Marital Counseling

We receive little if any education or training for dealing with hetero-sexual relationships. Most of what we learn comes first from observation of parents, then from observation of other adults, then from discussions with same-sex peers, and, finally, from direct associations with opposite-sex peers. Although these relationships help us learn how to relate and satisfy our needs, the absence of any direct education in preparing for male-female relationships leaves us unprepared for the demands of marriage and parenthood. Most people expect or want to get married, yet few know what they want out of marriage, what they can give to a marriage, what they expect from a partner, how to solve problems together, or how to cope with every-day problems.

Intimacy is a frequent issue in counseling. Some people do not find closeness because they have not learned to be open with their feelings. In other cases, people are afraid that closeness will make them vulnerable. Some feel threatened by a partner's need for intimacy.

Marriage partners often have trouble maintaining the passion of their courtship. Sometimes partners have not been honest in terms of their real personality characteristics and behaviors, and when the real self becomes apparent in marriage, dissatisfaction ensues. Or, one or both partners may unrealistically expect passion to remain at the same level for years. Group counseling helps couples verify that it is common for passion to diminish.

Sexual dysfunction in a couple may result from lack of knowledge or of willingness to experiment, or it may be a symptom of a poor relationship. Despite the availability of sexual information, many people do not know how to behave in sexual relationships. Information on anatomy, techniques of foreplay and arousal, expressions of sexual pleasure to one's partner, and variations in sexual intercourse are helpful for these people. Others are reluctant to try various forms of sexual activity with their partner and need reassurance or permission. Marital groups are an ideal place to discuss these issues and share attitudes. When sexual dysfunction is a symptom of a poor relationship, the problems in the relationship rather than the sexual activity must be discussed. Chronic anger toward a partner, for example, is not conducive to satisfying sex.

In many instances, the partners have never really learned to communicate, and negative feelings of resentment, anger, jealousy, and bitterness have built up into fighting, degrading each other, excessive criticism, withdrawal, or avoiding each other. Under this negativism, there may be enough positive feelings to salvage the marriage. An outside source, such as the counselor and the group, is necessary to help the partners break the destructive pattern.

Other recommended marital counseling books are those of Gurman (1975), Koch and Koch (1976), Landis (1975), and Lederer and Jackson (1968).

One reason for more divorces and marital problems is that people feel they have a right not to be bored or dissatisfied with a marriage. More people want greater fulfillment and generally greater satisfaction in their lives. They are less willing to maintain a "bad" marriage, or are simply less willing to make sacrifices and meet the demands of marriage. Changes in the role of women in our society present new issues for couples. Some men are not ready to recognize greater freedom for their wives; others are threatened by their wives' earning power. Women also have trouble with the new roles. Some want a career but do not want so much independence and responsibility; others want a family, yet feel the financial pressure to work and delay having children. The many recent social changes have left many couples confused as to what they really want and what roles are comfortable for them. A group is an ideal place to discuss these issues.

Preparation for Marriage Counseling in Groups

The *intake interview* takes place between the counselor and couple before the first group session. The counselor explains the group and has the couple present what they see as problems. The discussion soon focuses on each member of the couple, their pain, and how the pain relates to their behavior. The counselor tries to have each person focus on his or her problems and how to alleviate them without blaming or criticizing the partner so that the one who is listening is less likely to be defensive and more likely to cooperate. After each person defines goals for counseling and sets observable objectives, they define goals as a couple, although this step must often wait for the group sessions. Individuals sometimes need to achieve their personal goals before they can commit themselves to improving the marriage. Some counselors prefer to meet each person alone first to allow freer self-expression. Some concerns may be shared later when they meet as a therapeutic triad—counselor, wife, husband.

Throughout counseling, the partners learn to establish *supportive dyads* with the counselor, other group members, and the partner. Each dyad serves a different purpose, and the frequency and type of dyadic relationships change over time. A wife may initially use the counselor for protection from an abusive husband, then use members of the group for the same purpose, and after learning to protect herself, seeks dyads that support her new assertiveness. The *therapeutic triad* is simply the beginning triad around which much of the therapeutic progress evolves.

The intake interview is also a good time to explore each person's relative commitment. If one person is reluctant to work on the marriage, he or she may need to delay joining the group. The counselor looks for ability to identify problems, communicate with others, and set goals for behavioral change. In the absence of willingness or motivation, it is best to work with the individual alone until there is some degree of commitment. If the group agrees, the uncommitted member might be admitted to the group on a temporary basis, although this person must still have some goals for participation in the group.

At the intake interview, the counselor answers client questions about the group and the individual's role in the group. The counselor tries to teach the couple how to identify their problems. To set goals, they must have behavioral objectives and work toward them. The counselor interacts with understanding and respect, to model how he hopes group members will interact with one another. The intake interview is a time for the couple to learn expectations for their behavior in the group. They also learn to differentiate therapeutic discussion from social conversation, vague goals from specific goals, talking about problems as opposed to doing something about them, and motivation from manipulation. Ability to detect pain, focus on feelings, and to openly discuss values and opinions are encouraged in the intake phase so that prospective group members have a good idea of what is expected of them as clients and as helpers. Their ability to meet these expectations evolves over the course of the group sessions.

Selection of clients for group counseling or a particular group is partly the counselor's responsibility; in an open group, which admits new members while it is in progress, participants share the responsibility. As with any group, those who would be harmed by the group, who would harm others, and who would simply interfere with others' progress should be excluded. Some people are too fragile or easily influenced by a group and probably need individual or couple counseling first. Others are insensitive to others' feelings, too self-centered, or too aggressive to be helpful in a group. The counselor wants members who can be facilitative to others and who will not inhibit others' growth because they do not want to openly explore their own problems and pain.

Other factors may not apply to every situation but deserve consideration. Significant differences in communication ability can interfere with interaction. Differences in educational background may forestall acceptance of fellow group members, and different religious beliefs may interfere with effective group work. In making selection decisions, the counselor must strive to achieve an atmosphere in which members have the greatest opportunity to grow and change, where marital concerns are the focus, and in which the group can avoid issues that will lead to its ultimate failure.

Group Process and Techniques

The process and techniques of marriage counseling groups are the same as those of other therapeutic groups, with some differences, modifications, or unique applications.

Beginning the Group

Marital group counseling involves dyads who have had some kind of intimate relationship. These two people know each other better than they know the other group members and their feelings for each other are more intense than toward other participants. They have set goals for themselves that will somehow have an impact on their relationship. These dynamics are absent from other therapeutic groups. The presence of both members of a couple can be useful from the beginning; for example, when one member is reluctant to reveal feelings, the other can be a source of encouragement. Self-disclosure and behavior change can occur outside the group because the couple has ongoing interactions. The group thus includes both special marital relationships and the total group relationships. We can say that group participants enter with primary dyadic relationships, which is not true of other groups; as the group evolves, other dyads form that may become more important in one way or another than the initial dyads.

Another unique dimension is that each couple brings a usually troubled communication pattern that becomes obvious in the group process. Typical problems—not listening to one another, demanding, power struggles, inconsideration, phoniness, manipulation—cannot be hidden very long from the group. The counselor and the members have an opportunity to examine and work on the communication problems directly rather than indirectly, as would be the case if each member of a pair attended separate groups.

Another advantage to couples in a group is that each interacts with other members of the group. This allows one person to observe the partner's interactions with others and learn from them. In the group, for example, Don treats Susan and Jenny very kindly, but is brusque and condescending with his wife. She points out the difference, and a group discussion ensues.

Couples can share similar problems or help others with different problems. Reactions and observations from several couples to a target couple can have a greater impact than the same information coming to the wife or husband alone from another member of a group. Conflict comes into the open for the counselor and group to discuss. Other couples state similar frustrations, and someone tries to get at the hurt feelings involved. As the interaction progresses, couples share similar feelings, get at the hurt, and work together to address the problem.

Marital Group Techniques

Role playing forces clients to act out their feelings, attitudes, and perceptions of others, and gives the group an opportunity to view member behavior firsthand. Role playing brings to the surface behavior and feelings that have not been expressed in the group. The advantage to the role players is that they act out feelings rather than hold them in or talk *about* them. They become more aware of themselves or the person whose role they are playing and receive feedback that helps them understand their situation. Group participants receive at least two benefits: seeing the behavior gives a more accurate picture of the problem and affords more accurate perceptions and reactions, and couples may see behavior that relates to their own marital relationship. Couples usually role play something, such as expressing anger, that most other couples must deal with in their marriage. Consequently, everyone learns from role playing; some benefit directly, others indirectly, and still others from being helpful.

Four role playing techniques are useful. The couple may role play themselves. The group leader may focus on a specific situation a couple has discussed (talking "about" a problem) or ask the couple for a specific instance of the problem. The problem may be one of expressing anger to each other, for which the couple gives the example of conflict over where to spend Christmas Day. Roger wants to alternate going to each set of parents' homes on Christmas. But Gail's mother lives alone and Gail is an only child, so Gail wants to go to Roger's parents on Christmas Eve because Christmas Day is special to her mother, who would spend it alone if they did not visit. Gail's mother lives in another city, so they can't visit both parents. In the first type of role playing, Gail plays herself and Roger plays himself. They are asked to sit in front of the group facing each other and recreate the scene, then discuss the conflict. Many group leaders encourage couples to express feelings as well as thoughts, opinions, and values. As with all role playing, the couple and group members are led in a discussion of what they learned from the interaction. Videotape is especially helpful; the couple can view the videotape between sessions and discuss it themselves, and if there is enough time, the counselor can replay the tape for everyone to discuss. Playing a section, stopping the tape, and discussing what went on allows more careful examination of statements and responses, a focus on nonverbal behaviors, and time to discuss specific behaviors.

A second type of role playing is role reversal, which is particularly effective with couples because until they join a group, they are exclusively concerned with themselves, and have been unable or unwilling to truly understand the other. Although each member of a couple believes he or she "knows" the other, couples with problems demonstrate great difficulty in truly understanding their mates. In this type of role playing Gail is asked to play the role of Roger and Roger plays Gail. When the action ends, there are various ways to lead the discussion. One might ask Gail to state where Roger was accurate or inaccurate and what he left out. She might say he did not reflect how concerned she is about her mother's loneliness; Roger might point out that Gail did not reflect the extent of his mother's jealousy and how it affects their relationship with her. The leader can also solicit the group's reaction to the role playing.

A third role playing method is to have other members of the group role play the target couple. Gail can play herself and select another man to play Roger. She acts as director, telling him how Roger behaves and how to approach the situation; Gail thus stages how she perceives the conflict. Roger learns from observing the interaction, which gives him a different perspective. There are many variations on this method: the role playing may be reenacted with a substitute for Gail and Roger playing himself, or other group members might play both Roger and Gail. This technique shows Gail and Roger how fellow group members perceive them, but more importantly, they can see how each hurts the other and begin to take steps to prevent the pain. The focus must be on understanding each other, which leads to greater motivation to solve the problem.

Role-play modeling blends two useful counseling techniques. Modeling teaches useful behavior through observation of those behaviors in other people. Couples have often learned self-destructive, conflictual, or poor communicative behavior by observing poor role models, or because they have not had role models. Gail grew up without a father, so she was not able to observe her mother relating to a husband. In Roger's home, his father made all the important decisions. Gail had little personal information and few examples of how a wife relates to a husband, while Roger thought he was supposed to be the boss, but had not learned the role well. In the group, members can role play healthy ways of dealing with conflict, demonstrating how to listen to one another, how to communicate thoughts and feelings, how to help each other meet needs, and how to make joint decisions that satisfy both parties. Another couple can role play Roger and Gail, but in a "healthy" way. This technique shows a couple alternative ways of relating to each other. Two or more couples may role play a situation to show that there is more than one useful way to handle a conflict situation. The other couples who are willing to show how someone else's problems could be handled probably have similar difficulties, and in the safer process of helping someone else, learn a more positive way of handling marital problems.

Another group technique is the *magic shop* (Carpenter & Sandberg, 1973), which Ohlsen adapts for marital groups. A group member is invited to go the magic shop, where the spouse is the proprietor; they subsequently barter for new behaviors, relationships, or personal characteristics. Schutz (1967) recommends an *approach-avoidance* technique that seems especially helpful when people are asked to stand at opposite ends of the room, remain silent, and walk toward each other while looking into each other's eyes. When they become close, they are to do whatever they feel impelled from within to do, continuing the exercise as long as they wish, following with group discussion. The leader urges them to respond to their feelings rather than plan what to do. Schutz gives an example of two people who had ambivalent feelings about the opposite sex. As George and

Marla met, George kept going. They stood still, with their backs to each other for five minutes. The group urged them to do something. Marla walked back, turned George so that she was facing his back, and gave him a hard kick in the rear, sending him several feet across the room. Marla invited him to kick her back. George refused until she held a pillow behind her, then he kicked her gently. The group then discussed the encounter. Marla felt strong and elated, and her participation increased. George became depressed as he realized that his problems with women, which he had avoided until then, were serious. Ohlsen also suggests the technique of *soliloquy* in the approach-avoidance context. This gives the client a chance to reveal "feelings and wished-for behaviors, and even to solicit suggestions from other group members on how to cope with their situation."

Ohlsen suggests the *fiddler game* as a way to help couples cooperate in decision making. (He derived this from *Fiddler on the Roof*, where Tevye presented sides to an argument by saying "on the other hand.") The counselor asks a couple to work together on a decision by making a point or points for deciding one way, followed by "on the other hand," until each side of the issue is exhausted. Gail and Roger, for example, list the desirability, rationale, and advantages of going to Gail's mother's for Christmas Day each year, as well as the points for alternating. They discover that their parents control their decisions and realize they have not been looking at what *they* want to do. In the end, they decide to spend Christmas Day alone with their children this year. After discussion in the group, the members support their decision. Gail and Roger feel better about each other and are better able to make decisions together.

Bach and Wydan (1970) use a variation of the approach-avoidance technique and interpret the difference between two people in preferred distance as an indication of each partner's tolerance for closeness. Lange and Jakubowski (1978) take a skill training approach to relationship problems. In a *lifestyle inventory*, a couple expresses in writing their preferences for such things as allocation of time, selection of friends, activities with family, time alone, work-related activities, church involvement, significance of social life, importance of financial success, managing money, place of children in the home, commitment to the marriage, and involvement in the community. The leader helps group members determine their lifestyle goals, arrange the items in priority, share the list with their spouse, then discuss the inventories with the group. Areas of compatibility as well as conflict emerge as couples make their wants and values explicit. The group helps each couple and watches each other struggle with problems and work toward resolution.

Other techniques in marital group counseling may include or deal with:

Use of formal contracts (Sager, 1976)

Jealousy (Clanton & Smith, 1977)

Fighting fairly (Bach & Wyden, 1968)

Early discovery and management (for example, dealing with revenge) (Ohlsen, 1979, pp. 158–61)

Cooperative decision making (Smaby & Tamminen, 1978)

Sexual dysfunction (Ohlsen, 1979, pp. 134–36; Kaplan, 1975; Mace, 1976; Masters & Johnson, 1971, 1976)

Conflict management: Top-dog–Underdog (Polster & Polster, 1973)

Family choreography, prescribed tasks (Papp, 1976)

Summary

Marriage counseling in groups is a relatively recent trend that has advantages beyond the lower cost involved. Couples can give each other feedback that might not be as readily accepted from the counselor and can share similar experiences.

A therapeutic triad consists of the two marriage partners and the counselor. As the group matures, members are able to replace the counselor with another therapeutic person in triadic interactions. Many ongoing triads exist in a group.

Usual group techniques, such as role playing, role reversal, and modeling help overcome marriage partners' troubled communications. Unique methods such as the magic shop, the fiddler game, a lifestyle inventory, and cooperative career planning have proved useful.

Discussion Questions

1. What issues do couples frequently deal with in group counseling? How can the group help them?

2. How does one get ready to form and lead a group of couples?

3. List some good ideas for beginning a couples' group.

4. Give examples of techniques that are applicable to couples' groups.

PART 4

Special Applications

16

Vocational Development Groups

In recent years, group procedures have come to be used with individuals who are dealing with some aspect or another of vocational development. This trend reflects economic realities; agencies, services, or programs, faced with increasing constraints on time, money, and professional expertise, see group procedures as a less expensive way to provide service, as compared to individual intervention.

Beyond this legitimate economic consideration, there are advantages for individuals; for example, groups provide peer pressure and/or peer support, opportunities to test one's personal reality against the experienced reality of others in the group, and opportunities to learn and practice social and communication skills. A job search is often difficult and discouraging, especially when jobs are not plentiful. The support of others who face the same difficulties and their expectation that one will continue to try can be a source of support as well as motivation. Others can help one see opportunities previously overlooked, and help someone keep his feet on the ground. To the extent that most types of work involve some social interaction, a group helps prepare more effectively for work by helping to refine personal interaction skills.

Group procedures also have advantages for the individual counselor who works with vocational development. They allow the coun-

Contributed by Anne Chandler, University of South Carolina

selor to disseminate information efficiently and assess clients in a more natural setting than can be done individually. Again, because work is often a social activity, the group allows the counselor to observe the client in a social setting, which can have important implications for remediation of problems in either a group or individual therapeutic setting.

Vocational Development

We will use *vocational development* to describe those aspects of growth, in terms of knowledge, attitudes, and skills, that specifically result in an individual's satisfactory establishment in the world of work. We will deal only with those aspects of individual development that are most critical and specifically related to attaining employment—concepts of vocational exploration, development and exploration of work values, decision making regarding vocational alternatives, and vocational placement.

We can categorize vocational development into the areas of career counseling and job placement. Career counseling includes vocational exploration, values and self-exploration, and establishing vocational alternatives. Job placement includes those tasks most directly related to securing employment. We will examine group procedures in both areas.

Group Purposes

Career Counseling Groups

Career counseling groups can be designed to meet diverse needs. To some extent, the purpose and design of any group reflect the leader's theoretical orientation to vocational development, the factors he considers significant in the individual's vocational development. These factors include such diverse variables as the nature of the parent-child relationship, personality type, presence of role models, individual ego needs, effects of the environment, and even "accident." Theorists do not agree, and research does not explain, as to how or why career development occurs. This lack of agreement reflects the complexity of the process, which you will quickly see in career counseling practice.

The emphasis of the group will vary depending upon the leader's orientation. In general, however, career counseling groups attempt to help participants arrive at a vocational objective, or objectives, or general area of vocational emphasis, consistent with the individual's interests and abilities. The concept of an adequate vocational objective has increasingly broadened to include the notion that an adequate choice is one the individual has a satisfactory chance of achieving in the present and projected labor market.

Job Placement Groups

The primary purpose of job placement groups, on the other hand, is specifically to prepare individual participants to compete successfully in the job market, after a career choice has been made. Unlike career counseling groups, job placement groups function more independently of the group leader's theoretical orientation, and there is greater consensus as to the necessary skills that must be addressed to reach the desired outcome.

Despite the apparent similarity in the purposes of career counseling and job placement groups (that is, both are oriented to producing a measurable outcome related to work), there is actually considerable difference in the two purposes. Because career counseling groups are intended to help individuals attain some self-direction in one sphere of their lives, they bear some resemblance to growth groups. Job placement groups, on the other hand, are more heavily oriented to skills acquisition, and thus more closely resemble educational groups. In addition, the job-seeking phase of vocational development is generally presumed to follow completion of other career development tasks.

Leader Preparation

Individuals interested in leading any type of vocational development group require two primary areas of preparation. One is that of group counseling skills. As with all groups, vocational development groups require the leader to understand human behavior and how best to facilitate human growth in the group situation. In addition, one who wishes to lead career counseling and job placement groups needs a solid understanding of the issues and tasks of these content areas.

The counselor who chooses to work with vocational development groups should begin preparation by learning about theoretical approaches in career counseling. Understanding these approaches will help the counselor better understand individual clients and allow him to impose some order on the process, at least intellectually.

Knowledge of the world of work as well as the more specific needs of employers will be invaluable. As one example, group leaders need to know that wearing a coat and tie is inappropriate when a man applies for most skilled trades positions. Although such information may seem trivial, it is critical for the prospective employee. If points such as these are not presented correctly, the leader's credibility will diminish, as will the effectiveness of the group. For individuals interested in leading job placement groups, it is productive to study teaching strategies, so that one can present information effectively and so as to maximize learning. To use specific structured vocational development programs effectively, the potential group leader must be familiar with their content and methodology.

Selection of Participants

The criteria for selecting participants differ somewhat for career counseling and job placement groups. Career counseling groups seem to work most effectively for participants who have at least a general interest in the world of work and some curiosity about their place in it, but this is not always essential, because participation occasionally evokes interest and curiosity in members who had previously seemed disinterested.

Leaders must also address the area of the level of emotional and intellectual functioning of potential participants. Effective career counseling depends to some extent upon the individual's ability to assess himself, to process information, and to make realistic decisions. If a potential participant has severe difficulties that preclude success in these activities, he might fare better either in individual counseling or by waiting to join a group after appropriate remediation of the other problems. Leaders must not, however, be overly restrictive in applying this criterion. For instance, if a client wishes to be a graphic designer, but has had no relevant experience and has dropped out of high school, she should not be excluded simply because her present choices are unrealistic. Actually, she might be a very good candidate for the group, since the group often functions well in helping individuals form both realistic and long-term plans for career choices.

Both career counseling and job placement groups often use activities that involve reading and writing, so the leader may find it useful to determine potential participants' general level of functioning in these areas. Many leaders prefer to group people according to educational level so that activities can be tailored to basic literacy skills, but it can be better to have some mix of skill levels, particularly in job placement groups, to allow group members to give each other concrete assistance, for example, in writing résumés. Helping each other enhances group cohesion and the members' commitment to each other.

When selecting participants for job placement groups, we generally assume that the individual has completed the process of exploring the world of work; has done an adequate self-appraisal; has selected appropriate vocational alternatives; and is ready to make the transition to employed status. In reality, however, the counselor seldom finds participants this "job ready." When screening participants for job placement groups, the counselor should look at issues as as these:

1. Does the participant have a clear vocational objective?

2. Has the participant identified possible alternative objectives?

3. Does the individual have adequate skills (training, experience, and so on) to obtain these objectives?

4. Does the participant have adequate job retention skills, such as the ability to get along with others and to maintain standards of attendance and promptness?

5. Does the individual want to go to work?

There may be other issues to address, but participants who rate highly on these factors seem likely to derive the most benefit from a job placement group.

Unfortunately, even clients who seem well-prepared for a job placement group often seem to become distracted from the placement goal after they are in the group, partly because of the content. For instance, an individual with clearly defined vocational objectives may discover in the course of the group that there is a poor labor market for those objectives, and may need to reexamine her goals.

On the other hand, some clients who at first seem poor candidates for job placement groups may benefit considerably from the group process. Occasionally, individuals who for one reason or other are either ambivalent about or disinterested in obtaining employment undergo a marked change in attitude and behavior as a result of inclusion in a job placement group. The change comes partly from peer support and enthusiasm and partly from the behavioral strategies that allow the individual to experience a measure of success. One sometimes finds that ambivalence has been a defense mechanism to protect the individual against anticipated failure in the job search.

It is difficult to establish stringent criteria for selecting members for a job placement group. Self-selection into the group and the presence of clear vocational goals seem to be the best indicators of maximum benefit. In reality, however, most practitioners have minimal control over participant selection, so it makes sense for the counselor to prepare herself to deal with a wide variety of personal and vocational issues, despite the group's seemingly narrow focus.

Group Process and Dynamics

Vocational development groups share with other groups many of the same phenomena of process and dynamics, so the leader needs considerable expertise in general group counseling skills. Differences in process and dynamics seem to reflect the purposes of these groups.

Career counseling groups tend to emphasize self-assessment and personal exploration along with education. Some groups may have a therapeutic emphasis as well, especially if part of the group's purpose is to change behavior or attitudes that are inimical to productive career development. Where the focus is on skill development (for example, decision-making skills), behavioral counseling strategies are often used. In general, career counseling group leaders seem to use a directive style, especially in information-giving phases. Career counseling groups usually encourage peer support. Members learn how others perceive them and share the information they gather during vocational exploration. Group interaction seems especially helpful to members who have inaccurate or unrealistic perceptions of their own skills or the world of work. Feedback from another group member seems to make a far greater impression than does equivalent feedback from the leader.

To a large extent, job placement groups are educational as opposed to therapeutic. Thus, much of their content consists of didactic instruction, skills training, and rehearsal of job-seeking skills. Some groups include assessment of assets and liabilities with respect to the job market, either through standardized assessment procedures or participants' self-assessments. Most job placement groups tend to rely on behavioral strategies—shaping, reinforcement, modeling, and behavioral rehearsal—as described in chapter 2.

With respect to group process, many job placement groups use peer pressure and peer support to enhance the learning process and stimulate behavior change. This is generally an informal process by which other members' interest and involvement tend to encourage the individual to remain persistent in his job search, although a structured program may build peer support into "buddy systems," with members pairing off to give each other support and assistance during each phase of the job search (Azrin & Besalel, 1980). Other groups use purposeful peer pressure; for instance, the Pounce program (Walker, 1969) used peer pressure and confrontation to deal with clients who failed to take personal responsibility for their unemployment. Whether peer support and pressure are structured, they can decrease the individual's sense of "aloneness" in his job search.

Structure

Vocational development groups vary greatly in amount of structure, but nearly all of them tend to be more structured than groups that deal with general issues of personal development and growth, perhaps because vocational groups have specific and measurable purposes.

In career counseling groups, the amount of structure often reflects the leader's theoretical orientation in terms of both career development theory and counseling theory in general. Thus, one leader may encourage general verbal exploration of self and past experiences, while another may use highly structured verbal and written exercises to elicit similar kinds of information.

Job placement groups tend to be more heavily structured. Most have an underlying assumption that participants have either a skills deficit with respect to job search skills or that the skills are inadequate because of lack of reinforcement. Thus, the group leader carries the responsibility of arranging a comfortable learning environment and using structured techniques to increase participants' skill levels. Even in job placement groups, however, structure is variable, especially when the group's purposes include components such as managing stress and effects of unemployment on oneself and others.

Because all vocational development groups involve dissemination of information about the world of work, one who is interested in leading such groups may find it helpful initially to use a highly structured, packaged program, which we will discuss later. Eventually the leader will create a more personalized structure based on materials and approaches from many programs and on her own experiences.

General Content Areas

Career Counseling Groups

Regardless of the theoretical orientation of career counseling groups, the nature of group activities, or the amount of structure, content areas tend to be similar, although some programs emphasize certain areas over others.

Self-Appraisal Most career counseling groups encourage partici-pants to assess themselves in a number of areas. Some use standard-ized assessment devices such as paper-and-pencil tests; other groups rely less on standardized instrumentation and more on individual reflection and introspection. There may also be semistructured activ-ities such as writing one's autobiography. Other group members may also contribute to a member's self-assessemnt in their feedback on their perceptions of the individual. Assessment areas may include individual interests, aptitudes or abilities, and past achievements. The purpose of this phase is to help the individual understand his current level of functioning and to provide a foundation upon which to build future group phases.

Identification of Work Values Although identification of work values can be part of the self-appraisal process, it is important enough to discuss separately. People work for many reasons and to meet a wide variety of personal needs. By examining an individual's values, we can discover valuable information about what kinds of work they will find satisfying and thus be motivated to pursue. We often assume that a good salary is the most critical work value, but that is not the case for many individuals; they repeatedly fail to maintain jobs that, to the outside observer, would seem to be excellent. As an example, let us look at the case of Harry. Harry had excellent mechanical abil-ity and enjoyed putting things together and working with machines. He took a job assembling heavy farm equipment at a handsome wage. Harry learned his job quickly and was meeting production standards within a few days. Three weeks after taking the job, Harry quit. Why? He disliked the repetitiveness of the job. Harry highly val-ued variety in his work. A job as an apprentice to an automobile mechanic, at lower wages, turned out to be much more satisfying to Harry, and became the start of his career. Had Harry received some assistance in identifying his work values from the start, both he and his first employer might have avoided an unfortunate occurrence.

Careful individual assessment is particularly important in diffi-cult economic times. While it is unrealistic to think that a person's career choice at, say, age 21, is immutable, it nevertheless makes sense to make as well-informed decisions as possible. Few people can afford the luxury of frequent job changes in an attempt to find sat-isfactory employment, nor is this even possible for most people in a tight job market. Greater self-knowledge helps one narrow choices and make a choice that is more likely to result in personal satisfaction.

Vocational Exploration Adequate knowledge about interests, abilities, and values allows one to move productively into the phase of vocational exploration. During this phase, individuals gather data about the world of work in general and about specific areas that particularly interest them. The individual can pursue a wide range of activities and resources. Basic information about career options and projections of employment trends are available from various publications, and most school and public libraries have a career development section with such standard references as the *Occupational Outlook Handbook* and *Guide to Occupational Exploration,* as well as pamphlets or systems about specific occupations.

Vocational exploration can also revolve around more action-oriented strategies. Participants may interview jobholders, visit worksites or participate in "shadow" experiences where they accompany an employee throughout a full workday, often performing job tasks in the "shadow" of the employee. This concept is sometimes extended to short-term actual job tryouts in one or two selected areas.

Regardless of the strategy or combination of strategies in the group setting, members generally exchange information with one another. This, of course, gives each member a considerable amount of information about the world of work in a relatively brief time and frequently gives one ideas or options he might not have encountered on his own.

Decision-Making Skills After the information-gathering process is under way, participants usually receive instruction and practice in decision making, for which a number of different models are available. The general process involves generating alternatives, evaluating alternatives in light of relevant criteria, then ranking alternatives in terms of desirability. Decision-making skill is important in many phases of vocational development, from choosing a vocational objective to choosing one job offer over others.

Development of a Career Plan The last content area is often developing career plans for the individuals in the group. This plan may include the vocational objective or objectives, plans for further exploration, information about necessary skill development or education, and plans for either employment or training in job-placement skills. Sometimes plans for life areas other than vocational may be included; for instance, most of us meet our needs and pursue our interests through a combination of vocational and avocational activities. A plan might thus address leisure activities as well as career issues.

Job Placement Groups

Although job placement groups may differ somewhat in the emphasis on various skill areas, several areas tend to be consistent across groups.

Development of a Résumé or Fact Sheet The résumé or fact sheet presents those aspects of an individual's educational and/or work history that are salient to her vocational objective. Participants learn how to write the résumé and how to develop an attractive format for the material. The résumé represents the individual when she cannot physically be present to speak for herself, for example, when contact with a potential employer is by mail. As a result, most groups spend considerable time on the résumé. There are many styles and formats for résumé preparation, and choosing a style depends on factors such as the type of job for which one is applying, the presence of past employment problems, and so on. Proponents of the various styles agree that the résumé should be short, concise, and written in clear language.

Application Completion Participants receive instruction in correctly completing job applications and in the importance of correctness. Groups generally place greater emphasis on this phase of instruction when:

- Group participants have characteristics that may place them at a disadvantage when applicant screening is based on an employer's review of application information (persons with disabilities, ex-offenders, those with gaps in their employment histories, and so forth).

- Group participants are dealing with particularly complex application forms, such as those for the Federal government; completing the application may be a critical step in securing employment, so more time is allotted to this topic, while other groups will give it only perfunctory attention.

Identifying Job Leads Identifying potential employers in a geographical location is often difficult and time-consuming. Group participants learn the importance of a comprehensive search. Participants learn various strategies for identifying employers and organizing this information effectively. Group members usually learn about the relative effectiveness of traditional methods of job search, such as using want ads, versus less traditional methods, such as personally contacting employers. Group leaders may also include instruction on obtaining in-depth information about a potential employer and encourage group members to share information about employers and the employment market. The group setting thus allows each member access to a far wider range of information and opportunities than a single individual could generate alone.

Contacting Employers Methods of contacting employers generally comprise another section of job placement groups, covering strategies for dealing with potential employers by mail (use of a cover letter), by phone, and in person. Time spent on each strategy is proportional to participants' needs; for example, participants seeking jobs in a large geographical area such as the Southwest will generally need more instruction on the use of cover letters than those who are seeking jobs in a small town.

Interviewing Techniques The employment interview is probably the single most critical step in the job search process. Regardless of one's credentials, the personal interview confirms or contradicts the employer's hypothesis that an individual is the appropriate choice for a particular job. Therefore, most job placement groups emphasize interviewing skills. They discuss appropriate grooming and dress for various jobs, and stress positive nonverbal behavior (posture, eye contact) and appropriate communication skills. Individuals are encouraged to focus on effective presentation of their relevant work skills and are coached on the differences between interviewing and social conversation. Frequently, participants role play interviews, receive feedback from group members, and shape appropriate interview behavior as guided by the group leader. Videotapes of the mock interviews are often used as an aid to behavior change. This area of job placement counseling often includes strategies for interview follow-up and self-assessment of interview behavior.

Structured Vocational Development Groups

Career Counseling Groups

Although there are many structured approaches, most career counseling groups do not use a specific structured program. Materials and activities for individual career counseling are often simply modified for the group setting; however, if the counselor's need is consistent with the purposes and activities of a structured approach, it may be more efficient to use the package than to develop a group program from scratch.

Vocational Exploration Group

The Vocational Exploration Group (VEG) was developed by Daane (1972), based on the premise that individuals usually know much more about the world of work than they realize. Small-group interaction taps that knowledge and helps group members better understand the relationship between the worker and the job. A recent revision (Daane, 1983) extends the VEG to leisure-activity exploration.

Structural Components   VEG groups have four to six members who meet for approximately six hours. Over the course of the group, participants go through a prescribed sequence of 17 steps designed to help members identify work activities that have the potential of meeting their individual needs. The program introduces the concept of a job's variety of components and teaches members to analyze jobs from the standpoint of environments, requisite skills, and satisfactions. Members also assess themselves along the same dimensions, identifying the skills or abilities they can use in the world of work and examining the satisfactions they wish to derive from a job. From the vocational exploration phase, participants select several alternatives consistent with their self-assessments. In the final phase, members develop action plans that specify the steps individuals will take to meet objectives.

Throughout the process, the leader's role and actions are clearly specified, as are each of the steps the participants complete. The program provides handouts, resource materials, and other teaching aids.

PATH

The PATH system was developed by Figler (1979) to help liberal arts students develop appropriate vocational alternatives. The assumption is that these students have developed some skills in the areas of communication and problem solving, but are often at a loss when it comes to perceiving the transferability of these skills to the job market or effectively marketing these skills to employers. In its present format, the PATH system may be used individually, but the group setting appears preferable.

Structural Components   A skilled leader can handle groups of as many as 24 participants. Subgroups of four members form for exercises, and remain intact through the program. Group sessions should not run longer than two and one-half hours at a time, and approximately 13–15 hours of group time are required to complete the program.

The PATH program is made up of 18 structured exercises that all participants complete. The *Workbook* (Figler, 1979) provides stimulus questions and space for responses, as well as some resource information for each exercise. It also gives specific instructions for the group leader, both for structuring the exercise and for discussing and using the response material. There are examples of responses, and group leaders are encouraged to use their personal responses to the exercises as examples. The sessions encourage certain principles, such as:

1. Flexibility—participants are encouraged to keep an open mind about vocational alternatives and to assume no limitations

2. Openness—participants are asked to react openly to exercises, although self-disclosure of the reaction is at the participant's discretion

3. Creativity—participants create individualized alternatives, with an emphasis on meeting a wide range of their individual interests and needs

4. Ongoing nature of the process—participants are not expected to settle on a single alternative, but are urged to think of the process as ongoing and for use at various times throughout life

The 18 structured activities are designed to stimulate both self-exploration and vocational exploration. Early in the program, participants explore childhood fantasies about the world of work, assess their attitudes toward work and the notion of creating a balance between work and play, and examine their personal values with respect to work. Because the program is designed for liberal arts students, another of the early exercises deals with the choice of college major and explores the desirability of graduate education.

Further on in the program, participants evaluate their interests by examining the activities they find enjoyable. Additional self-assessment is stimulated by listing significant life experiences and analyzing those personal attributes that contributed to the success or failure of the experiences.

Participants then go through a process of obtaining occupational information and begin to generate career ideas. As noted, the program stresses creativity and encourages participants to combine their self-assessment data and the occupational information they gather to produce unique and individualized options for themselves.

Toward the end of the program, participants look at various strategies for evaluating career options, review the general process of career choice, and explore ways to use the process in further decision making.

Job Placement Groups

Many of the structured approaches to the job search process are not specific only to groups. The counselor should review a variety of the structured programs, whether designed for individuals or groups; often, the programs can be used interchangeably with individual clients or groups of clients (Carkhuff, Pierce, Friel, & Willis, 1975; Keith, 1976).

Job Seeking Skills

The Job Seeking Skills (JSS) program (Bakeman, 1971) was developed by the Minneapolis Rehabilitation Center (now the Multi Resource Center) and uses three criteria for client selection:

1. The client is presumed to have an appropriate job goal

2. The client is employable

3. Any client problem (medical, etc.) that might preclude employment must be at least close to resolution (Bakeman, 1971).

As you can see from these criteria, the JSS program was originally designed to aid disabled or disadvantaged job seekers. The intent is to teach a set of skills that will allow for self-placement, both immediately following training and in the future.

Structural Components   Each JSS group has six to ten members and lasts for two days. Members watch a videotape that models good interviewing behaviors (Prazak, 1969). After group discussion of this videotape, the clients are videotaped in brief mock interviews with group leaders. Members and the leader reinforce positive behavior and begin identifying skills deficiences.

The next step involves direct skills teaching, with specific instruction for completing application blanks, especially when dealing with questions that may present difficulties, for example, "Have you ever been fired from a job?" Participants are coached to reveal specific, relevant skills in the job interview by preparing an asset review and citing specific experiences or skills that will clearly demonstrate their ability to do the job (Prazak, 1969).

Learning effective interview behaviors is a major focus of the JSS program, and because JSS was developed to meet the needs of those with serious employability problems, it emphasizes dealing with problem questions in the interview and turning liabilities into assets. For example, the older worker might be encouraged to emphasize that he is settled and mature, knows what work is about, and is interested in finding a job to "stick with." The younger worker, on the other hand, is coached to stress assets of eagerness to learn, with the potential as a worker who can learn to do things the employer's way.

The JSS program also addresses appearance and grooming, along with fine points of interviewing such as nonverbal behavior and use of the "call back" closing, a strategy in which the job applicant arranges to call the interviewer back at a specific time, rather than allow the interview to end with "We'll be in touch."

There is relatively little attention to résumé preparation and identification of job leads; rather, the approach focuses more intensively on the potential applicant's interpersonal skills, particularly with respect to the interview situation. Modeling, reinforcement, and behavior rehearsal are used extensively, and videotaping is used both as a teaching and motivating device and is considered an important adjunct to the group process (Prazak, 1969).

Job Club

The Job Club concept was developed in the early 1970s under the primary leadership of Nathan Azrin. The major components and processes are summarized in a counselor's manual (Azrin & Besalel, 1980). The Job Club is a systematic, behaviorally-oriented program that presumes each participant is employable and that the group's and the leader's commitment to helping each person find a job is permanent. The group leader bears the major responsibility for directing the group; however, specific activities and time lines are clearly delineated for the leader and each participant is expected to complete every step without exception. Peer support not only is encouraged, but is considered essential (Azrin & Besalel, 1980).

Structural Components   Groups of ten to twelve new Job Club members are recommended, and since the Job Club is a continuing program, up to eight "carry-overs" from previous groups may increase group size to a maximum of 20. An underlying assumption is that group members will seek employment on a full-time basis until they find suitable employment, so the individual's time in a group is open-ended. The structured format includes a *Counselor's Manual* that outlines specific activites for each day of the group. The manual provides forms for generating lists of contacts, references, and the like, and gives members precise behavioral goals for each activity undertaken; for example, job seekers are to contact ten potential employers each day. After the initial session, participants spend only half a day in groups and the rest of the day actually interviewing or seeking out jobs.

The counselor's active role includes a directive style and high levels of positive reinforcement. Counselors provide brief didactic instruction, but behavior rehearsal is considered more effective. Another important feature of the counselor's role is that he should spread his attention rapidly over all group members (Azrin & Besalel, 1980). Despite the considerable amount of structure, the Job Club manual continually stresses the need for encouragement, and personal involvement of the group leader with each participant.

Placement Preparation Program

Where the Job Club is limited in focus (job search skills) and goal (attaining employment), the Placement Preparation Program (PPP) developed by ICD Rehabilitation and Research Center looks at a broad range of employment issues beyond those of the job search.

PPP was developed in response to observed client behavior as individuals began the placement process. Clients seemed to find the placement process threatening and evinced concerns about the potential "losses" represented by employment, such as loss of disability payments or medical coverage. Many clients also failed to demonstrate minimal adequacy in such basic skills as appearing on time for appointments. PPP was thus developed to deal not only with job search issues, but also with clients' emotional and cognitive responses to the placement process (Weisinger & Schultz, 1979). Although initially developed for work with a disabled/disadvantaged population, many of the concerns PPP addresses are common to job-seekers in general.

Structural Components   PPP uses audiotapes to stimulate group discussion. Group leaders use guides and handout materials for each ten sessions. The goals of the PPP are as follows:

1. To resolve client-centered problems related to placement on a job and keeping a job

2. To provide activities to help clients consider the attitudes and social skills required to get and hold a job

3. To relate training program experiences to what will be expected on a job

4. To help clients realize the importance of knowing their goals, skills, and abilities

5. To develop clients' understanding of the formalities of job-seeking (Weisinger & Schultz, 1979)

We can see from the stated goals that the Placement Preparation Program is in many ways a cross between a job placement and a career placement group.

Research on Effectiveness

Career Counseling Groups

Most of the literature on group approaches to career counseling is descriptive; in most cases, the only evaluative information we find is that of subjective participant evaluations or equally subjective impressions of the leaders. This information can be valuable, but more empirical data would allow group leaders to make better decisions about which programs or components are most likely to be effective with a particular group.

Most of the empirical research does not deal with structured group programs but with career counseling groups in general, with the exception of the VEG. Daane (1972) studied the effects of the VEG on a group of 400 clients deemed ready for employment. Those exposed to the process found jobs at twice the rate of those in a control group. Tests of job knowledge and ability to relate job demands to self demonstrated a significant increase in scores among experimental (VEG) clients as compared to control group clients.

In another study, Tichenor (1977) studied the effect of the Life Work Planning program (Kirn, 1974) on the level of self-actualizing attitudes and values of participants. Using a personality inventory to measure change, no significant differences were found on overall scores between experimental and control groups either immediately after treatment or five months following treatment. Significant differences between the groups were found immediately post treatment on two subscales of the inventory; however, this finding did not hold up at the five month follow-up.

Other studies focus on a comparison of approaches. Graff, Danish, and Austin (1972) compared the effect of three approaches to career counseling—individual, group, and programmed self-instruction. Participants rated seven areas of skill/knowledge; subjects in all the experimental conditions rated themselves higher on the seven scales than did control group subjects. Group and individual approach subjects had similar ratings on the scales, while programmed self-instruction subjects rated higher than the other two experimental conditions on three of the scales.

In contrast, Swails and Herr (1976) studied the effectiveness of three types of group procedures using a measure of vocational maturity. The three experimental conditions involved (1) relationship counseling; (2) use of taped models; and (3) use of the Life Career Game. Ninth graders were assigned, using stratification procedures, to one of the experimental groups or a control group. No significant differences were found among groups on the vocational maturity inventory following treatment.

More positive results were found in a study by Jepsen, Dustin, and Miars (1982) with eleventh graders who were randomly assigned to either the control or one of three experimental conditions. In the experimental groups, participants took guided field trips to observe jobs; or received didactic instruction on problem-solving techniques, including behavior rehearsal of the techniques; or observed a video-taped role model of an individual using problem-solving techniques. Four inventories and one behavioral measure were used to ascertain the treatment effect on career exploration and decision making. Results indicated that both problem-solving treatments had a significant influence on career exploration, but there was no difference among groups on career decision making. Of the two problem-solving techniques, the didactic instruction treatment resulted in more requests for further career information.

As we can see, the effectiveness of group approaches to career counseling is far from defined. It is unlikely that the use of group procedures will diminish in the future, especially in view of the economic climate, so it is important for leaders of career counseling groups to seek out relevant research and carefully evaluate the programs and activities they use.

Job Placement Groups

Among the many structured group job placement programs, the Job Club (Azrin, Flores, & Kaplan, 1975) is the most thoroughly researched. Studies indicate that Job Club clients find jobs more quickly than do control group clients, at a statistically significant level; the findings hold for:

"Typical job seekers" (Azrin et al., 1975)

Clients receiving Aid to Families with Dependent Children (AFDC) (Azrin, Philip, Thienes-Hontos, & Besalel, 1980)

Disabled/disadvantaged clients (Azrin & Philip, 1979)

Each study compared Job Club participants to clients in a non-treatment control group.

A fourth study (Azrin, Besalel, Wisotzek, McMorrow, & Bechtel, 1982) used subjects from the general population and compared job-finding rates between clients receiving the Job Club treatment with behavior supervision and those receiving comparable information, but without direct supervision of the job seeking behaviors. Again, the former group showed a significantly higher rate of job placement.

Other findings from these studies indicate the Job Club method may have other advantages for participants, including less time finding employment (Azrin et al., 1975; Azrin & Philip, 1979), and somewhat higher salaries upon employment (Azrin et al., 1976; Azrin & Philip, 1979; Azrin et al., 1980). Despite the encouraging nature of these findings, we must still exercise caution in interpreting the results; for instance, two studies used volunteer subjects and one excluded individuals receiving unemployment benefits; thus, in practice, where selection of clients may not be possible, the "success rates" an individual counselor experiences may be somewhat lower. On the other hand, the *Job Club Counselor's Manual* (Azrin & Besalel, 1980) provides a clear definition of the strategy and should allow for future replication of the experimental studies.

Special Applications

Over the last 10 to 15 years, career counselors have noticed several areas of special need among the working population. Three areas have received much attention: mid-life career changes, dual career marriages, and preretirement counseling.

Mid-Life Career Changes More and more, we tend to view career choice as continuous; it is becoming fairly common to see individuals make a substantial career change during their middle years. This may be related to the societal pressure to "maximize one's potential," but in another respect, these changes may be more reflective of changes in the world of work. The growing emphasis on computer technology creates new opportunities for individuals at the same time that it eliminates the needs for some skills. As another example, many teachers face fewer opportunities in their field as the effects of the declining birth rate appear in declining school enrollments. Regardless of the motivation for career change, those who make such a change face common issues: "What kind of job do I want next? How can I best use the skills I already have in a new job? Do I need further education or training? What does the future hold?"

Dual Career Marriages   As women continue to enter the job market in increasing numbers, couples often find themselves dealing with issues foreign to even their parents' generation. Along with decisions about their careers, many couples must also consider the impact of their career decisions on their personal relationship. Dual career relationships give couples many opportunities, financial and otherwise, as well as a great deal of stress. Each partner's roles may change: males may find that their careers are no longer the determining factor in decisions about where the couple lives, and females may experience severe distress trying to balance traditional and nontraditional roles. Demanding work schedules can also make each partner less available to the other.

Preretirement Counseling   As longevity increases, more individuals have the luxury of planning for productive years after formal retirement from a structured job at age 65 or 70, and for many, the prospect of an unstructured lifestyle often provokes strong anxiety. There are concerns about how to best utilize time, to meet needs previously met by a job, and how retirement will affect personal relationships.

For all these situations, group counseling may help. Often, merely sharing common experiences reduces an individual's sense of isolation. Participants may also supply mutual assistance simply by sharing solutions they have found successful for themselves. Because work is a common issue in each situation, the career development counselor is in a unique position to offer assistance. She can use career counseling skills with retirees to help them identify ways to satisfy interests through avocational rather than vocational activities; and with dual-career partners to help them identify values and make decisions.

Job placement group strategies are expanding. Originally, many of the formal strategies were developed to meet the needs of individuals with serious employability problems, including physical or mental disability, poor or no employment history, a prison record, lack of education and/or marketable skills, and so on. Individuals with one or more of these problems continue to be at a disadvantage when competing in the employment market. In the past, client preparation for placement was often handled on an individual basis by counselors in human service agencies, but there has been a trend toward strategies in the face of financial constraints.

The range of candidates for job search skills training is also expanding. Soaring unemployment rates combined with technological changes that render whole industries obsolete both increase the number of individuals looking for work and result in different types of individuals falling into the unemployment ranks. Employment counselors reveal concerns about the greater numbers of skilled and professional workers who are becoming unemployed. Many of these individuals made their last job search many years ago and their job search skills are mediocre at best. These inadequacies combined with the current employment market create a new demand for job placement groups.

Similarly, workers whose job skills have been rendered obsolete by industry changes often need the assistance of job placement groups to make the requisite career change. Young people are emerging into a tighter job market than before, and job placement groups can help them enhance their competitive stance.

Thus, whereas job placement groups were once designed primarily for disabled or disadvantaged individuals, they are now relevant to a far greater proportion of the working population. Educational and training institutions can use them to help graduates make the best use of acquired skills; human service agencies—rehabilitation programs, mental health and family services programs, substance abuse programs, and employment services—find them valuable for the clients they have traditionally served as well as for the new, more highly skilled clientele who are victims of the economy. Industry is also beginning to use the techniques of group job placement to deal with large-scale layoffs; through *outplacement*, some companies help employees who are being laid off with the job search for new employment (Teague, 1981). Yet another application of the group job placement concept is with self-help groups, where individuals with similar, specialized concerns (for example, those who have been laid off or those over age 45) work together to help group members find employment.

Technology and Vocational Development

An interesting development in the area of vocational counseling is the arrival of computer software packages that complement the process of vocational development. Counselors and clients are able to rely on microcomputers to catalog and call up information about the world of work. Information that once took an hour or more to find can be accessed almost instantaneously on the computer.

Ability Information Systems (AIS)

The Ability Information Systems (AIS) is a computer-based occupational information system, accessible through the user's computer terminal system which is then connected via telephone to the main program in Spokane, Washington. Results of a system search are displayed on the user's terminal and/or printed on the user's printer.

There are a variety of uses for the AIS data base. For our purposes, the most important uses are for vocational exploration, identification of job leads, and identification of vocational alternatives. Regardless of the purpose, similar steps are performed to obtain the needed information. The major steps are as follows:

1. The user selects a major program mode (for example, placement).

2. Information about the client (especially past work history) is recorded on the computer.

3. The computer analyzes this information and constructs a profile of the individual's skills, abilities, interests and other factors. Using standard occupational information descriptions, this profile reflects the individual's maximum level of functioning.

4. Adjustments to the profile are made as necessary. For example, a client who wants to determine available vocational alternatives when he completes a course of schooling can adjust the educational level upward to reflect this change. Or, an injured worker who has previously done heavy work may need to adjust the exertion level of possible alternatives to consider only those that involve light or sedentary work.

5. The computer then searches through over 12,000 job titles and profiles and selects those that are compatible with the client's profile and displays them on the user's screen.

6. At this point, the user can exercise a number of options; for example, (a) if the titles selected are not of interest, the client profile can be adjusted and a new search initiated; (b) labor supply and demand statistics can be presented for the jobs of interest; or (c) a list of potential employers in the user's geographic area can be generated for a job of interest.

7. Results of the computer search or searches are printed in a format chosen by the user.

Two other particularly useful features of the AIS include:

The ability to generate a description of a desired vocational objective along with a given client profile. AIS can then be used to delineate discrepancies between the job-client match, providing information on what the client must do, perhaps in regard to educational level, to achieve the desired objective.

The ability to interface with a job bank. Thus, the system allows not only identification of potential employers for a given alternative, but also generates a list of known job openings for that alternative. (This is not a standard part of the AIS package, but is available as an optional service.)

AIS includes other options and features not mentioned here. Training on the system takes two to five days, depending on one's experience and expertise. The obvious advantage of a system such as AIS is its speed and thoroughness. It is not a substitute for counselor expertise, but it does minimize the time for routine information collection. Because of its rapidity, it also allows greater flexibility in information searches. In addition, the computer does not tire of searching, so it can make a much more thorough and complete search than can humans.

Although software packages like AIS are not a panacea for problems of vocational development, they can be enormously helpful to the vocational development counselor. When working with groups, counselors can use such packages to quickly provide individualized occupational information to group members. The time that is saved can then be used more productively to focus on the group process and clients' noninformational needs. Counselors who work with vocational development groups need to stay abreast of the opportunities computer technology presents and seek ways to use that technology creatively in their groups.

Discussion Questions

1. Name the various types of vocational development groups and the goals of each. How do they compare in terms of their structure and how they are led?

2. List some basic guidelines for selecting group members.

3. How are group process and dynamics in vocational development groups different from or similar to those of other groups, such as therapeutic groups?

4. What are some specific tasks to be accomplished by these groups?

5. How would you form and lead a job placement group?

17

Skill Training Groups

Over the past two decades, the phrase "skills training," with its many qualifiers, has become common nomenclature in group counseling. "Social-skills training," "assertiveness training," "social competency training," "social problem-solving training," "communication skills training" and other skills training programs and procedures have emerged as alternatives and/or supplements to more traditional approaches to group counseling. Although these skills training groups vary in terminology and technique, all focus on increasing an individual's skills in social or interpersonal situations. Skills training groups offer the counselor a wide range of group techniques applicable to a variety of individuals who have difficulty in interpersonal relationships or in social settings.

Traditional approaches to group counseling (psychoanalytic, neopsychoanalytic, and self-concept theories) typically view difficulties or deficits in interpersonal behavior as symptoms or results of an underlying psychological condition. A passive, unassertive, or shy individual, for example, may be seen as insecure, or to have a poor self-concept or low self-esteem. Similarly, someone who acts withdrawn, has a flat affect, or expresses apathy or self-deprecation may be diagnosed as a "depressive personality." The traditional approaches generally assume that treating the underlying cause, that

---

Contributed by Steven Ostby, University of North Carolina

is, increasing self-concept or reducing depression, will improve the individual's interpersonal behavior. With more severe disorders, such as schizophrenia, chronic depression or anxiety, mental retardation, learning disabilities, and other cognitive disfunctions, the a priori assumption of treating the underlying condition can frustrate both the counselor and the client.

Skills training groups are based on learning or behavioral theory and therefore propose different assumptions regarding human behavior and counseling intervention. As we saw in chapter 7, behavior theory assumes that human behavior is learned in a variety of ways: through reinforcement, conditioning, shaping, modeling, and so forth. According to the behavioral paradigm, one also learns social skills through these means. Hence, one may experience difficulty in social or interpersonal situations for a variety of reasons. One person may have "learned to be anxious" in a social interaction, while another may lack experience or appropriate role models.

For conceptual clarity, we can categorize social skills deficits into two basic types. The first type is demonstrated by the individual who cognitively "knows what to do" but, because of past failure, punishment, or other experiences, is inhibited from interacting successfully. With this type of problem, a circular pattern may develop. Imagine an individual who is engaging in a particular social situation for the first time—a job interview, asking for a date, being called upon in the classroom, or introducing himself to a social group. He *knows* he should remain calm, speak in an even tone, and try to make a good impression, but because it is his first experience with the situation, he instead blushes and perspires, his pulse increases, and his voice quavers. Most of us have had an experience like this; however, with *practice* and *reinforcement*, we gradually overcome our anxiety and enhance our social behavior repertoire. Conversely, without practice and reinforcement, the individual may continue to respond ineffectively in the situation. The inappropriate response does not come from lack of knowledge as to what is required by the situation; rather, the individual's emotional reaction restricts his behavioral repertoire and may prevent the development and practice of new, more appropriate responses. If appropriate responses are not exhibited, they cannot be reinforced. Thus, a cycle may form that prevents the individual's learning appropriate social behavior.

We find the second category of social skill deficits in those who, for various reasons, have never learned appropriate interpersonal skills. This type of skill deficit may be seen in persons with chronic mental illness or mental retardation or in other special populations. Persons with moderate to severe emotional or cognitive disabilities may, under certain circumstances, experience atypical socialization.

Placement in special education classrooms, institutionalization, or any experience that prevents the individual from participating fully in "normal social interaction" may eclipse the development of interpersonal skills. Frequently, the opportunity to engage in and learn from socialization is diminished by negative social attitudes. People with emotional, cognitive, or physical disabilities often have limited social experiences, and those in institutional settings may lack not only "normal" experiences and social models, but may learn inappropriate behaviors from others in their environment. At the same time, people who are receiving service from an institution, such as a state hospital or sheltered workshop, who attempt to behave assertively or independently may be seen by some staff members as "uncooperative" or unable to deal with authority figures. Someone with a chronic emotional or cognitive disability may thus lack appropriate social skills not because of the nature of the disability but because of limited exposure to appropriate interpersonal behavior.

The impact of a social skill deficit on the individual can be dramatic. Besides emotional discomfort, lack of social skills can affect vocational adjustment, personal adjustment, acceptance in the community, or, potentially, any activity relating to human society. Numerous studies of people with psychiatric disabilities or mental retardation document the importance of adequate social skills in maintaining job tenure and community placement (Anthony, 1978; Eagle, 1967; Gold, 1973; Goldstein, 1964; Neuhaus, 1967; Pierce & Drasgow, 1969; Stacy, Doleys, & Malcolm, 1979).

Social Skills Training Groups

Overview and Pre-Treatment Considerations

As we have said, people may require social skills training for a variety of reasons. Before forming a group, the counselor needs to consider the populations he will include. While a variety of presenting problems or personal backgrounds may stimulate the group process by providing a wide range of interactive styles, extreme differences may be detrimental.

Social skills training groups are relatively structured, not only as to techniques, but in the number of sessions and the content or theme of each. The setting and the population are the main determinants in structuring the training program. In an in-patient or institutional environment, such as a hospital setting, school system, or work adjustment program, one-hour sessions may be scheduled on a daily basis or several times per week for four to five weeks. For social skills training in an outpatient setting, ninety-minute sessions are typically scheduled on a weekly basis for 10 to 14 weeks. The number of sessions usually depends on the number of social skill areas to be addressed during the training.

The content of the sessions should be determined by and tailored to the needs of the population. For example, in working with adolescent or young adult populations, content themes may include: dating, interacting with parents, dealing with authority figures, or sexuality. In contrast, in a rehabilitative setting that emphasizes return to work and community, sessions may focus on employer relations, co-worker relationships, interview skills, and similar work-related social interactions.

The size of the group also requires consideration. The number of members depends partly on whether there will be a single counselor or a cocounseling team. With a solitary counselor, group size may range from six to eight; fewer clients may have trouble in role playing or role reversal activities, and groups larger than eight may make it difficult for the counselor to attend to all members adequately. Cotherapists offer several advantages. First, a larger number of members, usually 10 to 12, may be included, and while one counselor is instructing the group or operating audiovisual equipment, the other may attend to group behavior. Also, if there is both a male and female counselor, there is opportunity to model or role play a wider variety of social situations. Cotherapists may share responsibilities such as staff meetings with referring agencies, scheduling equipment, and preparing handouts. Perhaps the greatest advantage to cotherapists' regime is that of peer-consultation. It is frequently useful to "debrief" with another therapist after a training session, for the purpose of modifying the program format or comparing impressions of client progress. Finally, coleading a group with an experienced therapist is an excellent method for the beginning counselor to enhance her skill in social skills training.

As with any group counseling experience, the initial session may have a significant impact on the relative success of the training process. The initial session usually begins with introducing the counselor to the group and describing the goals and objectives of the social skills training group. The major goal is to help group members increase their skills in a variety of interpersonal situations and decrease anxiety or emotional discomfort in relating with others. Emphasis is on the practicality of the training, and group members are assured they will not be "forced into" situations they are averse to. The counselor should also explain that the training procedures are meant to enhance existing methods of relating interpersonally, not to "teach" them how to "act."

After discussing goals and objectives, the counselor introduces the various content themes of the sessions, for example, initiating conversations, giving and receiving criticism, giving and receiving compliments. At this point, group members are encouraged to "brainstorm" to develop other possible session themes. The themes need to be relevant to members' difficulties for the training to enhance their skills, and the leader must stress the importance of implementing and practicing the skills acquired in group. Group members become aware that increasing social skill involves nonverbal behaviors (gestures, facial expression) and verbal behaviors (vocal expression as well as content). These behaviors do not develop by listening to others or by thinking about them; knowledge and instruction is necessary and helpful, but to develop the *skill*, one must practice.

During the first session, group-building exercises help develop a sense of cohesion. A common exercise is to have each member introduce herself to the group, state her reasons for coming, and tell what skills she hopes to gain during the group sessions. Monti, Corriveau, and Curran (1982) use a less threatening variation of this exercise. They suggest counselors have group members pair off and assign the letter *A* or *B* to each member. The counselor instructs all *A* members to talk to the *B* members for approximately five minutes, and try to find out something interesting about that person. Following this five-minute period, each *A* member reports back to the group about each *B* member. During this process, the counselor reinforces, with praise, those who report interesting facts about their counterparts. Members then reverse roles, with *B* members interviewing *A* members and reporting back to the group. Monti et al. report several advantages to this exercise, including acquiring baseline behavior on each member in a nonthreatening fashion and introducing members to group exercises in general.

After the exercise, the therapist may facilitate discussion about difficulties the members encountered while interviewing other group members. Through role playing, the therapist models both appropriate and inappropriate behavior when "trying to get to know someone for the first time." The initial session thus serves as a preview of future sessions and familiarizes group members with each other and with social skills training procedures.

Treatment Techniques

Social skills training groups employ a variety of behavioral techniques, discussed by Bellack and Hersen (1977) for general behavioral group counseling and by Monti et al. (1982) for social skills training. Our overview of these techniques draws primarily from Monti et al.

Instruction

The counselor uses instruction to introduce the various behavioral components in interpersonal interaction. Along with verbal presentation, the counselor may choose instructional aids such as chalkboards, audiotapes, videotapes, and written materials. For example, a counselor who is conducting a group session on interview skills or employer relations may give instruction in the areas of appropriate dress and hygiene, preparing for employer questions, and appropriate questions to ask the employer about benefits and wages.

Modeling

Modeling is used throughout training, but particularly when introducing a social skill for the first time. It is extremely important for the counselor to *always* model the behavior before asking group members to role play the behavior. Modeling appropriate behavior *after* group members make mistakes can be frustrating and counterproductive. Modeling is especially useful during early sessions, and enhances instruction. For example, after presenting material about accepting criticism, the counselor can model the behaviors and help members translate the cognitive information into practical skills.

Behavioral Rehearsal

Instruction and modeling help present new social skills; behavioral rehearsal gives members opportunities to practice and refine the new skills. The initial behavioral rehearsal takes place between the therapist and individual group members. Later in the group process, after members gain skill in role playing, behavioral rehearsals progress to involve two or more group members and the therapist participates less frequently. These techniques can be employed sequentially to aid in skill development. The new skill (for example, initiating a conversation or asking for a date) is first presented via instruction. Next, the counselor *models* the behavior. Then, group members practice the skill through *behavioral rehearsal.*

Reinforcement and Shaping

A group member's initial behavior rehearsal is rarely at his optimal level of performance. The counselor can use reinforcement in the form of verbal praise to shape and enhance the member's social skills, but must remain constantly aware of which behaviors need reinforcement. Therapists who praise or compliment members regardless of actual performance diminish their effectiveness in shaping behavior. Another source of reinforcement for shaping behavior is the group's other members. The therapist can elicit positive reinforcement from members after a behavioral rehearsal by requesting that each member make a positive comment about the role playing. Possibly the most powerful reinforcer is that of the "natural" environment. When group members begin to practice appropriate social behaviors in their daily lives and receive positive feedback or reinforcement, the skills are strengthened and will occur more frequently. The counselor should encourage members to begin practicing easily attainable goals and gradually engage in more difficult social situations. (We will discuss this process in greater depth in regard to "homework.")

Feedback

Along with reinforcement and shaping, feedback should also follow each behavioral rehearsal. Feedback provides constructive criticism regarding the group member's performance in a social situation. The counselor is initially responsible for providing feedback, but should gradually involve group members in the process. Useful feedback may come from the other person or persons involved in the behavioral rehearsal. After role playing, the role-playing partner can tell how she felt about or reacted to statements and behaviors during the behavioral rehearsal. It is sometimes helpful to have members repeat the role playing several times with different approaches to the same situation and receive feedback on each approach. Another form of feedback is videotaping the behavioral rehearsals to allow members to view and critique their own behaviors. Although some individuals may be uncomfortable viewing themselves, the anxiety generally diminishes as members become used to the technique.

Role Reversal

Role reversal is a technique to help group members become aware of the impact of their social behavior on others. By reversing roles (for example, the client takes on the role of his boss, spouse, or neighbor), the group member gains insight into the effectiveness of his own behavior. Whoever assumes the role of the group member can rehearse several different behaviors, such as passive, aggressive, and assertive, so the member in the reversed role can see the contrast between appropriate and inappropriate behavior.

Homework

The purpose of homework in social skills training is to encourage group members to begin practicing their new interpersonal behaviors in their everyday lives. Modeling, behavioral rehearsal, and reinforcement are effective in learning new social behaviors, but for training to have true impact on one's behavior outside the treatment setting, there must be transference of that behavior from the group setting to the "outside world." At the end of each session, the counselor gives homework assignments pertaining to the topic or skill emphasized during the session. Initial assignments should be relatively simple and brief, so that members can experience success in their first attempts. The first portion of each session is spent discussing the members' homework experiences, with each member reviewing her successes and failures. Role playing these experiences, accompanied by feedback, can help the group in future homework assignments.

All the treatment techniques we have described are common components of a social skills training group. When combined and used sequentially by a competent therapist, these techniques can effectively enhance interpersonal skills.

Themes for Training Sessions

When selecting content themes for group sessions, the counselor should assess the members' unique needs and structure the training to meet those needs. Monti et al. (1982) have developed ten session themes for use on both an inpatient and outpatient basis with persons who have psychiatric disabilities. Monti says these typical areas should be considered very general, and sessions within each area should focus on the needs of the individuals in the group. These themes are applicable in a wide variety of settings and represent a wide range of social situations.

Session One: Starting Conversations

This session begins with the counselor's presenting the importance of interpersonal communication in casual and intimate relationships in everyday life *(instruction)*. Monti lists the following points for the counselor to stress during instruction:

1. Selecting an appropriate time and place for initiating a conversation

2. Selecting an appropriate topic

3. Determining the appropriate amount of self-disclosure

4. Close-ended statements

5. Ending the conversation appropriately

After instruction and group discussion on these basic points, the counselor then *models* the conversational skills and engages group members in a *behavioral rehearsal*. After each rehearsal, participants receive *feedback* and *reinforcement* for appropriate responses. *Homework* may involve initiating two or three conversations during the next week and maintaining one conversation for at least three minutes. (The amount and difficulty of homework should be determined by the counselor's observation of baseline behavior.

Session Two: Nonverbal Behavior

The second session is the time to address a variety of nonverbal interpersonal behaviors. The counselor should model both appropriate and inappropriate facial expressions, eye contact, posture, and gestures, as well as extreme behaviors such as staring at a person and looking down at the floor to make the group aware of the range of nonverbal behaviors. Behavior rehearsal, feedback, and role reversal will also promote skill development.

Session Three: Giving and Receiving Compliments

In the third session, group members receive instruction in the importance of compliments in social contexts. The group gets a brief explanation of behavior modification and how to use compliments in establishing social relationships. Members are told to give compliments in terms of their own feelings or thoughts, rather than in concrete terms, for example, "I think that was very nice of you."

Session 4: Negative Thoughts and Self-Statements

Monti says the fourth session differs significantly from the other sessions; in essence, the group receives instruction in cognitive-behavioral techniques such as those of Ellis's Rational-Emotive Therapy. The focus of this session is to help members understand the relationship between cognition (thinking), emotion (feeling), and behavior (acting) and the impact of negative cognition on social interaction. Each member is encouraged to explore and identify negative self-statements, and strategies are devised to help them reduce or eliminate these statements.

Session 5: Giving Criticism

Through modeling, role playing, or videotaping, group members learn how to give criticism more assertively and effectively. They learn to:

1. State criticism in terms of feelings, not in concrete terms

2. Criticize a specific behavior rather than the whole person

3. Make requests specific

4. Begin and end interaction on a positive note

5. Speak in a normal tone of voice without sounding angry

The focus of this session is on enhancing assertiveness skills, with practice in the form of behavioral rehearsals.

Session 6: Receiving Criticism

The group learns, in the sixth session, to distinguish between two types of criticism: *aggressive criticism*, directed at the individual, and *assertive criticism*, focusing on the individual's behavior. These guidelines help members cope with aggressive criticism:

1. Never deny the criticism

2. Find part of the criticism that may be valid and restate it more clearly

3. Request a specific behavioral explanation of which behaviors are unsatisfactory

To handle assertive criticism, the group practices these methods:

1. Acting as if the behavior is nothing to get upset about

2. Requesting clarification as to the exact nature of the criticism

3. Proposing a realistic compromise

Session 7: Listening Skills and "Feeling Talk"

Monti includes two skill areas in the seventh session. *Listening skills* refer to attentive behaviors during a conversation. The counselor models inappropriate listening skills, such as looking away, sighing, or tapping fingers or toes, then contrasts them with more appropriate behaviors. Perceiving how others "feel" is stressed as an important listening skill.

Feeling talk refers to appropriate self-disclosure, with modeling of a range of self-disclosure and discussion of how this technique can be used to establish friendships.

Session 8: Assertiveness in Business Settings

The eighth session briefly reviews the skills learned in the previous sessions and investigates how to apply these skills in business situations—with salespersons, employer problems, difficulties with co-workers, and so on. Job interviews may be role played, if appropriate.

Session 9: Close Relationships

As in the previous session, the ninth session reviews the skills developed earlier and applies them to members' daily lives, focusing on problems that arise in close interpersonal relationships. A common problem is the fear of hurting the other person's feelings. The group reviews the various techniques of giving criticism and discusses the advantages of "not letting things build up." Group members are encouraged to role play real-life problems, using role-reversal and feedback.

Session 10: Intimate Relationships

The tenth session focuses on special problems in intimate relationships or with very close friends. While the content may be more sensitive, it is important for group members to realize that social skills are valuable in a wide range of relationships. Intimate relationships pose unique problems in giving and receiving criticism, assertiveness, and communication in general. Behavior rehearsals, role reversals, and modeling help explain appropriate and comfortable methods for dealing with these areas.

The final social skills session is generally an overview of the previous sessions, with discussion of the skills the members have gained and the applicability of these skills to existing and future relationships.

Social Problem-Solving Training Groups

D'Zurilla and Goldfried (1971) define social problem solving (SPS) as "a behavioral process, whether overt or cognitive in nature, which (a) makes available a variety of potentially effective response alternatives for dealing with a problematic situation, and (b) increases the probability of selecting the most effective response from among these various alternatives" (p. 108). D'Zurilla and Goldfried's behavioral definition is based on learning theory approaches to problem solving proposed by Harlow (1949) and Gagné (1966). Harlow emphasized that the problem-solving process is not simply the development of learning sets, or skills, but involves transference of learning. Gagné (1966) feels that the skill acquired in problem solving is that of *applying a role* to a number of situations. Thus, rather than focusing on specific social skills or problem situations, the emphasis of social problem-solving training is on teaching a process for ameliorating social problems or difficulties.

As we have said, SPS training is a unique form of social skills training, and requires the same type of pretreatment consider-ations—population, setting, duration, and session themes. The coun-selor should also be familiar with the basic tenets of SPS. The major emphasis of all SPS sessions is application of a problem-solving approach to group members' problems in daily life.

A Model of Social Problem Solving

D'Zurilla and Goldfried (1971) propose a model for social problem solving which, as modified by D'Zurilla and Nezu (1982), contains five stages or skills: (1) problem orientation; (2) problem definition; (3) generation of alternatives; (4) decision making; and (5) solution implementation and verification. The authors stress that a stage-model approach should be viewed as a method of organizing the SPS process for study and training, not as an actual "description" of the process.

The first stage, *problem orientation,* focuses on reducing or dis-tracting attention from thoughts or emotional states that may inhibit SPS, and refocusing attention on internal and external stimuli that are likely to enhance SPS behavior. In essence, the individual devel-ops a "problem-solving set" involving (a) the ability to identify a problem when it occurs; (b) accepting problems as a manageable part of life; (c) believing that they can solve problems; and (d) the ability to "stop and think" (D'Zurilla & Nezu, 1982).

D'Zurilla and Nezu describe the *problem definition and formation* stage as an assessment process that results in identifying a realistic objective. This stage involves describing the situation in operational terms, differentiating irrelevant from relevant data, and setting a desired goal. The third stage, *generation of alternatives,* focuses on producing possible solutions and makes two assumptions. First, if the individual can "suspend judgement" until later, it is more likely that a high number of quality solutions will be generated. Second, the more solutions generated, the higher the probability of finding the "best" solution.

The fourth stage, *decision making*, requires evaluation of solutions that have been generated, determining the "goodness" of each, and selecting the "best" or most effective option. During this stage, the person is encouraged to consider the various effects of each solution in terms of short-term and long-term consequences and the possible impact of the solution on oneself and others. Finally, during *solution implementation and verification*, the individual performs or implements the "chosen" solution, observes its impact, and evaluates the solution by comparing the observed outcome to the expected outcome or the goal identified during stage two. If the observed outcome satisfies the goal, the individual is reinforced through successfully resolving the situation (D'Zurilla & Nezu, 1982).

Social Problem-Solving Group Therapy

George Spivack and his associates at the Hahnemann University Preventive Intervention Research Center in Philadelphia have contributed substantially to SPS. Spivack et al. have investigated the differences in SPS skills of "normal" and "impaired" populations and the effects of training on SPS skills. Spivack, Platt, and Shure (1976) outline a number of group SPS programs developed for kindergarten children, third- and fourth-grade children, fourth- and fifth-grade children, chronic psychiatric patients, young adults and adults, and hospitalized psychiatric patients. Except for some minor, semantic differences, Spivack et al. follow the same SPS model described earlier. The SPS program for young adults and adults outlines SPS procedures that are applicable to a variety of populations and settings.

This SPS program consists of 19 units or sessions, with the first half of the sessions focusing on prerequisite skills and the second half emphasizing specific SPS skills. The program, however, emphasizes these themes at all stages of training:

- Problems are solvable

- The program's focus is on problems of an interpersonal nature

- Everyone encounters social problems in daily life

- Group members should bring in current interpersonal problems to work on

- The focus of the group is on the present and future, not the past

Unit 1 Spivack et al. (1976) describe the initial session as an attempt to create a positive group atmosphere and to help members recognize interpersonal problems. Group members are asked how to tell if a problem exists, with discussion focusing on subjective feelings. Through discussion, members generate the various cues they use to recognize problems (for example, how one feels, how people look, and how people act). Next, the group lists all the common interpersonal problems they can think of. The purpose of this exercise is to illustrate the commonality of interpersonal problems and that, generally, everyone has had them. Finally, as a homework assignment, the group is to work on a problem (for example, "your boss yells at you") and each member is to write down all the possible solutions he can think of.

Units 2, 3, and 4 These sessions focus on differentiating between fact and opinion, paying attention to details (cues) in the environment, and obtaining additional information from the environment. The emphasis is on discriminating between reality and fantasy by focusing attention on what is *actually* seen or heard. The counselor can use pictures, such as Thematic Apperception Test cards, and have members role play exercises, after which members must identify only what they saw or heard. The counselor also gives instruction on how people infer or form opinions based on experience and explains that members must attend to the stimuli of their environment. During Unit 4, the group discusses ways of gaining more information, and discusses and practices the various ways to ask questions. As a homework task, members are asked to call on another group member and gather data as to what types of problems the member is having, then help the member generate possible solutions.

Unit 5 The goal of this session is for group members to understand that individuals may have different perspectives regarding a problem situation, which can be helpful in SPS. Differences in opinion can be illustrated nonthreateningly by having group members identify favorite foods, movies, and so on. Next, the counselor can present an ambiguous TAT card and ask group members to identify characters or activities. The different interpretations are then extended to interpersonal situations, with group members participating in role playing situations.

Units 6 and 7 Units 6 and 7 concentrate on recognizing how others feel by attending to verbal and nonverbal cues. Discussion centers on how to combine those cues with previously learned skills for solving problems. From pictures, group members can identify the emotion depicted in facial expressions. Members are encouraged to recall experiences in which they encouraged these emotions in others or in themselves. Unit 7 focuses on members' becoming more aware of their own facial expressions and nonverbal communications by practicing with mirrors and pairing off to give each other feedback on the emotion one is portraying nonverbally. Often, people who lack social skill are unintentionally exhibiting emotional behaviors of which they are unaware. These exercises help reduce or eliminate inappropriate or inaccurate affect, as well as increase skills in recognizing affect in others and portraying one's feelings appropriately.

Units 8, 9, 10, and 11 In these units, Spivack introduces several "tricks of the problem-solving trade" with attention to memory aids and applying techniques members have used in other situations to remembering conversational content. Unit 9 continues to build on emotional cue recognition and increasing memory of faces. In various exercises, the member must pick out a photo he has been shown from a large number of photos. Visual cues such as hair color, eye color, shape of face, and distinguishing characteristics are emphasized as memory aids in identifying previous acquaintances, and the counselor may talk aloud while demonstrating these cues: "O.K. I'm going to find Joe in this picture of a crowd. I know he has blond hair, blue eyes, a square jaw, and kind of a big nose. Is that . . . no, his hair is too long. I don't have to hurry, it's important that I take my time. There, I found him." The counselor tells group members to use this type of "self-talk" when solving "mock" problems in group and solving problems in real life. The intention is to shape the behavior of "stopping and thinking before acting." Group members attend to their self-statements while they engage in SPS and notice what they are saying to themselves when they are unsuccessful. They must then determine what they could have done differently and what they would say to themselves while doing it. Gradually, talking aloud changes to "talking to yourself." Through homework, members practice "self-talk" when they notice a problem or when they feel bad, with statements such as "Why do I feel like this?" "What if I . . . ?" "Or could I . . . ?" and always, "I don't need to hurry, I'll take my time and solve this thing." Finally, Session 11 emphasizes the role of thinking aloud in defining problems. With pictures of problem situations and self-talk, members define a problem; after identifying all possible problems, the group begins to generate possible solutions.

Unit 12 This session focuses completely on generating alternatives to a problem situation. The group examines a series of interpersonal problem situations and generates as many solutions as possible without critically appraising them.

Social Problem-Solving Sessions

The twelve central sessions were designed to be somewhat similar and repetitious in structure so that behaviors and expectations generated in one session would be applicable to later sessions. Each session follows the Butler and Ayer (1970) SPS model, which is similar to that of D'Zurilla and Nezu (1982), and has the following objectives:

- That group members be able to identify at least three verbal and/or nonverbal signals or cues that indicate the reactions of the characters in the video vignettes to the problem.

- That, given a social problem situation similar to that portrayed in the vignette, group members will be able to role play the appropriate problem solution selected by the group in previous discussion.

Each session begins with a brief discussion of the homework assigned at the end of the previous session and a review of the theme of that session. The facilitator solicits relevant experiences group members have had since the previous session. Discussion focuses on how group members attempted to solve the social problem.

After the homework discussion, the leader introduces the video vignette for that session and identifies its characters. Each vignette portrays a social problem situation with a unique theme. The whole vignette is shown, and repeated if requested or if the facilitator feels it necessary.

Next, group members are asked to identify and conceptualize the problem portrayed in the vignette. The facilitator should encourage discussion at this stage by inquiring if any group members have had a similar experience, and if so, asking them to describe their reaction. The importance of verbal and nonverbal cues or signals is emphasized. The videotape is then viewed in parts to demonstrate the cues the characters give in the vignette. After this discussion, group members identify possible solutions to the problem portrayed in the vignette while the leader lists the suggestions on a chalkboard. The group then assesses the consequences of each proposed solution and selects the best.

To check their comprehension, the leader asks group members to identify at least three verbal or nonverbal cues indicating the reaction of the vignette's characters to the social problem. The group then role plays a social problem situation similar to that portrayed in the vignette using the solution members have selected earlier.

Finally, the leader asks group members to practice the social problem-solving model if they encounter problems at home, work, or school, and to bring examples of problems if they occur to the next session.

Wrap-up Session

The purpose of the wrap-up session is to give the subjects a review of the treatment procedures. The various themes of the SPS sessions are reexamined and the problem-solving process restated. Each group member is asked to state what she has learned from the program and how it may or may not help her daily life.

Summary

This chapter has presented an overview of skills training groups with an example of a social-skills training group and two examples of SPS training groups. Social problem solving is a unique form of social skills training that uses many similar techniques, such as instruction, modeling, behavioral rehearsal, reinforcement, and feedback. The two SPS group procedures approach treatment slightly differently. Spivack and his associates (1976) introduce SPS skills individually, with individual sessions for training in problem definition, alternative generation, and so on. In contrast, the Butler and Ayer (1970) approach presents the group with all the SPS skills during each session, and sessions focus on applying these skills in varying situations. These approaches to group counseling may serve as primary or supplementary service components, or as adjuncts to individual counseling for those who experience difficulty in interpersonal relationships.

Discussion Questions

1. What are the basic assumptions and unique procedures for skills training groups?

2. Describe how you would set up and lead a social skills training group for a population of your choice. What would be your goals? How would the group be structured? What techniques would you employ? What specific tasks would you want each participant to accomplish?

3. Do the same for a social problem-solving group.

References

Ability Information Systems. P.O. Box 15228, Spokane, WA, 99215.

Ackerman, N. (1938). The unity of the family. *Archives of Pediatrics, 51,* 55.

Ackerman, N. (1958). The psychodynamics of family life. New York: Basic Books.

Adler, A. (1925). *Individual psychology.* Tatowa, NJ: Littlefield, Adams & Co.

Adler, A. (1939). *Social interest.* New York: Putnam.

Alger, I. E. (1976). Multiple couple therapy. In P. J. Guerin (Ed.), *Family therapy.* New York: Gardner Press.

Altholz, J. A. S. (1978). Group psychotherapy with the elderly. In I. M. Burnside (Ed.), *Working with the elderly: Group processes and techniques.* North Scituate, MA: Duxbury Press.

Ansbacher, H., & Ansbacher, R. (1956). *The individual psychology of Alfred Adler.* New York: Basic Books.

Anthony, W. (1978). *The principles of psychiatric rehabilitation.* Amherst, MA: Human Resources Development Press.

Anthony, W. (1980). A rehabilitation model for rehabilitating the psychiatrically disabled. *Rehabilitation Counseling Bulletin, 24* (1), 6–21.

Asch, S. E. (1956). Studies of independence and conformity: A minority of one against a unanimous majority. *Psychological Monographs, 70* (9, Whole No. 416).

Axline, V. (1947). *Play therapy.* Boston: Houghton Mifflin.

Ayllon, T., & Michael, J. (1959). The psychiatric nurse as a behavioral engineer. *Journal of Experimental Analysis of Behavior, 2,* 323–334.

Azrin, N. H., Besalel, V. A., Wisotzek, I., McMorrow, M., & Bechtel, R. (1981). Behavioral supervision versus informational counseling of job seeking in the Job Club. *Rehabilitation Counseling Bulletin, 25* (4), 212–218.

Azrin, N. H., & Besalel, V. A. (1980). *Job Club Counselor's Manual.* Baltimore: University Park Press.

Azrin, N. H., Flores, T., & Kaplan, S. J. (1975). Job-finding club: A group assisted program for obtaining employment. *Behavior Research and Therapy, 13,* 17–27.

Azrin, N. H., Philip, R. A., Thienes-Hontos, P., & Besalel, V. A. (1980). Comparative evaluation of the Job Club program with welfare recipients. *Journal of Vocational Behavior, 16,* 133–134.

Bach, G. R. (1954). *Intensive group psychotherapy.* New York: Ronald Press.

Bach, G., & Wyden, P. (1970). *The intimate enemy: How to fight fair in love and marriage.* New York: Avon.

Bakeman, M. (1971). *Job Seeking Skills: Reference Manual.* Minneapolis: Multi-Resource Center.

Bales, R. F. (1950). *Interaction processes analysis.* Cambridge, MA: Addison-Wesley.

Bales, R. F. (1955). How people interact in conferences. *Scientific American, 192*(3), 31–35.

Bales, R. F. (1958). Task roles and social roles in problem-solving groups. In E. E. Maccoby, T. M. Newcomb, & E. L. Hartley (Eds.), *Readings in social psychology.* New York: Holt, Rinehart and Winston.

Bales, R. F. (1970). *Personality and interpersonal behavior.* New York: Holt, Rinehart & Winston.

Bales, R. F. (1980). *SYMLOG case study kit.* New York: Free Press.

Bandura, A. (1965). Behavioral modifications through modeling procedures. In L. Krasner & L. P. Ullman (Eds.), *Research in behavior modification.* New York: Holt, Rinehart and Winston.

Bandura, A. (1969). *Principles of behavior modification.* New York: Holt, Rinehart and Winston.

Bandura, A. (1971a). Analysis of modeling processes. In A. Bandura (Ed.), *Psychological modeling: Conflicting theories.* New York: Aldine-Atherton.

Bandura, A. (1971b). Psychotherapy based upon modeling principles. In A. E. Bergin & S. L. Garfield (Eds.), *Handbook of psychotherapy and behavior change: An empirical analysis.* New York: John Wiley.

Bandura, A., & Menlove, F. L. (1968). Factors determining vicarious extinction of avoidance behavior through symbolic modeling. *Journal of Personality and Social Psychology, 8,* 99–108.

Barch, J. P. M., & Liberto, M. L. (1980). Heterogeneous grouping: Its effectiveness in disability related psychotherapy. *Archives of Physical Medicine and Rehabilitation, 61,* 481–482.

Barclay, J. (1971). *Foundations of counseling strategies.* New York: John Wiley & Sons.

Baron, R. S., Baron, P. H., & Miller, N. (1973). The relation between distraction and persuasion. *Psychological Bulletin, 80,* 310–323.

Bauelas, A. (1948). A mathematical model for group structures. *Applied Anthropology, 7,* 16–30.

Beck, A. (1981). The research evidence for distributed leadership in therapy groups. *International Journal of Group Psychotherapy, 31,* 43–71.

Bedell, J., & Weathers, L. (1979). A psycho-educational model for skill-training: Therapist facilitated and game-facilitated applications. In D. Upper & S. Ross (Eds.), *Behavioral group therapy.* Champaign, IL: Research Press.

Bednar, R. L., & Battersbu, C. P. (1976). The effects of specific structure on early group development. *Journal of Applied Behavioral Science, 12,* 513–522.

Bellack, A. S. (1976). A comparison of self-monitoring and self-reinforcement in weight reduction. *Behavior Therapy, 7,* 68–75.

Bellack, A. S., & Hersen, M. (1977). *Behavior modification: An introductory textbook.* Baltimore: Williams and Wilkins.

Bellack, A. S., & Hersen, M. (Eds.). (1979). *Research and practice in social skills training.* New York: Plenum Press.

Bellack, A. S., Rozensky, R. H., & Schwartz, J. A. (1974). A comparison of two forms of self-monitoring in a behavioral weight reduction program. *Behavior Therapy, 5,* 523–530.

Benjamin, A. (1978). *Behavior in Small Groups.* Boston: Houghton Mifflin.

Berman, E. (1982). Authority and authoritarianism in group psychotherapy. *International Journal of Social Psychiatry, 2,* 275–280.

Berne, E. (1961). *Transactional analysis in psychotherapy.* New York: Grove Press.

Berne, K. D., & Sheats, P. (1948). Functional roles of group members. *Journal of Social Issues, 2,* 42–47.

Berzon, B., Pious, C., & Parson, R. (1963). The therapeutic event in group psychotherapy: A study of subjective reports by group members. *Journal of Individual Psychology, 19,* 204–212.

Berzon, B., & Solomon, L. N. (1966). The self-directed therapeutic group: Three studies. *Journal of Counseling Psychology, 13* (4), 491–497.

Bickman, L. (1974). The social power of a uniform. *Journal of Applied Social Psychology, 4,* 47–61.

Biddle, B. J. (1979). *Role theory: Expectations, identities, and behavior.* New York: Academic Press.

Bieber, D. (1957). The emphasis on the individual in psychoanalytic group therapy. *International Journal of Social Psychiatry, 2,* 275–280.

Blinder, M. (1965). MCFT: Simultaneous treatment of several families. *American Journal of Psychotherapy, 19,* 559.

Bloch, D. (Ed.). (1973). *Techniques of family therapy.* New York: Grune and Stratton.

Bolstad, O., & Johnson, S. (1972). Self-regulation in the modification of disruptive classroom behavior. *Journal of Applied Behavior Analysis, 5,* 443–454.

Bonney, M. E. (1974). Popular and unpopular children: A sociometric study. *Sociometry Monographs* (No. 9).

Bowen, M. (1976). Principles and techniques of multiple family therapy. In P. J. Guerin (Ed.), *Family Therapy.* New York: Gardner Press.

Bozarth, J. D., & Rubin, S. E. (1975). Empirical observations of rehabilitation counselor performance and outcome: Some implications. *Rehabilitation Counseling Bulletin, 19* (3), 294–298.

Bradford, J. P., Gibb, J. R., & Berne, K. D. (1964). *T-group theory and laboratory method.* New York: John Wiley & Sons.

Bratter, T. (1972). Group therapy with affluent, alienated adolescent drug abusers: A reality therapy and confrontation approach. *Psychotherapy, Theory, Research and Practice, 9,* 308–318.

Bratter, T. (1974). Reality therapy: A group psychotherapeutic approach with adolescent alcoholics. *Annals of the New York Academy of Sciences, 233,* 104–114.

Brody, W. (1959). Some family operations and schizophrenia. *Archives of General Psychiatry, 1,* 379–402.

Brower, I. C. (1983). Counseling Vietnamese. In D. R. Atkinson, G. Morten, & D. W. Sue (Eds.), *Counseling American Minorities: A cross cultural perspective* (2nd ed.). Dubuque, IA: W. C. Brown.

Burfe, P. J. (1967). The development of task and social-emotional role differentiation. *Sociometry, 30,* 379–392.

Butler, A. J., & Ayer, M. J. (1970). *Problem solving and development of social skills in the mentally retarded.* University of Wisconsin-Madison. The Social and Rehabilitation Service, Department of Health, Education and Welfare, Washington, D.C. (Project No. 15-P-55212/5-02). Unpublished progress report.

Cantor, D. (1977). School based groups for children of divorce. *Journal of Divorce, 1,* 183–187.

Capell, R. (1979). *Changing human systems.* Toronto: International Human Systems Institute.

Capuzzi, D., & Gross, D. (1980). Group work with the elderly: An overview. *Personnel and Guidance Journal, 59,* 206–211.

Carkhuff, R. R. (1969). *Helping and human relations: Vol. 1. Selection and training.* New York: Holt, Rinehart and Winston.

Carkhuff, R. R. (1971). *The development of human resources, education, psychology, and social change.* New York: Holt, Rinehart and Winston.

Carkhuff, R. R., & Berenson, B. G. (1977). *Beyond counseling and therapy.* New York: Holt, Rinehart and Winston.

Carkhuff, R. R., Pierce, R. M., Friel, T. W., & Willis, D. G. (1975). *Get a Job.* Amherst, MA: Human Resource Development Press.

Carpenter, P., & Sandberg, S. (1973). The things inside: Psychodrama with delinquent adolescents. *Psychotherapy: Research and Practice, 10,* 245–247.

Cartwright, D. A. (1959). A field theoretical conception of power. In D. Cartwright (Ed.), *Studies in social power.* Ann Arbor, MI: Institute for Social Research.

Cartwright, D., & Zander, A. (1968). *Group dynamics: Research and theory* (3rd Ed.). New York: Harper & Row.

Cautela, J. R. (1966). Treatment of compulsive behavior by covert desensitization. *Psychological Record, 16,* 33–41.

Chubon, R. A. (1982). Group practices in the rehabilitation of physically disabled persons. In M. Seligman (Ed.), *Group Psychotherapy and Counseling with Special Populations.* Baltimore: University Park Press.

Clanton, G, & Smith, L. (1977). *Jealousy.* Englewood Cliffs, NJ: Prentice-Hall.

Clark, J. B., & Culbert, S. A. (1965). Mutually therapeutic perception and self-awareness in a T-group. *Journal of Applied Behavioral Science, 1,* 180–194.

Clement, P., & Milne, D. (1967). Group play therapy and tangible reinforcers used to modify the behavior of 8-year-old boys. *Behavior Research and Therapy, 5,* 301–312.

Cofer, D., & Nir, V. (1975). Theme-focused group therapy on a pediatric ward. *International Journal of Psychiatry in Medicine, 6,* 541–550.

Cohen, E., & Rietma, K. (1981). Utilizing marathon therapy in a drug and alcohol rehabilitation program, *International Journal of Group Psychotherapy, 31,* 117–123.

Corder, B., Whiteside, R., McNiell, R., Brown, T., & Corder, R. (1981). An experimental study of the effect of structured videotape feedback on adolescent group psychotherapy process. *Journal of Youth and Adolescence, 10*(4), 255–261.

Corey, G. (1981). *Theory and practice of group counseling.* Monterey, CA: Brooks/Cole.

Corey, G., & Corey, M. S. (1977). *Groups: Process and practice.* Monterey, CA: Brooks/Cole.

Corey, G., Corey, M. S., Callanan, P. J., & Russell, J. M. (1982). *Group Techniques.* Monterey, CA: Brooks/Cole.

Corsini, R. (Ed.). (1973). *Current psychotherapies.* Itasca, IL: F. E. Peacock.

Cunningham, J. M., & Matthews, K. L. (1982). Impact of multiple-family therapy approach on a parallel latency-age/parent group. *International Journal of Group Psychotherapy, 32* (1), 91–102.

Curran, J. P., & Monti, P. M. (Eds.). (1982). *Social skills training: A practical handbook for assessment and treatment.* New York: Guilford Press.

Curry, A. (1965). Therapeutic management of multiple family groups. *International Journal of Group Psychotherapy, 15,* 90.

Daane, C. (1972). *Vocational exploration group: Theory and research.* Washington, DC: U.S. Department of Labor, Manpower Administration.

Daane, C. J. (1983). *Work and leisure satisfactions.* Tempe, AZ: Studies for Urban Man.

Dailey, R. C. (1977). The effects of cohesiveness and collaboration on work groups: A theoretical model. *Group and Organizational Studies, 2,* 261–269.

Davis, F. (1971). *Inside intuition: What we know about nonverbal communication.* New York: Signet.

DeCecco, J., & Richards, A. (1974). *Growing pains: Uses of school conflict.* New York: Aberdeen Press.

DeCecco, J., & Richards, A. (1975, November). Civil war in the high schools. *Psychology Today, 175* (9), 51–58.

Dick, B., Lessler, K., & Whiteside, J. (1980). A developmental framework for cotherapy. *International Journal of Group Psychotherapy, 30,* 273–285.

Dickoff, H., & Lakin, M. (1963). Patient views of psychotherapy: Retrospections and interpretations. *International Journal of Psychotherapy, 13,* 61–73.

DiLoreto, A. (1971). *Comparative psychotherapy.* New York: Aldine-Atherton.

Dinkmeyer, D. C., & Muro, J. J. (1971). *Group counseling: Theory and practice.* Itasco, IL: F. E. Peacock.

Drabman, R., Spitalnik, R., & O'Leary, K. D. (1973). Teaching self-control to disruptive children. *Journal of Abnormal Psychology, 82,* 10–16.

Dreikurs, R. (1951). The unique social climate experienced in group psychotherapy. *Group Psychotherapy, 3,* 292.

Dreikurs, R. (1957). Group psychotherapy from the point of view of Adlerian psychology. *The International Journal of Group Psychotherapy, 7,* 363.

Dreikurs, R., Corsini, R., Lowe, R., & Sonstegard, M. (1959). *Adlerian family counseling.* Eugene: University of Oregon, The University Press.

Durrell, V. (1969). Adolescents in multiple family group therapy in a school setting. *International Journal of Group Psychotherapy, 15,* 90.

D'Zurilla, T. J., & Goldfried, M. (1971). Problem solving and behavior modification. *Journal of Abnormal Psychology, 78* (1), 107–126.

D'Zurilla, T. J., & Nezu, A. (1982). Social problem solving in adults. In P. Kendall (Ed.), *Advances in cognitive-behavioral research and therapy* (Vol. 1, pp. 202–274). New York: Academic Press.

Eagle, E. (1967). Prognosis and outcome of community placement of institutionalized retardates. *American Journal of Mental Deficiency, 72,* 232–243.

Effron, A. (1980). Children and divorce: Help from an elementary school. *Social Casework, 10,* 305–312.

Egan, G. (1976). *Interpersonal living: A skills/contract approach to human-relations training in groups.* Monterey, CA: Brooks/Cole.

Egan, M. (1975). Dynamisms in activity discussion group therapy (ADGT). *International Journal of Group Psychotherapy, 25,* 199–218.

Ekman, P., & Friesen, W. (1968). Nonverbal behavior in psychotherapy research. In J. Shlien (Ed.), *Research in psychotherapy* (Vol. 3, pp. 179–216). Washington, DC: American Psychological Association.

Ellis, A. (1962). *Reason and emotion in psychotherapy.* Secaucus, NJ: Lyle Stuart.

Ellis, A. (1973). Rational-emotive therapy. In R. Corsini, *Current psychotherapies.* Itasca, IL: F. E. Peacock.

Erikson, E. H. (1963). *Childhood and society* (2nd ed.). New York: W. W. Norton.

Erkskine, R., & Maisenbacher, J. (1975). The effects of transactional analysis on socially maladjusted high school students. *Transactional Analysis Journal, 5* (3), 252–254.

Falbo, T. (1977). The multidimensional scaling of power strategies. *Journal of Personality and Social Psychology, 35,* 537–548.

Festinger, L. (1957). *A theory of cognitive dissonance.* Stanford, CA: Stanford University Press.

Figler, H. E. (1979). *PATH: A career workbook for liberal arts students.* Cranston, RI: The Carroll Press.

Foley, V. (1974). *An introduction to family therapy.* New York: Grune and Stratton.

Folk, R., & Johnson, D. W. (1973). The effects of perspective taking and egocentrism on problem solving in heterogeneous and homogeneous groups. *Journal of Social Psychology, 102,* 63–72.

Folkins, C., Pepitone-Arreola-Rockwell, F., Vando, A., Spensley, J., & Rockwell, D. (1982). A leaderless couples group postmortem. *International Journal of Group Psychotherapy, 32* (3), 367–373.

Forsyth, D. (1983). *An introduction to group dynamics.* Monterey, CA: Brooks/Cole.

Fox, D., & Lorge, I. (1962). The relative quality of decisions written by individuals and by groups as the available time for problem solving is increased. *Journal of Social Psychology, 57,* 227–242.

Fox, L. (1962). Effecting the use of efficient study habits. *Journal of Mathematics, 1,* 76–86.

Frank, J. (1978). A weekly group meeting for children in a pediatric ward: Therapeutic and practical foundations. *International Journal of Psychiatry in Medicine, 6,* 541–550.

French, J. R. (1941). The disruption and cohesion of groups. *Journal of Abnormal and Social Psychology, 36,* 361–377.

French, J. R., & Raven, B. H. (1959). The basis of social power. In D. Cartwright (Ed.), *Studies in social power.* Ann Arbor: University of Michigan Press.

Fromm-Reichmann, F. (1950). *Principles of intensive psychotherapy.* Chicago: University of Chicago Press.

Furst, W. (1953). Homogeneous versus heterogeneous groups. *International Journal of Psychotherapy, 3,* 59–66.

Gagné, R. M. (1966). Human problem solving: Internal or external events. In B. Kleinmuntz (Ed.), *Problem solving: Research, method and theory.* New York: John Wiley.

Galinsky, M. J., & Schopler, J. H. (1974). The social work group. In J. B. Shaffer and M. D. Galinsky, *Models of group therapy and sensitivity training.* Englewood Cliffs, NJ: Prentice-Hall.

Gans, R. (1957). The use of group co-therapists in the teaching of psychotherapy. *American Journal of Psychotherapy, 11,* 618–625.

Garfield, S. & Bergin, A. (1978). *Handbook of psychotherapy and behavior change: An empirical analysis.* New York: John Wiley & Sons.

Gazda, G. (1968). *Basic approaches to group psychotherapy and group counseling.* Springfield, IL: Charles C. Thomas.

Gazda, G. M. (Ed.). (1976). *Theories and methods of group counseling in the schools* (2nd ed.). Springfield, IL: Charles C. Thomas.

Gazda, G. M. (1978). *Group counseling: A developmental approach.* Boston: Allyn and Bacon.

Gazda, G. M., Asbury, F. R., Balzer, F. J., Childers, W. C., & Walters, R. P. (1977). *Human relations development: A manual for educators* (2nd ed). Boston: Allyn and Bacon.

Geiser, R. (1971). An experimental program of activity in a child care center. *Child Welfare, 50* (5), 290–297.

Gerstein, A. (1974). Variations in treatment technique in group activity therapy. *Psychotherapy: Theory, Research and Practice, 11*(4), 343–350.

Gesell, A., Ilg, F. L., Ames, L. B., & Bullis, G. E. (1946). *The child from five to ten.* New York: Harper.

Gesell, A., Ilg, F. L., & Ames, L. B. (1956). *Youth: The years from ten to sixteen.* New York: Harper.

Gibb, J. R. (1961). Defensive communication. *Journal of Communication, 11,* 141–148.

Gibb, J. R. (1972). Tori theory: Nonverbal behavior and the experience of community. *Comparative Group Studies, 3,* 461–472.

Ginott, H. (1961). *Group psychotherapy with children.* New York: McGraw-Hill.

Ginott, H. (1968). Group therapy with children. In G. Gazda (Ed.), *Basic approaches to group psychotherapy and group counseling.* Springfield, IL: Charles C. Thomas.

Glasser, W. (1965). *Reality therapy.* New York: Harper & Row.

Gold, M. W. (1973). Research on the vocational habilitation of the retarded: The present, the future. In N. Ellis (Ed.), *International review of research in mental retardation.* New York: Academic Press.

Goldfried, M., Decenteceo, E., & Weinberg, L. (1974). Systematic rational restructuring as a self-control technique. *Behavior Therapy, 5,* 247–254.

Goldman, M. A. (1965). A comparison of individual and group performance for varying combinations of initial ability. *Journal of Personality and Social Psychology, 1,* 210–216.

Goldstein, A., Sprafkin, R., Gershaw, N., & Klein, P. (1980). *Skill-streaming the adolescent.* Champaign, IL: Research Press.

Goldstein, A. J., & Wolpe, J. (1971). Behavior therapy in groups. In H. I. Kaplan & B. J. Sadock (Eds.), *Comprehensive group psychotherapy.* Baltimore: Williams and Wilkins.

Goldstein, H. (1964). Social and occupational adjustment. In H. Stevens & R. Heber (Eds.), *Mental retardation: A review of research.* Chicago: University of Chicago Press.

Goldstein, P., Heller, K., & Sechrest, L. B. (1966). *Psychotherapy and the psychology of behavior change.* New York: John Wiley & Sons.

Graff, R. W., Danish, S., & Austin, B. (1972). Reactions to three kinds of vocational-educational counseling. *Journal of Counseling Psychology, 19* (3), 224–228.

Gratton, L., & Rizzo, A. (1969). Group therapy with young psychotic children. *International Journal of Group Psychotherapy, 19,* 63–71.

Green, B. (1978). Helping children of divorce: A multimodal approach. *Elementary School Guidance and Counseling, 12,* 31–45.

Gurman, A., & Rice, D. (1975). *Couples in conflict.* New York: Jason Aronson.

Gustafson, J. P. (1978). Schismatic groups. *Human Relations, 31,* 139–154.

Haas, D. F., & Deseran, F. A. (1981). Trust and symbolic exchange. *Social Psychology Quarterly, 44,* 3–13.

Haley, J. (Ed.). (1971). *Changing families.* New York: Grune and Stratton

Haley, J., & Hoffman, L. (Eds.). (1967). *Techniques of family therapy.* New York: Basic Books.

Hansen, J., Niland, T., & Zani, L. (1969). Model reinforcement in group counseling with elementary school children. *Personnel and Guidance Journal, 47* (8), 741–744.

Hardy-Fanta, C., & Montana, P. (1982). The Hispanic female adolescent: A group therapy model. *International Journal of Group Psychotherapy, 32,* 351–366.

Hare, A. P. (1976). *Handbook of small group research* (2nd ed.). New York: Free Press.

Harrison, R. P. (1974). *Beyond words: An introduction to nonverbal communication.* Englewood Cliffs, NJ: Prentice-Hall.

Harshbarger, C. (1980). Group work with elderly visually impaired persons. *Visual Impairment and Blindness, 74,* 221–224.

Heckel, R., & Salzberg, H. (1976). *Group psychotherapy: A behavioral approach.* Columbia: University of South Carolina Press.

Hersen, M., & Bellack, A. S. (1977). Assessment of social skills. In A. R. Ciminero, K. S. Calhoun, & H. E. Adams (Eds.), *Handbook for behavioral assessment.* New York: John Wiley & Sons.

Hervells, J. (1971). *Theory and practice of family psychiatry.* New York: Brunner/Mazell.

Hill, W. F. (1965a). *Group-counseling training syllabus.* Los Angeles: University of Southern California, Youth Studies Center.

Hill, W. F. (1965b). *HIM, Hill interaction matrix.* Los Angeles: University of Southern California, Youth Studies Center.

Ho, M. K. (1981). Social work with Asian-Americans. In R. H. Dana (Ed.), *Human services for Cultural Minorities,* Baltimore: University Park Press.

Hoffer, E. (1951). *The true believer.* New York: Harper & Row.

Homans, G. C. (1950). *The Human group.* New York: Harcourt Brace & World.

Howells, J. (1971). *Theory and practice of family psychiatry.* New York: Brunner/Mazell.

Isaacs, W., Thomas, J., & Goldiamond, I. (1960). Application of operant conditioning to reinstate verbal behavior in psychotics. *Journal of Speech and Hearing Disorders, 25,* 8–12.

Ivey, A. (1974). Microcounseling and media therapy: State of the art. *Counselor Education and Supervision, 13,* 172–182.

Jackson, D. (Ed.). (1968). *Communication, family, and marriage.* Palo Alto, CA: Science and Behavior Books.

Jacobson, E. (1938). *Progressive relaxation.* Chicago: University of Chicago Press.

Janis, I. L. (1971). Group think. *Psychology Today, 5* (6), 36–43, 74–76.

Jepsen, D. A., Dustin, R., & Miars, R. (1982). The effect of problem-solving training on adolescents' career exploration and career decision-making. *Personnel and Guidance Journal, 61* (3), 149–153.

Johnson, D. W. (1974). Communication and the inducement of cooperative behavior in conflicts. *Speech Monographs, 41,* 64–78.

Johnson, D. W. (producer). (1980). *Belonging* [Film]. Minneapolis: J & J Book Co.

Johnson, D. W., & Johnson, F. P. (1982). *Joining together: Group therapy and skills.* Englewood Cliffs, NJ: Prentice-Hall.

Johnson, K. A., & Growick, B. S. (1982). Holistic rehabilitation applied to a job placement program for disabled public welfare recipients. *Journal of Rehabilitation, 48*(3), 44–46.

Jourard, S. (1971). *The transparent self.* New York: Van Nostrand Reinhold.

Kadis, A. (1973). Co-ordinated meeting and group psychotherapy. In M. Rosenbaum & M. Berger (Eds.), *Group psychotherapy and function.* New York: Basic Books.

Kagan, N. (1967). *Studies in human interaction, interpersonal process recall, stimulated by video-tape* (Final Report Project No. 5-0800). Washington, DC: Department of Health, Education and Welfare.

Kahn, M. W., Williams, C., Galvez, E., Lejero, L., Conrad, R., & Goldstein, G. (1981). The Papago Psychology Service: A community mental health program on an American Indian reservation. In R. H. Dana (Ed.), *Human Services for Cultural Minorities.* Baltimore: University Park Press.

Kanfer, F. H. (1975). Self-management methods. In F. H. Kanfer & A. P. Goldstein (Eds.), *Helping people change.* New York: Pergamon Press.

Kanfer, F. H., Karoly, P., & Newman, A. (1975). Reduction of children's fear of the dark by competence-related and situational threat-related verbal cues. *Journal of Consulting and Clinical Psychology, 43,* 251–258.

Kantorovich, N. V. (1929). An attempt of curing alcoholism by associated reflexes. *Novoye v Refleksologii i Fiziologi Nervnoy Sistemy, 3,* 436.

Kaplan, H. (1975). *The illustrated manual of sex therapy.* New York: Quadrangle, The New York Times Book Company.

Kapp, F. T. (1964). Group participation and self-perceived personality change. *Journal of Nervous and Mental Disorders, 139,* 255–265.

Keat, D. (1974). *Fundamentals of child counseling.* Boston: Houghton Mifflin.

Keith, R. D. (1976). *A study of self-help employment seeking preparation and activity of vocational rehabilitation clients.* Unpublished doctoral dissertation, Michigan State University.

Keith, R. D., Engelkes, J. R., & Winborn, B. B. (1977). Employment-seeking preparation and activity: An experimental job-placement training model for rehabilitation clients. *Rehabilitation Counseling Bulletin, 21* (2) 159–165.

Kelman, H. C. (1961). Processes of opinion change. *Public Opinion Quarterly, 25,* 57–78.

Kennard, W. W., & Shilman, R. P. (1979). Group services to the homebound. *Social Work, 24,* 330–332.

Kilham, W., & Mann, L. (1974). Level of destructive obedience as a function of transmitter and executant roles in the Milgram obedience paradigm. *Journal of Personality and Social Psychology, 29,* 696–702.

Kipnis, D. (1972). Does power corrupt? *Journal of Personality and Social Psychology, 24,* 33–41.

Kirn, A. (1974). *Lifework planning workbook and manual.* Wilton Center, NH: Published privately.

Knapp, M. (1972). *Nonverbal communication in human interaction.* New York: Holt, Rinehart and Winston.

Koch, J., & Koch, L. (1976). *The marriage savers.* New York: Cavard, McCann, and Geoghegan.

Kogan, J. (1976). The genesis of gestalt therapy. In C. Hatcher & P. Himelstein, *The handbook of gestalt therapy.* New York: Jason Aronson.

Kohlberg, L. (1973). Continuities and discontinuities in childhood and adult moral development revisited. In P. B. Baltes & K. W. Schaie (Eds.), *Life-span developmental psychology: Research and theory.* New York: Academic Press.

Kottler, J. (1983). *Pragmatic group leadership.* Monterey, CA: Brooks/Cole.

Kriegsman, K. H., & Celotta, B. (1981a). Creative coping: A program of group counseling for women with physical disabilities. *Journal of Rehabilitation, 47* (3), 36–39.

Kriegsman, K. H., & Celotta, B. (1981b). Sexuality in creative coping groups for women. *Sexuality and Disability, 4,* 169–172.

Krumboltz, J., & Potter, B. (1973, January). Behavioral techniques for developing trust, cohesiveness and goal accomplishment. *Educational Technology* (pp. 26–30).

Laing, R. D., & Esterson, A. (1964). *Sanity, madness, and the family.* Baltimore: Penguin.

Lakin, M., & Carson, R. C. (1966). A therapeutic vehicle in search of a theory of therapy. *Journal of Applied Behavioral Science, 2,* 27–40.

Landis, P. H. (1975). *Making the most of marriage.* Englewood Cliffs, NJ: Prentice-Hall.

Lange, A., & Jakubowski, P. (1978). *Responsible assertive behavior: Cognitive/ behavioral procedures for trainers.* Champaign, IL.: Research Press.

Lanier, E., & Robertiello, R. (1977). A small group of patients discuss their experiences and feelings about working with therapists of different races. *Journal of Contemporary Psychology, 9,* 42–44.

Laqueur, H. P. (1976). Multiple family therapy. In P. J. Guernin (Ed.), *Family Therapy.* New York: Gardner Press.

Larsen, J., & Mitchell, C. (1980). Task-centered strength-oriented group work with delinquents. *Social Casework, 61,* 154–163.

Laughlin, P. R., Branch, L. G., & Johnson, H. H. (1969). Individual versus triadic performance on a unidimensional complementary task as a function of initial ability level. *Journal of Personality and Social Psychology, 12,* 144–150.

Lazarus, A. A. (1961). Group therapy of phobic disorders by systematic desensitization. *Journal of Abnormal and Social Psychology, 63,* 504–510.

Lazarus, A. A. (1968). Behavior therapy in groups. In G. M. Gazda (Ed.), *Basic approaches to group psychotherapy and group counseling* (pp. 149–175). Springfield, IL: Charles C. Thomas.

Lazarus, A. A. (1972). *Clinical behavior therapy.* New York: Brunner/Mazel.

Leary, T. (1957). *Interpersonal diagnosis of personality.* New York: Ronald Press.

Leavitt, H. (1951). Some effects of certain communication patterns on group performance. *Journal of Abnormal Psychology, 46,* 38–50.

Lederer, W., & Jackson, D. (1968). *The mirages of marriage.* New York: W. W. Norton.

Lerner, M. J., Miller, D. T., & Holmes, J. G. (1976). Deserving and the emergence of forms of justice. In L. Berkowitz & E. Walster (Eds.), *Equity theory: Toward a general theory of social interaction. Advances in experimental social psychology* (Vol. 9). New York: Academic Press.

Leventhal, G. S. (1976). The distribution of rewards and resources in groups and organizations. In L. Berkowitz & E. Walster (Eds.), *Equity theory: Toward a general theory of social interaction. Advances in experimental social psychology* (Vol. 9). New York: Academic Press.

Lewin, K. (1943). Forces behind food habits and methods of change. *Bulletin of the National Research Council, 108,* 35–65.

Lewin, K. (1948). *Resolving social conflicts: Selected papers on group dynamics.* New York: Harper.

Lewin, K., & Lippitt, R. (1938). An experimental approach to the study of autocracy and democracy: A preliminary note. *Sociometry, 1,* 292–300.

Lewin, K., Lippitt, R., & White, R. (1939). Patterns of aggressive behavior in experimentally created social climates. *Journal of Social Psychology, 10,* 271–299.

Liberman, R. (1970). A behavioral approach to group dynamics: Reinforcement and prompting cohesiveness in group therapy. *Behavior Therapy, 1,* 141–175.

Lidz, T., Terry, D., & Fleck, S. (1958). The intrafamilial environment of the schizophrenic patient. *Archives of Neurological Psychiatry, 79,* 305–316.

Lieberman, M. A., Laken, M., & Whitaker, C. (1969). Problems and potential of psychoanalytic and group dynamics theories for group psychotherapy. *International Journal of Group Psychotherapy, 19*, 131–141.

Lieberman, M. A., Yalom, I. D., & Miles, M. B. (1973a). Encounter: The leader makes the difference. *Psychology Today, 6,* 16ff.

Lieberman, M. A., Yalom, I. D., & Miles, M. D. (1973b). *Encounter groups: First facts.* New York: Basic Books.

Lifton, W. M. (1966). *Working with groups.* New York: John Wiley & Sons.

Lippitt, R. A., & White, R. K. (1952). An experimental study of leadership and group life. In G. E. Swanson, T. M. Newcomb, & E. L. Hartley (Eds.), *Readings in Social Psychology* (rev. ed.). New York: Holt, Rinehart and Winston.

Lovaas, O. I., Schaeffer, B., & Simmons, J. Q. (1965). Building social behavior in autistic children by use of electric shock. *Journal of Experimental Research on Personality, 1,* 99–109.

Luft, J. (1969). *Of human interaction.* Palo Alto, CA: National Press Books.

Lurie, A., & Ron, H. (1971). Multiple group counseling of discharged schizophrenic young adults and their parents. *Social Psychiatry, 6,* 88.

Mace, D. R. (1976). Marital intimacy and the deadly love-anger cycle. *Journal of Marriage and Family Counseling, 2,* 131–137.

Mahoney, M. (1974). *Cognition and behavior modification.* Cambridge, MA: Ballinger.

Mahoney, M. (1977). Reflections on the cognitive learning trend in psychotherapy. *American Psychologist, 32,* 5–13.

Mainard, W., Burk, H., & Collins, G. (1965). Confrontation versus diversion in group therapy and chronic schizophrenic as measured by a "Positive incident" criterion. *Journal of Clinical Psychology, 31,* 725–729.

Marcovitz, R., & Smith, J. (1983). Patients' perceptions of factors in short-term psychotherapy. *International Journal of Group Psychotherapy, 33,* 21–39.

Masters, W., & Johnson, V. (1971). *Human sexual inadequacy.* Boston: Little, Brown.

Masters, W., & Johnson, V. (1976). *The pleasure bond: A new look at sexuality and committment.* Boston: Little, Brown.

Matthias, V. (1981). Baltimore's job squad for the handicapped. *Rehabilitation Counseling Bulletin, 24* (4), 304–307.

Max, L. W. (1935). Breaking up a homosexual fixation by the conditioned reaction technique: A case study. *Psychological Bulletin, 32,* 734.

McClure, D. P. (1972). Placement through improvement of clients' job-seeking skills. *Journal of Applied Rehabilitation Counseling, 3* (2), 188–196.

McGregor, D. (1967). *The human side of enterprise.* New York: McGraw-Hill.

McGuire, W. (1969). The nature of attitudes and attitude change. In B. Lindsey & E. Aronson (Eds.), *Handbook of Social Psychology* (Vol. 3). Reading, MA: Addison-Wesley.

McManus, M. (1971). Group desensitization of test anxiety. *Behavior Research and Therapy, 9,* 55–56.

McMurrian, T. T., & Gadza, G. M. (1974). Extended group interaction interpersonal functioning as a developmental process variable. *Small Group Behavior, 5,* 393–403.

Mehrabian, A. (1971). Nonverbal betrayal of feeling. *Journal of Experimental Research in Personality, 5,* 64–73.

Meichenbaum, D. (1971). Examination of model characteristics in reducing avoidance behavior. *Journal of Personality and Social Psychology, 17,* 298–307.

Meichenbaum, D. (1977). *Cognitive behavior modification.* New York: Plenum.

Menninger, K. (1958). *Theory of psychoanalytic technique.* New York: Harper & Row.

Midelfort, C. (1957). *The family in psychotherapy.* New York: McGraw-Hill.

Milgram, S. (1963). Behavioral study of obedience. *Journal of Abnormal and Social Psychology, 67,* 371–378.

Milgram, S. (1974). *Obedience to authority.* New York: Harper & Row.

Minuchin, S. (1974). *Families and family therapy.* Cambridge, MA: Harvard University Press.

Monti, P. M., Corriveau, D. P., & Curran, J. P. (1982). Social skills training for psychiatric patients: Treatment and outcome. In J. Curran & P. Monti (Eds.), *Social skills training: A practical handbook for assessment and treatment.* New York: Guilford Press.

Moreno, J. L., & Kipper, D. A. (1968). Group psychodrama and community-centered counseling. In G. M. Gazda (Ed.), *Basic approaches to group psychotherapy and group counseling.* Springfield, IL: Charles C. Thomas.

Morse, S., & Watson, R. (1977). *Psychotherapy: A comparative casebook.* New York: Holt, Rinehart and Winston.

Mosak, H., and Dreikurs, R. (1973). Adlerian psychotherapy. In R. Corsini, *Current psychotherapies.* Itasca, IL: F.E. Peacock.

Moustakas, C. E. (1959). *Psychotherapy with children: The living relationship.* New York: Harper & Row.

Muro, J., & Engels, D. (1980). Life coping skills through developmental group counseling. *Journal for Specialists in Group Work, 3,* 127–130.

Napier, R., & Gershenfeld, M. (1983). *Making groups work: A guide for group leaders.* Boston: Houghton Mifflin.

National Training Laboratories. (1962). *Issues in human relations training.* Selected readings series. Washington, DC: NTL.

Neuhaus, E. C. (1974). Training the mentally retarded for competitive employment. In L. Daniels (Ed.), *Vocational rehabilitation of the mentally retarded: A book of readings.* Springfield, IL: Charles C. Thomas.

Newcomb, T. M. (1961). *The acquaintance process.* New York: Holt, Rinehart and Winston.

Nichols, M. P., & Taylor, T. Y. (1975). Impact of therapy interventions on early sessions of group therapy. *Journal of Clinical Psychology, 31,* 267–276.

O'Connor, R. D. (1969). Modification of social withdrawal through symbolic modeling. *Journal of Applied Behavior Analysis, 2,* 15–22.

Ohlsen, M. (1979). *Marriage counseling in groups.* Champaign, IL: Research Press.

Orne, M. T., & Evans, F. J. (1965). Social control in the psychological experiment: Antisocial behavior and hypnosis. *Journal of Personality and Social Psychology, 1,* 189–200.

Ostby, S. S., & Butler, A. J. (1983). *Social problem-solving training: A working paper.* Unpublished, University of Wisconsin-Madison, Research and Training Center in Mental Retardation.

Papp, P. (1976). Brief therapy with couples groups. In P. J. Guerin (Ed.), *Family Therapy.* New York: Gardner Press.

Parloff, M., & Dies, R. (1977). Group psychotherapy outcome research 1966–1975. *International Journal of Group Psychotherapy, 27,* 281–319.

Parloff, M. B., Waskow, I. E., & Wolfe, B. E. (1978). Research on therapist variables in relation to process and outcome. In S. Garfield & A. Bergin (Eds.), *Handbook of psychotherapy and behavior change: An empirical analysis* (2nd ed.). New York: John Wiley & Sons.

Pasnau, R., Williams, L., & Tallman, F. (1971). Small activity groups in the school. *Community Mental Health Journal, 1,* 303–311.

Passons, W. R. (1975). *Gestalt approaches in counseling.* New York: Holt, Rinehart and Winston.

Patterson, C. (1973). *Theories of counseling and psychotherapy.* New York: Harper & Row.

Paul, G. L. (1966). *Insight versus desensitization in psychotherapy: An experiment in anxiety reduction.* Stanford, CA: Stanford University Press.

Paul, G. L., & Shannon, D. T. (1966). Treatment of anxiety through densensitization in therapy groups. *Journal of Abnormal Psychology, 71,* 124–135.

Paul, N., Bloom, J., & Paul, B. (1981). Outpatient multiple family group therapy—why not? In L. Wolberg & M. Aronson, *Group and family therapy.* New York: Brunner/Mazel.

Perez, J. (1965). *Counseling: Theory and practice.* Reading, MA: Addison-Wesley.

Perez, J. (1979). *Family counseling: Theory and practice.* New York: Van Nostrand.

Peterson, L., & Shigetomi, C. (1981). The use of coping techniques to minimize anxiety in hospitalized children. *Behavior Therapy, 12,* 1–14.

Phelan, J., Slavson, S., Epstein, N., & Schwartz, M. (1960). Studies in group psychotherapy in residential treatment of 'delinquent' boys. *International Journal of Group Psychotherapy, 10,* 174–212.

Piaget, J. (1955). *The language and the thought of the child.* London: Routledge and Kegan Paul.

Pierce, R., & Draskow, J. (1969). Teaching facilitative interpersonal functioning to psychiatric patients. *Journal of Community Psychology, 16,* 296–298.

Platt, J. J., & Spivack, G. (1976). *Workbook for training in interpersonal problem solving thinking.* Philadelphia: Department of Mental Health Services, Hahnemann Community Mental Health, Mental Retardation Center.

Plenk, A. (1978). Activity group therapy for emotionally disturbed preschool children. *Behavior Disorders, 3,* 210–218.

Polster, E., & Polster, M. (1973). *Gestalt therapy integrated.* New York: Brunner/ Mazel.

Prazak, J. A. (1969). Learning job-seeking interview skills. In J. D. Krumboltz & C. E. Thoresen (Eds.), *Behavioral Counseling.* New York: Holt, Rinehart and Winston.

Psathas, G., & Hardert, R. (1966). Trainer interventions and normative patterns in the T-group. *Journal of Applied Behavioral Science, 2,* 149–169.

Rachman, A. (1972). Group psychotherapy in treating the adolescent identity crisis. *International Journal of Child Psychotherapy, 1,* 97–119.

Rachman, S., & Teasdale, J. (1969). *Aversion therapy and behavior disorders: An analysis.* Miami, FL: University of Miami Press.

Radke, M., & Klisurich, D. (1947). Experiments in changing food habits. *Journal of the American Diatetics Association, 23,* 403–409.

Rappaport, R. C. (1982). Group therapy in prisons. In M. Seligman (Ed.), *Group Psychotherapy and Counseling with Special Populations.* Baltimore: University Park Press.

Raven, B. H., & Rietsema, J. (1957). The effects of varied clarity of group goal and group path upon the individual and his relation to his group. *Human Relations, 10,* 29–44.

Riess, M., Forsyth, D. R., Schlenker, B. R., & Freed, S. (1977). Opinion conformity as an impression management tactic following commitment to unpleasant behaviors. *Bulletin of the Psychonomic Society, 9,* 211–213.

Rimm, D. C., Saunders, W. D., & Westel, W. (1975). Thought stopping and covert assertion in the treatment of snake phobias. *Journal of Consulting and Clinical Psychology, 43,* 92–93.

Roethlisberger, F., & Dickson, W. (1940). *Management and the worker.* Cambridge, MA: Harvard University Press.

Rogers, C. R. (1957). The necessary and sufficient conditions of therapeutic personality change. *Journal of Consulting Psychology, 21,* 95–103.

Rogers, C. R. (1967). The process of the basic encounter group. In J. F. Bugental (Ed.), *Challenges of humanistic psychology.* New York: McGraw-Hill.

Rogers, C. R. (1970). *Carl Rogers on encounter groups.* New York: Harper & Row.

Roth, R. (1977). A transactional analysis group in residential treatment of adolescents. *Child Welfare, 56,* 776–785.

Ruesch, J., & Bateson, G. (1951). *Communication: The social matrix of society.* New York: W. W. Norton.

Sager, C. J. (1976). *Marriage contracts and couple therapy.* New York: Brunner/Mazel.

Sands, P. M., & Hanson, P. G. (1971). Psychotherapeutic groups for alcoholics and relatives in an outpatient setting. *International Journal of Group Psychotherapy, 21,* 23–33.

Sarason, I., & Ganzer, V. (1973). Modeling and group discussion in the rehabilitation of juvenile delinquents. *Journal of Counseling Psychology, 20,* 442–449.

Satir, V. (1967). *Conjoint family therapy.* Palo Alto, CA: Science and Behavior Books.

Satir, V. (1972). *Peoplemaking.* Palo Alto, CA: Science and Behavior Books.

Schachter, S. (1951). Deviation, rejection, and communication. *Journal of Abnormal and Social Psychology, 46,* 190–207.

Schauble, P. G., Parker, W. M., Probert, B. S., & Altmaier, E. M. (1979). Taking counseling to the students: The classroom as a delivery vehicle. *Personnel and Guidance Journal, 58,* 176–180.

Scheflen, A. (1973). *How behavior means.* New York: Gordon and Breach.

Schein, J. D. (1982). Group techniques applied to deaf and hearing-impaired persons. In M. Seligman (Ed.), *Group Psychotherapy and Counseling with Special Populations,* Baltimore: University Park Press.

Schulman, I. (1957). Modifications in group psychotherapy with antisocial adolescents. *International Journal of Group Psychotherapy, 1,* 310–317.

Schutz, W. C. (1958). *FIRO: A three-dimensional theory of interpersonal behavior.* New York: Holt, Rinehart & Winston.

Schutz, W. C. (1966). *The interpersonal underworld.* Palo Alto, CA.: Science and Behavior Books.

Schutz, W. C. (1967). *Joy: Expanding human awareness.* New York: Grove Press.

Schutz, W. C. (1971). *Here comes everybody.* New York: Harper & Row.

Senatore, V., Matson, J., & Kazdin, A. (1982). A comparison of behavioral methods to train social skills to mentally retarded adults. *Behavior Therapy, 13,* 702–714.

Seretsky, T. (1972). Resistance in a group as a function of the therapy counter transference expectations. *Psychotherapy: Theory, Research and Practice, 9,* 265–266.

Shaffer, J. B., & Galinsky, M. D. (1974). *Models of group therapy and sensitivity training.* Englewood Cliffs, NJ: Prentice-Hall.

Shaw, M. (1964). Communication networks. In L. Berkowitz (Ed.), *Advances in experimental social psychology* (Vol. I). New York: Academic Press.

Sheridan, C. L., & King, R. G. (1972). Obedience to authority with an authentic victim. *Proceedings of the 80th Annual Convention of the American Psychological Association, 7,* 165–166.

Sherif, M. (1936). *The psychology of social norms.* New York: Harper & Row.

Sherif, M. (1966). *In common predicament: Social psychology of intergroup conflict and cooperation.* Boston: Houghton Mifflin.

Shipiro, D., & Birk, L. (1967). Group therapy in experimental perspective. *International Journal of Group Psychotherapy, 17,* 211–224.

Shoben, E. (1962). The counselor's theory as a personal trait. *Personnel and Guidance Journal, 40,* 617–621.

Simkin, J. S. (1976). The development of gestalt therapy. In C. Hatcher & P. Himelstein, *The handbook of gestalt therapy.* New York: Jason Aronson.

Sisson, P. A., Sisson, C., & Gazda, G. M. (1973). Extended group counseling with psychiatric residents. *Small Group Behavior, 4,* 466–475.

Skinner, B. F. (1938). *The behavior of organisms: An experimental analysis.* New York: Appleton-Century-Crofts.

Skynner, A. (1976). *Systems of family and marital psychotherapy.* New York: Brunner/Mazel.

Slater, P. E. (1955). Role differentiation in small groups. *American Sociological Review, 20,* 300–310.

Slavson, S. R. (1955). Group psychotherapies. In J. L. McCary (Ed.), *Six approaches to Psychotherapy.* New York: Dryden.

Slavson, S. R. (1964). *A textbook in analytic group psychotherapy.* New York: International Universities Press.

Sloane, R. B., Staples, F. R., Cristo, A. H., Yorkston, N. J., & Whipple. K. (1975). *Psychotherapy versus behavior therapy.* Cambridge, MA: Harvard University Press.

Smaby, M., & Tamminen, A. (1978). Counseling for decisions. *Personnel and Guidance Journal, 57,* 106–110.

Sonnenshein-Schneider, M., & Baird, K. (1980). Group counseling children of divorce in elementary schools: Understanding process and technique. *Personnel and Guidance Journal, 59,* 88–91.

Spivack, G., Platt, J. J., & Shure, M. B. (1976). *The problem-solving approach to adjustment.* San Francisco: Jossey-Bass.

Stacey, D., Doleys, D., & Malcolm, R. (1979). Effects of social skills training in a community-based program. *American Journal of Mental Deficiency, 84*(2), 152–158.

Stefflre, B., & Matheny, K. (Eds.). (1968). *The function of counseling theory.* Guidance Monograph Series. Boston: Houghton Mifflin.

Stodgill, R. (1974). *Handbook of leadership.* New York: Free Press.

Stone, G. (1980). *A cognitive-behavioral approach to counseling psychology.* New York: Praeger.

Stotle, J. (1978). Power structure and personal competence. *Journal of Social Psychology, 38,* 72–83.

Strupp, H. (1973). *Psychotherapy: Clinical, research, and theoretical issues.* New York: Jason Aronson.

Sue, D. W. (1980). Asian-Americans. In N. A. Vacc & J. P. Wittmer (Eds.), *Let me be me: Special populations and the helping professions*. Muncie, IN: Accelerated Development, Inc.

Sue, D. W., & Sue, S. (1983). Counseling Chinese-Americans. In D. R. Atkinson, G. Morten, & D. W. Sue (Eds.), *Counseling American Minorities: A cross cultural perspective* (2nd ed.). Dubuque, IA: W. C. Brown.

Sullivan, H. S. (1953). *The interpersonal theory of psychiatry*. New York: W. W. Norton.

Super, D. E., Slarisheusky, R., Matlin, N., & Jordaan, J. P. (1963). *Career development: Self-concept theory*. New York: College Entrance Examination Board.

Sussman, A. E. (1979). Group therapy with the severely handicapped. In A. E. DellOrto & R. G. Lasky (Eds.), *Group Counseling and Physical Disability*. North Scituate, MA: Duxbury Press.

Swails, R. G., & Herr, B. L. (1976). Vocational development groups for ninth grade students. *Vocational Guidance Quarterly, 24* (3), 256–260.

Teague, C. H. (1981). Easing the pain of plant foreclosure: The Brown & Williamson experience. *Management Review, 70* (4), 23–27.

Thibaut, J. W., & Kelley, H. H. (1959). *The social psychology of groups*. New York: John Wiley.

Thoresen, C. E., & Mahoney, M. J. (1974). *Behavioral self-control*. New York: Holt, Rinehart and Winston.

Tichenor, J. M. (1977). Life work planning: A group career program evaluated. *Vocational Guidance Quarterly, 26* (1), 54–59.

Tjosvold, D. (1978). Alternative organizations for schools and classrooms. In D. Bart-Tal & L. Saxe (Eds.), *Social Psychology of Education*. Washington, DC: Hemisphere.

Torrance, E. (1954). Some consequences of power differences in decision making in permanent and temporary three-man groups. *Research Studies, State College of Washington, 22*, 130–140.

Triandis, H. C. (1978). Some universals of social behavior. *Personality and Social Psychology Bulletin, 4*, 1–16.

Trotzer, J. (1977). *The counselor and the group: Integrating theory, training and practice*. Monterey, CA: Brooks/Cole.

Truax, C. (1961). The process of group therapy: Relationship between hypothesized therapeutic conditions and interpersonal exploration. *Psychological Monographs, 75* (No. 5111).

Truax, C., & Carkhuff, R. (1967). *Toward effective counseling and psychotherapy*. Chicago: Adeline.

Tucker, R. C. (1977). Personality and political leaders. *Political Science Quarterly, 92*, 383–393.

Tuckman, B. W. (1965). Developmental sequences in small groups. *Psychological Bulletin, 63*, 384–399.

Tuckman, B. W., & Jensen, M. A. (1977). Stages of small group development revisited. *Group and Organizational Studies, 2,* 419–427.

Turkewitz, H., O'Leary, K. D., & Ironsmith, M. (1974). Generalization and maintenance of appropriate behavior through self-control. *Journal of Consulting and Clinical Psychology, 43,* 577–583.

Tylim, I. (1982). Group psychotherapy with Hispanic parents: The psychodynamics of idealization. *International Journal of Group Psychotherapy, 32,* 339–350.

Upper, D., & Cautela, J. R. (1979). *Covert conditioning.* Elmsford, NY: Pergamon Press.

Vander Kolk, C. (1973). Comparison of two mental health counselor training programs. *Community Mental Health Journal, 9,* 260–269.

Vander Kolk, C. (1976). Popular music in group counseling. *School Counselor, 23* (3), 206–210.

Vosen, L. M. (1966). *The relationship between self-disclosure and self-esteem.* Unpublished doctoral dissertation, University of California at Los Angeles.

Walker, R. A. (1969). "Pounce": Learning to take responsibility for one's own employment problems. In J. D. Krumboltz & C. E. Thoresen (Eds.), *Behavioral Counseling.* New York: Holt, Rinehart and Winston.

Walster, E., Walster, G., & Berscheid, J. (1978). *Equity: Theory and research.* London: Allyn and Bacon.

Walters, R. (1978). Nonverbal communication in group counseling. In G. M. Gazda, *Group counseling: A developmental approach.* Boston: Allyn and Bacon.

Walton, R. (1969). *Interpersonal peacemaking.* Reading, MA: Addison-Wesley.

Watson, G. (1931). Do groups think more effectively than individuals? In G. Murphy & L. Murphy (Eds.), *Experimental and social psychology.* New York: Harper.

Watson, G., & Johnson, D. W. (1972). *Social psychology: Issues and insights* (2nd ed.). Philadelphia: Lippincott.

Webster-Stratton, C. (1982). The long term effects of a videotape modeling parent-training program: Comparison of immediate and one-year follow-up results. *Behavior Therapy, 13,* 702–714.

Weinstein, I. (1971). Guidance of a choice of a co-therapist. *Psychotherapy: Theory, Research, and Practice, 8,* 301–303.

Weinstock, A. (1979). Group treatment of characterologically damaged, developmentally disabled adolescents in a residential treatment center. *International Journal of Group Psychotherapy, 29,* 369–381.

Weisinger, M., & Schultz, B. B. (1979). *Placement Preparation Program.* New York: ICD Rehabilitation and Research Center.

Whitaker, D. S., & Lieberman, M. A. (1965). *Psychotherapy through the group process.* New York: Atherton Press.

Wish, M., Deutsh, M., & Kaplan, S. J. (1976). Perceived dimensions of interpersonal relations. *Journal of Personality and Social Psychology, 33,* 409–420.

Wolfe, A., & Schwartz, E. K. (1962). *Psychoanalysis in groups*. New York: Grune and Stratton.

Wolpe, J. (1958). *Psychotherapy by reciprocal inhibition*. Stanford, CA: Stanford University Press.

Wolpe, J. (1969). *The practice of behavior therapy*. New York: Pergamon Press.

Wynne, L., Ryskoff, I., Day, J., & Hirsch, S. (1958). Pseudomutuality in the family relationship of schizophrenics. *Psychiatry, 21,* 202–220.

Yalom, I. D. (1970). *The Theory and Practice of Group Psychotherapy*. New York: Basic Books.

Yalom, I. D. (1975). *The Theory and Practice of Group Psychotherapy* (2nd ed.). New York: Basic Books.

Yalom, I. D., & Lieberman, M. (1971). A study of encounter group casualties. *Archives of General Psychiatry, 25,* 16–30.

Yalom, I. D., & Rand, K. H. (1966). Compatibility and cohesiveness in therapy groups. *Archives of General Psychiatry, 13,* 267–276.

Yalom, I. D., Tinklenberg, J., & Gilula, M. (1970). Curative factors in group therapy. In I. D. Yalom, *The theory and practice of group psychotherapy* (p. 42). New York: Basic Books.

Zeleny, L. D. (1956). Validity of a sociometric hypothesis: The function of creativity in interpersonal and group relations. *Sociometry, 8,* 439–449.

Zimet, C. (1979). Developmental task and crisis groups: The application of group psychotherapy to the maturational processes. *Psychotherapy: Theory, Research and Practice, 16,* 2–8.

Author Index

Subject Index